THE GREENING OF THEOLOGY
The Ecological Models of
Rosemary Radford Ruether, Joseph Sittler, and Jürgen Moltmann

American Academy of Religion
Academy Series

edited by
Barbara A. Holdrege

Number 91

THE GREENING OF THEOLOGY
The Ecological Models of
Rosemary Radford Ruether, Joseph Sittler,
and Jürgen Moltmann
by
Steven Bouma-Prediger

Steven Bouma-Prediger

THE GREENING OF THEOLOGY
The Ecological Models of
Rosemary Radford Ruether,
Joseph Sittler, and Jürgen Moltmann

Scholars Press
Atlanta, Georgia

THE GREENING OF THEOLOGY
The Ecological Models of
Rosemary Radford Ruether, Joseph Sittler,
and Jürgen Moltmann

by
Steven Bouma-Prediger

© 1995
The American Academy of Religion

Library of Congress Cataloging in Publication Data
Bouma-Prediger, Steven.
    The greening of theology : the ecological models of Rosemary
Radford Ruether, Joseph Sittler, and Jürgen Moltmann / Steven Bouma-
Prediger.
        p.   cm. — (American Academy of Religion academy series ; no.
91)
    Includes bibliographical references.
    ISBN 0-7885-0163-1 (alk. paper). — ISBN 0-7885-0164-X (pbk. :
alk. paper)
    1. Human ecology—Religious aspects—Christianity—History of
doctrines—20th century. 2. Ruether, Rosemary Radford. 3. Sittler,
Joseph. 4. Moltmann, Jürgen. I. Title. II. Series.
BT695.5.B693   1995
261.8'362'0904—dc20   95-33570
                                                        CIP

Printed in the United States of America
on acid-free paper

This work is dedicated
with love and hope

to
Anna Meredythe
Chara Kristine
and
Sophia Calvert

and to Celaine

TABLE OF CONTENTS

PREFACE

This book in an earlier incarnation was a dissertation. As is well known, the writing of books (at least scholarly books) is often an arduous and time-consuming process, perhaps especially so for dissertations. Indeed, this work would have been impossible for me to complete without the support and encouragement, advice and criticism, prayers and petitions of many people. I have been extremely blessed to have had many friends who provided me with such necessary sustenance and I here gratefully and humbly acknowledge them and their contributions to this project.

To my friends and colleagues at the Institute for Christian Studies in Toronto, Ontario, where I began my graduate studies many years ago and where I was first immersed in a tradition of vigorous scholarship from a Christian perspective, I offer many thanks. I owe a special debt of gratitude to Hendrik Hart and James Olthuis, my primary mentors at ICS. I also wish to thank Nik Ansell and Brian Walsh for their ever perceptive comments on earlier versions of chapters two and five.

To my teachers at Fuller Theological Seminary I also owe a debt of gratitude. Jack Balswick, Richard Muller, Jack Rogers, Gary Sattler, and Lewis Smedes, to name only a few, were not only stimulating teachers and admirable scholars but became good friends. I especially wish to thank Richard Mouw for his wise counsel and valued friendship. His sincere concern, honest advice, and wonderful sense of humor combine with a disciplined mind and discerning spirit to provide those of us who know him with an exemplary model of the Christian scholar-teacher.

As is well-known, the University of Chicago Divinity School is a place of rigorous scholarship and academic excellence. I was privileged to learn much from members of that community. Of the students I am especially indebted to Peter Bakken for invaluable assistance on chapters three and six. Among the faculty I particularly wish to thank Don Browning and Langdon Gilkey for their advice and support. I would also like to express my appreciation to Anne Carr and William Schweiker for their timely and helpful comments on this work. Finally, to David Tracy, my advisor at Chicago, I extend a most heartfelt thanks for wise words of counsel, perceptive criticism, and needed encouragement along the way. One could not have for a doctoral advisor a better model of erudite scholar, irenic spirit, and avid encourager than David--an incarnation of the virtues of conversation for which he is justly famous.

To friends at North Park College, with whom I labored for four years, I also owe many thanks, especially Sonia Bodi, Dean Ebner, David Horner, and Robert Johnston, who as administrators made North Park a very congenial place for me to engage in my scholarly pursuits. I especially wish to express my gratitude to faculty colleagues Cal Katter and Jack Levison who enthusiastically offered welcome encouragement on this endeavor.

To colleagues at Hope College, my alma mater and present scholarly home, I also offer gratitude, especially to department chair Allen Verhey, to dean Bill Reynolds, and to provost Jack Nyenhuis, for creating at Hope a place in which both teaching and scholarship are pursued with genuine enthusiasm and recognized excellence. I especially appreciated the Knight Fellowship for New Faculty made available by provost Nyenhuis which supported the final work on this project.

For those at Scholar's Press who shepherded this project through the publication process, I am very grateful. I appreciated both the helpful criticism and the honest affirmation provided by two anonymous reviewers. And I am especially grateful to Barbara Holdrege, whose careful attention to detail and editor's eye greatly improved the manuscript, and to Dennis Ford, for his enthusiasm and timely support.

One is truly fortunate to have parents whose love is steadfast and unwavering. For many years now my parents, while wondering where all this graduate school was leading, have shown their love and support in countless tangible ways. To them, Curt and Jean Prediger, I owe a debt of gratitude beyond all measuring. I am doubly blessed in having parents-in-law whose enthusiasm and support for my largely unintelligible academic projects seemingly knows no bounds. Cal and Barbara Bouma are deserving of so much more than this feeble thank you.

My daughter Anna Meredythe has been a never failing source of wonder and amazement, though at times unhappy that "Daddy at office." So also, Chara Kristine, who arrived on the scene as this work in its initial form was being finished, is every bit what her name means--a bundle of unspeakable joy. And newcomer Sophia Calvert already serves as an infant reminder that authentic wisdom resides in humble dependence and trust-- upon each other and upon God. It is all too true that we not only inherit the earth from our ancestors but also borrow it from our children. Thus my fervent prayer and impassioned hope is that Anna and Chara and Sophia, and all of the other children of God's good earth, will grow up to inhabit a world flourishing and filled with shalom because of the ways we their elders have lived.

Last but certainly not least, this book would not have seen the dawning light of day were it not for my wife Celaine. In this long endeavor she has been, in the most profound sense, the person without whom this work could not have been written. Words cannot express the depth of my gratitude to her. Truly she has been and continues to be my beloved and my friend.

CHAPTER 1

INTRODUCTION

Nature, the world, has no value, no interest for Christians. The Christian thinks only of himself and the salvation of his soul.[1]

Ludwig Feuerbach

The contempt for the world or the hatred of it, that is exemplified by the wish to exploit it for the sake of cash and by the willingness to despise it for the sake of "salvation," has reached a terrifying climax in our own time. The rift between soul and body, the Creator and the Creation, has admitted the entrance into the world of the machinery of the world's doom.[2]

Wendell Berry

The Contemporary Scene

It is rare that a day passes without our learning about some new ecological degradation. With each daily newspaper and television report, we are shaken from our comfortable ignorance about the state of our earthly home and confronted with an ecological crisis that, like a crescendo, is growing to unimaginable and genuinely frightening proportions. Global warming, holes in the ozone layer, toxic wastes, oil spills, acid rain, drinking water contamination, overflowing landfills, topsoil erosion, species extinction, destruction of the rain forests, leakage of nuclear waste, lead poisoning, desertification, smog--such is merely a partial litany of worry and woe.

If our non-scientific observations and intuitions need any confirmation, there are plenty of more highly trained earth-

---

[1]Ludwig Feuerbach, *The Essence of Christianity* (New York: Harper and Row, 1957), 287.

[2]Wendell Berry, "A Secular Pilgrimage," in *Western Man and Environmental Ethics: Attitudes Toward Nature and Technology*, ed. Ian Barbour (Reading, MA: Addison-Wesley, 1973), 135.

watchers ready and willing to speak out about the current state of the planet. For example, biologist Calvin DeWitt states that "a crisis of degradation is enveloping the earth"--a crisis genuinely unique in human history in its destructive capability.[3] He lists "seven major degradations brought on by our assault on creation": land conversion and habitat destruction, e.g., land lost due to deforestation or plowing; species extinction; degradation of the land, e.g., loss of topsoil to wind and water erosion; resource conversion and production of wastes and hazards; global toxification, e.g., chemical and oil spills; the greenhouse effect and ozone depletion; human and cultural degradation, e.g., the displacement of agriculture by agribusiness.[4] Such is the plight of the earth.

Many people blame Christianity for the present ecological crisis. Directly or indirectly the Christian tradition is held responsible. The Christian faith, many argue, underwrites the rape of the earth. There are four major arguments to this case against Christianity. For example, Arnold Toynbee asserts that

> some of the major maladies of the present-day world--for instance the recklessly extravagant consumption of nature's irreplaceable treasures, and the pollution of those of them that man has not already devoured--can be traced back in the last analysis to a religious cause, and that this cause is the rise of monotheism.[5]

In particular Toynbee argues that the Genesis 1:28 command to have dominion and subdue the earth not only permits but directs humankind to dominate and exploit creation.[6] Given this

---

[3]Calvin DeWitt, "Assaulting the Gallery of God: Human Degradation of Creation," *Sojourners*, February-March 1990, 19. See also "The State of the Planet", in *Earthkeeping in the 90's*, ed. Loren Wilkinson (Grand Rapids: Eerdmans, 1991); and Bill McKibben, *The End of Nature* (New York: Doubleday, 1989).

[4]DeWitt, "Assaulting the Gallery of God," 20-21.

[5]Arnold Toynbee, "The Religious Background of the Present Environmental Crisis," in *Ecology and Religion in History*, eds. David and Eileen Spring (New York: Harper and Row, 1974), 146.

[6]Ibid., 147. Many others make this same charge, e.g., Ian McHarg "The Place of Nature in the City of Man," in *Western Man and Environmental Ethics*, 174-175. See Jeremy Cohen, "The Bible, Man, and Nature in the History of Western Thought," *The Journal of Religion* 65 (April 1985) for

diagnosis, Toynbee claims that the remedy for what ails us "lies in reverting from the *Weltanschauung* of monotheism to the *Weltanschauung* of pantheism."[7]

In the quote at the beginning of this chapter Wendell Berry articulates a second argument for why Christianity is at fault for the current ecological crisis. Berry claims that the emphasis within the Christian tradition on dualisms of soul and body, spiritual and material, sacred and secular, denigrates the earth and sanctions its misuse and exploitation.[8] Specifically the argument is that since there is a dualism between spiritual and material such that the former is of greater value than the latter, and since lack of value implies lack of ethical duty, Christianity has fostered a care-less attitude toward things material and thus is at fault for the plundering of the earth.

A third argument often cited by critics derives from perceived inadequacies in Christian eschatology.[9] For example, it is argued that Christian eschatology negates any rationale for preserving the earth since the second coming of Jesus will usher in a completely new form of existence. Biblical texts like 2 Peter 3:10, with its little known yet profoundly significant mistranslation,[10] are often cited

---

the claim that the history of the idea of dominion, as exemplified in Gen. 1:26-28, has yet to be adequately written; and see Cohen's *"Be Fertile and Increase, Fill the Earth and Master It": The Ancient and Medieval Career of a Biblical Text* (Ithaca: Cornell, 1989) for such a history.

[7]Toynbee, "The Religious Background," 148.

[8]As we will see, this argument is also articulated by many feminists, including, e.g., Rosemary Radford Ruether.

[9]For example, Berry, "A Secular Pilgrimmage," 134.

[10]The last clause of 2 Peter 3:10, "and the earth and the works that are upon it will be burned up" (RSV), is one biblical text often cited to support a basic discontinuity between this world and the world to come. Almost all versions translate the Greek in a similar creation-negating manner. For example, "the earth also and the works therein shall be burned up" (KJV); "the earth and everything in it will vanish" (TEV); "the earth and everything in it will be laid bare" (NIV); the earth and everything in it will be stripped bare" (NEB); "the earth and everything in it will be burned up to nothing" (Phillips); the French and Spanish equivalents of the TEV render the last verb "will cease to exist" (*cessera d'exister*) and "will be burned up" (*sera quemada*) respectively.

The 1985 update of Luther's German Bible comes closer to the true reading when it translates the last clause "the earth and the works upon it will find their judgment" (*werden ihr Urteil finden*), as does the recently

in support of this position. James Watt, the Reagan era Secretary of Interior, exemplified this view when, in response to a question about why his agency was acting contrary to its expressed mandate, he reportedly said, "I don't know how many future generations we can count on before the Lord returns." In short, since the world is ephemeral, unimportant, and will ultimately be destroyed, we need not live in an ecologically sensitive way.

Fourthly and finally, Lynn White, Jr., in his oft reprinted 1967 essay entitled "The Historical Roots of Our Ecologic Crisis," claims that because of its role in the rise of modern science and technology, "Christianity bears a huge burden of guilt" for the present situation.[11] White argues that by emphasizing humanity's transcendence over nature and by desacralizing nature, Christianity made possible the growth of modern science and technology, which in turn led to uncontrolled power over nature and the current ecological crisis. Hence Christianity is at least partially responsible for the current plight of the earth. Such is the case against Christianity.[12]

---

completed *New RSV* when it translates the last clause "and the earth and everything that is done on it will be disclosed." However, only the new Dutch translation (*Nieuwe Vertaling*, 1975) faithfully captures the actual meaning of the best Greek text: and the earth and the works upon it will be found (*en de aarde en de werken daarop zullen gevonden worden*).

The Greek verb in question here is *heurethêsetai*, future passive indicative third singular from *heuriskein*, or "to find," from which we get the English expression "Eureka." Thus the text rightly rendered speaks of a basic *continuity* rather than discontinuity of this world with the next. Apparently a creation-negating worldview has played a decisive role in the translation of this text. See Albert Wolters, "Editorial: Worldview and Textual Criticism," *Anakainosis* 2 (June 1980): 1-2. For corroboration of this reading, see Richard Bauckham, *Word Biblical Commentary 50: Jude and 2 Peter* (Waco: Word, 1983), 303-322.

[11]Lynn White, "The Historical Roots of Our Ecologic Crisis," in *Western Man and Environmental Ethics*, ed. Ian Barbour (Reading, MA: Addison-Wesley, 1973), 27. Originally published in *Science* 155 (March 10, 1967): 1203-1207. The literature regarding the relationship between Christianity and the rise of modern science is vast. For an early and now classic essay, see Michael Foster, "The Christian Doctrine of Creation and the Rise of Modern Science," in *Creation: The Impact of an Idea*, ed. Daniel O'Connor and Francis Oakley (New York: Scribners, 1969).

[12]For presentation of a similar case against Christianity, see also Wesley Granberg-Michaelson, *Worldly Spirituality: The Call To Redeem*

In sum, many people view Christianity, especially Christian theology, as ecologically bankrupt and morally blameworthy--as an irremediable part of the disease and no possible part of the cure. If we do indeed have a serious ecological problem, and if Christian theology for the four reasons indicated is in large measure responsible for the problem, then, so the argument goes, in searching for a perspective which could provide an adequate response to the ecological challenges before us we must look to other than the Christian tradition. The Christian tradition is of no use since it is the cause or one of the major causes of the problem in the first place. Perhaps other traditions will be able to provide the intellectual and moral and spiritual resources appropriate to the ecological crisis. Or so it is argued.

The Various Tasks of a Christian Ecological Theology

Now a number of responses can be made to this argument. The initial premise that we today are facing a large and seemingly intractable ecological crisis--nightmare some would say--seems irrefutable.[13] While debate rages as to the precise extent of the

---

Life On Earth (San Francisco: Harper and Row, 1984), chapter 2, and James Nash, *Loving Nature: Ecological Integrity and Christian Responsibility* (Nashville: Abingdon, 1991), chapter 3. Each author also offers his own insightful response to this "ecological complaint against Christianity," to use Nash's words.

[13]A cursory review of any recent *Sierra, Wilderness,* or *Garbage* magazine will provide evidence of this claim. If these periodicals seem too partisan, then a recent *Newsweek* or *Time* will do. If these all seem too popular and unscientific, then consult the most recent *The State of the Earth.* Better yet, look around you. As I write these words, Holland, MI (population 34,000) is having an ozone alert, our Lake Michigan beach is offering up more dead fish than usual, and "development" continues to eat up rich agricultural land in Ottawa County. One need not live, as I did for many years, in large metropolitan areas like Los Angeles or Chicago to have a first-hand experience of many kinds of basic ecological degradation.

While perhaps accepting the claim that the ecological crisis is large, some will challenge its apparent intractability. Modern technology, some say, will come to the rescue and deliver us from our present situation. For a critique of this faith in technology, coupled with an informed and responsible Christian alternative, see Stephen Monsema, ed. *Responsible*

damage in certain cases, e.g., the exact size of the holes in the ozone layer or the rate at which certain species are being lost or the toxicity of various chemicals, almost all informed observers concur that the earth and its various ecosystems are groaning in travail. The plight of the earth is all too real.

The second premise is, however, more questionable. Indeed, this book, in part, is a modest attempt to repudiate the assertion that Christian theology, and the practices informed by that theology, are necessarily or irremediably or intrinsically ecologically bankrupt. There are, however, a number of possible strategies that may be employed here, and a variety of issues that require serious reflection. In the context of perceptively arguing that ecological theology and political theology must be conceived as two sides of the same coin, H. Paul Santmire outlines the possible, and in his view, necessary tasks involved in responding to the above arguments and in developing an "ecological theology."

First of all, there is "the historical and sociocritical task."[14] Largely a strategy of rebuttal and defense, this approach seeks to counter the "case against Christianity" by showing that such a claim is historically inaccurate, e.g., by demonstrating that there are in fact rich resources in the Christian tradition "which we ignore to our own impoverishment."[15] Santmire himself, while candidly admitting the at best "ambiguous ecological promise of Christian theology," nevertheless displays the not inconsiderable riches of the Christian tradition for matters ecological in what is to date the most thorough and sophisticated example of this historical project.[16] He points, for example, to Irenaeus, Augustine, Francis

---

Technology (Grand Rapids: Eerdmans, 1986). For a more in depth analysis, see Egbert Schuurman, *Technology and the Future: A Philosophical Challenge* (Toronto: Wedge, 1980).

[14]H. Paul Santmire, "Ecology, Justice, and Theology: Beyond the Preliminary Skirmishes," *The Christian Century,*12 May 1976, 461.

[15]Ibid.

[16]H. Paul Santmire, *The Travail of Nature: The Ambiguous Ecological Promise of Christian Theology* (Philadelphia: Fortress, 1985). Another informed and enlightening volume which sets forth the riches of the Christian tradition is Susan Power Bratton's *Christianity, Wilderness,and Wildlife: The Original Desert Solitaire* (Scranton: University of Scranton Press, 1991).

of Assisi, and to some extent Luther and Calvin as resources for the development of a Christian theology of nature. Similarly René Dubos retrieves the Benedictine tradition of responsible stewardship as a resource for "developing human activities which favor a creative, harmonious relationship between man and nature."[17]

This historical task also includes showing how Christian theology is "only one factor among many that helped to set the stage for the contemporary ecological crisis."[18] As Clarence Glacken conclusively demonstrates, ecological destruction is no respecter of religious or philosophical perspectives--having been around a long while before Christianity came on the scene.[19] In other words, Christian belief and practice are not a necessary condition for the domination of nature. As René Dubos states:

> In my opinion, the theory that Judeo-Christian attitudes are responsible for the development of technology and for the ecological crisis is at best a half-truth. Erosion of the land, destruction of animal and plant species, excessive exploitation of natural resources, and ecological disasters are not peculiar to the Judeo-Christian tradition and to scientific technology. At all times, and all over the world, man's thoughtless interventions into nature have had a variety of disastrous consequences or at least have changed profoundly the complexion of nature.[20]

Also often included in this defense of Christianity is the presentation of the argument that the modern scientific and technological worldview has in fact contributed more significantly to our current problems than has Christianity.[21] The Enlightenment, not Christianity, is the more basic cause of the ecological crisis.

---

[17]René Dubos, "Franciscan Conservation versus Benedictine Stewardship," in *Ecology and Religion in History*, 130-131. See also, Wilkinson, *Earthkeeping*.

[18]Santmire, "Ecology, Justice, and Theology," 461. See also Louis Moncrief, "The Cultural Basis of Our Environmental Crisis," in *Western Man and Environmental Ethics*, 31-42.

[19]Clarence Glacken, *Traces on the Rhodian Shore: Nature and Culture in Western Thought from Ancient Times to the End of the Eighteenth Century* (Berkeley: University of California, 1967).

[20]Dubos, "Franciscan Conservation," 120.

[21]There are many relevant works here. For example, see Wesley Granberg-Michaelson, *Worldly Spirituality*, chap. 3; Bob Goudzwaard, *Capitalism and Progress: A Diagnosis of Western Society* (Grand Rapids:

This first task, Santmire rightly argues, also must include renewed critical attention to biblical studies in order to reconsider and reconceive certain fundamental biblical concepts, e.g., the notion that creation is merely a stage for human action.[22] Santmire and others argue that since the Christian scriptures have been wrongly interpreted and used in ways which have fostered ecological destruction, renewed study of scripture is required in order to uncover distorted readings and reformulate important concepts.[23] In sum, this "historical and sociocritical task" seeks to argue that neither Christian theology nor the Christian scriptures is as ecologically bankrupt as is commonly believed.

Beyond the legitimate and necessary task of defense, however, lies the task of presenting a faithful articulation of a Christian perspective that adequately addresses the pressing needs of today. Into this category fall Santmire's four remaining tasks. There is the task, for example, within the domain of philosophical and theological anthropology of properly explicating the concepts of nature and history and their precise interrelationship. As Santmire notes, these concepts typically fall prey to one of two problems: either that which is distinctively human is submerged within the natural, or the natural is seen as merely a backdrop for the truly valuable realm of human action and history.[24] The challenge is to develop a position which does justice both to that which is uniquely human and to that which humans have in

---

Eerdmans, 1979); H. Paul Santmire, "Reflections on the Alleged Ecological Bankruptcy of Western Theology," in *Ethics for Environment: Three Religious Strategies*, eds. Dave Steffenson, Walter Herrscher, and Robert Cook (Green Bay: University of Wisconsin at Green Bay), 23-45.

[22]Santmire, "Ecology, Justice, and Theology," 462.

[23]For alternatives to the usual readings and for the best biblical commentators with respect to ecological issues, see, e.g., Bernhard Anderson, *Creation in the Old Testament* (Philadelphia: Fortress, 1984) and *Creation versus Chaos* (Philadelphia: Fortress, 1987); Richard Austin, *Hope for the Land: Nature in the Bible* (Atlanta: John Knox, 1988); Walter Brueggemann, *The Land* (Philadelphia: Fortress, 1977); C. F. D. Moule, *Man and Nature in the New Testament* (Philadelphia: Fortress, 1967); Odil Steck, *World and Environment* (Nashville: Abingdon, 1978); Claus Westermann, *Creation*, translated by John Scullion (Philadelphia: Fortress, 1974); Cal DeWitt, ed. *The Environment and the Christian: What Can We Learn from the New Testament?* (Grand Rapids: Baker, 1991).

[24]Santmire, "Ecology, Justice, and Theology," 462.

common with other creatures. Given both the similarities and the differences between human and non-human creatures, how should the categories of nature and history best be conceived?

The third fundamental task is to find a root metaphor or basic image, or a cluster of such images, that is able most adequately to inform a Christian perspective.[25] The task here is primarily the philosophical-theological and ultimately metaphysical task of articulating foundational analogies that are both faithful to the Christian tradition, e.g., attentive to the need to express both the transcendence and immanence of God vis-a-vis the world, and meaningful and evocative in today's world, e.g., conceptually coherent and emotionally able to empower appropriate action. For example, how is God most appropriately envisioned: as king, as clockmaker, as parent, as leader? And, correlatively, how is the world most adequately construed: as a realm overseen by a monarch, a machine produced by a designer, a child birthed by a mother, a community guided by a leader?

The fourth necessary component of a full-orbed response is the theological, scientific, and ultimately ethical task of sorting out certain basic issues regarding the natural world. For example, do non-human creatures have intrinsic value--worth in and of themselves irrespective of any utility for humans? Or do non-human creatures have merely instrumental value--value only in relation to their utility for humans? And if the natural world does have intrinsic value, what are the ethical implications of such a claim? For example, is it permissible to speak of the rights of non-human creatures, or at least of human duties toward such creatures? Much of the current debate in environmental ethics hinges upon how one answers these basic questions.[26]

---

[25]For the concept of root metaphor, see Stephen Pepper, *World Hypotheses* (Berkeley: University of California, 1942). The literature on the role of metaphor and analogy in science in general and in theology and philosophy in particular is enormous. For further references consult the works of McFague and Barbour in the bibliography.

[26]See, e.g., Holmes Rolston, III,*Environmental Ethics: Duties to and Values in the Natural World* (Philadelphia: Temple University, 1988); Robin Attfield, *The Ethics of Environmental Concern*, 2nd ed. (Athens, GA: University of Georgia Press, 1991); Roderick Nash, *The Rights of Nature: A History of Environmental Ethics* (Madison: University of Wisconsin, 1989);

Finally, Santmire outlines "perhaps the most difficult theological question of all," namely, the question of "our understanding of God as it relates to sexual dualism."[27] This basic task especially involves consideration of theology proper or the doctrine of God, but also impinges upon theological and philosophical anthropology. The challenge here is to construe the nature, character, and action of God in a way that brings shalom to both oppressed humans--especially women, people of color, and the poor--and an oppressed earth, since such a construal is at the very center of the Christian gospel, rightly interpreted.

The Task of this Project

This project is most concerned with the last four of Santmire's tasks, especially tasks two, three, and five. That is, the focus here is most directly on issues in anthropology, metaphysics, and theology proper. More exactly, this endeavor is primarily an attempt to show how the Christian tradition has within it considerable resources to develop an ecologically informed and affirming theology. In other words, I intend to show how Christian theology and philosophy can be an asset rather than a liability in the quest to bring shalom to our threatened earthly home. By critically examining the work of three contemporary Christian thinkers who themselves have striven to retrieve aspects of the Christian heritage and creatively reformulate that tradition, I hope

---

Ian Barbour, *Earth Might Be Fair: Reflections on Ethics, Religion, and Ecology* (Englewood Cliffs: Prentice Hall, 1972); J. Baird Callicott, *In Defense of the Land Ethic: Essays in Environmental Philosophy* (Albany: State University of New York, 1989); Robert Elliot and Aaran Gare, eds. *Environmental Philosophy: A Collection of Readings* (University Park: Penn State University, 1983); and Eugene Hargrove, *Foundations of Environmental Ethics* (Englewood Cliffs: Prentice Hall, 1989). One of the best introductory texts in ecological ethics is by Joseph DesJardins, *Environmental Ethics* (Belmont, CA: Wadsworth, 1993).

[27]Santmire, "Ecology, Justice, and Theology," 463. The literature on this issue is large and growing ever larger. For an introduction to Christian feminism, see Anne Carr, *Transforming Grace: Christian Tradition and Women's Experience* (San Francisco: Harper and Row, 1988). For an introduction to ecofeminism, see Carol Adams, ed. *Ecofeminism and the Sacred* (New York: Continuum, 1993).

to show that Christian ecological theology is not an oxymoron--
indeed that such a theology is not only possible, but a powerful
response to the problems of today's world.

In brief, the question to be addressed in this book is this: How
can Christians construct an ecological theology that is both faithful
to the best of the Christian tradition and sensitive to its past faults
and the present situation? What are the definitive contours of a
biblically informed, historically conscious, and creation-affirming
Christian theology? Given both the plight of the earth and the case
against Christianity, how might Christians today creatively and
faithfully develop an ecologically sound theology and thus engage
in discipleship which envisions care of creation as essential to the
practices of Christian faith?

It should be made clear that while there are obviously
compelling reasons within the present situation for engaging in
such a project as this, an equally if not more compelling reason for
reflection on this topic is found within the Christian faith itself. In
other words, in the inevitable and often muddy interplay between
present situation and Christian message,[28] cogent reasons for
reflection on and development of an ecological theology can be
given from the perspective of *both* situation and message. As a
Christian theologian and philosopher, my primary concern is that
the Christian gospel be faithfully understood and presented in *all*
of its liberating fullness. The integrity of the Christian message
demands nothing less. And thus while the current situation, as
indicated above, is an important factor in shaping the direction of
theological reflection, providing the context for why this particular
issue is of importance at this given time, the primary rationale for
concern with this issue is that the wholeness of the Christian gospel
demands it.[29] Other Christian thinkers express a similar point of
view. For example, Joseph Sittler affirms this when he says:

---

[28]On this issue of interplay between situation and message,
important texts are Paul Tillich, *Systematic Theology*, vol. 1 (Chicago:
University of Chicago, 1951); Langdon Gilkey *Message and Existence: An
Introduction to Christian Theology* (New York: Seabury, 1981); and David
Tracy, *Blessed Rage for Order: The New Pluralism in Theology* (New York:
Seabury, 1975), especially chap. 3.

[29]See, e.g., Nicholas Wolterstorff, *Until Justice and Peace Embrace*
(Grand Rapids: Eerdmans, 1983), chap. 8 for an articulation of how one's

> When we turn the attention of the church to a definition of the Christian relationship with the natural world, we are not stepping away from grave and proper theological ideas; we are stepping right into the middle of them. There is a deeply rooted, genuinely Christian motivation for attention to God's creation, despite the fact that many church people consider ecology to be a secular concern.[30]

In short, even if there were *not* ecological degradation of the kind and extent which we face today, there are *still* compelling reasons from within the Christian faith itself for reflecting theologically on this issue and ultimately for attending to the earth and caring for its many creatures.

Ruether, Sittler, Moltmann

The specific focus of this project is provided by the three thinkers specified in the title. Ruether has been chosen for a number of reasons. First, she was one of the first Christian theologians to perceive clearly and articulate forcefully the interconnections between liberation theology and theology of nature, making those connections in the late 1960's. While many today see ecological theology and political or liberation theology as separate and in fact antagonistic projects, Ruether was one of the first and is still one of the few to link these concerns and correctly see them as two sides of

---

Christian worldview should function both in shaping the direction of research and in theory acceptance and rejection, i.e., as providing both a governing interest and a controlling principle in one's scholarly activites. Alvin Plantinga says essentially the same thing in his "Advice to Christian Philosophers," in *Christian Theism and the Problems of Philosophy*, ed. Michael Beaty (Notre Dame: University of Notre Dame, 1990). Both of these contemporary Christian philosophers are indebted to the Dutch neo-Calvinist tradition of Abraham Kuyper.

[30]Joseph Sittler, *Gravity and Grace*, ed. Linda Marie Delloff (Minneapolis: Augsburg, 1986), 15. For confirmation of Sittler's firm conviction that the natural world is a fundamental theological issue, see Peter Bakken, "The Ecology of Grace: Ultimacy and Environmental Ethics in Aldo Leopold and Joseph Sittler" (Ph.D. dissertation, University of Chicago, 1991), 41.

a single issue.[31] Indeed, she has reformulated her entire theology from not only a feminist perspective but also from an ecological point of view, thus joining a growing number of ecofeminists.[32] One of the arguments presented in this work is that any relatively adequate Christian ecological theology must include as a central dimension a concern for and ability to address issues of social justice and human liberation.

In addition, Ruether is included here because feminism presents one of the major challenges to any theological perspective today, raising important and inescapable issues, particularly with respect to the doctrine of God.[33] Responsible Christian theology must address the various concerns raised by feminism, and by ecofeminism in particular. Ruether is one of the major Christian feminist theologians of our time--an excellent exemplar of the best in feminist thinking. She presents the challenges of feminism in a powerful way. If one is to address these challenges, one could do no better than to take Ruether's work seriously.

Third, Ruether has been chosen because she is relentlessly critical of every position and insightfully self-critical about feminism itself. She poses to every point of view uncomfortable but necessary questions about intellectual honesty and theological integrity. For example, to engage in dialogue with her is to risk hearing and being forced to respond to the marginal and muffled voices of women, the poor, and people of color, and thereby to risk

---

[31]For example, Rosemary Radford Ruether, *Liberation Theology* (New York: Paulist, 1972), 18, 123. Paul Santmire is another theologian who early on saw this interconnection; see, e.g., "Ecology, Justice and Theology."

[32]Rosemary Radford Ruether, *Sexism and God-Talk* (Boston: Beacon, 1983), 85. Sallie McFague is another such thinker; see, e.g., *Models of God* (Philadelphia: Fortress, 1987), and also McFague's *The Body of God: An Ecological Theology* (Minneapolis: Augsburg/Fortress,1993).

[33]In her book *Transforming Grace* Anne Carr presents this challenge particularly well. See also Carol Gould, *Beyond Domination: New Perspectives on Women and Philosophy* (Totowa, NJ: Rowman and Allanheld, 1983); Elizabeth Dodson Gray, *Green Paradise Lost* (Wellesley: Roundtable, 1981); Evelyn Fox Keller, *Reflections on Gender and Science* (New Haven: Yale, 1985); Marjorie Casebier McCoy, "Feminist Consciousness in Creation," in *Cry of the Environment*, ed. Philip Joranson and Ken Butigan (Santa Fe: Bear, 1984); Michelle Zimbalist Rosaldo and Louise Lamphere, eds., *Women, Culture, and Society* (Stanford: Stanford University, 1974).

being changed.[34]But such a risk is at the heart of the Christian gospel. Indeed, to hear the voices of and compassionately respond to today's equivalents of the Old Testament widows, orphans, and sojourners are essential to authentic Christian discipleship.

Sittler also has been chosen for a variety of reasons. First, he was one of the first Christian theologians in this century to talk seriously about the ecological implications of Christian theology and practice. Even before his famous 1961 speech to the World Council of Churches in New Delhi,[35] Sittler was theologizing in an ecological mode in the 1950's--long before the recent awareness of the plight of the earth and certainly long before it was theologically fashionable.[36] Sittler, from the beginning of his career, thought and wrote and preached with ecological concerns in mind.[37] As Paul Santmire, among many others, has noted, Joseph Sittler was a "pioneering Christian theologian of nature."[38]

Sittler is also included here because he is an all too neglected yet insightful and important figure. While well known in certain circles, e.g., within American Lutheranism, within the ecumenical movement, and at the University of Chicago, Sittler is still a relative unknown--a relative unknown who has much to offer current theological reflection, especially with respect to ecology and christology. Only recently has his work attracted the attention that it properly deserves.[39] One of the arguments of this endeavor

---

[34]Mary Hembrow Snyder confirms this when she says that Ruether "challenges us to hear the cry of the victims." In *The Christology of Rosemary Radford Ruether: A Critical Introduction* (Mystic, CT: Twenty-Third, 1988), 114.

[35]Joseph Sittler, "Called to Unity," *Southeast Asia Journal of Theology* 3 (April 1962): 6-15.

[36]Sittler's ecological ruminations go back at least to 1953. See, e.g., "God, Man, Nature" in *The Pulpit* 24 (August 1953): 16-17. This is confirmed by Bakken, "The Ecology of Grace," 41.

[37]See Sittler, *Gravity and Grace*, 83 where he mentions that he majored in both religion and biology in college in the 1920's. While ecology was not the household word and primary area of study then that it is now, it is interesting to note Sittler's early interest in matters biological.

[38]See, e.g., the dedication in Santmire's *The Travail of Nature*.

[39]The only in-depth examinations of Sittler's theology of which I am aware are Peter Bakken's aforementioned 1991 University of Chicago dissertation, "The Ecology of Grace: Ultimacy and Environmental Ethics in Aldo Leopold and Joseph Sittler;" and Moira Creede, "Logos and Lord: A

is that any relatively adequate Christian ecological theology must reformulate christology along the lines Sittler suggests. There is a goodly inheritance in Sittler's theology, the riches of which remain largely unknown and unappreciated.

Finally, Sittler offers for study the instructive example of a Protestant church theologian who creatively attempts to rework traditional categories and modes of thought, e.g., the concepts of nature and grace.[40] In other words, Sittler is a case study in the possibilities and limitations of a self-consciously pastoral and theological approach to the issues facing us today.[41] He in his work poses the question of how the orthodox Christian tradition can and must be reconceived in order to be adequate both to the demands of the tradition itself and to the demands of today. If those texts of scripture and those strands of tradition which speak in a more creation-affirming way are taken seriously, how would Christian theology (and the practices informed by it) change? If the groanings of a degraded world as well as the beauty of a flourishing earth are accurately perceived, how would Christian theology (and its practices) be different? And Sittler asks these questions in and with and for the Church.

Like the previous thinkers, Moltmann too has been chosen for a number of reasons. First of all, he has developed a creative Christian theology which takes seriously not only fidelity to the Christian tradition but also both the present ecological crisis and the worldwide struggle for liberation. That is, similar to Ruether, Moltmann has developed a theological perspective which attempts to address both concern for human liberation and concern for ecological wholeness. And like Sittler he has developed his theology not only in light of current ecological degradation, but also in

---

Study in the Cosmic Christology of Joseph Sittler" (Ph.D. dissertation, Louvain, 1977).

[40]See, e.g., Sittler, *Gravity and Grace*, 65, 67 for comments on the primary role of the pastorate and of preaching on his theology. See also the remarks about Sittler's self-perceived role preeminently as a *church* theologian, in Bakken, "The Ecology of Grace," 37, 43.

[41]For example, on pp. 100-101 of "In Appreciation of Joseph Sittler," *The Journal of Religion* 54 (April 1974), Jerald Brauer speaks of Sittler as a "pastoral theologian" who "remained a churchman, even a pastor, throughout his career at Chicago."

continuity with the Christian tradition[42] In short, Moltmann's theology represents an impressive attempt to combine a number of features crucial to any adequate Christian ecological theology.

Moltmann is also included here because he is a highly regarded and influential theologian from the Reformed tradition-- that strand of the tapestry of Christian faith that I call home. In fact, he has articulated the most creative and sophisticated ecological theology from the Reformed perspective of which I am aware.[43] So Moltmann represents an important dialogue partner from within my own theological and philosophical tradition--a thinker who exemplifies certain of the strengths and a number of the weaknesses of that tradition. He is, in short, someone from whom much can be learned.

---

[42]For example, Moltmann refers to his method as "an ecumenical method" which draws upon Protestant, Catholic, and Orthodox sources; see Jürgen Moltmann, *God In Creation: A New Theology of Creation and the Spirit of God* (San Francisco: Harper and Row, 1985), xiii.

[43]Other Reformed thinkers who have recently addressed the issue of a theology of nature include: Wes Granberg-Michaelson, *Worldly Spirituality* (San Francisco: Harper and Row, 1984), *Tending the Garden* (Grand Rapids: Eerdmans, 1987), *Ecology and Life* (Waco: Word, 1988), and various articles some of which are listed in the bibliography; Paul Fries, "Explorations in the Spirit and Creation," *Perspectives/Reformed Journal* 6 (January 1991): 10-13; and, more indirectly, Christopher Kaiser, *Creation and the History of Science* (Grand Rapids: Eerdmans, 1991).

Valentine Hepp's 1930 Princeton Seminary Stone Lectures, published as *Calvinism and the Philosophy of Nature* (Grand Rapids: Eerdmans, 1930), is not terribly helpful. Of more interest is Herman Bavinck's 1908-09 Stone Lectures, reprinted as *The Philosophy of Revelation* (Grand Rapids: Baker, 1979). Hepp followed Abraham Kuyper and Bavinck in the chair of systematic theology at the Free University of Amsterdam, and was succeeded by G. C. Berkouwer. The most relevant of Berkouwer's writings is *Alegemene Openbaring*, volume four of his "Studies in Dogmatics," and (poorly) translated into English as *General Revelation* (Grand Rapids: Eerdmans, 1955).

Of course the source for much of these reflections is John Calvin, especially chapters 1-5 of Book I of his *Institutio Christianae religionis*, translated by Ford Lewis Battles and edited by John McNeill as *Institutes of the Christian Religion* (Philadelphia: Westminster, 1960). A fine study of Calvin's theology of nature is Susan Schreiner's *The Theatre of His Glory: Nature and Natural Order in the Thought of John Calvin* (Grand Rapids: Baker, 1991).

Moltmann has been chosen, thirdly, because he has explored at length a fully trinitarian theology, emphasizing especially the role of the Holy Spirit. One of the arguments of this book is that any relatively adequate Christian ecological theology must take seriously the person and work of the Holy Spirit. A further and related argument is that an adequate Christian theology must be a trinitarian theology. For those convinced of these claims, Moltmann's work is a significant resource for further theological development. For those as yet unpersuaded, Moltmann presents a compelling case for each of these claims. In any event, his work illustrates both the considerable assets and the possible liabilities of a trinitarian theology.

Thus I am taking up H. Paul Santmire's suggestion that Sittler and Moltmann should be given more attention since they have offered some of the most creative and satisfactory reflections in the area of Christian ecological theology in the recent past. Santmire names John Cobb, Joseph Sittler, and Jürgen Moltmann as the Christian theologians who in his judgment have provided the most creative and fruitful reflections aimed at developing a theology of nature--on the first, second, and third persons of the Trinity, respectively.[44] In my own "holy trinity" I have replaced Cobb with Ruether since I find Cobb's process theology more problematic and less helpful than Ruether's feminist perspective,[45] and since some important work has already been done on the ecological dimensions of his theology.[46]

---

[44]H. Paul Santmire, "Healing the Protestant Mind: Beyond the Theology of Human Dominion," unpublished manuscript prepared for the "Theology and Ethics Symposium: New Perspectives on Ecojustice" (Chicago, March, 1990), 2. See also Santmire, "Studying the Doctrine of Creation," *Dialog* 21 (Summer 1982): 199; and "Toward A New Theology of Nature," *Dialog* 25 (Winter 1986): 47.

[45]For critiques of process thought, see, e.g., Robert Neville, *Creativity and God* (New York: Seabury, 1980); David Basinger, *Divine Power in Process Theism* (Albany: State University of New York, 1988); Langdon Gilkey, *Reaping the Whirlwind* (New York: Seabury, 1981); Ronald Nash, ed., *Process Theology* (Grand Rapids: Baker, 1987).

[46]See, e.g., Claude Stewart, Jr. *Nature in Grace* (Macon: Mercer, 1983), chap. 3.

Thesis Statement

The overall argument or thesis of this book has two parts. First, I argue that only a perspective which reconceives basic issues having to do with anthropology, ontology, and theology proper will be adequate to both the best of the Christian tradition and the present ecological crisis and--insofar as attitudes influence action, beliefs shape behavior, theology informs practice--lead to a more earth-affirming way of life. That is, a Christian ecological theology will be adequate both to its own central message and to the groanings of creation only if it reshapes certain fundamental theological concepts, namely, the concepts of humanity, world, and God. As Max Wildiers states: "All human reflection on the deeper meaning of life ultimately revolves around three concepts, or the metaphysical trinity as they have been called: God, man, and world."[47] In short, a revision of certain basic theological and philosophical categories is a necessary, but not sufficient, condition for an adequate Christian ecological theology.

Such a claim is, in a sense, purely formal. It specifies no substantive content; it gives no indication of the precise nature of the proposed reconceptions. It merely states the need for revision and identifies the particular theological and philosophical loci involved. While a necessary preliminary step in the overall argument, by itself this claim is insufficient. Some specification of the exact nature of the revisions is required.

Thus the second part of the thesis spells out proposed revisions. With respect to anthropology I argue, among other things, that the typical dualism between nature and history is mistaken and must be replaced by a perspective in which these basic categories are reconceived in less dichotomistic ways. On the basis of both the science of ecology, e.g., its contention about the interdependent character of all things, and the study of scripture, e.g., the testimony to the one covenant of creation, I claim that we must move beyond the dualism of nature and history--which sets non-human and human over against each other such that nature is

---

[47]N. Max Wildiers, *The Theologian and His Universe* (New York: Seabury, 1982), 1.

inevitably devalued--by redefining history as inclusive of all being and nature as inclusive of human being. As Ian Barbour claims, this project is possible since the "distinctive features of human existence can be acknowledged without denying man's fundamental unity with nature."[48] And as David Tracy and Nicholas Lash maintain, this task is necessary: "History cannot be understood without nature" and thus "contemporary Christian theology needs to recover a theology of nature--even to develop an adequate theology of history."[49]

With respect to ontology I argue, for example, that the common view of "nature" as essentially autonomous and basically unresponsive is mistaken and must be replaced by a perspective in which the natural world is seen as a grace-full and response-able creation. Indeed I contend that the term nature itself should be replaced by the term creation. A theocentric perspective in which the relatedness and responsiveness of creation are central is more adequate than either an anthropocentric view which divests creation of its grace-full character or a cosmocentric view which re-enchants creation with some sort of quasi-divine status. As Sittler suggests:

> Man is not alone is this world, not even when his aloneness is unalleviated by the companionship of the fellowman. The creation is a community of abounding life--from the invisible microbes to the highly visible elephants, the vastness of the mountains, the sweep of the seas, the expanse of land. These companions of our creaturehood are not only *there*; they are there as things without which I cannot be at all! They surround, support, nourish, delight, challenge, and talk back to us.[50]

Santmire similarly proposes that given "a certain *mysterious activity*" of non-human creatures, we must speak of a third type of

---

[48]Ian Barbour, "Attitudes Toward Nature and Technology," in *Earth Might Be Fair*, ed. Ian Barbour (Engelwood Cliffs: Prentice Hall, 1972), 152.

[49]David Tracy and Nicholas Lash, eds. *Cosmology and Theology* (New York: Seabury, 1983), 87, 89.

[50]Joseph Sittler, "Evangelism and the Care of the Earth," in *Preaching in the Witnessing Community*, ed. Herman Stuempfle (Philadelphia: Fortress, 1973), 102.

relation beyond the I-Thou or I-It relations, namely, "the I-Ens relation," if we are to capture the responsiveness of creation.[51]

With regard to theology proper, the argument has three distinct sub-claims. First, I argue that a doctrine of God that relies exclusively on patriarchal images must give way to a more inclusive view of the first person of the Trinity that includes images of God as, for example, caregiver and nurturer--as Ruether advocates--if the doctrine of God is to serve, as it must, as an integral part of a Christian ecological theology. Second, a christology that tends to focus exclusively on humanity must be replaced by a christology that is cosmic in scope, including within its purview not merely human history but also the entire natural world--as Sittler argues--if the doctrine of Christ is to be, as it must, of genuine assistance within a Christian ecological theology. And third, the typical view of the Holy Spirit as unimportant must be replaced by an acknowledgment of the role of the Holy Spirit as the authentic presence of God in and with creation, especially within a social theory of the Trinity--as Moltmann maintains--if the doctrine of the Holy Spirit is to play, as it must, a significant role in a Christian ecological theology. In short, an adequate Christian ecological theology will involve certain reformulations with respect to the first, second, and third persons of the Trinity-- taking cues from Ruether, Sittler, and Moltmann, respectively.

In summary, my argument involves two basic claims. First, a necessary condition for any relatively adequate Christian ecological theology is the examination and reformulation of certain issues in anthropology, ontology, and theology proper. This theology must reconceive its views of the nature and role of humankind, of the relationship between God and the cosmos, and of the character and action of God. Such a Christian theology may involve more reformulation, but if adequate it will not involve less.

Second, with respect primarily to theology proper, certain revisions are necessary *if* the doctrines of God, Christ, and the Holy Spirit are to play more integral roles in grounding a Christian ecological theology, and given the assumption that theology

---

[51]H. Paul Santmire, "I-Thou, I-It, and I-Ens," *The Journal of Religion* 48 (July 1969): 266.

informs practice, if such a Christian theology is to function constructively in bringing shalom to the earth. Something like Ruether's claim that God must be like a Mother as well as like a Father, Matrix as well as Creator; and something like Sittler's claim that Christ must be cosmic, Lord of "nature" as well as "history," agent of creation as well as redemption; and something like Moltmann's claim that the Holy Spirit permeates all creation, in, with, and under all being--something akin to these three claims are necessary if not sufficient conditions if theology, christology, and pneumatology are to be an integral part of a Christian ecological theology.

Methodology and Outline

In the three chapters that follow, my methodology is to expound systematically the thought of each of the three theologians under consideration. In other words, first with respect to Ruether, then Sittler, and finally Moltmann, I explain those aspects (and only those aspects) of each person's thought that pertain to a Christian ecological theology. In each case the exposition differs. With Ruether I expound chronologically the development of her thought with regard to a single multifaceted topic, namely, ecojustice. With Sittler I set forth thematically various dimensions of his thought as they bear on a particular position, i.e., cosmic christology. And with Moltmann I elucidate certain selected works within the context of his larger theological project, viz., primarily the first two volumes of his ongoing systematic theology.

These three chapters of exposition are followed in chapters five, six, and seven by analysis and critique. Here I carefully examine and evaluate each thinker's perspective. Taking cues from Wildiers' "metaphysical trinity" and Santmire's tasks, this task of analysis and critique falls under three headings: anthropology, ontology, and theology. That is, I am adopting the threefold rubric of humanity, world, and God as a general interpretive framework, and thus am concentrating on Santmire's tasks two, three, and five: the philosophical-theological and anthropological task of elucidating the nature of human being and its place in the world, especially the relation between nature and history; the metaphorical-metaphysical task of finding a root metaphor or foundational analogy or basic image that best expresses the relation between God and creation; and the strictly theological task of understanding the attributes and action of God.

These three chapters of analysis and critique are followed in the concluding chapter--chapter eight--by a critical comparison which presents the major contributions of each of these thinkers and which points to some of the revisions necessary for a more adequate Christian ecological theology. In this chapter I also begin to develop my own constructive position. By concentrating on the metaphysical trinity of the human, world, and God and by incorporating various of the distinctive contributions of Ruether, Sittler, and Moltmann, I begin to develop a perspective which moves beyond the typical dualism of nature and history, which more adequately expresses the responsiveness of creation, and which articulates a social theory of the Trinity. Needless to say, this exploration will be unfinished.

CHAPTER 2

BEYOND GOD THE FATHER:
THE THEOLOGY OF ROSEMARY RUETHER

We cannot criticize the hierarchy of male over female without ultimately criticizing and overcoming the hierarchy of human over nature.[1]

Rosemary Radford Ruether

Women must see that there can be no liberation for them and no solution to the ecological crisis within a society whose fundamental model of relationships continues to be one of domination. They must unite the demands of the women's movement with those of the ecological movement to envision a radical reshaping of the basic socioeconomic relations and the underlying values of this society.[2]

Rosemary Radford Ruether

The Significance of Ruether

As indicated in chapter one, Rosemary Radford Ruether is one of the leading contemporary feminist theologians. She has written or edited nearly two dozen books and written literally hundreds of articles and reviews. Her writing spans the disciplines, from history to sociology to theology proper, and is recognized for its critical insight, thought-provoking creativity, and prophetic power.[3] She is, simply put, one of the most important theologians alive today.[4]

---

[1] Ruether, *Sexism and God-Talk*, 73.

[2] Rosemary Radford Ruether, *New Woman/New Earth: Sexist Ideologies and Human Liberation* (San Francisco: Harper and Row, 1975), 204.

[3] For example, William Ramsey includes Ruether, along with Walter Rauschenbusch, Martin Luther King, Jr., and Gustavo Gutierrez, in his *Four Modern Prophets* (Atlanta: John Knox, 1986).

[4] For example, Ruether is one of twenty-one theologians, and only one of two women, included in the *Christian Century* series "How My

As also indicated previously, while taking seriously the feminist critique of Christianity, Ruether wishes to remain within the Christian tradition. She attempts to take seriously "both the radical feminist critique of Judaism and Christianity and the experience of many thoughtful women who remain within the synagogues and churches."[5] Like Elizabeth Schussler Fiorenza, Anne Carr, Phyllis Trible, and Letty Russell, Ruether undertakes "a critical retrieval of the central Christian symbols understood in the context of the wider discussion in contemporary Christian theology."[6] Unlike some feminists, e.g., Mary Daly, Ruether is unwilling to abandon the Christian scriptures and tradition.

While much has been written about Ruether, there are few in depth examinations of her theology.[7] Needless to say, this is not a comprehensive exposition and analysis of her thought. Rather, given the circumscribed scope of this project, the focus in what follows is assiduously on only those aspects of Ruether's theology which concern the development of an ecological theology. That is, while acknowledging that the thought of most theologians is of a piece, in this chapter I am concerned only with those dimensions of Ruether's theology which are germane to the issues of this endeavor. The outline for this chapter is straightforward. After a short section on the theme of double domination, I present, in chronological order, an exposition of selected aspects of Ruether's theology. As mentioned in chapter one, an analysis and critique of Ruether's theology will be offered in chapter five.

Mind Has Changed," edited by James Wall and published as *Theologians in Transition* (New York: Crossroad, 1981).

[5]Carr, *Transforming Grace*, 92.

[6]Ibid. Important titles by the others mentioned include Elizabeth Schussler Fiorenza, *In Memory of Her: A Feminist Theological Reconstruction of Christian Origins* (New York: Crossroad, 1983); Carr, *Transforming Grace*; Phyllis Trible, *God and the Rhetoric of Sexuality* (Philadelphia: Fortress, 1978); Letty Russell, *Human Liberation in a Feminist Perspective: A Theology* (Philadelphia: Westminster, 1974).

[7]See, e.g., Snyder, *The Christology of Rosemary Radford Ruether*; Judith Vaughan, *Sociality, Ethics, and Social Change: A Critical Appraisal of Reinhold Niebuhr's Ethics in the Light of Rosemary Radford Ruether's Works* (Lanham: University Press of America, 1983); and Mary Kathryn Williams Weir, "The Concept of Freedom in the Work of Rosemary Radford Ruether" (Ph.D. dissertation, University of St. Andrews, 1982).

Double Domination

Rosemary Ruether was one of the first contemporary thinkers to perceive and articulate the interconnections between two seemingly disparate issues. Since at least 1971 Ruether has seen the connections between the domination of nature and the domination of women (and humans more generally) and has provided insightful and passionate accounts of this inter-relationship.[8] In addition, she has offered arguments for a religious and social vision which would address *both* ecological degradation *and* social injustice, especially injustice to women.

To be sure, there are others who have made the connection between environmental destruction and female subordination. For example, Elizabeth Dodson Gray in *Green Paradise Lost*, previously published with the provocative title *Why the Green Nigger?*, explores the identification and consequent domination of women and nature.[9] As the original title strikingly suggests, Gray seeks to understand how the earth has come to be treated as a "green nigger"--abused, dominated, exploited. Borrowing from Dorothy Dinnerstein and Nancy Chodorow, Gray insightfully describes the "feminizing of nature" evident in such a common and seemingly benign expression as "Mother Nature."[10] Gray moves beyond diagnosis to a prescription that includes insights from, among others, Whitehead, St. Francis, and Aldo Leopold. Her prescription for what ails us also involves taking seriously God's

---

[8]The earliest reference in Ruether's work to the interconnection between the domination of nature and the domination of women that I have been able to locate is "Mother Earth and the Megamachine," *Christianity and Crisis*, 13 December 1971.

[9]Elizabeth Dodson Gray, *Why the Green Nigger?: Remything Genesis* (Wellesley: Roundtable, 1979). As indicated previously, *Green Paradise Lost* was published in 1981.

[10]Ibid., chap. 4. See also Dorothy Dinnerstein, *The Mermaid and the Minotaur: Sexual Arrangements and Human Malaise* (New York: Harper and Row, 1976); Nancy Chodorow, "Family Structure and Feminine Personality," in *Women, Culture, and Society*, eds. Michelle Zimbalist Rosaldo and Louise Lamphere (Stanford: Stanford University, 1974).

covenant in Genesis 9--a covenant with *all* creation in its interdependent diversity.[11]

As William French perceptively points out, however, Gray has a tendency toward reverse sexism "based on reductionistic generalization and biological determinism."[12] As French indicates, Gray tends to claim female superiority because of women's connection to nature, whereas Ruether, as we will see, "makes a more accurate and limited claim that some classes of women have a superior social and cultural awareness...afforded them by their experience of systematic victimage and oppression."[13] In other words, it is not biology but cultural experience that provides women with greater insight. Notwithstanding this criticism, Gray's work is an important if neglected treatment of this issue.

Another example of someone who has perceived the connections between the oppression of women and the exploitation of nature is Carolyn Merchant. In her fine historical study *The Death of Nature: Women, Ecology, and the Scientific Revolution* Merchant persuasively argues that "we must reexamine the formation of a world view and a science that, by reconceptualizing reality as a machine rather than a living organism, sanctioned the domination of both nature and women."[14] She further states that her book

---

[11]Gray, *Why the Green Nigger?*, 146-149. Gray has pointed to a significant yet often overlooked biblical resource. Unlike the subsequent covenants, the covenant in Genesis 9 involves more than just humans. Six times in verses 8-17, like a constant drumbeat, the text tells us that God made a covenant with much *more* than humans. For example, the covenant is between God and 1) every living creature (*kol basar hayyah*) that is with you (vss. 10, 12); 2) the earth (*haeres*) (vs. 13); 3) every living creature of all flesh (*kol nephesh hayyah bekol basar*) (vs. 15); 4) every living creature of all flesh that is upon the earth (*kol nephesh hayyah bekol basar asher al haeres*) (vs. 16); 5) all flesh that is upon the earth (*kol basar asher al haeres*) (vs. 17). God's original and unconditional covenant is *not* an anthropocentric covenant.

[12]William French, "Christianity and the Domination of Nature" (Ph.D. dissertation, University of Chicago, 1985), 315.

[13]Ibid., 317.

[14]Carolyn Merchant, *The Death of Nature: Women, Ecology, and the Scientific Revolution* (San Francisco: Harper and Row, 1980), xvii.

elaborates an ecological perspective that includes both nature and
humankind in explaining the developments that resulted in the
death of nature as a living being and the accelerating exploitation of
both human and natural resources in the name of culture and
progress.[15]

However, while attentive to religion, Merchant's work is primarily
historical and thus offers fewer resources for an ecological
theology than Ruether's explicitly theological perspective.

Hence while some have perceived and addressed the
interconnections between the subjugation of women and the
subjugation of nature, there are few people who have
comprehensively addressed *both* of these issues as frequently and
insightfully as Ruether, or done so in as theologically rigorous a
way. Having an inclusive vision--a vision of the wholeness of all
things--that breaks down the divisions between people is rare.
Indeed, as Sallie McFague says, citing Ruether as an example,
"only in a few instances has this vision been extended to the
nonhuman world."[16] This relatively unique feature of Ruether's
theology--her attempt to address both the domination of women
and the domination of nature, both androcentrism and
anthropocentrism--serves as an excellent entry point into her
theology and its contributions to a Christian ecological theology.

In order to grasp accurately the scope and vigor of Ruether's
argument, it is most advantageous to trace chronologically the
development of her thought on this topic of double domination.
While her views have not changed in any substantive way over the
last twenty-five years, she has added certain insights and
emphasized particular themes as warranted by the situation,
thereby constructing a web of various strands when viewed over
time and as a whole.

As indicated above, awareness of this issue first surfaces in
"Motherearth and the Megamachine: A Theology of Liberation in a
Feminine, Somatic and Ecological Perspective," which appeared in
Christianity and Crisis in 1971, and was included as a chapter in
the book *Liberation Theology* published in 1972. Ruether begins her

---

[15]Ibid., xvii-xviii.
[16]McFague, *Models of God*, 7.

argument with historical-cultural explorations. In this essay, Ruether claims that Christianity is the synthesis of two world-negating religions, namely, apocalyptic Judaism, with its male warrior god and heavenly messianic king, and Neo-Platonism, with its exaltation of intellect over body and vision of a transcendent logos of immutable Being.[17] This combination of world-negating religious traditions in late antiquity bequeathed to Christianity an unfortunate legacy of dualisms: mind/body, intellect/emotion, spirit/matter, culture/nature, and male/female, to name just a few. But, argues Ruether, "the alienation of the masculine from the feminine is the primary sexual symbolism that sums up all these alienations."[18] Or alternately, the "subjugation of the female by the male is the primary psychic model" for the various other forms of oppression.[19] Ruether thus argues that the world-view which places culture over against nature, thereby sanctioning the exploitation of nature, has its origin in the dualism of male over female and consequent domination of the latter by the former.

Ruether traces "the psycho-social history of the domination of women" through three stages.[20] What began as the holistic, communal worldview of the neolithic village--a worldview in which there were no dualisms between male and female or society and nature--started to break down some time in the first millennium B.C. Both in Hebrew religion, e.g., in apocalyptic, and in classical philosophy, e.g., in Plato, the individual became alienated from the world, male deities were elevated while female deities were repressed, and nature was seen as an alien reality. For example, in Hebrew religion "hopes for a renewal of nature and society, projected into a once and for all historical future, now came to be seen as less and less realizable in history itself," ultimately ending in "the apocalyptic negation of history itself."[21]

---

[17]Ruether, *Liberation Theology*, 115.
[18]Ibid., 115-116.
[19]Ibid., 118.
[20]Ibid., 118-123.
[21]Ibid., 120.

To use the language of Charles Murphy, the earth had come to be seen as our hotel rather than our home.[22]

According to Ruether, despite the emphasis on creation and incarnation in Christianity, this dualistic worldview with its body-negating, anti-feminine spirituality became enshrined as the dominant worldview within the Christian tradition. And it is this worldview, with its "emphasis upon the transcendent consciousness" and "will to transcend and dominate the natural and social world," that has over time created "the urban earth" and given birth to *both* the ecological crisis and the oppression of women.[23] In others words, "social oppression in Western culture is very closely related to the mentality that has created body-alienation and earth-exploitation," and so "it is not accidental that the most devastated environments, whether in Appalachia or in the ghetto, are found where poor people live."[24] The oppression of persons and the oppression of the earth stem from the same mentality--a mentality which, according to Ruether, was ingredient in Christianity from the very beginning and which Christianity has actively fostered.

Then, in 1971, Ruether presciently saw that both "nature and society are giving clear warning signals that the usefulnesss of this spirituality [of domination] is about to end."[25] In words that still ring true today, over twenty years later, she observes that there are two "revolutions" going on: a human potential movement seeking communal, egalitarian, and ecological patterns of livings, and a liberation movement seeking social justice. Unfortunately in her view, these two revolutions "are running in contrapuntal directions." That is to say, the human potential and environmental movements remain "elitist, privatistic, esthetic, and devoid of a profound covenant with the poor and oppressed of the earth," while the liberation movement, in contrast, relies on "technological

---

[22]Charles Murphy, *At Home On Earth: Foundations for a Catholic Ethic of the Environment* (New York: Crossroad, 1989), chap. 2.

[23]Ruether, *Liberation Theology*, 122.

[24]Ibid., 18.

[25]Ibid., 123.

domination of nature and antagonistic, competitive relationships between peoples."[26]

It is in this situation, still largely the case today, that Ruether asserts that "women must be the spokesmen for a new humanity arising out of the reconciliation of spirit and body."[27] The women's movement, she observes, is uniquely located in the center of the clash between the two above-named revolutions, since women are both the oldest oppressed people and have been identified with a subjugated earth. In short, Ruether maintains that in order to "build a new cooperative social order out beyond the principles of hierarchy, rule, and competitiveness," we must get beyond *both* motherearth *and* the megamachine.[28] If we are to move beyond both "the romanticized primitive jungle" and "the modern technological wasteland," then "we must create a living pattern of mutuality between men and women, between parents and children, among people in their social, economic, and political relationships, and finally between mankind and the organic harmonies of nature."[29] And, in her opinion, the women's movement is strategically placed to effect just such a pattern of socio-cultural transformation.

The Biblical Vision of the Ecological Crisis

In an essay published a year later, "Paradoxes of Human Hope: The Messianic Horizon of Church and Society," Ruether delves more deeply into the Hebrew heritage of Christianity in order to retrieve and emphasize certain aspects of an oft forgotten tradition. More specifically, she affirms that "the biblical prophetic message brought together as a single vision the dualisms between the sacred and the secular, the individual and society, the spiritual and the material, which Christianity absorbed through the

---

[26]Ibid.
[27]Ibid., 124.
[28]Ibid., 124-125.
[29]Ibid., 125.

religious culture of later Hellenism."[30] Thus "Israel's hope for
salvation did not split the human community from the cosmos, but
looked forward to a total transfiguration of man and nature in the
kingdom of God."[31] Ruether proceeds to trace how "the holistic
world view of the Psalms was broken up into a number of
contradictions," e.g., dualisms between individual and society, this-
worldly and other-worldly hope.[32]

Ruether claims, for example, that the early Hebrews viewed
all of life in terms of a single unified covenant. There was no sharp
contrast between individual and society, private and public, since
"man and nature, as one covenant of creation, wept together and
rejoiced together."[33] Future life did not involve "the salvation of
the individual psyche," but rather "the transfiguration of creation,
embodying not only each man's inward obedience to God, but
justice and peace between man and man, man and animal, animal
and animal."[34] With the coming of imperial conquest, e.g., the
empires of Persia, Greece, and Rome, however, this collective
consciousness was eroded and eventually replaced by an ecologically destructive individualism.

In light of this alienation of the individual from society and of
humankind from the nonhuman world, Ruether argues that we
must "return to the holistic vision of messianism"--to "a world
view in which man, society, and nature form a single community of
life."[35] We must renew a vision

> that perceives the interdependence of all living things in a global
> community where personal morality cannot be divorced from how
> we live our lives with our fellows, even on the other side of the
> earth, or how we situate our social and economic systems in
> relation to the organic systems of animal and plant, earth and sky,
> air and water.[36]

---

[30]Rosemary Radford Ruether, "Paradoxes of Human Hope: The
Messianic Horizon of Church and Society," *Theological Studies* 33 (June
1972): 235.

[31]Ibid.

[32]Ibid., 239.

[33]Ibid.

[34]Ibid.

[35]Ibid., 241.

[36]Ibid.

Ruether concludes that a theology of messianic hope, similar to that of ancient Israel, can provide significant resources for a more world-affirming perspective that moves beyond "the spirituality of domination and subjugation" common today.[37] Indeed, she declares that the "unfinished effort of classical Christian theology" is "to synthesize the world-affirming and world-negating traditions of religious hope"--to combine "the world-renewing Ba'al with the world-transcending Yahweh-Christ"--so as to bring reconcilation with the earth.[38] In other words, while Ruether here insists that any relatively adequate Christian ecological theology must include both the transcendence and immanence of God, given the predominant emphasis on a world-negating otherness within the tradition, greater emphasis must be placed on God as restorer of the natural world.

In the 1975 essay "Women, Ecology and the Domination of Nature," which is entitled "New Woman and New Earth: Women, Ecology and Social Revolution" in its form as a chapter in the 1975 publication *New Women, New Earth: Sexist Ideologies and Human Liberation*, Ruether further nuances her historical argument and provides some practical proposals that flesh out her alternate vision. Ruether here distinguishes between pre-exilic Hebrew religion and the later developments of Judaism and Christianity, and maintains that, unlike both of the later religions, pre-exilic Hebrew religion "is not a religion that views nature as inferior or evil" since, like ancient Canaanite religion, "it is a religion of socionatural renewal."[39] In the religion of pre-exilic Israel, "society and nature cohere in a single created community under the sovereignty of God"--a community bound together by "a single socionatural covenant."[40] Ruether cites Isaiah 24 as a biblical text which clearly articulates this cojoining of a social or human covenant with a covenant with the natural world, and she refers to

---

[37]Ibid., 251.
[38]Ibid.
[39]Ruether, *New Women/New Earth*, 187.
[40]Ibid., 187-188.

this covenant as a "cosmic covenant" involving not just "the brotherhood of man" but also "the fellowship of life."[41]

Thus Ruether claims that while pre-exilic Old Testament religion is patriarchal, unlike Greek, later Jewish, and Christian traditions, its "religion of socio-natural renewal" did *not* result in a world-negating spirituality. Since it lacks both a spirit/matter or mind/body dualism and any projection of that dualism onto class or sex relations, such that lower classes and women are viewed as inferior, pre-exilic Hebrew religion, while patriarchal, does not involve an alienated view of nature.[42] However, these two ideas, which form the basis for a worldview of world alienation and view of salvation as flight from material existence, are found in apocalyptic Judaism and classical Greek philosophy and are inherited by Christianity. According to Ruether, despite the best attempts to unite the God of creation with the God of redemption, "cosmic alienation and spiritual dualism triumphed in classical Christian spirituality."[43] And so "the Christian view of nature split creation into two opposite possibilities: sacramentality and demonization," such that "nature could be sacramental or demonic, but never secular, i.e., never neutral and 'value-free'."[44]

In Ruether's opinion, this religious synthesis, with its concomitant view of nature as decidedly unsecular, continued until the seventeenth century, at which time the tie between science and this "magical worldview" was broken, most notably by Francis Bacon. Bacon argued that the domination of nature through science was identical to the Christian redemption of nature, but, claims Ruether, "created a quite unchristian split between the moral redemption of the human soul and the restoration of nature," i.e., between the spheres of religion and science.[45] The subjugation of nature to human, viz., male, reason was thus

---

[41]Ibid., 31. See also Rosemary Radford Ruether, "Rich Nations/Poor Nations and the Exploitation of the Earth," *Dialog* 3 (Summer 1974): 207 for a previous discussion of Isaiah 24 and the idea of a single covenant involving both society and nature.
[42]Ruether, *New Women/New Earth*, 188.
[43]Ibid., 190.
[44]Ibid.
[45]Ibid., 191. For a more extensive analysis of this move, see Carolyn Merchant, *The Death of Nature*.

legitimated on religious grounds. Liberalism, despite its own noble intentions, became the social philosophy of scientific rationalism, thus perpetuating domination based upon sex, class, and race. And since "the fruits of domination belonged to the dominant class, sex, and cultural group," i.e., European white males, "the crisis of ecology and technology reflects this context of social injustice and unequal power relations."[46] In other words, the ecological crisis is fully understandable only if it is seen in terms of social justice. In terms Ruether will later use, the movements for ecological wholeness and social justice must be seen as interconnected and ultimately as two sides of a single movement for ecojustice.

This interrelationship is borne out by the fact that, for example, romanticism was a reaction to liberalism that "did not grapple with a socioeconomic or structural dissolution of domination."[47] By stressing the differences between men and women, and specifically positing that women are closer to nature and hence less rational, romanticism perpetuated the domination of both women and the natural world. In the end, according to Ruether, women were caught on the horns of a false dilemma: "emancipation through identification with a misogynist male rationality or identification with a concept of 'nature' and 'femininity' which ever returns them to powerless, inarticulate subjugation."[48] Ruether astutely recognizes that romanticism, now as then, is a form of escapism that ignores important aspects of reality and so evades the actual problem.

The primary and usually implicit assumption of this whole historical development, in Ruether's reading, is "the male ideology of transcendent dualism."[49] This involves seeing reality in terms of a whole chain of dualistic relations--male/female, soul/body, spirit/matter, culture/nature--in which the second half of each pair is seen as alien and subject to the first. The primary characteristic of this ideology is the inability to treat the "other" as subject rather than object. The "other" is merely an alien object for conquest, whether in the case of the domination of women by men, the

---

[46]Ruether, *New Women/New Earth*, 193.
[47]Ibid.
[48]Ibid., 194.
[49]Ibid., 195.

control of the body by the soul, or the exploitation of the nonhuman world by humans.

Furthermore, the socio-economic patterns of industrial society, Ruether argues, have reinforced and intensified the subjugation of both women and the natural world. For example, industrialization changed the home from a producer to a consumer unit in society, thereby reducing the role of women to "interpersonal emotionality, extended child nurture, and the primary physical support of male work" and giving rise in the nineteenth century to "a new type of family and a new definition of woman's 'place.'"[50] The proper place for women was the private sphere of hearth and home. In short, a whole new set of dualisms was added to the previous group: work/leisure, public/private, competition/nurture, business and politics/morality and religion, immoral society/ moral man. One effect of this last dualism with respect to the ecological crisis is to see the crisis solely in terms of individual responses within the so-called private sector, since morality is reduced to that sphere of action. This, of course, leaves unchallenged and unchanged the entire system of domination, whether of the earth or of women.

In light of her historical analysis, Ruether concludes with a summary statement--one which was included at the beginning of this chapter:

> Women must see that there can be no liberation for them and no solution to the ecological crisis within a society whose fundamental model of relationships continues to be one of domination. They must unite the demands of the women's movement with those of the ecological movement to envision a radical reshaping of the basic socioeconomic relations and the underlying values of society. [51]

The domination of "nature" by "man" is intimately related to the social domination of women by men. Hence if the movement for women's liberation is to succeed, then so must the ecological movement succeed, and conversely. The success of one is a necessary condition for the success of the other, and *both* require a overthrow of the current social structure of domination. Both must

---

[50]Ibid., 197.
[51]Ibid., 204.

be replaced by a transformative worldview in which reciprocity and mutuality, equality and solidarity, function as the new norms for society.

Ruether offers some relatively specific proposals on how to incarnate this alternative vision. For example, she contends that a vision of harmony between human and non-human communities "has nothing to do with anti-intellectual or anti-technological primitivism."[52] The problem is not with technology per se, but rather with its misuse by those in power. Technology, for Ruether, is not intrinsically evil, but held captive by the ruling class. The remedy, therefore, is to democratize the decision-making process and equalize the benefits of technological development. More specifically, Ruether advocates "a total overhaul of the present method of transportation that is based on the private auto and the freeway system."[53] Public mass transit, bicycles, and electric cars should be substituted for gasoline-burning and street congesting automobiles. Also, there should be a general shift away from non-renewable and heavily polluting energy sources to renewable and relatively less polluting sources like sun, wind, and water.

In order to actualize such proposals, Ruether eschews both free-market capitalism and Marxist or state socialism by advocating a form of "democratic socialism" or "communitarian socialism" based on strong self-governing local communities.[54] Only in this way, she argues, can the current relationship between power, home, and work--a relationship which produces "the caste status of women"--be overcome, since both free-market capitalism and state socialism support the present system of exploitation. A communitarian socialist society, on the other hand, would allow for the communalization of tasks like housekeeping and child-raising and would spread such activities between both men and women. A decentralized economy would reintegrate home and work and "allow men and women to take an equal hand in both nurturing and supportive roles and also in work and political life."[55] Instead of being forced into social roles that are harmful and

---

[52]Ibid., 205.
[53]Ibid.
[54]Ibid., 206-207.
[55]Ibid., 210.

destructive for both sexes, each person "could shape a complex whole from the full range of human psychic potential for intellect and feeling, activity and receptivity."[56]

In short, Ruether paints a picture of a new social order based on a radically new social vision--a vision of "reciprocal interdependence" rooted in "our actual solidarity with all others and with our mother, the earth, which is the actual ground of our being."[57] Elsewhere Ruether refers to this new vision as "a new mandate to redeem our sister, the earth, from her bondage to destruction."[58] Thus, she concludes:

> The exorcism of the demonic spirit of sexism in the Church touches off a revolution which must transform all the relations of alienation and domination--between self and body, between leaders and community, between person and person, between social groups, between Church and world, between humanity and nature, finally our model of God in relation to creation--all of which have been modeled on the sexist schizophrenia.[59]

Ruether here clearly articulates one of the fundamental theological tasks facing anyone who takes the feminist perspective seriously, namely, the task of transforming the dominant model of the God-creation relation. Ruether herself takes up this challenge most directly in her subsequent work, as we will see.

While having identified the essential dynamics of the concept in previous writings, Ruether first employs the newly coined term ecojustice in a 1978 essay "The Biblical Vision of the Ecological Crisis." This article presents in a succinct and clear manner her views on the basic issues and her own alternative biblical vision. Ruether describes two perspectives which sharply criticize the Western-style industrialization model of development prevalent until the 1960's: the Third World liberation movement and the First World ecological movement. She perceptively notes, however, that these two movements "soon appeared to be in considerable conflict

---

[56]Ibid.
[57]Ibid., 211.
[58]Ibid., 83.
[59]Ibid.

with each other."[60] Many thought, and many still think, that social justice and ecological harmony are ethical norms necessarily in conflict with each other.

Ruether also notes that there are two general religious responses to the ecological crisis. On the one hand, there are those who view all traditional religion as ecologically bankrupt, Christianity especially, and who opt for some form of romanticism or neoanimism. On the other hand, some people defend the biblical tradition, usually advocating a dominion as stewardship rather than a dominion as domination model as an alternative. This stewardship position usually expresses itself in terms of an ethic of conservationism. Ruether points out how both of these religious responses refuse to acknowledge how a particular socio-economic system structures various relationships of exploitation. Both countercultural primitivism and stewardly conservationism are unable or refuse to recognize systemic injustice. Both approaches, in other words, "never deal with the question of ecojustice."[61] Ruether asks "if there is a third approach that has been overlooked by both the nature mystics and the puritan conservationists?"[62] She asks if and how ecological harmony and economic justice can be wedded into a single socio-economic system.

In answer to her own query, Ruether suggests that "our best foundation lies precisely in the Hebrew Bible."[63] She turns again to Isaiah 24 for an alternative vision to both conservationism and romanticism. Over against the history/nature dualism typical of nineteenth century conservationism, the vision of Isaiah 24 does not limit God's presence to history, but rather sees the natural world "as a powerful medium of God's presence or absence."[64] In the Old Testament, Ruether insists, God is related to and active in the trees and the rivers. In contrast to romanticism, on the other

---

[60]Rosemary Radford Ruether, "The Biblical Vision of the Ecological Crisis," *The Christian Century*, 22 November 1978, 1129. For background on the use of the term and the development of the concept of ecojustice, see William Gibson, "Eco-Justice: Burning Word," *Foundations* 20 (October-December 1977).

[61]Ruether, "The Biblical Vision," 1131.
[62]Ibid., 1130.
[63]Ibid., 1131.
[64]Ibid.

hand, Isaiah 24 illustrates that scripture is not to be blamed for what is in fact the quite modern view of nature as merely an object to be controlled and exploited. The view of human reason as "outside and above nature," often attributed by advocates of romanticism to the Bible, "does not properly correspond to any of the earlier religious visions of nature."[65] In short, Ruether asserts that "it is precisely the vision of the Hebrew prophets that provides at least the germ of that critical and prophetic vision" which will allow us "to review and critique where we have gone wrong in our relationship to God's good gift of the earth."[66]

According to Ruether, this prophetic vision implies that "human interaction with nature has made nature itself historical."[67] In other words, nature is historical because "nature no longer exists 'naturally' for it has become part of the human social drama, interacting with humankind as a vehicle of historical judgment and a sign of historical hope."[68] That is, the nonhuman world is mixed, so to speak, with human actions, and in such a way that the natural order represents either judgment or hope on human action in history. In addition, Ruether maintains that "humanity as a part of creation is not outside of nature but within it."[69] That is to say, if we take this and other biblical texts seriously, we cannot deny the creatureliness of humankind, e.g., our finitude and bodiliness. Thus not only is "nature" an inescapable part of history, but humans are inextricably embedded in the natural. Given both of these conclusions, there can be no dualism between nature and history or nature and culture.

This is the case, argues Ruether, preeminently "because nature itself is part of the covenant between God and creation."[70] There is a single covenant that includes *both* humans and non-humans and which entails not only that we as humans have ethical obligations toward God and other people, but also that we have ethical obligations to nonhuman creatures. This further implies, as

---

[65]Ibid.
[66]Ibid.
[67]Ibid.
[68]Ibid.
[69]Ibid.
[70]Ibid.

hinted above, that "nature's responses to human use or abuse become an ethical sign."[71] Air pollution, soil erosion, and water contamination are not just interesting facts about the world, but ethical judgments on human action in the world. On the other hand, rejuvenated lakes, flourishing forests, and air free from sulphur dioxide are signs of hope. For Ruether, both poverty and pollution, social oppression and exploitation of the earth, are violations of this "covenant of creation" since human and nonhuman creatures "are profoundly linked together in the biblical vision as parts of one covenant."[72]

In summary, Ruether reaffirms that in at least certain portions of the Bible "the raping of nature and the exploitation of people in society are profoundly understood as part of one reality, creating disaster in both."[73] Given this affirmation, she draws the conclusion that "the covenant of creation can be rectified and God's Shalom brought to nature and society" only if we engage in "social repentance and conversion to divine commandments."[74] The realization of a full-orbed vision of the flourishing of all creation necessarily requires nothing less. Only "a vision of ecojustice" is adequate for "the sort of ecological theology we need today."[75]

Ecology and Human Liberation

Ruether explores in more detail the unfortunate legacy of a nature/culture dualism and the possibilities of an alternative perspective in the essay, "Ecology and Human Liberation: A Conflict between the Theology of History and the Theology of Nature?", originally given as part of the 1980 Kuyper Lectures at the Free University of Amsterdam and subsequently published in 1981 as a chapter in the book *To Change The World*. Here Ruether not only reiterates some previously developed themes of her historical and socio-cultural analyses but also provides more

---

[71]Ibid.
[72]Ibid., 1132.
[73]Ibid.
[74]Ibid.
[75]Ibid.

substantive constructive proposals, especially in a section entitled "Towards a new world view of eco-justice."

Once again Ruether emphasizes the connections between the ecological crisis and social domination. In her view, "social domination is the missing link in the question of the domination of nature."[76] That is, the environmental crisis is insoluable as long as the present social system allows (mostly male) decision-makers "to maintain high profits for the few by passing on the costs to the many in the form of low wages, high prices, bad working conditions, and toxic side effects of the techniques of extraction."[77] Social justice is a necessary condition for ecological wholeness and harmony. Hence we cannot assume, as many people today do, that the ecological crisis "can be resolved by adopting a new personal ethic and world view of symbiosis and enjoyment of nature."[78] As Ruether strongly asserts:

> An ecological ethic cannot stop at protection of parks and rivers for wilderness hiking and camping for the leisured classes. We must recognize the hidden message of social domination that lies within the theological and ideological traditions of domination of nature. 'Man's' domination of nature has never meant humans in general, but ruling-class males. The hidden link in their domination of nature has always been the dominated bodies, the dominated labor of women, slaves, peasants, and workers.[79]

Any traditional ecological ethic is insufficient for the problems besetting us. Only a more inclusive ethic which acknowledges and criticizes social domination will be adequate to the present task.

As in previous writings, Ruether explicates a theory of the socio-historical origins of this connection between the subordination of nature and social domination. According to Ruether, the theological basis for the ecological crisis is found in the Judaeo-Christian tradition of "man's" domination over nature. Instead of falling heir to an ecological model of interdependence and mutuality, classical patriarchy inherited from both Hebrew

---

[76]Rosemary Radford Ruether, *To Change The World: Christology and Cultural Criticism* (New York: Crossroad, 1981), 59.

[77]Ibid.

[78]Ibid., 60.

[79]Ibid.

Law and Greek philosophy a model which connected the subordination of the natural world with social domination, e.g., the subordination of women by men.

In the case of Hebrew Law, the language for the God-world relationship is borrowed from the language of patriarchal domination over wives, children, and slaves, and thus both world and women are seen as under the dominion of a male hierarch. In the case of Greek philosophy, both nature and women are identified with the body and the world of material existence and hence viewed as under the control of the higher realm of mind, reason, and the world of spiritual existence.[80] In either case, like Ernest Becker, Ruether argues that fear of the revolt of the body and ultimately the fear of death, of finitude, lie behind the domination of body, women, and nature.[81]

After tracing the responses to scientific and industrial domination in liberal progressivism, Marxism, and romanticism, and noting both the elements in each which can be affirmed and their common failure to address adequately the underlying problems of ecology and human liberation, Ruether offers "some outlines" of "an ecological-libertarian world view."[82] First, she argues that we must replace the dream of infinitely expanding power and wealth with a culture that accepts limits and finitude. This requires "conversion," a rediscovery of "the finitude of the earth as a balance of elements, which together harmonize to support life for all parts of the community."[83] It means a non-hierarchical model of reality in which all parts of creation are not just interconnected but interdependent--where "ecological harmony is based on diversity in which each part has an equally vital part to play in maintaining the renewed harmony and balance of the whole."[84] Indeed, on this view, no part of reality has higher or lower ontological or moral value than any other part. Reality is, in Ruether's analogy, like "the connecting links of a dance in which

---

[80]Ibid., 60-61.

[81]See Ernest Becker's brilliant studies, *The Denial of Death* (New York: Macmillan, 1973) and *Escape From Evil* (New York: Macmillan, 1975).

[82]Ruether, *To Change The World*, 66.

[83]Ibid., 67.

[84]Ibid.

each part is equally vital to the whole."[85] Obviously central concepts here are interdependence, harmony, and equality.

Secondly, Ruether insists that such a non-hierarchical world-view must challenge many Western theological assumptions, e.g., the dualism between, as the rhetorical question in the subtitle of this essay suggests, a theology of history and a theology of nature. In contrast, Ruether contends that we need to recover the Hebrew notion that "there is one covenant of creation that includes nature and society"--which includes both the norms of harmony with the earth and justice in society.[86] Ruether again notes the importance of such a concept "for the construction of an ethic of ecojustice."[87] Thirdly and finally, Ruether maintains that we must question "the linear model of history that sees it moving, either in an evolutionary or revolutionary manner, to some final static end-point of salvation" since this notion is "intrinsically contrary to created existence."[88] In other words, in light of the dynamic and open-ended character of creation, we must question the pre-dominant belief that history has an unchanging telos.

In the place of either the model of infinite growth or of final revolution, Ruether would substitute the concept of conversion, since this idea provides "certain ingredients of a just and liveable society" without positing "a utopian system of humanity that lies back in a paradise of the past."[89] To fill out her model of messianic redemption as conversion, Ruether appeals here to the Hebrew idea of Jubilee, of periodic revolutionary conversion, with its vision of a society where "humanity and nature recover their just balance."[90] Ruether claims that this vision of justice and balance--of "conversion back to the centre rather than to a beginning or end-point in history"--is more consonant with temporal existence and is especially characteristic of Jesus' idea of the Kingdom of God.[91]

---

[85]Ibid.
[86]Ibid., 68.
[87]Ibid.
[88]Ibid.
[89]Ibid.
[90]Ibid., 69.
[91]Ibid. See also p. 11 where Ruether argues that the Kingdom of God proclaimed by Jesus "means both reconciliation with God when people obey God from the heart, *and* justice on earth and harmony between humanity

This perspective has the distinct advantage, in Ruether's view, of helping us recover "the mortal limits of covenantal existence" since it acknowledges that change and death are part of the natural limits of life and as such good, and thus that any attempt to escape either mutability or death is misguided and in fact impossible.[92] Ruether claims that such a recognition of finitude and limits, both for ourselves and for all creation, is a necessary move toward a new worldview of ecojustice.

Sexism and God-Talk

In Ruether's much-discussed book *Sexism and God-Talk: Toward A Feminist Theology* these issues are taken up explicitly in the chapter entitled "Woman, Body, and Nature: Sexism and the Theology of Creation." Ruether begins by recalling Sherry Ortner's postulation of a universal devaluation of women based upon the cultural assumption of a hierarchy of culture over nature. Specifically, Ortner argues that because the realm of culture "asserts itself to be not only distinct from but superior to nature," and since for various reasons women are symbolized "as being closer to nature than men," therefore women are universally seen as subordinate to men.[93] In other words, since male is to female as culture is to nature, and since culture is viewed as superior to nature, not only is nature devalued, but so are women. Women are universally "seen as representing a lower order of being, as being less transcendental to nature than men are."[94] The upshot of this, states Ruether, is that "we cannot criticize the hierarchy of male over female without ultimately criticizing and overcoming the

---

and nature. These are not two different things, but, in fact, two sides of the same thing. There is no possibility of divorcing the two sides from each other."

[92]Ibid.

[93]Sherry Ortner, "Is Female to Male as Nature Is to Culture?" in *Women, Culture, and Society*, eds Michelle Rosaldo and Louise Lamphere (Stanford: Stanford University Press, 1974), 73.

[94]Ibid.

hierarchy of humans over nature."[95] The fate of women and the fate of the earth are intimately related.

Ruether hypothesizes about the roots of domination in male consciousness, e.g., in male puberty rites, before launching into her characteristic historical analysis of the correlation between dominated woman and dominated nature. She, however, questions Ortner's claim that dominated woman and dominated nature are *universally* correlated. According to Ruether, Ortner fails to see that *both* woman and nature as cultural symbols are ambivalent, viz., they can be seen as either negative or positive. For example, femaleness can symbolize "that which is lower than male (real humanity)," or it can represent "woman as mother, as original source of life, primary mediator of nature and culture."[96] Likewise, nature can be viewed "as that which is beneath the human, a realm to be controlled," or it can be seen positively "as cosmos, as the encompassing matrix of all things, supported by or infused with divine order and harmony."[97] In other words, the situation is more complex than Ortner allows.

Against Ortner Ruether claims that in the shift from Babylonian to Hebrew to Greek thought there is an increasing rather than constant correlation between dominated woman and dominated nature, i.e., an increasing tendency to see the male/female distinction in terms of the culture/nature dualism. In fact, Ruether cites Hebrew religion as a partial counter-example to Ortner's claim of any strict correlation. Ruether states:

> There is not a direct correlation between women and nonhuman nature because nonhuman nature is not seen as a sphere subject directly to human (male) control. Rather it is an encompassing sphere in which God acts out wrath or reward. God's covenantal relation with humanity links the human and natural communities in one creation. Nature suffers along with humanity in the ups and downs of relationship with God.[98]

---

[95] Ruether, *Sexism and Godtalk*, 73; see also the critique of "humanocentrism" on p. 20.

[96] Ibid., 75.

[97] Ibid., 75-76.

[98] Ibid., 78.

According to Ruether, it is only with Greek thought that "a more radical dualism and alienation between male consciousness and nonhuman nature take place."[99] In Greek philosophy, e.g., in Aristotle's *Politics*, "women are symbolized as analogous to the lower realm of matter and body, to be ruled by or shunned by transcendent mind."[100] And so, insists Ruether, the correlation of dominated woman and dominated nature comes to complete fruition within the Greek inspired chain of being: God, spirits, male, female, nonhuman nature, matter.

This ontology, as with all ontologies, implies a soteriology. Ruether argues that this "great chain of being" ontology of late antiquity posits a "world-fleeing spirituality" of salvation as alienation from the natural world. In late medieval culture this took the form of contempt for both the natural world and women, both of which represented the demonic insofar as they lay outside the realm of grace. With the Renaissance and scientific revolution, there was a revolt against this other-worldlinesss and demonization of nature, and the natural world was increasingly secularized. Ruether then traces the rise of liberalism and romanticism as further developments of this historical trajectory.

In the last section of the chapter, entitled "Toward an Ecological-Feminist Theology of Nature," Ruether outlines her own constructive proposal. In an opening statement, she claims:

> An ecological-feminist theology of nature must rethink the whole Western theological tradition of the hierarchical chain of being and chain of command. This theology must question the hierarchy of human over nonhuman nature as a relationship of ontological and moral value. It must challenge the right of the human to treat the nonhuman as private property and material wealth to be exploited. It must unmask the structures of social domination, male over female, owner over worker, that mediate this domination of nonhuman nature. Finally, it must question the model of hierarchy that starts with non-material spirit (God) as the source of the chain of being and continues down to nonspiritual "matter" as the bottom of the chain of being and the most inferior, valueless, and dominated point in the chain of command.[101]

99Ibid.
100Ibid., 79.
101Ibid., 85.

For Ruether, the tradition of hierarchy and chain of being must give way to a theology of "the God/dess who is primal Matrix, the ground of being-new being" and who is "neither stifling immanence nor rootless transcendence."[102] Drawing on the new physics and the thought of Teilhard de Chardin, Ruether also claims that spirit and matter are "the inside and outside of the same thing."[103] Elaborating, she asserts that consciousness is "the most intense and complex form of the inwardness of material energy itself as it bursts forth at that evolutionary level where matter is organized in the most complex and intensive way--the central nervous system and the cortex of the human brain."[104] Given a Teilhardian interpretation of evolution, Ruether contends that we can "no longer make the dichotomy between nature and history" since "nature itself is historical."[105] The being of nature is becoming, and is thus historical, even before the appearance of humans.

However, lest the hierarchicalism of evolutionary theory reinstate a new, more perverse chain of being ontology, Ruether wishes to make a number of modifications. For example, she posits that our intelligence, though "a special, intense form of this radial energy" of matter, is "not without continuity with other forms" of life.[106] That is to say, while unique in terms of self-consciousnss, we also have much in common with nonhuman forms of life, and so "we must respond to a 'thou-ness' in all beings."[107] This, insists Ruether, is not romanticism or anthropomorphic animism, but rather a response "to the spirit, the life energy that lies in every being in its own form of existence"--a response which implies that "the 'brotherhood of man' needs to be widened to embrace not only women but also the whole community of life."[108] In other words, there is a spirit or life energy in all living things, and we humans, as the most complex and intelligent form of evolutionary existence, have the "responsibility to become the caretaker and cultivator of

[102]Ibid.
[103]Ibid.
[104]Ibid., 86.
[105]Ibid.
[106]Ibid., 87.
[107]Ibid.
[108]Ibid.

the welfare of the whole ecological community upon which our whole existence depends"[109] We have "the responsiblity and the necessity to convert our intelligence to the earth."[110]

Such a conversion requires learning "how to convert intelligence into an instrument that can cultivate the harmonies and balances of the ecological community and bring these to a refinement."[111] This implies "understanding the integrity of the existing ecological community and learning to build our niche in that community in harmony with the rest."[112] And such knowledge itself is a result of a recognition of the interdependence of humans with nonhuman forms of life. This conversion demands "a new form of human intelligence" and "different kind of rationality" in which left-brain linear thought and right-brain spatial and relational thought are integrated.[113] And so Ruether disavows any putative "new" relation between "man" and "nature"--any rearrangement of essentially unchanged categories. Rather, we must convert our minds "to nature's logic of ecological harmony"-- to a "new creation in which human nature and nonhuman nature become friends in the creating of a livable and sustainable cosmos."[114] Reiterating a familiar theme, Ruether maintains:

> Any ecological ethic must always take into account the structures of social domination and exploitation that mediate domination of nature and prevent concern for the welfare of the whole community in favor of the immediate advantage of the dominant class, race, and sex. An ecological ethic must always be an ethic of eco-justice that recognizes the interconnection of social domination and domination of nature.[115]

We must combine concern for the earth with care for others.

Ruether further elaborates on these themes in other portions of the book. For example, in chapter nine, entitled "The New Earth: Socioeconomic Redemption from Sexism," Ruether presses her

---

[109]Ibid., 88.
[110]Ibid., 88-89.
[111]Ibid., 89.
[112]Ibid.
[113]Ibid., 89-90.
[114]Ibid., 91-92.
[115]Ibid., 91.

contention that socioeconomic liberation is "an intrinsic part of the meaning of redemption."[116] After evaluating liberal, socialist, and radical feminism, and finding each of them wanting, she asks rhetorically if there is an integrative feminist vision of society. Ruether's own response is to advocate a "democratic socialist society" that: 1) "affirms the equal value of all persons;" 2) "dismantles sexist and class hierarchies" and "restores ownership and management of work to the base communities of workers themselves;" 3) builds "organic community" which allows "both men and women to share the child nurturing and homemaking and also creative activity and decision making in the larger society;" and 4) integrates both "human and nonhuman ecological systems" into "harmonious and mutually supportive, rather than antagonistic, relations."[117]

And in chapter ten, entitled "Eschatology and Feminism," Ruether suggests a different model of hope--a different eschatology--based upon the idea of "conversion." Drawing on the Jubilee tradition in the Old Testament and ecological ideas of embeddedness, process, and balance, she advocates a concept of social change as "conversion to the center, conversion to the earth and to each other, rather than flight into the unrealizable future."[118] Ruether asserts that we need a "historical eschatology" that takes seriously the realities of our *present* temporal existence and which holds up a "just and livable" society as normative in *this* age, rather than subjecting ourselves "to the tyranny of impossible expectations of final perfection."[119] Eschatology, Ruether vigorously affirms, must be this-worldly.

Ruether also addresses the topic of "personal eschatology." In her view, at death "our existence ceases as individuated ego/organism and dissolves back into the cosmic matrix of matter/energy," and it is "this matrix, rather than our individuated centers of being, that is 'everlasting.'"[120] In other words, there is no individual existence after death. But while death means the end of

---

116Ibid., 214-215.
117Ibid., 232-233.
118Ibid., 255-256.
119Ibid., 254-256.
120Ibid., 257.

an individual center of existence, "all the component parts of matter/energy that coalesced to make up our individual self are not lost" since they "change their form and become food for new beings to arise from our bones."[121] Typical burial patterns thus represent "a fundamental refusal to accept the earth as our home and the plants and animals of earth as our kindred" and so "fail to recognize the redemptive nature of our own disintegration-reintegration back into the soil."[122] Our achievements and failures "are gathered up, assimilated into the fabric of being, and carried forward into new possibilities" by "the great organism of the universe itself"--"that great collective personhood" which is the "great matrix" and "the Holy Being" and "Holy Wisdom."[123] This, Ruether exclaims, is a genuine mystery. Therefore "religion should not make this the focus of its message;" rather "our responsiblity is to use our temporal life span to create a just and good community for our generation and for our children."[124]

Beyond God the Father

As should be obvious, Ruether's entire discussion of ecojustice leads ultimately to the conclusion that some radical theological reconstruction is needed. Perhaps most especially, there is a need for a reconception of God. As stated previously, Ruether argues that "the exorcism of the demonic spirit of sexism in the Church touches off a revolution which must transform...finally our model of God in relation to creation."[125] And this transformation, more specifically, must involve a rejection of the tradition of hierarchy and chain of being in favor of a theology of "the God/ess who is primal matrix, the ground of being-new being"--who is "neither stifling immanence nor rootless transcendence."[126] In sum, Ruether's main intention is to challenge the exclusively male image of God. This challenge is particularly important since "the

---

[121]Ibid., 258.
[122]Ibid., 254-258.
[123]Ibid.
[124]Ibid.
[125]Ruether, *New Woman/New Earth*, 83.
[126]Ruether, *Sexism and God-Talk*, 85.

exclusively male image of God in the Judaeo-Christian tradition has become a critical issue of contemporary religious life"--an issue that "originates in the experience of alienation from this male image of God experienced by feminist women."[127]

While there are many places in her writings where this issue is addressed, perhaps the place where her views are most succinctly expressed is chapter two of *Sexism and God-Talk*, entitled "Sexism and God-Language: Male and Female Images of the Divine." Here Ruether first explores female imagery for the divine in the ancient Near East. Ruether claims that "the root human image of the divine" is "the Primal Matrix, the great womb within which all things, Gods and humans, sky and earth, human and nonhuman beings, are generated."[128] This female image of the divine is later paired with a male deity, but in such a way that "gender complementarity is absent" since "the Goddess and God are equivalent, not complementary, images of the divine."[129] In other words, in this stage of development both God and Goddess are imaged in terms of both masculine and feminine traits, e.g., both are characterized as powerful and loving.

This view of the divine, contends Ruether, gave way to "male monotheism"--the view that there is only one God and that God is to be viewed exclusively in terms of male images. In this view, the social hierarchy of patriarchy is religiously legitimated and a hierarchy of God-male-female is established. In short, "male monotheism begins to split reality into a dualism of transcendent Spirit (mind, ego) and inferior and dependent physical nature."[130] According to Ruether, this hierarchical ordering is evident in both the Old and New Testaments.

However, in Ruether's judgment, male monotheism did not entirely supplant the Goddess tradition. For example, in the interaction between Yahwism and Canaanite religion "the

---

[127]Rosemary Radford Ruether, "The Female Nature of God: A Problem in Contemporary Religious Life," in *God As Father?*, eds. Johannes-Baptist Metz and Edward Schillebeeckx (New York: Seabury, 1981), 61.

[128]Ruether, *Sexism and God-Talk*, 48.

[129]Ibid., 52.

[130]Ibid., 54.

Goddess is not so much eliminated as she is absorbed and put into a new relationship with Yahweh as her Lord."[131] In addition, Ruether claims that "Yahwism appropriates female images for God at certain points," e.g., in the Wisdom tradition.[132] So too in Christianity, female imagery for the divine is evident, even if marginalized by the predominantly male imagery. For example, the person of the Holy Spirit often incorporates the female imagery resident in the Hebraic ideas of Sophia and Hokmah. In sum, there are both male and female images of God within both Jewish and Christian traditions.

Ruether cautions, however, against any view of this dual imagery that would see it in terms of "the androgyny of God," i.e., the view that "God has both mothering or feminine as well as masculine characteristics."[133] Such an approach, e.g., identifying the feminine aspect of God with the Holy Spirit, "falls easily into an androcentric or male-dominant perspective" in which "the female side of God then becomes a subordinate principle underneath the dominant image of male divine sovereignty."[134] Ruether argues that "we need to go beyond the idea of a 'feminine side' of God."[135] What is needed is a new definition of humanity which includes *both* typical "masculine" and "feminine" traits as characteristic of *both* men and women.

In developing her own constructive position, Ruether turns to the Bible itself to criticize male monotheism and the exclusive use of male imagery for God. As she states elsewhere: "I see in biblical religion an important key for any genuine theology of liberation, including liberation from sexism, which we cannot afford to discard."[136] Ruether draws upon four sources: the prophetic

---

[131]Ibid., 56.

[132]Ibid.

[133]Ibid., 60.

[134]Ibid.

[135]Ibid., 61. For another discussion of this issue and insightful argument that the very concept of "feminine" (and "masculine") itself is a creation of patriarchy and thus in need of revision, see Ruether, "The Female Nature of God: A Problem in Contemporary Religious Life," in *God As Father?*

[136]Rosemary Radford Ruether, "Sexism, Religion, and the Social and Spiritual Liberation of Women Today," in *Beyond Domination: New*

tradition of the Bible, the biblical idea of the liberating sovereign, biblical proscriptions against idolatry, and equivalent images for God as male and female. In the case of the prophetic tradition, Ruether affirms that God is seen as "a champion of the social victims," a perspective that is radicalized in the New Testament to include class, ethnicity, and gender.[137] The biblical idea of the liberating sovereign implies, to put it concisely, that "because God is our king, we need obey no human kings."[138] The Reign of God is not only a community of equals, but, to use Elizabeth Schussler Fiorenza's phrase, involves a "discipleship of equals."[139]

The proscription against idolatry, Ruether argues, must extend to include words as well as pictures, language in addition to objects. That is, if "the word *Father* is taken literally to mean that God is male and not female, represented by males and not females, then this word becomes idolatrous."[140] Following Thomas Aquinas, Ruether affirms that "classical Christian theology teaches that all names for God are analogies;" thus "God is both male and female and neither male nor female."[141] Finally, Ruether finds references to God in the Bible which employ truly gender equivalent images, e.g., in some of the parables of Jesus. Ruether offers the term "God/ess" as a feminist alternative to exclusively male language for God. Such a term attempts to capture female imagery on equal par with male imagery. While we should use "Mother" as well as "Father" to describe God, Ruether questions the use of parental langauge to refer to God, since it may "prolong spiritual infantilism" and "make autonomy and assertion of free will a sin."[142] We need, rather, "to start with language for the Divine as redeemer, as liberator, as one who fosters full personhood and, in that context, speak of God/ess as creator, as source of being."[143]

Perspectives on Women and Philosophy, ed. Carol Gould (Totowa, NJ: Rowman and Allanheld, 1983), 121.

[137]Ruether, *Sexism and God-Talk*, 62.
[138]Ibid., 65.
[139]Schussler Fiorenza, *In Memory of Her*, 97.
[140]Ruether, *Sexism and God-Talk*, 66.
[141]Ibid., 67.
[142]Ibid., 69.
[143]Ibid., 70.

Merely to focus on God as liberator, however, is insufficient, since such an approach may still perpetuate male monotheism. In fact, Ruether criticizes partiarchal liberation theologies for emphasizing God as Liberator while negating God as Matrix, as ground of being. By mistakenly "identifying the ground of creation with the foundations of existing social systems," and also associating being, matter, and nature with women, such theologies define liberation as "liberation out of or against nature into spirit" and thus are "hostile to women as symbols of all that 'drags us down' from freedom."[144] That is to say, by identifying God the Creator and Sustainer with present unjust and oppressive social systems, and by accepting the dualisms of male/female and spirit/nature, many theologies of liberation envision liberation as an escape from nature, matter, women. A further implication of this view is that redemption is essentially divorced from creation, new being unrelated to original being.

Ruether strenuously rejects any dualism of spirit and nature. While acknowledging that "feminist theology needs to affirm the God of the Exodus, of liberation and new being," Ruether also maintains that the God of liberation must be "rooted in the foundations of being rather than as its antithesis."[145] She insists that "the God/ess who is the foundation (at one and the same time) of our being and our new being embraces both the roots of the material substratum of our existence (matter) and also the endlessly new creative potential (spirit)."[146] In other words, God is both Creator and Redeemer, and this creating and redeeming God encircles both matter and spirit, body and soul. God/ess is, in summary, the "Shalom of being" who heals "our broken relations with our bodies, with other people, with nature."[147]

---

[144]Ibid.

[145]Ibid.

[146]Ibid., 71.

[147]Ibid. See also "Sexism, Religion, and the Social and Spiritual Liberation of Women," p. 121, where Ruether states that "underneath this history [of sexism] lies an alternative reality of harmony, with each other, with God, with nature, as our true nature."

Gaia and God

Many of the themes found in the writings explicated above are recapitulated in Ruether's recently published *Gaia and God*.[148] As the subtitle indicates, in this long-awaited volume Ruether pulls together her reflections on religion and ecology from the previous twenty years and presents her most systematic constructive contribution to feminist ecological theology. A brief exposition of selected sections of this volume highlights her emphasis on double domination, her insistence on the importance of ecojustice, and her retrieval of important biblical traditions.

The central question which Ruether asks--put forward on the very first page of the introduction--is this: "Are Gaia, the living and sacred earth, and God, the monotheistic deity of the biblical traditions, on speaking terms with each other?"[149] In other words, is a Christian ecological theology and ethic possible? Ruether's whole project is an attempt to answer this question affirmatively and show with some precision just how to construct such a theology. So in contrast to those who argue that the Christian tradition is ecologically bankrupt, Ruether contends: "For Christian ecological thinkers, however, the biblical God and Gaia are not at odds; rightly understood, they are on terms of amity, if not commingling."[150] Biblical religion and care for creation are in fact integrally related.

The key phrase here, for Ruether, is "rightly understood." It is not self-evident that ecology and Christianity are or can be on such good speaking terms. And so a right understanding or proper perspective is necessary. According to Ruether the critical perspective which makes possible this "amity" and "commingling" is ecofeminism, for it "explores how male domination of women and domination of nature are interconnected, both in cultural ideology and in social structures."[151] Ecofeminism, in other words, is that critical theory best able to expose relationships and patterns

---

[148]Rosemary Radford Ruether, *Gaia and God: An Ecofeminist Theology of Earth Healing* (San Francisco: Harper/Collins, 1992).
[149]Ibid., 1.
[150]Ibid., 240.
[151]Ibid., 2.

of domination and thereby lead to genuine and lasting healing. It is the means most ably suited to achieve the goal of "a healed relationship between men and women, between classes and nations, and between humans and the earth."[152] Hence Ruether argues that "a healed relation to the earth cannot come about simply through technological 'fixes'," but rather "demands that we must speak of eco-justice."[153] Only a perspective which joins concern for the full equality of women with concern for the wholeness of creation will be able to achieve the telos of healing and reconciliation.

This ethic of ecojustice must, furthermore, be seen as part of a "new consciousness" or "spirituality" in which "our inner psyches and the way we symbolize the interrelations between men and women, humans and the earth, humans and the divine, the divine and the earth" are transformed. For example, given the new scientific creation story we must acknowledge our kinship with all creatures. "Recognition of this profound kinship," Ruether stoutly maintains, "must bridge the arrogant barriers that humans have erected to wall themselves off" from other living and non-living beings.[154] We need "scientist-poets" who can tell the story of the cosmos "in a way that can call us to wonder, to reverence for life, and to the vision of humanity living in community with all its sister and brother beings."[155] Thus, concludes Ruether, ecojustice and spirituality are "the inner and outer aspects of one process of conversion and transformation."[156]

In short, ecofeminism, and more exactly the ethical norm of ecojustice, undergirds a new spirituality and provides the lens through which Ruether evaluates the causes of double domination and appropriates resources both past and present. As Ruether herself puts it, her project is "to assess the cultural and social roots that have promoted destructive relations" of various sorts and also to "sift through the legacy of the Christian and Western cultural

---

152Ibid., 1.
153Ibid., 2.
154Ibid., 48. See also Thomas Berry, *The Dream of the Earth* (San Francisco: Sierra Club, 1988).
155Ruether, *Gaia and God*, 58.
156Ibid., 4.

heritage to find usable ideas that might nourish a healed relation to each other and to the earth."[157] That is, hers is both a hermeneutic of suspicion and a hermeneutic of retrieval.

In this sifting process Ruether identifies two distinct Christian traditions which in her judgement must be retrieved. There are, she avers, "two lines of the biblical thought and Christian traditions which have reclaimable resources for an ecological spirituality and practice: the covenantal tradition and the sacramental tradition."[158] While each of these traditions must be reinterpreted and stripped of the legacy of patriarchalism, they nonetheless provide "profoundly valuable themes for ecological spirituality and practice."[159] For example, in Ruether's construal the covenantal tradition emphasizes the single unified covenant between God and all creatures, thereby contravening the history/nature dualism. It speaks of the the finitude of creaturely reality and the limits of human power, and thus engenders humility and a sense of place in the face of the arrogant grasping for More. This tradition reminds us that we are but stewards, not owners, of the land and are called to be a just community, attentive to the needs of strangers, animals, and the poor. In short, for Ruether the covenantal tradition--especially when the covenant is properly expanded to include not just marginalized humans but also the natural world--provides "prophetic self-criticism" necessary for any adequate ecological perspective.[160]

The sacramental tradition, on Ruether's reading, emphasizes the presence and manifestation of God in creation, and so well complements the covenantal tradition's insistence on God's otherness. Indeed, according to Ruether, "we need both of these holy voices."[161] In particular she draws on the Pauline and Johannine references to Christ as cosmic and to Irenaeus' incarnational theology. To be more specific, in Ruether's view the

---

[157]Ibid., 2.

[158]Ibid., 205; see also p. 5.

[159]Ibid., 206.

[160]Ibid., 217.

[161]Ibid., 255. David Tracy employs a similar distinction, though he calls these two traditions the prophetic and the mystical. See *Dialogue With the Other* (Grand Rapids: Eerdmans, 1990), ch. 5.

sacramental tradition, especially with its cosmic christology, stresses the pervasive sustaining power of God in creation, thereby repudiating any de facto deism. It witnesses to the continuity between creation and redemption and thus precludes any eschatology which devalues the earth. And insofar as this tradition celebrates bodiliness--with its emphasis on the incarnation, all gnostic attempts to flee the corporeal world are denied. In sum, for Ruether the sacramental tradition allows us "to restore for today the cosmological center of theology and spirituality."[162]

The upshot of these theological retrievals is the unmasking of "cultures of domination and deceit" and the development of "cultures of critique and compassion." [163]Her underlying ethical value, in keeping with her ethic of ecojustice, is equity.

> This vision [of a good society] must start with a principle of equity: equity between men and women; between human groups living within regions; equity across human communities globally; equity between the human species and all other members to [sic] the biotic community of which we are a part; and finally equity between generations of living things, between the needs of those alive now and those who are to come.[164]

Ruether offers a variety of specific proposals which flesh out this ethical vision. For example, given the intrinsic value of both individual animals and species, and given the need to feed one billion starving people, Ruether argues that "there are compelling moral reasons for a mostly vegetarian diet, particularly for affluent people."[165] She contends that given both the increasing scarcity of and continuing pollution caused by fossil fuels, "we need to phase out petroleum and other fossil fuels as the primary energy sources of production, transporation, and home heating."[166] Given the increasing ecological unacceptability of the private automobile, we must develop whole new systems of transportation and, beyond that, reorganize our cities and towns "so that much less

---

[162]Ruether, *Gaia and God,*,229.
[163]Ibid., 258.
[164]Ibid.
[165]Ibid., 225.
[166]Ibid., 259.

transportation is required to connect the segments of daily life."[167]
Like many today she calls for a "return to seasonal patterns of food,
produced and distributed in one or several contiguous bio-
regions."[168] We must shift from agribusiness back to agriculture,
with more, not less, people living and working on the land.

Concretely embodying this vision of the good society will also
require, Ruether affirms, "recovering something of the biorhythms
of the body, the day, and the seasons from the world of clocks,
computers, and artificial lighting."[169] This vision requires more of
us to compost our wastes and recycle our "disposables." It means
that, given the exponential growth in the number of humans on our
planetary home, we have "no real alternative to population
control."[170] This implies "the empowerment of women as moral
agents of their own sexuality and reproduction"--a change which
itself entails that men "overcome the illusion of autonomous
individualism" and "integrate themselves into life-sustaining
relations with women as lovers, parents, and co-workers."[171]
Realizing this ethical vision requires, Ruether insists, "genuine
demilitarization across the board" since that is "the *sine qua non* of
any genuine, ecologically sustainable, biospheric economy."[172]

To carry this vision forward and actually begin to develop
such an equitable and sustainable world, Ruether concludes, we
must build "communities of celebration and resistance." We need to
be part of communities whose corporate liturgies express and
engender this new consciousness and which become bases of
political action. We need, in sum, "neither optimism nor pessimism"
but rather "committed love" since "being rooted in love for our real
communities of life and for our common mother, Gaia, can teach us
patient passion, a passion that is not burnt out in a season, but can
be renewed season after season."[173]

[167]Ibid., 260.
[168]Ibid., 261. See also, e.g., Wendell Berry, *The Unsettling of America*
(San Francisco: Sierra Club, 1977).
[169]Ruether, *Gaia and God*, 262.
[170]Ibid., 263.
[171]Ibid., 264-266.
[172]Ibid., 268.
[173]Ibid., 269-273.

While much time has been spent merely explicating Ruether's views, there is, needless to say, much left unexplained. As one commentator puts it, "Ruether is greatly to be respected for the penetrating quality of her thought and the breadth of her *oeuvre*."[174] The focus in the above, as stated previously, has been on only those aspects of Ruether's thought which are germane to the issues under investigation here, and so we have seen only a glimpse of the breadth of Ruether's work. It is beyond the scope of this project to delve into topics which, while important, are less central to a Christian ecological theology.

---

[174]Kathyrn Allen Rabuzzi, "The Socialist Feminist Vision of Rosemary Radford Ruether: A Challenge to Liberal Feminism," *Religious Studies Review* 15 (January 1989): 8.

CHAPTER 3

THE COSMIC CHRIST:
THE CHRISTOLOGY OF JOSEPH SITTLER

The world is not God, but it is God's.[1]

Joseph Sittler

When we turn the attention of the church to a definition of the Christian relationship with the natural world, we are not stepping away from grave and proper theological ideas; we are stepping right into the middle of them. There is a deeply rooted, genuinely Christian motivation for attention to God's creation, despite the fact that many church people consider ecology to be a secular concern. "What does environmental preservation have to do with Jesus Christ and his church?" they ask. They could not be more shallow or more wrong.[2]

Joseph Sittler

The Significance of Sittler

As mentioned previously, Joseph Sittler was an important, even if often overlooked, theologian. One indication of his significance can be found in his influence within and on the ecumenical movement. For example, in his chronicle of the christology of the Faith and Order Movement of the World Council of Churches, Conrad Simonson points to the pivotal role of Sittler, especially his New Delhi speech of 1961 "Called to Unity," in challenging and prodding the church to expand the scope of its christological vision to include nothing less than all of reality. As Simonson says:

---

[1]Joseph Sittler, "Ecological Commitment as Theological Responsibility," *Zygon* 5 (June 1970): 178.
[2]Sittler, *Gravity and Grace*, 15.

Time magazine ventured the opinion that the most original and challenging address to the Assembly was given by Dr. Joseph Sittler, Lutheran professor at the University of Chicago Divinity School. ...What is needed, he [Sittler] concluded, is an all-encompassing Christian vision...with a core of spirituality illuminating "economics, politics, and all other areas of human affairs."[3]

Sittler's unique and lasting contribution, according to Simonson, is his "christology of nature"--a christology "as large as the nature and destiny of man" and "expanded to its cosmic dimensions."[4]

Moira Creede also traces Sittler's not inconsiderable influence in ecumenical circles. She claims that what most distinguishes Sittler's theology and that which put him "in the vanguard" of Christian theologians of his time was "his concern to provide a theological basis for the present ecological crisis."[5] That is, Sittler was concerned to understand theologically the ecological crisis and, beyond mere diagnosis, to offer a revised and expanded christology as a prescription for our ailing earth. As Creede shows, Sittler came to this realization as early as 1954 when, in his article "A Theology for Earth," he "found his real subject"--that topic which "in the years that followed this provided the organizing theme for his theology."[6]

Peter Bakken likewise remarks that because of "his early attention to the environmment as a theological issue," Joseph Sittler "has been called 'the most original American theologian of his time.'"[7] Echoing Creede's comment about Sittler being in the vanguard of theologians concerned with ecology, Bakken refers to Sittler a someone who "is widely recognized as a pioneer in bringing environmental concerns into Christian theology."[8] Indeed, Bakken asserts that "Sittler's main concern was to expand Christians' understanding of grace to include *more* than the individual's relationship to Jesus."[9] So also Jerald Brauer speaks of

---

[3]Conrad Simonson, *The Christology of the Faith and Order Movement* (Leiden: Brill, 1972), 94.
[4]Ibid., vii, 94.
[5]Creede, "Logos and Lord," 355.
[6]Ibid., 83.
[7]Bakken, "The Ecology of Grace," 35.
[8]Ibid., 45.
[9]Ibid., 390.

Sittler's "prophetic role in American theology."[10] Sittler was a prophet, states Brauer, because "long before ecology became a household word in America, Sittler was using the concept as a means of explicating Christian faith"--first with respect to the inner dynamics of faith itself and then with regard to the presence of God in the natural world.[11]

Finally, as mentioned in chapter one, Paul Santmire, one of the most informed and insightful thinkers in the area of ecological theology, includes Sittler in his short list of the three Christian theologians who have offered the most creative and fruitful reflections on a Christian ecological theology. According to Santmire:

> The inner-theological challenge that Sittler presents to Western theology must be perceived as both radical and revolutionary. His challenge is in fact a call for a kind of paradigm shift in Christian thought, away from an exclusively the-anthropological soteriology, to what can be called an inclusive or universal soteriology, which envisions the final salvation of all things as the *telos* of creation, not just the salvation of a kingdom of rational spirits, in the fashion of most post-Kantian Protestant theology.[12]

Others who point to Sittler's significance could be mentioned, e.g., William French[13] and David Engel,[14] but it should be sufficiently clear that Joseph Sittler, who died in December of 1987, was an important Christian theologian, especially with respect to the devlopment of an ecological theology.

The outline for this chapter is staightforward. After a brief section on the theme of cosmic christology, I present an exposition of those aspects of Sittler's theology that contribute to a Christian ecological theology, especially his christology. As indicated in chapter one, an analysis and critique of Sittler's work are given in chapter six.

---

[10]Brauer, "In Appreciation," 100.

[11]Ibid.

[12]Santmire, "Studying the Doctrine of Creation," 199; see also Santmire, "Toward a New Theology of Nature," 43, 47.

[13]French, "Christianity and the Domination of Nature," 146ff.

[14]David Engel, "Elements in a Theology of Nature," *Zygon* 5 (September 1970): 224.

Cosmic Christology

Sittler is the theologian, at least in the West, who in the recent past has most forcefully and eloquently advocated a cosmic christology. But while Sittler has been the person perhaps most closely associated with cosmic christology, other contemporaries have also addressed this issue. For example, when it comes to biblical studies, there have been others besides Sittler who have explored the scriptural basis for cosmic christology. In fact, ever since Sittler's New Delhi speech exegetes have debated with great vigor the acceptability of the use of Col. 1:15-20 as a scriptural warrant for cosmic christology. Creede reviews this exegetical discussion and in the end "vindicates his [Sittler's] use of Paul, and therefore his presupposition of the ecological nature of theology."[15] In concluding his exegetical study of Colossians 1 James Burtness affirms that "the decision forced upon us by Col. 1:15-20 is that what Bultmann calls 'gnostic'--that is, the cosmic dimension of the work of Christ--is actually very close to the heart of the New Testament message."[16] Burtness also notes that "this emphasis [on the cosmic work of Christ] was, of course, the center of lively discussion at New Delhi, in relation to the remarkable address of Joseph Sittler."[17]

In an extensive survey of the issues, including a discussion of various problems of interpretation, John Gibbs argues that "cosmic christology, far from being a late addendum, belongs to the core of the Pauline concept of Lord, no less than does the theology of the cross."[18] Including in his survey texts from Romans, I Corinthians,

---

[15]Creede, "Logos and Lord," 455.

[16]James Burtness, "All the Fullness," *Dialog* 3 (Autumn 1964): 260. Similarly Roy Harrisville surveys the biblical debate surrounding the Col. 1 text and concludes that "the concept of a cosmic, creation-wide deliverance is native to the New Testament." If human redemption is warranted by the Bible, then so is cosmic redemption and a cosmic Christ; see "The New Testament Witness to the Cosmic Christ," in *The Gospel and Human Destiny*, ed. Vilmos Vajta (Minneapolis: Augsburg, 1971), 53.

[17]Burtness, "All the Fullness," 263.

[18]John Gibbs, "Pauline Cosmic Christology and Ecological Crisis," *The Journal of Biblical Literature* 90 (December 1971): 466.

Philippians, and Ephesians, as well as the much contested Col. 1:15-20, Gibbs reaches on more thorough and solid exegetical grounds many of the same conclusions as Sittler. Gibbs concludes that "man and the whole creation are bound together in redemption" and, furthermore, that "Christ's cosmic work was no less essential to Paul's christology than Christ's redemptive work."[19]

Turning to more systematic efforts, Loren Wilkinson also develops a cosmic christology. He argues that "the *concept* of Christ as God's creating Word, the controlling Wisdom of the universe, is pervasive" in the New Testament, and that this has clear ethical implications for "the Christian's role in creation."[20] More specifically, if humans are made in the image of God, and if this imaging means following "not only Christ the Saviour but also Christ the Creator," then we are "to participate with him [Christ] in the care of, the sustaining, and even, in some sense, the *creation* of the world."[21] In short, a cosmic christology necessarily entails an ethic of care for creation.

Allan Galloway, whom Sittler quotes numerous times,[22] presents probably the most philosophically informed cosmic christology. The presentation of his own constructive position is preceded by a historical overview of the idea of cosmic redemption from the Old Testament through Hegel. Galloway argues that since "man's life as a person is so intimately bound up with his life as a physical creature in a physical environment that anything that involves man as a person also involves him as a physical creature," it follows that cosmic redemption is "an implicate of the idea of personal redemption."[23] Galloway argues that if to be a person is to be physical, and if redemption is personal, then redemption must necessarily include the physical and thus be cosmic in scope. Hence

---

[19]Ibid., 472, 479.

[20]Loren Wilkinson, "Cosmic Christology and the Christian's Role in Creation," *Christian Scholar's Review* 11 (1981): 28, 35.

[21]Ibid., 35, 38. See also Colin Gunton, *Christ and Creation* (Grand Rapids: Eerdmans, 1992), especially chapter 3, for a stimulating set of reflections on the role of Christ in creation and the implications of a cosmic christology.

[22]For example, Sittler, "Called to Unity," 7, 9.

[23]Allan Galloway, *The Cosmic Christ* (New York: Harper and Brothers, 1951), 204-205.

Galloway contends that "physical nature cannot be treated as an indifferent factor--as the mere stage and setting of the drama of personal redemption. It must either be condemned as in itself evil or else it must be brought within the scope of the redemptive act."[24] Since the former option is unacceptable, the latter option must be adopted. Redemption must include all creatures.

In yet other words, Galloway argues that since "self and world are correlative terms"--since "there is no sharp disjunction between the subjective and objective elements of human experience"--personal and cosmic redemption "are correlative aspects of one and the same thing."[25] And cosmic redemption entails a cosmic Christ. Only a Christ who is the preeminent Logos is powerful enough and only a Christ whose work is cosmic in scope is large enough to overcome the meaningless and the demonic.

While others have explored the topic of cosmic christology,[26] few have done so with as much imagination, eloquence, or singleness of purpose as Sittler. And so even given the limitations of his theology--its unfinished character, its nonlinearity, its poetic language[27]--Sittler's reflections on theology in general and cosmic christology in particular warrant further investigation. In what follows, various themes in Sittler's theology are elucidated in order better to comprehend his christology.

The Scope of Grace

It is entirely fitting that we begin our exploration of Sittler's christology with the topic of grace, since Sittler himself again and again points to this theme as being of central importance to his theological project and, in his view, to the future of Christian theology. For example, Sittler states that

---

[24]Ibid., 205.
[25]Ibid., 240.
[26]In addition to those mentioned above, in chapter four of "Logos and Lord" Creede explores the views of Gerard Manley Hopkins, Pierre Teilhard de Chardin, and Karl Rahner.
[27]See, e.g., Creede, "Logos and Lord," 426, and Bakken, "The Ecology of Grace," 46-47.

I am interested in the reality or the presence of the grace of God in the creation, because only the doctrine of grace will be adequate to change the spirit of our minds whereby we deal with timber and oil, fish and animals, and the structure of cities, urban design, homes for people, places to work--all these mundane, concrete things that yet constitute the anchorage of our hearts, the home of our daily lives.[28]

Sittler elaborates on this claim when, in referring to the ecological or relational character of reality as the necessary context for doing theology, he asserts: "If we are to ask which of the comprehensive Christian doctrines is the one large enough and ready enough and interiorly most capable of articulating a theological relationship between theology and ecology, I would suggest that the doctrine of grace is the one."[29] And in his conclusion to a long discussion on christology and grace, Sittler movingly says:

You fly over southern Indiana and look at the wretched earth where the strip mining has gone on for fifty years, and you almost feel as if you are looking at a torn and tattered body. This is going on more and more. "The earth groans in travail, waiting . . ." What is she waiting for? If you put it into idiomatic English, she is waiting for the sons of God to "act like it" and take care of their Sister, to have a new sense for the common grace, created grace. That is where I see the doctrine of grace as a potential to be at the center of a renovation of Christian theology apposite to man's new opportunities with nature.[30]

In other words, of all the various theological loci that one could choose to address the ecological crisis, e.g., creation or incarnation or eschatology, Sittler contends that only the doctrine of grace has the sufficient power and scope and centrality within the Christian tradition to effect the kind of drastic change of thought and action that is required.

[28]Sittler, *Gravity and Grace*, 14. See also p. 13 where Sittler says that "nothing less than the doctrine of grace would be an adequate doctrine to shape the Christian community's mind and practice in a way appropriate to the catastophe in the environment."

[29]Sittler, "Ecological Commitment," 180.

[30]Joseph Sittler, "The Sittler Speeches," in *Center for the Study of Campus Ministry Yearbook 1977-78*, ed. Phil Schroeder (Valparaiso: Valparaiso University, 1978), 45.

Sittler argues, however, that no traditional doctrine of grace will be adequate. The doctrine of grace must, rather, be reformulated to meet both the demands of scripture and the needs of the modern world. For example, in speaking of the presence of God, Sittler claims:

> The content of that presence, even when negatively envisioned, is certainly identical with the meaning of grace, the most comprehensive term the scripture uses for the reality and presence and acts of the triune God. If presence and grace belong together, and if this presence and grace are to be confessed by men who have their existence within the realms of nature and of history...then nothing short of a restudy of the doctrine of grace can suffice to illuminate the relation of God to nature and history.[31]

And in his magnum opus, *Essays on Nature and Grace,* Sittler clearly states both the problem before us and his own understanding of its solution:

> In virtue of what gift, love, understanding, and appropriate behavior can man live with the world-as-nature so as rightly to enjoy and use it? That is the problem. It is the thesis of these chapters that nothing short of a radical relocation and reconceptualization of the reality and the doctrine of grace is an adequate answer to that problem.[32]

Sittler's entire life project could fairly be described as an attempt to reconceive the doctrine of grace in such a way that its full cosmic scope is visible. Indeed, Philip Hefner so describes Sittler's life work when he says that Sittler sought to carry "the implications of the unrestricted scope of grace to their farthest conclusions."[33]

---

[31]Joseph Sittler, "The Presence and Acts of the Triune God in Creation and History," in *The Gospel and Human Destiny,* ed. Vilmos Vatja (Minneapolis: Augsburg, 1971), 99.

[32]Joseph Sittler, *Essays on Nature and Grace* (Philadelphia: Fortress, 1972), 6.

[33]Philip Hefner, "Presentation to Joseph Sittler," in *The Scope of Grace: Essays on Nature and Grace in Honor of Joseph Sittler,* ed. Philip Hefner (Philadelphia: Fortress, 1964), vii. Jerald Brauer comments that Sittler's "career from its very beginning, has reflected a remarkable integrity and wholeness...a single commitment," namely, "the freedom of God in his creativity, exhibited throughout the cosmos and documented by his Word in history, especially by Jesus Christ;" see p. 101 of "In Appreciation."

In various places Sittler traces the history of the narrowing of the scope of grace--an important story but one that lies beyond the bounds of our project here.[34] His main conclusion is that "the doctrine of grace has been almost exclusively administered in relation to man as sinner."[35] That is, grace has been "completely identified with the work of God according to the Second Article, the grace of God in Jesus Christ."[36] In yet other words, "christology is reduced to soteriology."[37] Sittler insists that this "almost exclusive elaboration of Christology under the article of redemption is reductive of biblical scope and of the richness of theological tradition."[38] For example, Sittler argues at length that any "radical christocentrism" fails to take seriously "the growing magnitude in the christological utterances of the New Testament."[39] And with respect to tradition, Sittler asserts that while "in his understanding of the grace of God in and with the creation Augustine stands with the catholic tradition" of Irenaeus and Athanasius, "it is very clear, however, that almost exclusive attention to grace within the rubric of *sin* and grace has fated his teaching to have been understood in such a diminished way" that the presence of grace in all of creation is not recognized.[40] Viewing grace solely or exclusively in terms of sin and redemption fails to do justice both to the riches of the biblical testimony to grace and to the expansive scope of grace articulated within the Christian tradition.

The most serious consequence of this reduction of grace is that "the realms of history and the moral" are identified "as the sole realm of grace" so as "to shrink to no effect the biblical Christology of nature."[41] In other words, because grace has often been reduced to the human or cultural or historical realm, the cosmic scope of Christ's work and the creation-wide extent of God's grace have

---

[34]For example, Sittler, "Speeches," 42-43; *Essays*, 76ff; "Nature and Grace: Reflections on an Old Rubric," *Dialog* 3 (Autumn 1964): 255-256.

[35]Sittler, *Essays*, 14.

[36]Sittler, "Speeches," 42.

[37]Sittler, "Nature and Grace," 255.

[38]Sittler, *Essays*, 11.

[39]Sittler, "Nature and Grace," 255; *Essays*, 11; see also chapter two of *Essays* entitled "Grace in the Scriptures."

[40]Sittler, *Essays*, 65-66.

[41]Sittler, "Called to Unity," 10.

gone unrecognized and the pressing problems of the earth have been ignored. Concludes Sittler, this

> concentration of the whole doctrine of God the Creator at the incarnated point of God the Redeemer...has to some degree crippled theology in its necessary contemporary engagement with problems demanding an ultimate word about the abuse and promise of the world-as-nature, and it has so evacuated the doctrine of the Holy Spirit as to leave it nebulous, recondite, and in practice, unavailable to human need.[42]

In short, Sittler refers to "the necessity to speak of the Triune God and his grace in a way that breaks out of a Protestant disposition to confine the reality of grace to the second article."[43] While "grace came by Jesus Christ" and "has in him its absolute embodiment," grace "was not created by Jesus Christ."[44] God's grace is larger than the work of Jesus.

One of the analogies Sittler uses to explain both the reduction of grace and the proper view of grace is the relationship between the center and the circumference of a circle. Sittler declares that

> the grace of God whereby "Christ Jesus has made me his own" establishes the center. But the center is not the circumference; the circumference of the grace which is redemption is not smaller than that theatre of life and awareness which is the creation. The grace that *came* in enpersonalized Incarnation in Jesus Christ is no other than the grace of God who is the Creator, Sustainer, and Law-giver.[45]

The center, redemption, is not the circumference, creation. While redemption in Christ may be a singular concentration of grace, it does not exhaust the scope of grace. The grace of redemption must be seen in the context of a grace-full creation.

If then it is clear what Sittler sees as problematic, what precisely is Sittler's own view? This crucial question is somewhat difficult to answer since Sittler's ruminations on grace are varied

---

[42]Sittler, "Nature and Grace," 255.
[43]Sittler, "The Presence and Acts," 125.
[44]Ibid.
[45]Sittler, *Essays*, 35; cf. Sittler, "The Presence and Acts," 106, and "Speeches," 11.

and complex. Indeed, Sittler describes his theological method in the following way: "If I have a theological method, that is it: to walk around the question or the issue or the problem and see it as carefully as I can from several perspectives and then hope that the outcome is useful. Often it is, and often it is not."[46] In describing Sittler's method Creede remarks that "one sometimes has the awkward feeling of taking great theological leaps, now hither, now thither, with both feet firmly planted in mid-air."[47] While Creede exaggerates somewhat, she points to a genuine problem. The results of Sittler's method are not easily summarized. The following is one attempt to piece together Sittler's "leaps" with respect to the doctrine of grace.

If, first of all, we "ask what grace is as a sheer phenomenon," we find, claims Sittler, that grace is "the sheer *givenness*-character of life, the world, and the self--the plain *presentedness* of all that is."[48] Grace is "the sense of the sheer giftedness of wheat, of the wind, of the colors of the year, the fact of the miracle that what man cannot live without he cannot bring into existence, the fecundity of the earth, the ability of the sea to multiply by millions of times."[49] According to Sittler: "The grace of God is not simply a holy hypodermic whereby my sins are forgiven. It is the whole giftedness of life, the wonder of life, which causes me to ask questions that transcend the moment."[50] Grace, in other words, is an answer to questions about the contingency of existence. It is a response to both the question of ontological contingency--Why is there *anything* at all?--and the question of existential contingency--Why does *this particular* world exist?[51] At this level, grace describes the need-not-have-been character of being, including human being.

---

[46]Sittler, "Speeches," 20.

[47]Creede, "Logos and Lord," xx. On p. 20 of "Speeches" Sittler says, in response to Creede's work, that "she knows me better than I know myself." He remarks that his wife, having read Creede's description, was "so convulsed with laughter...that she could not continue."

[48]Sittler, *Essays*, 88.

[49]Sittler, "Speeches," 44.

[50]Sittler, *Gravity and Grace*, 14.

[51]For this distinction, see Robert Russell, "Cosmology, Creation, and Contingency," in *Cosmos As Creation*, ed. Ted Peters (Nashville: Abingdon, 1989), 195.

Continuing his phenomenological inquiry, Sittler posits that "the underside of this sheer gratuity, the givenness quality of things, supplies the subjective vocabulary by which that unaccountability is recognized."[52] The sheer gratuity of being, the giftedness of existence, evokes "surprise, wonder, Tillich's 'ontological shock.'"[53] In a summary statement of sorts, Sittler insists that

> whenever men encounter grace it is the shock and the over-plus of sheer gratuity that announces the presence, as indeed, it invented the name. By gratuity is meant primal surprise, the need-not-have-been of uncalculated and incalculable givenness. "Amazing" is the only adequate adjective; wonder is the ambience.[54]

As Sittler never tires of saying: "Grace is always a strangeness, a gift, a surprise."[55]

Beyond this general phenomenology, however, Sittler describes grace theologically. Grace is the reality, energy, and essence of God. For example, Sittler acknowledges that "grace is indeed commonly postulated as the elemental character of God in his relation to all that is not God" and goes on to affirm that "grace is that God-as-communicating nothing less or other than himself as Presence."[56] God in relation to the world is nothing other than God in Godself, a reality fundamentally characterized by grace. In the economy of God, grace is basic and pervasive: "The reality of grace is the fundamental reality of God the Creator in his creation, God the Redeemer in his redemption, and God the Sanctifier and Illuminator in all occasions of the common life where sanctifying grace is beheld, bestowed, and lived by."[57] Employing the distinction between divine essence and energy, *ousia* and *energeia*, that goes back at least to Gregory of Nyssa, Sittler affirms that

---

[52]Sittler, *Essays*, 88.
[53]Ibid.
[54]Ibid., 104.
[55]Ibid., 19.
[56]Ibid., 75.
[57]Ibid., 88.

grace is "a proper divine energy of the Trinity as such."[58] Put simply, grace is "the energy of love."[59]

For Sittler grace is not only a characteristic of God, but also of creation. "The fundamental meaning of grace," says Sittler, "is the goodness and lovingkindness of God and the activity of this goodness in and toward his creation."[60] Borrowing from Athanasius, Sittler affirms that grace is "both a comprehensive term for the created goodness of all reality, and a term wherewith to specify the incarnated presence and historical focus of that Light which is God."[61] God is grace, and since God created and continually creates all things, grace is built into the very structure of being. Grace describes the goodness of creation as well as the love of God.

Beyond describing merely the divine energy or work *ad extra*, however, Sittler views grace as that property most descriptive of the inner trinitarian life itself.

> The one comprehensive reality of this Trinitarian God is grace. ...When grace is postulated as the reality of God, as the reality of the life of the Father in the Son witnessed to by the "internal testimony of the Holy Spirit," then literally all that is must be invested with an interpretation congruent with that postulate.[62]

While Sittler's use of terms often lacks precision, in perhaps his clearest statement on this issue he states that "grace is the fundamental ascription that Christian faith must make in the God-relationship. It is that particular 'attribute,' or reality, or energy, essence, or substance of the God of Abraham, Isaac, and Jacob and of Jesus Christ."[63] For Sittler, grace is constitutive of the being and action of God, and thus all creation and all creatures must be understood in light of that fact.

---

[58]Sittler, "The Presence and Acts," 127.

[59]Sittler, *Essays*, 87.

[60]Ibid., 24.

[61]Ibid., 64.

[62]Joseph Sittler, *Grace Notes and Other Fragments*, selected and edited Linda Marie Delloff (Philadelphia: Fortress, 1981), 88-89.

[63]Sittler, *Essays*, 82.

One important consequence of the above affirmation, according to Sittler, is that we must see grace as pervasive in all God does and all creation is. In contrast to a delimitation of grace to only certain acts within the biblical drama, Sittler argues that "in the great catholic tradition grace comes in creation, in redemption, in sanctification or the unfolding and maturation of the Christian life."[64] And since "the God of grace *is* a God of grace in the fullness of his being as Creator, Redeemer, and Sanctifier...the region of grace is all that is, has been, and will be."[65] Grace is not a partial feature of God's being or characteristic only of certain divine actions, nor is grace limited to only certain regions or spheres of existence. Grace dare not be confined to some marginalized "sacred" realm in contrast to the "secular." In typical trinitarian fashion Sittler affirms that "if grace is postulated of God the Creator, God the Redeemer, and God the Sanctifier, then the presence and power and availability of grace must be postulated with equivalent scope."[66]

In presenting his views on grace, Sittler employs the classical distinction between common and special grace.

> We have sometimes talked about "created grace and uncreated grace" or "common grace and special grace." By "created grace" the early Church meant that grace which is a power and gift of God the Creator and with which he endows his creation. There is a gracious reality present in the things that are made--in this created world, the world which we are equipped to enjoy, study, criticize. To be human in the midst of God's world is to dwell in created grace, that is the grace which is inherent in and given in, with, and under the creation. By "uncreated grace" the old Church meant grace which comes over and above the creation by the incarnation, the sacrifice, the teaching, the presence of Jesus Christ.[67]

Common or created grace is the gratuitous need-not-have-been character of existence. It is grace inherent in creation simply as a result of its being the work of a gracious God. Special or uncreated

---

[64]Sittler, "Speeches," 11.
[65]Sittler, *Essays*, 86.
[66]Ibid., 83.
[67]Sittler, "Speeches," 43.

grace is the authentic manifestation of that same gracious God in the person of Jesus. Elsewhere Sittler elaborates on this distinction:

> By created grace is meant the ecological matrix Psalm 104 talks about. When the Psalm sings a doxology by and out of a man of the earth, there is a celebration of the grace which comes to man in virtue of the Creation and precisely because of man's placement in it. This man is not singing a doxology because he is a gaseous spirit with no relation to chipmunks and corn and wine and oil; these gifts are rather the matrix and occasion whereby he knows the joy out of which he now praises God as creature. Created grace is exactly the grace that inheres in the world by virtue of the fact that it is a creation of a gracious God.
> Uncreated grace points to that specification, incandescence, concentration, humanization, and incarnation of grace which comes not as a naked nonhistorical or nonnatural word but precisely as a historical man born of the Virgin Mary.[68]

While Sittler employs this distinction, he also affirms that "grace is single."[69] While there are different types of grace, grace has a single source--God the Father.

Creation as the Theatre of Grace

This all too brief explication of Sittler's doctrine of grace quite naturally leads to an investigation of his views on creation. Sittler's prescient and timely articulation of "a theology for earth" can be traced, at least in part, to his life-long interest in the natural world.[70] As Sittler himself says:

> For reasons that have nothing to do with Christian commitment, I have always been interested in nature and I just kept acting on that interest, not out of a service to God but because I enjoyed it. Then I found that what I did for enjoyment served well to help me relate theology to the environmental problem.[71]

---

[68]Sittler, "Ecological Commitment," 178-179.

[69]Sittler, *Essays*, 46.

[70]Sittler's 1954 article "A Theology For Earth," *The Christian Scholar* 37 (September 1954) is the work in which, according to Creede, Sittler "found his real subject." See Creede, "Logos and Lord," 83.

[71]Sittler, *Grace Notes*, 15.

Sittler traces this interest in things natural back to his earliest school days. As he puts it, my "lover's relationship with the physical world" began in elementary school with a "remarkable teacher" who would read "writing of memorable beauty"--lines from Shakespeare, Keats, and Whitman.[72] It was in hearing and reading such literature, Sittler recalls, that his partial blindness toward the world was overcome--that, for example, "I learned to look at the sky in a different way."[73] This influence of literature, combined with living in the country, greatly contributed to Sittler's "love affair with the natural world."[74] As he eloquently affirms:

> All my life I've been a passionate lover of our rich American land's variety: the lonely beauty of New England, the great chain of the Appalachians and the Green and White Mountains, the sweep of the praires, the majesty of the Rockies, the unbelievable fecundity of the West Coast valleys.[75]

In this context Sittler queries: "Is it not possible that we can learn to regard the world as a place of grace, because there have been those among our fellows who have celebrated it in such language that the transcendent grace of God resonates and is reflected in the common grace of the creation?"[76]

These reflections by Sittler on the origins of his interest in the natural world are important not only because they help explain why he was one of the first Christian theologians of our time to speak of a "theology for nature" or "theology of ecology."[77] They are also important because they point to the crucial role of perception and of having "a sense for the world" in developing an adequate ecological theology.[78] Sittler often contrasts two ways of

---

[72]Ibid., 83-84.

[73]Ibid., 84.

[74]Ibid. As Sittler says on p. 83, his interest in the natural world, especially in living things, led him to major in biology as well as religion as an undergraduate.

[75]Ibid., 85.

[76]Ibid.

[77]Sittler, "A Theology for Earth," 373, and "Ecological Commitment," 172; cf. Sittler, *Essays*, 58.

[78]See, e.g., Sittler, *Essays*, chapter 5 which is entitled "Grace and a Sense for the World."

attending to the world: looking and beholding. To look at something is simply "an act of perception"; in contrast, to behold a thing "means to regard it in its particularity--its infinite preciousness, irreplaceability, and beauty."[79] Peter Bakken elegantly captures the significance of this distinction:

> It is only by learning to behold the natural world as the bearer of ultimate value and meaning--only by knowing ourselves and all things to be bound together in an ecology of grace--that we will be moved to that love without which neither humanity nor our strange and wonderful companions can long endure.[80]

Only if we behold the natural world as, to use Sittler's language, "a place of grace" and see all creation as an interconnected web of grace will we be sufficiently moved to act responsibly toward nonhuman creatures. And only with such beholding will creation--including us--endure.

Like many others, Sittler points to the eclipse of the Christian doctrine of creation as a significant factor in the loss of a vision of the natural world as graced.[81] Because of "this virtual demise of a vigorous doctrine of the Creation," argues Sittler,

> it is difficult but possible to get men to understand that pollution is biologically disastrous, aesthetically offensive, equally obviously economically self-destructive and socially reductive of the quality of human life. But it is a very difficult job to get even Christians to see that so to deal with the Creation is *Christianly* blasphemous. A proper doctrine of creation and redemption would make it perfectly clear that from a Christian point of view the ecological crisis presents us not simply with moral tasks but requires of us a freshly renovated and fundamental theology of the first article.[82]

---

[79]Sittler, *Gravity and Grace*, 16; cf. 84.

[80]Bakken, "The Ecology of Grace," 414-415.

[81]Others who note this *Schöpfungsvergessenheit* are Per Lønning, *Creation--An Ecumenical Challenge*, 5; Ian Barbour, *Religion in an Age of Science* (San Francisco: Harper and Row, 1990), 217; and Gustaf Wingren, "The Doctrine of Creation: Not an Appendix but the First Article," *Word and World* 4 (Fall 1984): 353ff.

[82]Sittler, "Ecological Commitment," 179.

Only renewed attention to and a creative reconception of the doctrine of creation will provide the necessary theological and ethical resources to think and act responsibly.

Lest anyone think that the Christian tradition is ecologically bankrupt and thus incapable, even with renewed attention to the first article, of providing the resources sufficient to address the ecological crisis, Sittler contends that "at the heart of the Christian and Judaic tradition, there does indeed lie an organic and holistic way of regarding man in the world which is profound and ample enough to address us in our cultural need."[83] As stated in the epigraph at the beginning of this chapter, Sittler claims that

> when we turn the attention of the church to a definition of the Christian relationship with the natural world, we are not stepping away from grave and proper theological ideas; we are stepping right into the middle of them. There is a deeply rooted, genuinely Christian motivation for attention to God's creation, despite the fact that many church people consider ecology to be a secular concern. "What does environmental preservation have to do with Jesus Christ and his church?" they ask. They could not be more shallow or more wrong.[84]

Attention to the natural world is at the very center of the Christian faith, rightly understood.

Sittler gives a variety of reasons for a shrunken and truncated sense for the world.[85] He also delineates "two ways by which man has sought to do justice to the realm of meaning in the natural world."[86] First of all, "nature can be subsumed under man," i.e., "reduced to a resource for his needs."[87] From this anthropocentric point of view, the nonhuman world has no intrinsic value; it has, rather, merely instrumental value. On the other hand, humankind can be "subsumed under nature."[88] In the case of this naturalistic perspective, it is the human which is

---

[83]Joseph Sittler, "The Perils of Futurist Thinking," in *Shaping the Future*, ed. John Roslansky (Amsterdam: North Holland, 1972), 76.

[84]Sittler, *Gravity and Grace*, 15.

[85]Sittler, *Essays*, 101.

[86]Sittler, "A Theology for Earth," 371.

[87]Ibid.

[88]Ibid.

reduced in ontological value since humankind is seen as nothing but a product of nature. The human is reducible to the natural.

Sittler argues that "neither of these ways is adequate" since "neither one does justice either to the amplitude and glory of man's spirit or to the felt meaningfulness of the world of nature."[89] In contrast to both of these views, Sittler insists that "Christian theology, obedient to the biblical account of nature, has asserted a third possible relationship: that man ought properly stand alongside nature as her cherishing brother, for she too is God's creation and bears God's image."[90] Drawing on Psalm 104, among other biblical texts, Sittler claims that this alternative of a "holy naturalism" regards the nonhuman world as "a matrix of divine grace in which all things derive significance from their origin, and all things find fulfillment in praise."[91]

The challenge, then, as Sittler sees it is to develop an ecological theology--a "holy naturalism"-- which creatively steers a course between utilitarian anthropocentrism and reductionistic naturalism.

> The largest, most insistent, most delicate task awaiting Christian theology is to articulate such a theology for nature as shall do justice to the vitalites of earth and hence correct a current theological naturalism which succeeds in speaking meaningfully of earth only at the cost of repudiating specifically Christian categories. Christian theology cannot advance this work along the line of an orthodoxy-- neo or old--which celebrates the love of heaven in complete separation from man's loves in earth, abstracts commitment to Christ from relevancy to those loyalties of earth which are elemental to being. Any faith in God which shall be redemptive and regenerative in actuality dare not be alien to the felt ambiguities of earth or remain wordless in the resounding torments of history and culture. For the earth is not merely a negative illustration of the desirability of heaven![92]

---

[89]Ibid., 372.

[90]Ibid.

[91]Ibid. As Creede observes, with this alternative perspective Sittler wishes to affirm that nature is a theatre that exists for the glory of God. Sittler's views here are similar to those of Calvin; see, e.g., *Institutes* 1.5.8; 1.14.20; and 2.6.1.

[92]Sittler, "A Theology for Earth," 373-374.

In other but less eloquent words, a Christian ecological theology must be informed by natural science and attentive to both the natural and cultural worlds. But it must also be shaped and guided by the Christian categories of creation (not just nature), sin, redemption, grace, and the like. Neither an ecologically uninformed orthodoxy nor an ecologically informed heterodoxy is adequate to the challenge of developing a "holy naturalism."

Sittler spells out this "holy naturalism" in a number of ways. First, with respect to naturalism, Sittler insists that Christian theology must take seriously one of the basic deliverances of the science of ecology, namely, the fact that the world is an ecosystem. The "fundamental postulate of ecology," says Sittler, is "that anything is related to everything."[93] Sittler repeatedly refers to the "ecologically intricate structure" and the "closely woven, ecologically integrated, and delicate structure" of the world.[94] He maintains that "the environment is not just just a dumb resource, but it is a living organism."[95] Echoing John Muir, Sittler affirms that "nature is like a fine piece of cloth: you pull a thread here, and it vibrates throughout the whole fabric."[96] This implies, states Sittler, that "the ecological structure of the human reality" is "the 'web' apart from which I cannot think."[97] The earth is "an interlaced web of origin and sustenance without which man is not."[98] In language reminiscent of Ruether, Sittler affirms that creation is "the entire vast, cosmic, all-engendering, and all-enfolding matrix" without which human life is inconceivable.[99] Using one of his more arresting metaphors, he asserts that "the natural world" is the "life-sustaining placenta of self-consciousness."[100] Like a baby in the mother's womb, nourished by

---

[93]Sittler, *Essays*, 113; cf. p. 3 where Sittler claims that ecology "insists that no thing exists apart from all things."

[94]Sittler, *Gravity and Grace*, 21; *Grace Notes*, 92; *Essays*, 85.

[95]Sittler, "Speeches," 37.

[96]Sittler, *Gravity and Grace*, 22; cf. John Muir, *My First Summer in the Sierra* (San Francisco: Sierra Club, 1988), 110.

[97]Sittler, *Essays*, 3; cf. p. 114 where Sittler refers to the earth as "an ecological web of some astonishing subtlety."

[98]Ibid., 89.

[99]Ibid., 109.

the placenta, without the nonhuman world we cannot exist. Says Sittler at his aphoristic best: "I am no-thing apart from everything."[101]

Therefore Sittler insists that any adequate theology of nature must presuppose an ontology of relations. We must acknowledge "that life is indeed a bundle, that 'all things' is the context of anything, that physics by nature demands a metaphysics."[102] In perhaps his clearest statement of his own ontology, Sittler posits:

> Reality is known only in relations. This statement conflicts with the very structure of a good deal of post-Enlightenment thought in the Western world. I mean by such a statment that we must think it possible that there is no ontology of isolated entities, or instances, of forms, of processes, whether we are reflecting about God or man or society or the cosmos. The only adequate ontological structure we may utilize for thinking things Christianly is an ontology of community, of communion, ecology--and all three words point conceptually to thought of a common kind. "Being itself" may be a relation, not an entitative thing.[103]

"An ontology of relations," maintains Sittler, "begets a beholding in relations, and this begets a thinking in relations."[104] Such an ontology is a necessary ingredient of any genuine solution to the ecological crisis. A relational ontology, furthermore, comports well with the Bible since "the biblical mode of speech about God and man is relational in fundamental structure and image."[105] Indeed, Sittler asks: "Is it not further possible that the relational-dynamic concepts of contemporary physics and biology might be peculiarly apposite to the uses of biblical language?"[106]

---

[100]Ibid., 108; cf. "Presence and Acts," 132. On p. 408 of "Feminism and the Grace-full Thought of Joseph Sittler," *The Christian Century*, 9 April 1980, 408, Thetis Cromie speaks of Sittler as "the man with the placental mind."

[101]Sittler, *Essays*, 111.

[102]Joseph Sittler, "The Scope of Christological Reflection," *Interpretation* 26 (July 1972): 337.

[103]Sittler, "Ecological Commitment," 174. In *Essays*, 106-107, Sittler acknowledges the influence on his own thinking of "an ontology of communion" articulated by his colleague Joseph Haroutunian.

[104]Sittler, "Ecological Commitment," 176.

[105]Sittler, *Essays*, 128.

[106]Ibid.

Mention of the dynamic as well as relational character of reality introduces another conclusion of science that Sittler believes must be taken seriously: the natural world is not only interdependent, it is evolving and in process. We must speak of "an evolutionary ecosystem."[107] We must understand "anthropology as not extractable from the story of *man* in an evolving world-process."[108] We must, contends Sittler, see "life as dynamic, in-motion, developmental. Progress is a moot question; change is not. From astrophysics to gene-mutation the evidence is conclusive: there is no such thing as a steady-state."[109] This recognition of the historical nature of all creation is, maintains Sittler, terrifying. Borrowing a phrase from Dilthey, Sittler acknowledges the "terrifying dynamism of the historical" and extends this to include the natural world. We can and must talk about the "terrifying dynamism of the natural world" as well--a world ever-changing, developing, evolving, being transformed.[110] In sum, as Sittler sharply and memorably puts it: "The history of nature is the context for the nature of history."[111]

While Sittler insists, in the ways just indicated, on taking seriously the "naturalism" side of the expression, he also insists on taking seriously the qualifier "holy" in the phrase "holy naturalism." In his doctrine of creation he not only seeks to avoid a utilitarian anthropocentrism, but also a reductionistic naturalism. In other words, natural science does not have the only or the final word on how we should properly view creation. For example, Sittler argues against any separation between nature and history on biblical as well as scientific grounds. Sittler affirms that "later large categories under which life was divided into life-as-nature and life-as-history are useless for grasping the structure of Israel's faith."[112] There is a congruence of modern scientific and biblical worldviews on this matter. According to Sittler, "the life-world that characterizes our time and to which an adequate christology must

---

[107]Ibid., 42.
[108]Sittler, "The Presence and Acts," 91.
[109]Ibid., 123.
[110]Sittler, "Speeches," 32.
[111]Sittler, "Scope," 330.
[112]Sittler, *Essays*, 24.

be proposed includes both the world as nature and the world as history. I would suggest to you that so does the biblical world."[113]

In his attempt to develop a naturalism shaped by Christian categories Sittler makes one central claim: "The world is not God, but it is God's. Or to put the issue another way, nature and grace belong together."[114] As he elaborates elsewhere, paraphrasing God's message to the ancient Hebrews: "Nature is God's, but it is not God. Nature is not to be worshipped, but it is my gift, and you are to exercise care for my gift."[115] Creation implies a Creator. The world is neither divine nor autonomous--to be neither worshipped nor viewed as empty of divine presence.

It follows, Sittler argues, that the earth is most properly seen not as mother, but as our fellow creature--indeed our sibling. Emphasizing the importance of "beholding" Sittler states:

> Therefore, to "behold" actuality from the standpoint of reality understood as relational is not just a quip of language; it is rather a rhetorical acknowledgment of a fundamental ecological understanding of man whose father is God but whose sibling is the whole creation.[116]

More specifically, while calling the term "Mother Nature" a "pagan phrase," Sittler asserts that

> in Christian faith, God is our Father, the Church is our Mother (she is the one who brings forth all believers, in Luther's phrase and back of him Augustine), but nature is our Sister; nature is God's other creation who stands alongside of us with her own individuality, integrity, vitality, and which has limits to what you can do.[117]

With references to both scripture and tradition--Romans 8 and St. Francis--Sittler affirms that the earth is "man's sister, sharer of his sorrow and scene and partial substance of his joys," who "unquenchably sings out her violated wholeness, and in groaning

[113]Sittler, "Speeches," 32.

[114]Sittler, "Ecological Commitment," 178; cf. Joseph Sittler, *The Anguish of Preaching* (Philadelphia: Fortress, 1966), 63.

[115]Sittler, *Gravity and Grace*, 18.

[116]Sittler, "Ecological Commitment," 175.

[117]Sittler, "Speeches," 38.

and travail awaits with man the restoration of all things."[118] Combining scientific and theological perspectives, Sittler eloquently affirms: "This radioactive earth, so fecund and so fragile, is his [God's] creation, is our sister and the material place where we meet the brother in Christ's light."[119]

All of the above may be summarized in what is perhaps Sittler's most pervasive theme with respect his attempt to fashion a *holy* naturalism. In a variety of ways Sittler affirms that creation is the locus of grace. He argues, for example, that because "God creates his creation in grace" therefore "the creation itself is a realm of grace."[120] Sittler states that references to the "ecological facts of life" are "descriptions of the *field* of grace, expositions of the actuality of man's life and placement within the web of nature."[121] Sittler insists that "despite human rapacity and despoilation" the natural world is still "a field of grace."[122] In yet other words, Sittler simply speaks of creation as the place of grace. For example, in a sub-section of *Essays on Nature and Grace* entitled "The Place of Grace" Sittler asserts that "the focal region of God's grace is not less than the whole creation."[123] After quoting a poem by Whitman, Sittler asks whether it is "possible that we can learn to regard the world as a place of grace?"[124] And with a typical reference to the ecological matrix of existence, Sittler posits that "the place of grace must be the webbed connectedness of our creaturely life"--a connectedness which "does not indeed bestow grace" but "is necessarily the theatre" for grace.[125]

The characterization of creation as a "theatre of grace" is Sittler's most common way of speaking of the grace-full character of reality. For example, Sittler argues that "the reality of grace is not severable from that web and bundle of life out of which the human emerges and is defined" and which "constitutes the theatre

[118]Sittler, "A Theology for Earth," 370; cf. 372.
[119]Sittler, *Grace Notes*, 115.
[120]Sittler, *Gravity and Grace*, 13; cf. Sittler, *Anguish*, 41, 59.
[121]Sittler, *Essays*, 2; see also, Joseph Sittler, "Commencement Address," *The Chicago Lutheran Seminary Record* 64 (November 1959): 36.
[122]Sittler, *Grace Notes*, 86.
[123]Sittler, *Essays*, 86; cf. 69, 120.
[124]Sittler, *Gravity and Grace*, 85.
[125]Sittler, *Grace Notes*, 80; cf. 88-89.

of our redemption by grace."[126] Indeed, Sittler maintains that "ecology, that is, the actuality of the relational as constitutive of all that live [sic], is the only theatre vast enough for a modern playing out of the doctrine of grace."[127] This image of creation as a theatre of grace is a prominent image in Sittler's famous New Delhi speech. He declares that "nature, as well as history, is the theatre of grace and the scope of redemption."[128] Elsewhere, sounding a familiar theme, Sittler affirms that "the grace of God must find the theatre of its acknowledgement not just in the forgiveness of sins and the sacrament and the sermon, etc., but in the very giftedness of the natural world as itself a theatre of grace."[129]

Sittler's basic argument is fairly straightforward:

> Grace is intrinsic to all that God has made. When encountered in his deed of grace in Jesus Christ, it so places the child of grace within existence that the world of persons, things, processes, and all mortal engagements with them is proposed to the mind and spirit as a veritable theatre of grace.[130]

Grace is fundamental to the being of God. So that which God creates is characterized by grace. When humans encounter God in Jesus Christ, they are epistemically able to see creation for the grace-full reality that it in fact is. In summary:

> There is a gracious reality present in the things that are made--in this created world, the world which we are equipped to enjoy, study, criticze. To be human in the midst of God's world is to dwell in created grace, that is, the grace which is inherent in and given in, with, and under the creation.[131]

Sittler continually affirms that "the presence of grace is beheld and celebrated in and through the creation."[132]

---

[126]Ibid., 85; cf. 115, and Sittler, *Essays*, 106.

[127]Sittler, "Ecological Commitment," 180.

[128]Sittler, "Called to Unity," 11; cf. 7, 14.

[129]Sittler, "Perils," 82; cf. 81.

[130]Sittler, *Essays*, 13; cf. 89, 116.

[131]Sittler, "Speeches," 43; cf. Sittler, *Essays*, 75.

[132]Sittler, *Essays*, 19. See also Sittler, *Gravity and Grace*, 14, and Joseph Sittler, *The Ecology of Faith* (Philadelphia: Muhlenburg, 1961), 47 for additional references to "grace *in* the natural."

The Triune God

In addition to the topics of grace and creation, one other theme must be addressed before Sittler's christology can be adequately understood, namely, Sittler's views on God and the Trinity. Sittler contends, first of all, that divine being is a function of divine action. As Sittler succinctly says, "What God is...is an organic function of what God does."[133] Or as he insists elsewhere: "Scriptural speech about God is always dynamic. God is what God does. God is that from which all things come. This means that God language is fundamentally functional--not propositional."[134] This functionally constituted God is, following the Creed, "the maker of heaven and earth--God of all that is."[135] That God is creator is basic for Sittler. In a favorite image Sittler posits that God is "the fountain of life from whose eternal livingness all things are brought forth."[136] Borrowing from Calvin's statement that "God is the fountain of all livingness," Sittler affirms that "God is the name for that one from whom all things flow."[137] The universe is dependent upon God its creator since God is the ultimate Source of all things.

Despite the fountain metaphor, which can suggest an inner necessity to divine creation, Sittler maintains that God is free. Indeed, as indicated previously, Sittler articulates the core of the

---

[133]Joseph Sittler, *The Structure of Christian Ethics* (Baton Rouge: Louisiana State University, 1958), 5. In *Anguish*, 63, Sittler says that "Christian affirmation [is] grounded in a doctrine of a God whose isness is his doesness in historical liberations."

[134]Sittler, *Gravity and Grace*, 83. See also p. 43 where Sittler states that "God in Scripture is not the one who *is* but the one who *does*. This is a functional definition of God, not a dictionary definition."

[135]Ibid., 35.

[136]Sittler, *Structure*, 4. Sittler also speaks of the eternity of God in "Speeches," 50-54, and *Gravity and Grace*, 126-127.

[137]Sittler, "Ecological Commitment," 174; cf. 173, and *Essays*, 104. Sittler does not give a citation for this quotation of Calvin, and I have been unable to locate the precise textual source. It does not sound like something Calvin would say; however, Calvin sometimes says things that one does not expect. For example, in *Institutes* 1.5.5 he states: "I confess, of course, that it can be said reverently, provided that it proceeds from a reverent mind, that nature is God." While he immediately qualifies this statement, it is nonetheless quite surprising.

Christian faith in terms of divine freedom and grace. The "freedom of God in his grace," says Sittler, is "a right designation of the central substance of the Christian confession."[138] Hence while God is the one from whom all things flow, God is in no way compelled to create. *That* God creates and that God creates *what* God creates are, Sittler reminds his readers, always surprises, since as a free agent God need not create at all. God is the freely creating ultimate Source of all things.

Sittler affirms, in addition, that God and the world are different. As Sittler simply puts it: "God is not the same as the world--and grace is not the same as nature."[139] Furthermore, says Sittler, "the awesome, mystical, stunning difference between God and the creatures is an important difference."[140] This difference is important because we must speak about God with the necessary respect and reverence and because it "points to that central humility which one has in the presence of the knowledge that he is a creature and not the Creator."[141] As the freely creating ultimate Source of all things, God is distinct from all that is not-God.

However, while Sittler claims that creator and creation are distinct in some sense, he also maintains that they are intimately related. God is other than creation, but God is also present in and with creation. For example, Sittler asserts that "our modern view of nature as by definition not having anything to do with the divine is in complete hiatus with the Old Testament view. There nature comes from God, cannot be apart from God, and is capable of bearing the 'glory' of God."[142] Quoting Thomas Aquinas, Sittler affirms that "God is above all things by the excellence of his nature; nevertheless he is in all things as causing the being of all things."[143] As Sittler insists: "God is not identical with but is present in what he creates, is present in the redemption of what he creates, and is present in all restoration, uniting, and upholding of his redeemed

---

[138]Sittler, *Essays*, 86. See also Brauer, "In Appreciation," 101, and Hefner, *The Scope of Grace*, vi, for statements which point to the centrality of this summary statement in Sittler's theology.

[139]Sittler, "Commencement Address," 37.

[140]Sittler, *Gravity and Grace*, 78.

[141]Sittler, "Speeches," 46.

[142]Sittler, *Essays*, 37.

[143]Ibid., 89.

creation."[144] Thus with typical concreteness Sittler acknowledges: "I have never been able to entertain a God-idea which was not integrally related to the fact of chipmunks, squirrels, hippopotamuses, galaxies, and light years."[145]

In sum, God is neither identified with the world nor separate from the world. As mentioned previously, Sittler states that "the world is not God, but it is God's." On this basis he argues that because "nature is acknowledged as God's but not God," we are free to "really care for and love the world."[146] In other words, if nature is not divine, then nature worship is illegitimate. Worship should be given instead to the God who creates the natural world, for only then will knowledge of God's intentions for the world become clear, namely, that we should care for the world around us. As Sittler puts it in one of his many fetching aphorisms: "God is not identified with the world, for he *made* it; but God is not separate from his world, either. For *He* made it."[147]

These remarks form the background for Sittler's discussion of the Trinity. In Sittler's opinion, the "old ways of speaking about the doctrine of the trinity" are "not now useful to the clarification of the doctrines of God or of grace" since the language of Nicea and Chalcedon is embedded in "an ontological schema which is no longer congruent with most men's perception of reality or language about it."[148] Sittler wishes "to honor the richness and operational adequacy of the traditional confessions of the trinity" and affirm "the interior relations of Father, Son, and Spirit in a manner that preserves faith's intentions," but he wishes to do so in a way appropriate to people of today.[149] We must, claims Sittler, "try to find a conceptuality appropriate to our time" since "we must not simply assume theirs [the categories of the early Church] will carry the mail for us."[150] According to Sittler, the basic affirmation of the doctrine of the Trinity is that "creation, redemption, and

---

[144]Sittler, "The Presence and Acts," 91.
[145]Sittler, "Ecological Commitment," 173.
[146]Sittler, *Anguish*, 63-64.
[147]Sittler, *Structure*, 4.
[148]Sittler, "The Presence and Acts," 91.
[149]Ibid.
[150]Sittler, "Speeches," 25-26.

sanctification have their source in God, that this God is not identical with but is present in what he creates, is present in the redemption of what he creates, and is present in all restoration, uniting, and upholding of his redeemed creation."[151] From this Sittler concludes:

> If this indeed be the reality to which the doctrine points, then the terms of ascription and the language of confession must be appropriate to a time that understands creation as continuous, and understands anthropology as not extractable from the story of *man* in an evolving world-process.[152]

Sittler's own reformulation of this doctrine involves a number of moves. First, Sittler not surprisingly argues that the Trinity must be viewed in terms of grace. Grace is characteristic of God in *all* God is and does. There must be "a relocation of the reality of grace" because "the God of grace *is* a God of grace in the fullness of his being as Creator, Redeemer, and Sanctifier."[153] Sittler firmly reminds us that "grace characterizes the whole of Christian theology--God the Father, God the Son, and God the Holy Spirit."[154] Grace, for Sittler, is simply the most accurate and comprehensive descriptor of God, regardless of whether God is viewed in terms of functions or persons. And so Sittler repeatedly affirms that "the one comprehensive reality of this Trinitarian God is grace."[155]

Sittler's favorite way of talking about the Trinity is in terms of what God *does*--God as creator, redeemer, and sanctifier. For example, when referring to eschatology Sittler insists that our "vision of the New Creation is a product of God who is affirmed in faith to be Creator of the world, Redeemer of the world, and Sanctifier of the world."[156] When discussing the temptation to reduce christology to soteriology, Sittler maintains: "The doctrine of the Holy Trinity is an effort to secure faith against that

---

[151]Sittler, "The Presence and Acts," 91.
[152]Ibid.
[153]Sittler, *Essays*, 86; cf. 83.
[154]Sittler, *Gravity and Grace*, 20; cf. 14.
[155]Sittler, *Essays*, 120; cf. 88.
[156]Ibid.; cf. 42, 83, 88.

temptation. There is one God. We know him as God the creator, God the Redeemer, and God the Sanctifier."[157] And with respect to Christian ethics Sittler most often speaks of God as Creator, Redeemer, and Sanctifier.[158] God is as God does, and the triune God creates, redeems, and sanctifies.

Sittler's second move, alluded to previously, is to use the typically Eastern Orthodox language of the energy of God to speak of the action of the Trinity. Divine action is a kind of unified operation or energy. Sittler posits that "a triadic-organic way of speaking about what the Psalms called 'the energies of God' would seem to offer a presently promising way to honor the richness and operational adequacy of the traditional conceptions of the trinity."[159] This approach is promising, says Sittler, not only because it captures the heart of the tradition, but because that "wonderful phrase"--"the energies of God"--"brings a way of talking about God that intersects with the contemporary worldview in which this table top and rug are but transformed energies."[160] Sittler finds this category of divine energy extremely helpful in attempting to correlate classical tradition and contemporary times.[161] In sum, God is a "function of energy and the energies of God have various forms."[162] For Sittler, grace is "a proper divine energy of the Trinity as such."[163]

The upshot of Sittler's ruminations on the Trinity can be summarized in terms of three basic claims. Sittler argues that the

---

[157]Sittler, *Anguish*, 39; cf. 55. See also *Gravity and Grace*, 19 where Sittler states that the three affirmations in the Apostles' Creed "are ways of speaking of the activity and reality of one God."

[158]Sittler, *Structure*, 87; cf. Sittler, *Grace Notes*, 72-73.

[159]Sittler, "The Presence and Acts," 91. For a clear elucidation of the traditional understanding of the concept of divine energy as, e.g., "an existentially perceivable manifestation" of a nature or essence, see John Meyendorff, *Byzantine Theology* (New York: Fordham, 1979), 185-188.

[160]Sittler, "Speeches," 43.

[161]For Sittler's method, see, e.g., "A Theology for Earth," 368, where Sittler states that the "Professor of Christian Theology" has a "double vocation: a vocation to work at the task of Christian theology, and a vocation to citizenship in the twentieth century." Or, as Sittler says on p. 68 of *Essays*, the challenge is to do theology "in continuity with the church's faith and in ways useful for our time." See also *Essays*, 22, 93.

[162]Sittler, "Speeches," 43.

[163]Sittler, "The Presence and Acts," 127.

doctrine of the Trinity, especially with the emphases and nuances that he highlights, is necessary to express adequately the scope of grace, to develop coherently a cosmic christology, and to ground sufficiently an earth-affirming ecological theology. As Sittler insists with respect to the development of dogma in the early church: "When, later, a conceptualization of the scope of grace was compelled to give dogmatic precision to these organic images [in Colossians, Ephesians, etc.] of the energy of grace operating in so wide a range, nothing short of the dogma of the Holy Trinity was adequate to set it forth."[164] So also, given "the recognition of man's actuality within nature as creation," i.e., human embeddedness in the webbed connectedness of the natural world, Sittler argues that "the effort to elaborate a Christology to the size of *that* ecological placement of man will not be able to stop short of a fresh go at the venerable doctrine of the Holy Trinity."[165] In a summary statement of sorts Sittler draws out the implications of his doctrine of the Trinity for a Christian ecological theology:

> The Christian doctrine of the creation acknowledges this [that the earth is the Lord's]; the Christian doctrine of redemption by its affirmation of the incarnation declares that God who created man in the garden of history and nature does not will to redeem him in any other garden--or in some angelic removal from all gardens. And the doctrine of the Holy Spirit declares that God, as Sanctifier, sticks by his earthly decision as Creator and Redeemer. When the presence and gift of the Holy Spirit "filled all the house where they were sitting" the same Spirit made clear that God does not empower a holy balloon-ascension out of nature and history, but rather that he empowers a new heaven and new earth to be constituted for men for whom "all things have become new."[166]

Christ as Cosmic and a Christology for Nature

Sittler's conviction that the categories of traditional Christian theology must be reformulated, evident in his views on grace and creation, is never more prominent than with regard to his christology. Like a steady drumbeat, Sittler again and again

---

164Sittler, *Essays*, 48; cf. Sittler, "The Presence and Acts," 114.
165Sittler, "Scope," 330.
166Sittler, *Anguish*, 55.

asserts the need to rethink the received views of Christ. For example, Sittler argues, largely as a result of his work with the Faith and Order Commission, that "Christology remains formally imprisoned in categories which are felt by the initiated to be inadequate and by the uninitiated to be irrelevant."[167] Furthermore, Sitler claims that "this inadequacy and this irrelevancy are made the more painful because we recognize that the classical Christology of the Creeds perpetuates formulations which operate with a way of speaking about God which is incongruent with our time and its ways of thinking.[168] Sittler states that "the center of my own theological work" is "the effort to fashion a more comprehensible and intelligible and relevant christology to a quite new age, the twentieth century."[169] As with his discussion of "holy naturalism," in which both fidelity to the Christian faith and openness to contemporary science are important, Sittler describes his task in terms of developing a christology "which shall be pulled through but also taken beyond the traditional language" of the person and work of Christ.[170]

But Sittler does not merely express the need to reformulate christology; he articulates the need to *expand* the scope of christology to encompass all that has being. The task is "to recognize that the traditional scope of christological understanding is under pressure to achieve vaster amplitude in virtue of contemporary man's apprehension of the world-as-nature."[171] The pressure to enlarge the scope of christology also arises, Sittler insists, from the Bible.

> Positive theological work, it seems to me, must operate with the event of the Incarnation with a depth and amplitude as least as wide and far ranging and as grand as that of the New Testament. We may not be able to go beyond Ephesians, Colossians, and the eighth chapter of Romans; but we dare not stop short of the incomparable boldness of those utterances.[172]

---

[167]Joseph Sittler, "A Christology of Function," *Lutheran Quarterly* 6 (May, 1954): 122.
[168]Ibid.
[169]Sittler, "Speeches," 29.
[170]Ibid.
[171]Sittler, *Essays*, 51.
[172]Sittler, "A Theology for Earth," 374.

Hence whether on scientific or biblical-theological grounds, Sittler affirms the need to expand the scope of christology. As he eloquently puts it in his famous New Delhi speech:

> The address of Christian thought is most weak precisely where man's ache is most strong. We have had, and have, a christology for the moral soul, a christology for history, and, if not a christology for the ontic, affirmations so huge as to fill the space marked out by ontological questions. But we do not have, at least not in such effective force as to engage the thought of the common life, a daring, penetrating, life-affirming christology for nature. The theological significance of cosmic christology lies, for the most part, still tightly folded in the Church's innermost heart and memory.[173]

A necessary dimension in the development of a "christology for nature" is the articulation of a cosmic christology. As Sittler asserts: "The way forward is from Christology expanded to its cosmic dimensions."[174]

In addressing this task, Sittler makes a number of important distinctions. First, Sittler distinguishes between two *styles* of christology: Western and Eastern. He contrasts these two styles according to various emphases:[175]

Western	Eastern
redemption from sin	divinization of humanity
the passion of Christ	the cosmos-ruling Christ
atonement	participation/illumination
restoration	reunification
Savior	Pantocrator
corpus	*Christus rex*

Sittler illustrates this contrast by explicating the christological views of Gregory of Nyssa, Gregory Palamas, Ireneaus, and Athanasius.[176] Sittler argues that while "a Christology of the total

---

[173]Sittler, "Called to Unity," 12. See also p. 10 for another reference to a "Christology of nature."

[174]Ibid., 14; cf. Sittler, *Grace Notes*, 115.

[175]Sittler, *Essays*, 52ff.

[176]The influence of such Eastern thinkers is pervasive in Sittler. See, e.g., *Essays*, 13, 52ff; "The Presence and Acts," 116ff, 126ff; "Speeches," 36.

cosmos with the force and scope necessary to constitute Christian illumination of Western man's absurd and suicidal operations with nature is not a prominent or even popularly accepted strand within the churches of the West," nevertheless the "catholic tradition does indeed include such a possibility."[177] In other words, Sittler claims that there are important resources within the Christian tradition for developing a cosmic christology, but those resources are most pervasive and powerful in the Eastern Orthodox tradition. If Western Christians desire to develop a cosmic christology, then they will have to learn from Eastern theology.

Sittler also distinguishes between two *types* of christology: functional and essential. "Within the New Testament," says Sittler, "there are, on the main, two ways of trying to understand Christ...he is who he is because he does what he does, or he does what he does because he is who he is."[178] In other words, Christ "is called the Son of God...because he does what he does," especially because of "the things which he suffers;" or he "is ontologically one with the Father and therefore does the works of God."[179] The first view states that Christ "became the Son" because of "the things that he suffered," while the second posits that in Christ "the substance of God is reenacted."[180] According to Sittler, the first is characteristic of the Synoptics while the second is found in the gospel of John. The first is "a christology of function" while the second is "a christology of essence."[181]

Sittler, however, does not simply distinguish between these types of christology. He advocates a functional christology over an

---

Sittler also speaks appreciatively of Gustaf Wingren and Karl Rahner; see, e.g., "The Presence and Acts," 120, 127-128.

[177]Sittler, *Essays*, 55. See also "Speeches," 36, where with reference to cosmic christology Sittler says "I discovered that in the Eastern fathers particularly this theme is not only fully present but much more fully elaborated than in Western Christendom."

[178]Sittler, "Speeches," 24. In *Anguish*, 31, Sittler acknowledges: "We are both told that he [Christ] is who he is because he does what he does; we are also told that he does what he does because he is who he is. There is in the New Testament a Christology of essence become function and a Christology of godly function interpreted as essence."

[179]Sittler, "Speeches," 24.

[180]Ibid.

[181]Ibid., 26.

essential or ontic christology. While acknowledging that the New Testament employs both types and that the church should not necessarily give up saying the Nicence Creed, Sittler nevertheless insists that an ontic christology is "no longer adequate or appropriate or fitting or intelligible."[182] Furthermore, the early Church, affirms Sittler, "could say 'Immanuel' even in the absence of a philosophical *logos* or hypostatic theology" because Jesus' contemporaries "saw a man do something and said, 'God is with us.'"[183] That is to say, while it may be articulated in terms of philosophical categories, e.g., essence, substance, christology is first and foremost a description of the action of Jesus--of how Jesus functioned. In addition, Sittler argues that "the functional strand in the New Testament testimony to Christ" has been obscured since "so strong has been the insistence upon the assertion that Christ does what he does because he is who he is."[184] Sittler concludes that "inadequate attention has been paid to the testimony that he also is affirmed to be who he is because he does what he does."[185]

Sittler also distinguishes, thirdly, between a theocentric and christocentric christology, and argues in favor of the former. For example, Sittler repudiates any "Jesus only" christology since "Jesus never would have said such a thing."[186] As Sittler contends with respect to Jewish-Christian dialogue: "There is no future in Christians trying to be more Christocentric than Jesus was. And Jesus was not Christocentric at all. His whole life, his words, actions, disposition, and final act were radically theocentric."[187] The "witnessing Christocentrism" of the early Christian community was not intended to be a modification of "the theocentrism of the faith of Israel;" rather, "when the community spoke of Christ's

---

[182]Ibid., 25-26.
[183]Ibid., 26-27.
[184]Sittler, *Structure*, 47-48.
[185]Ibid., 48.
[186]Sittler, "Speeches," 23. As Sittler remarks on the same page, "this 'Jesus only' thing is really bad biblical theology as well as bad christology."
[187]Sittler, *Gravity and Grace*, 106. See also *Essays*, 87-88, where Sittler says that "Jesus was not centered in Jesus at all;" and "Speeches," 23, where Sittler contends that "Jesus is radically theocentric always." In this context Sittler is fond of quoting the texts in the gospel of John in which Jesus continually points to God the Father.

doing they were speaking of God's doing."[188] Christ was the "center and intention" of all their symbols and terms, but "the Christ to whom they bore witness was in continuity with the God of Abraham, Isaac, and Jacob."[189] Sittler thus argues for a kind of christocentrism, but one qualified by a theocentric perspective.

Sittler turns to the Bible to ground his christology for nature and in so doing squarely faces a crucial hermeneutical issue: how can one acknowledge the undeniable variety of the New Testament witness to Christ and yet also account for the apparent momentum in the New Testament toward a christology cosmic in scope? As Sittler asks:

> Is it possible to speak of this variety in such a way as, on the one hand, to honor the warning against dogmatic "arangement," and, on the other, to acknowledge that there is movement in this witness, that the referential amplitude is vastly wider in some voices than in others . . .?[190]

On the one hand, "the New Testament witness to God and to Christ discloses a process...of fusion, transformation, and clarification" which admits of "no single or simple way of speaking of God and man and grace and the natural world."[191] If scripture is to be taken seriously and fairly, "the huge variety of the New Testament witness to Christ" must be acknowleged.[192]

On the other hand, Sittler claims that "it is possible and legitimate to see a growing magnitude in the christological utterances of the New Testament"--"an ever-widening orbit of christological meaning, scope, and force."[193] There are not only differences in the biblical testimony to Christ, argues Sittler, but "differences-in-motion" such that talk of a "christological momentum may be the most accurate term for what the literature of the New Testament discloses."[194] Especially in Paul there is an

---

[188]Sittler, *Essays*, 27.
[189]Ibid.
[190]Ibid., 29.
[191]Ibid., 26.
[192]Ibid., 28.
[193]Ibid., 11.
[194]Ibid., 29.

"imperial christological momentum" or trajectory of thought toward a truly cosmic christology.[195] In short, while Sittler acknowledges that there is a genuine plurality in the New Testament witness to Christ that cannot be systematized, he also insists that "there clearly is a momentum and a directionality at work in the scope and variety of the New Testament witness to Jesus as the Christ"--a momentum characterized by "widening circles of reference" until in Colossians and Ephesians "all things" are enfolded within the work of Christ.[196]

Sittler thus speaks of a "rhetoric of cosmic extension" in the Bible.[197] There is "an undilutable momentum, a 'blooming' of the language of Christ-testimony, in the New Testament" that has its roots in Israel's faith and finds its fullest expression in Colossians 1, Ephesians 1, and Romans 8.[198] As Sittler states in his New Delhi address--which actually is an extended meditation on Col. 1:15-20, "the sweep of God's restorative action in Christ is no smaller than the six-times repeated *ta panta*."[199] Indeed, says Sittler, "all things are permeable to his [Christ's] cosmic redemption because all things subsist in him. He comes to all things, not as a stranger, for he is first-born of all creation, and in him all things were created."[200] As Sittler later puts it in summarizing the thesis of that famous address: "Only a Christology capable of administering the cosmic scope of biblical and catholic Christ-testimony would be adequate to the question about Christ and his meaning as it is necessarily put by men of modernity."[201]

As intimated previously, Sittler also looks to the early Church, and especially Ireneaus, for examples of and resources for "a Christology of the total cosmos."[202] What attracts Sittler to "the cosmic Christology of Ireneaus" is "the idea that the Incarnate Word is in himself the unity and harmony not only of men, but also of the entire material universe," especially as Ireneaus works out

---

[195]Ibid., 46.
[196]Sittler, "Scope," 334.
[197]Sittler, *Essays*, 36ff.
[198]Ibid., 30.
[199]Sittler, "Called to Unity," 6.
[200]Ibid.
[201]Sittler, *Essays*, 8.
[202]Ibid., 55.

that idea using the language of recapitulation.[203] In other words, "the God who is man's Redeemer dare not be acknowledged as other or less than the Creator of the world" and thus "the scope of Lordship dare not be specified as less than the scope of all that is."[204] Sittler thus argues that "if there is postulated a logos-toward-redemption at work in history, and if the Lord who is disclosed there is postulated as the Lord of all that is, then this same comprehensiveness must inhere in an adequate Christology."[205] Our Redeemer must be our Creator, and the Creator must be the Creator of everything.

In his christology Sittler describes Christ as "the personal concentration of the grace of God."[206] All creation is grace, but there is an "absolute concentration of the reality of grace at the point of Christ."[207] Therefore the scope of grace must be understood "both in its Christ-concentration and its extent."[208] And so for Sittler, grace is not only "a comprehensive term for the created goodness of all reality," but also a term "to specify the incarnated presence and historical focus of that Light which is God."[209] Grace is evident in all creation, but Christ is the incarnation of grace--God's special grace.

An important implication for Sittler of this view of Christ is that it is precisely the earth that is the place where God's glory became flesh. "The Christian is to accept," says Sittler, "what God gives as Redeemer: the earth and all human life as the place wherein God's glory became flesh and dwelt among us."[210] And the presence of the glory of God implies the "indubitable, unassailable presence and action of God."[211] Hence the glory of God "is simply a sign of the ineffable which meets us through the effable, the

[203]Ibid., 63.
[204]Ibid., 116.
[205]Ibid., 89.
[206]Sittler, *Anguish*, 59. See also *Gravity and Grace*, 106, where Sittler refers to Jesus as "the incomparable and incandescent concreteness" of God.
[207]Sittler, *Essays*, 77.
[208]Ibid., 25.
[209]Ibid., 64.
[210]Sittler, *Structure*, 87; cf. Sittler, *Grace Notes*, 72.
[211]Sittler, "Speeches," 21.

material, the ordinary."[212] All creation is a sacrament. The natural world is a sign of divine presence. So Sittler warns that "we dare not exclude as a theatre of grace that same order of creation within whose form and substance God willed in Christ to make the place of his gracious presence."[213] Sittler's theology is thus an incarnational theology. As he insists, distinguishing his incarnational theology of nature from other theological perspectives, e.g., natural theology: "My theology is not one derived from nature; it is a theology of the incarnation applied to nature--which is quite different."[214] One does not properly start with the natural world and proceed to make inferences about the being and action of God; rather one draws conclusions about creation based upon the incarnation of Christ.

One final aspect of Sittler's christology must yet be explicated. Sittler accurately perceives in modern life what he calls "the contemporary crisis of presence."[215] There is, says Sittler, a perceived absence of divine presence. The figure of Jesus is a "strange presence" amidst "the human diminishment and debacle of an 'absence.'"[216] And this absence of divine presence is compounded by "an increasingly impersonal culture."[217] Yet, states Sittler, the term presence "is nevertheless the term upon which must turn all speech about God in creation and in history."[218] There is a crisis of presence, and yet the very idea and, more importantly, experience of personal presence is a crucial requirement if religious language is to be meaningful since religious language is by its very nature, among other things, language of presence.[219]

For Sittler this crisis of presence finds its most profound expression in the "ineffable, inexplicable, almost unimaginable suffering" of Jesus.[220] In the cross one comes face to face with

---

212Ibid.
213Sittler, *Essays*, 132.
214Sittler, *Gravity and Grace*, 67.
215Sittler, *Essays*, 97.
216Sittler, "The Presence and Acts," 98.
217Ibid., 99.
218Ibid., 98-99.
219See, e.g., Merold Westphal, *God, Guilt, and Death: An Existential Phenomenology of Religion* (Bloomington: Indiana University Press, 1984).
220Sittler, "Speeches," 28.

complete absence and utter abandonment. However, for Sittler the suffering of Jesus also represents God's response to the crisis of presence. Affirms Sittler: "The sufferer in the presence of the cross somehow knows he is not alone, that that which is ultimate, that which is the ground of all, is somehow engaged in the profoundest levels of his knowledge of his own humanity."[221] Pondering the logic of incarnation, Sittler argues:

> Unless the God before whom we sit, and at whom we gaze, and about whom we think--unless that God has the tormented shape of our human existence, he isn't God enough. We ask, "Why did God become human?" And the answer is that the God who wants to be the source of our order must become the horror of our disorder, or he has no authority.[222]

In one of his earliest published articles, Sittler reflects on the brokenness and ambiguity of life--what he calls "the cruciform character of human existence."[223] He concludes that "because life itself is cruciform it must be addressed, if it is to be savingly struck, in an action which itself is cruciform."[224] The incarnation is such an action. Commenting on John 1:14, Sittler expresses amazement at the words "The Word became flesh and dwelt among us." Declares Sittler: "Flesh--because that is *what* we are. Dwelt among us!-- because that is *where* we are."[225] God took flesh and tented among us. The cruciform character of life has been addressed by the crucified Christ.

Such claims lie at the very core of the Christian faith. At the heart of the Christian story lies the bold and joyful insistence, incredible though it seems, that the Creator of the universe enters into our pain and undergoes our suffering. God tents with us. The cosmic Christ is a crucified God. In Sittler's words, only "the crucified God" is God enough to have "enabled generation after generation, century after century, to sustain so great a weight of

---

[221]Ibid., 28-29.

[222]Sittler, *Gravity and Grace*, 34.

[223]Joseph Sittler, "The Cruciform Character of Human Existence," *The Chicago Lutheran Seminary Record* 54 (October 1949), 18.

[224]Ibid., 20.

[225]Ibid.

human woe."[226] Only a crucifix "could absorb all of the worries and apprehensions heaped upon it."[227] As Sittler explicitly affirms with characteristic honesty and elegance:

> The cross is the symbol [of Christian faith] because the whacks of life take that shape. Our lives are full of abandonments, infidelities, tragedies. The affirmation is always crossed by a negation. The vitalities of life move toward death. And unless you have a crucifed God, you don't have a big enough God.[228]

[226]Sittler, *Gravity and Grace*, 33.
[227]Ibid.
[228]Sittler, *Grace Notes*, 118.

CHAPTER 4

THE SPIRIT IN CREATION: THE PNEUMATOLOGY OF JUERGEN MOLTMANN

The sciences have shown us how to understand creation as nature. Now theology must show how nature is to be understood as God's creation.[1]

Jürgen Moltmann

Through his Spirit God himself is present in his creation. The whole creation is a fabric woven and shot through by the efficacies of the Spirit.[2]

Jürgen Moltmann

The Significance of Moltmann

As indicated to some extent in the introductory chapter, Jürgen Moltmann is one of today's most important theologians. Richard Bauckham, author of an informed and insightful exposition of Moltmann's theology, claims that "Jürgen Moltmann has probably had more influence worldwide than any other Protestant dogmatic theologian alive today."[3] James Carpenter seconds that assessment when he asserts that "anything Jürgen Moltmann writes is of immediate interest and importance" and affirms that Moltmann is "a frontrunner in theological scholarship and skill."[4]

Moltmann's importance takes on increased significance with respect to a Christian ecological theology. For example, Paul Santmire contends that Moltmann is one of the few contemporary

---

[1]Moltmann, *God in Creation*, 38.

[2]Ibid., 212.

[3]Richard Bauckham, *Moltmann: Messianic Theology in the Making* (Hants: Marshall Morgan and Scott, 1987), 1.

[4]James Carpenter, *Nature and Grace* (New York: Crossroad, 1988), 85.

Christian thinkers who have "valiantly continued to explore, in depth, theological issues related to the concerns of ecology and the environment."[5] Santmire names Joseph Sittler and John Cobb along with Moltmann as "more or less solitary explorers" in developing a Christian ecological theology.[6] Santmire points especially to Moltmann's work on the third person of the Trinity.

William French also acknowledges Moltmann's importance. Because of "Moltmann's thorough scholarship, creative insights, and prophetic energy over the years," states French, his reputation as "one of the premier Protestant voices of our day" is insured.[7] French points in particular to what he calls the "grand reversal of theological direction and sensibility" and "the great sea change" that is represented in Moltmann's more ecologically affirming recent work, e.g., his *God in Creation*, in comparison to his writings of the 1960's and 1970's.[8] While French has some serious criticisms of Moltmann, he nonetheless admits that

> Moltmann's remarkable turnabout does display his questing intellect, powerful openness to new views and concerns, his sensitivity and compassion for societal problems as well as his disarming courage to leave himself vulnerable to precisely the sort of obvious criticism I have noted here.[9]

Finally, to mention only one more aspect to Moltmann's significance, in his study of the doctrine of God in both process theology and in the theology of Moltmann, John O'Donnell astutely observes that "the context of Moltmann's theological enterprise" is "the suffering of the world."[10] Moltmann's messianic theology, in other words, arises out of what could be called the contemporary crisis of divine presence. As O'Donnell remarks, "the question which troubles Moltmann is whether [Christian] belief is an honest option in the face of injustice and an apparently godless

---

[5]Santmire, "Healing the Protestant Mind," 2.

[6]Ibid.; cf. 12.

[7]William French, "Returning to Creation: Moltmann's Eschatology Naturalized," *Journal of Religion* 68 (January 1988): 86.

[8]Ibid., 79, 81.

[9]French, "Christianity and the Domination of Nature," 171.

[10]John O'Donnell, *Trinity and Temporality* (Oxford: Oxford University Press, 1983), 109.

world."[11] Can there be an authentic theology after Auschwitz? After Hiroshima? After the killing fields of Cambodia? O'Donnell concludes that for Moltmann, "any authentic theology today must come to terms with the theodicy question."[12]

As Moltmann himself reveals in a number of places, his experience as a German prisoner of war during and after World War II has profoundly influenced both his life and his theology. He endured his own indeliable "experience of misery and forsakenness and daily humiliation."[13] And yet in the midst of this suffering he found comfort--indeed a "rebirth to new life."[14] The Psalms, for example, "gave me words for my own suffering."[15] In this experience of "God's presence in the dark night of the soul," Moltmann confesses, he found reason for hope: "This experience of not sinking into the abyss but of being held up from afar was the beginning of a clear hope, without which it is impossible to live at all."[16] In short, Moltmann is also significant because he writes not only out of a deep recognition of the suffering Other--whether exploited peasants or the groaning earth--but also out of remembrance and acknowledgement of his own suffering. Such honest acknowledgments are important dimensions of any

---

[11]Ibid.

[12]Ibid., 110. For a fine exposition of Moltmann's theology with respect to the issue of theodicy, see W. Waite Willis, Jr., *Theism, Atheism, and the Doctrine of the Trinity* (Atlanta: Scholars Press, 1987). Willis argues that "the doctrine of the Trinity as formulated by Karl Barth and Jürgen Moltmann provides the basis for a cogent response to the charges brought against faith by contemporary atheism." (p. 3) While Moltmann would most likely repudiate the suggestion that Barth's theology is sufficiently trinitarian to provide adequate resources for such a response--see, e.g., Moltmann, *The Trinity and the Kingdom: The Doctrine of God* (San Francisco: Harper and Row, 1981), 139ff, where Moltmann characterizes Barth's putative trinitarianism as a form of monarchianism--Willis nonetheless makes a number of insightful observations about the whole theism-atheism debate.

[13]Jürgen Moltmann, *Experiences of God* (Philadelphia: Fortress, 1980), 7.

[14]Ibid.

[15]Ibid., 8.

[16]Ibid. For another "autobiographical note," see A. J, Conyers, *God, Hope, and History: Jürgen Moltmann and the Christian Concept of History* (Macon: Mercer, 1988), 203ff.

authentic theology today--in an age characterized by "the interruption of those who suffer."[17]

The outline for this chapter is, like the previous two, straightforward. After a short section on the place of the Holy Spirit in theology, I present an exposition of certain aspects of Moltmann's thought that pertain to a Christian ecological theology. My focus is on Moltmann's more recent work, especially the first three volumes of his ongoing five volume "messianic theology." As indicated in chapter one, an analysis and critique are given in chapter seven.

The Eclipse of the Spirit

If, as a number of people have noted, there has been in recent times a *Schöpfungsvergessenheit*,[18] it could be said with equal validity that there also has been an eclipse of the Spirit--or more accurately, an eclipse of interest in the Spirit. As John O'Donnell puts it: "In the history of Christian theology, the Holy Spirit has often appeared as the unknown God."[19] At least in the West, the Spirit has often been a forgotten member of the Trinity and a neglected locus within systematic theological discussion, despite the presence in the church of the vigorous charismatic movement in its many forms. While there is no dearth of biblically oriented studies on the Holy Spirit, there appears to be relatively little attention given to the Spirit in more systematic studies.[20] For example, in one popular and much-used introduction to Christian

---

[17]Rebecca Chopp, *The Praxis of Suffering: An Interpretation of Liberation and Political Theologies* (Maryknoll: Orbis, 1986), 2. See also David Tracy, *Plurality and Ambiguity: Hermeneutics, Religion, Hope* (San Francisco: Harper and Row, 1987).

[18]See, e.g., footnote 81 in chapter three.

[19]John O'Donnell, *The Mystery of the Triune God* (London: Sheed and Ward, 1988), 75.

[20]The works of James D. G. Dunn, e.g., *Jesus and the Spirit* (Philadelphia: Westminster, 1975), and George Montague, e.g., *The Holy Spirit: Growth of a Biblical Tradition* (New York: Paulist, 1976), are especially important in biblical studies. Dunn's work contains a 500 item bibliography of related works, and there is a nice (though now dated) bibiography of mostly biblical studies titles in Michael Green, *I Believe in the Holy Spirit* (Grand Rapids: Eerdmans, 1975).

theology, interest in the Spirit is noticeable by its absence. Neither the chapter on "God" nor the chapter on "The Spirit and the Christian Life"--two places where one would expect to find such interest--gives much serious attention to the Spirit.[21]

A sample of other theologians confirms this observation about the relative lack of attention given to the Spirit. For example, there is precious little about the Spirit in Rahner's *Foundations of Christian Faith*.[22] Until recently Wolfhart Pannenberg had written only one article directly on the doctrine of the Spirit.[23] Karl Barth, even with his expressly trinitarian perspective, gives much less attention to the Spirit than to Father and Son.[24] And in his *Studies in Dogmatics* Dutch Reformed theologian G. C. Berkouwer devotes not a volume explicitly to the Holy Spirit.[25]

---

[21]Peter Hodgson, and Robert King, eds., *Christian Theology: An Introduction to its Traditions and Tasks*, second edition (Philadelphia: Fortress, 1985).

[22]Karl Rahner, *Foundations of Christian Faith* (New York: Crossroad, 1987).

[23]Wolfhart Pannenberg, "The Doctrine of the Spirit and the Task of a Theology of Nature," *Theology* 75 (January 1972); but now see his *Systematic Theology*, (Grand Rapids: Eerdmans, 1991).

[24]Karl Barth, *Church Dogmatics* (Edinburgh: T. and T. Clark, 1975; 1932-1968 in German).

[25]G. C. Berkouwer, *Studies in Dogmatics* (Grand Rapids: Eerdmans, 1952-1972), 14 vols. in English and 18 vols. in Dutch. Many would argue, however, that Berkouwer is something of an exception in this regard. For example, Garth Wilson observes: "Theologians in the Reformed tradition show a keen interest in pneumatology," from "The Doctrine of the Holy Spirit in the Reformed Tradition: A Critical Overview," in *The Holy Spirit*, ed. George VanderVelde (Winfield, BC: Institute for Christian Studies, 1989), 57. Wilson's remark is supported not only by the considerable attention Calvin gave to the doctrine of the Holy Spirit, but also by the works of subsequent Reformed thinkers. For example, both Abraham Kuyper and Hendrikus Berkhof produced substantial treatments of this often neglected topic. See, e.g., Abraham Kuyper, *The Work of the Holy Spirit* (Grand Rapids: Eerdmans, 1969), originally published in Dutch in 1888 and first published in English in 1900; and Hendrikus Berkhof, *The Doctrine of the Holy Spirit* (Grand Rapids: Eerdmans, 1962).

More recently, Paul Fries has, like Moltmann, begun to explore a theology of creation based on the doctrine of the Spirit. While Fries argues that "Reformed theology has articulated a fuller and more extensive doctrine of the Spirit than perhaps any other in the Western church," he

Less traditional theologies also seem to share in this eclipse of the Spirit. For example, while she wishes to retrieve aspects of the Hebrew Sophia tradition and early Christian Spirit christology, Rosemary Radford Ruether actually says very little about the Holy Spirit, at least understood in any classical, i.e., recognizably trinitarian, sense.[26] Similarly, Gustavo Gutierrez, while speaking at length about a liberation spirituality, does not say much about the Holy Spirit.[27] Leonardo Boff's *Trinity and Society* is an exception to this Spirit-eclipsing trend.[28]

As the above all-too-brief review shows, this eclipse of the Spirit has been, to continue the metaphor, a partial and not complete eclipse. For example, as suggested above, in the Eastern tradition the Holy Spirit has received much more attention.[29] And even in the West there is increasing attention being given to the Spirit. Perhaps the clearest indication of this concern for the Spirit can be found in recent movements within the World Council of Churches. For example, the recent WCC General Assembly in Canberra, Australia had as its theme "Come Holy Spirit--Renew the Creation" and recently an entire volume of the *Ecumenical Review* is devoted to reflections on the Spirit, creation, and the

---

concludes that "no expansion or modification of covenant theology, as it has been developed in the post-Reformation period, will yield a satisfactory theology and ethic of creation. It is, I believe, in an expanded and re-oriented doctrine of the Spirit that a view of creation that does not depend on the 'subject-object' or the 'creation-salvation' opposition may be developed," from "Explorations in the Spirit and Creation," 10, 13.

[26]See, e.g., Ruether, *Sexism and God-Talk*, chapter 2.

[27]See, e.g., Gustavo Gutierrez, *A Theology of Liberation*, revised edition (Maryknoll: Orbis, 1988), 116-120; and Gutierrez, *We Drink From Our Own Wells* (Maryknoll: Orbis, 1984), 64. Unlike Ruether, who is not a trinitarian in any recognizable sense, Gutierrez assumes the truth of the doctrine of the Trinity; however, he says little about it in general or the Spirit in particular.

[28]Leonardo Boff, *Trinity and Society* (Maryknoll: Orbis: 1988). Frederick Dale Bruner's fine work on Pentecostalism also stands out as an exception to the general neglect given to the third person of the Trinity. See, e.g., *A Theology of the Holy Spirit: The Pentecostal Experience and the New Testament Witness* (Grand Rapids: Eerdmans, 1970).

[29]For example, see John Meyendorff, *Byzantine Theology*, 168ff; and Alexander Schmemann, *For the Life of the World* (New York: National Student Christian Federation, 1963).

links between them.[30] As WCC participant James Van Hoeven says: "a rethinking of traditional theologies of creation" must involve "a recovery of the immanence of the Creator in creation"--a project which "can best be helped forward by the rehabilitation of the christological concept of creation through the word of God and the pneumatological concept of creation in the Spirit of God."[31] We need, maintains Van Hoeven, "a Spirit-recast theology of creation" and "a Spirit-filled ecological ethic."[32]

The recent work of Jürgen Moltmann, especially on the Spirit in creation, has greatly contributed to this renewal of interest in pneumatology. And Moltmann's insistence that the doctrine of the Spirit be integrally linked with the doctrine of creation represents a creative and stimulating attempt to address, from the perspective of Christian theology, the profound and pressing concerns of the ecological crisis. In the following exposition, various themes in Moltmann's theology are set forth in order better to comprehend his pneumatology.

Creation as the Home of God

Like many people today, Moltmann acknowledges that the "environmental crisis" puts before us novel and profound questions. Especially in the context of both the Christian faith and the current crisis, Moltmann asks: "Faced as we are with the progressive industrial exploitation of nature and its irreparable destruction, what does it mean to say that we believe in God the Creator, and in this world as his creation?"[33] And given certain deleterious effects in history due to the Christian belief in creation, Moltmann poses the question: "How must the Christian belief in creation be interpreted and reformulated, if it is no longer to be itself one factor in the ecological crisis and the destruction of nature, but is instead to become a ferment working towards the

---

[30]*Ecumenical Review*, volume 42.

[31]James Van Hoeven, "Renewing God's Creation: An Ecumenical Challenge," *Reformed Review* 44 (Winter 1990): 141.

[32]Ibid., 148.

[33]Moltmann, *God in Creation*, xi.

peace with nature which we seek?"[34] In response to these and other questions, in the very first paragraph of the very first chapter of his work *God in Creation* Moltmann clearly states that his intention with respect to the doctrine of creation is to develop an "ecological doctrine of creation."[35] It is, therefore, with this doctrine of creation that we begin.

With respect to this central concept of creation, Moltmann makes a number of important distinctions. First, he distinguishes between three types of creation: *creatio originalis, creatio continua,* and *creatio nova. Creatio originalis* is "creation in the beginning" or "God's initial creation;" *creatio continua* is "creation in history" or God's "historical creation;" and *creatio nova* is "the creation of the End-time" or God's "perfected creation."[36] In other words,

> we can see *initial creation* as the divine creation that is without any prior conditions: *creatio ex nihilo;* while *creation in history* is the laborious creation of salvation out of the overcoming of disaster. The *eschatological creation* of the kingdom of glory, finally, proceeds from the vanquishing of sin and death, that is to say, the annihilating Nothingness.[37]

These types of creation, however, are dimensions of "a meaningfully coherent process."[38] That is, these aspects of creation are not disjunctive or disparate but part of one coherent whole. We can, therefore, speak of "a 'tripartite' concept of creation."[39]

The concept of *creatio originalis,* asserts Moltmann, implies a number of distinct claims. First, creation in the beginning means "creation without any preconditions or presuppositions."[40] According to Moltmann: "Wherever and whatever God creates is

---

[34]Ibid., 21.

[35]Ibid., 1; cf. p. 12 where Moltmann refers to "the ecological doctrine of creation which we are looking for and need today."

[36]Ibid., 55. See also Jürgen Moltmann, *The Future of Creation* (Philadelphia: Fortress, 1979), 119ff; and also *The Way of Jesus Christ: Christology in Messianic Dimensions* (San Francisco: HarperCollins, 1990), 286-287.

[37]Moltmann, *God in Creation,* 90; cf. 193.

[38]Ibid., 55; cf. 206.

[39]Ibid., 208.

[40]Ibid., 207. See also, Moltmann, *The Future of Creation,* 120.

without any precondition. There is no external necessity which occasions his creativity, and no inner compulsion which could determine it."[41] This is what is meant by the affirmation of *creatio ex nihilo*. As Moltmann puts it: "If this world has been *created* by God, then it is not necessarily existent; it is contingent."[42] In short, God is free and creation is contingent.

Second, creation in the beginning implies the creation of time. "The initial creation," posits Moltmann, "has to be understood as *creatio mutabilis*."[43] Thus creation is "not closed within itself" but "open for history," and so must be seen as "an 'open system', which has neither its foundation, nor its goal, nor its equilibrium within itself, but which is from the very outset ec-centrically designed, and aligned in the direction of the future."[44] Creation in the beginning is creation subject to change and development--incomplete and in process. In sum, creation is "not a *factum* but a *fieri*."[45]

Third, as suggested above, creation in the beginning is "aligned in the direction of the future." As Moltmann claims with respect to the "traditional doctrine":

> The notion of a perfect, self-sufficient equilibrium in the resting, stable cosmos contradicts the biblical--and even more the messianic--view of creation aligned towards future glory. The idea of the future as a *restitutio in integrum* and a return to the original paradisal condition of creation (*statis integritatis*) can neither be called biblical nor Christian.[46]

The goal of creation "is not a return to the paradisal primordial condition" but rather "the revelation of the glory of God."[47] Consequently, according to Moltmann, "even creation in the

---

[41]Moltmann, *God in Creation*, 41; cf. 86ff, 311.

[42]Ibid., 38.

[43]Ibid., 207.

[44]Ibid.

[45]Moltmann, *The Future of Creation*, 119. See also p. 190 where Moltmann defines what he means by the openness of a system. An open system is characterized by four things: the genuine possibility of change; the fact that future behaviour is not totally determined by past behaviour; the ability to communicate with other systems; the fact that the final state is different than the initial state.

[46]Moltmann, *God in Creation*, 208.

[47]Ibid., 207.

beginning already points beyond salvation history towards its own perfected completion in the kingdom of glory."[48] This implies, furthermore, that "creation is the framework of history" and so the natural world is "more than merely a stage for God's history with men and women."[49]

The concept of *creatio continua* also involves a number of different claims, especially since Moltmann distinguishes between two types of *creatio continua*. Creation in history can mean, first of all, "God's activity in preserving creation from the powers of annihilation;" it is "the continuous sustaining of the creation which was once brought into being."[50] Continuous creation does not in this sense mean that God creates anything genuinely new. It refers, rather, to the traditional concepts of the preservation and sustenance of creation by God--concepts typically found as aspects of the doctrine of the *providentia Dei*.

However, there is, insists Moltmann, another meaning of *creatio continua*. In this second sense it means the bringing into being of the beginning of the consummation of creation. It is "the preparation of its [the world's] completion and perfecting."[51] Hence *creatio continua* is not merely divine preservation and sustenance, but the creation of something new. That is, continuous creation in this second sense as "the anticipation of the salvation in which creation will be consummated" is "not merely *creatio continua*," but is "at the same time *creatio nova*" and "*creatio anticipativa*."[52] Thus, in contrast to both the theological tradition, which "has laid a one-sided stress on the preservation of the world," and the new theologies of process and evolution, in which there is "a one-sided stress on the world's development," the "unremitting creative activity of God" is "an activity that both preserves *and* innovates."[53] And so here too Moltmann affirms that creation is an open system--evolving, developing, and unfinished.[54] Indeed, he

---

[48]Ibid., 56.
[49]Ibid.
[50]Ibid., 208-209.
[51]Ibid., 209.
[52]Ibid.
[53]Ibid.
[54]Ibid., 196, 199, 204-205; see also Jürgen Moltmann, *Creating a Just Future* (Philadelphia: Trinity, 1989), 78.

describes God's action in history as consisting "essentially in opening up systems which are closed in on themselves."[55]

Finally, with respect to his "tripartite concept of creation," Moltmann makes a number of claims about *creatio nova*. First, *creatio nova* signifies "the consummated new creation of all things."[56] That is, the concept of new creation refers to the consummation and complete realization of the kingdom of glory-- the perfected creation.[57] The eschatological creation, furthermore, is characterized by "the openness *par excellence* of all life systems, and hence their eternal livingness, not their finite petrification."[58] Indeed, Moltmann argues that "in the kingdom of glory there will be time and history," but "to an unimpeded degree and in a way that is no longer ambivalent."[59] Thus instead of speaking of "timeless eternity" we should speak of "eternal time," and "instead of the 'end of history' we should talk about the end of pre-history and the beginning of the 'eternal history' of God, human beings and nature."[60] Hence in the new creation there will be "change without transience, time without the past, and life without death."[61] Yet, Moltmann cautions, "even in the kingdom of glory the world remains God's creation and will not become God himself."[62] In other words, "the resurrection creates an immortal life for the dead, a life finite and created, but not infinite and divine."[63] Finite created beings will always be finite created beings.

In sum, there are three types of creation, or better, three aspects to the process of creation. And consonant with the orientation for which he has become famous, Moltmann contends that "this process acquires its signficance from its eschatological goal."[64] In other words:

[55]Moltmann, *God in Creation*, 211.
[56]Moltmann, *The Way of Jesus Christ*, 286.
[57]Moltmann, *God in Creation*, 206, 213.
[58]Ibid., 213.
[59]Ibid.
[60]Ibid.
[61]Ibid.
[62]Ibid., 184
[63]Ibid.
[64]Ibid., 55.

> Creation in the beginning points beyond itself to the history of promise given with Abraham, Isaac, and Jacob. This history of promise points to the messianic history of the gospel of Christ, and both point to the coming kingdom which will renew heaven and earth, filling everything with the divine radiance. In this process of creation, which is consistently and coherently aligned towards the kingdom of God, we can none the less (in accordance with the different conditions of being and time) distinguish between creation in the beginning, the creations of history, and the eschatological new creation.[65]

In Moltmann's view, the transformation of the world in "the eschatological new creation" means that the world will be the home of God. With the completion and consummation of creation, God will be present in creation in a new, direct and unmediated way.[66] In the future sabbath of creation, when "God's creation and revelation will be one," God will dwell in the whole creation and the whole creation will be "the manifestation and mirror of his glory."[67] Through the Holy Spirit, "*the world will be transfigured*, transformed into God's world, which means into God's own home"--a hope which is "expressed in continually new visions of *the indwelling of God* (*Einwohnung Gottes*) in this new world."[68] In the new creation, through the indwelling of the Spirit "the whole world will become God's home" such that God is "*in the world* and *the world in God*."[69] In such a "panentheistic" vision, the world will then be "*the home of the Trinity*."[70]

God in the World and the World in God

The claim that the world will be the home of God raises the question of the precise relationship between God and the world. And as the quote above indicates, Moltmann's answer to this basic question is in terms of a form of panentheism. In the opening chapter of his book on the Trinity, he states that "by taking up

---

[65]Ibid., 55-56.
[66]Ibid., 280, 287.
[67]Ibid., 288.
[68]Moltmann, *The Trinity and the Kingdom*, 104.
[69]Ibid., 104-105.
[70]Ibid., 105.

panentheistic ideas from the Jewish and the Christian traditions, we shall try to think *ecologically* about God, man and the world in their relationships and indwellings."[71] In other words, Moltmann's panentheism is an attempt to describe the relationship between God and creation in a more wholistic and intimate way. Traditional theology must be revised so that "we shall no longer be able to separate God and nature but will see God in nature and nature in God."[72] In sum, according to Moltmann, the relationship between God and the world must be envisioned such that "God [is] *in* the world and the world *in* God."[73]

Moltmann's motivation for thinking of God and creation in this way lies, in part, in what he perceives to be the deleterious consequences of an overemphasis on divine transcendence. For example, he argues that "the ruthless conquest and exploitation of nature which fascinated Europe during this period [modernity] found its appropriate religious legitimation in that ancient distinction between God and the world."[74] In short, too much stress on divine transcendence vis-a-vis creation too easily leads to severe ecological degradation. Furthermore, Moltmann insists:

> An ecological doctrine of creation implies a new kind of thinking about God. The centre of this thinking is no longer the distinction between God and the world (*die Unterscheidung von Gott und Welt*). The centre is the recognition of the presence of God *in* the world and the presence of the world *in* God.[75]

Therefore, while the distinction between God and the world "is a truth that must not be surrendered," it is also true that "an ecological doctrine of creation today must perceive and teach

---

[71]Moltmann, *The Trinity and the Kingdom*, 19; cf. 105, 110, 122, 161. See also *The Crucified God: The Cross of Christ as the Foundation and Criticism of Christian Theology* (New York: Harper and Row, 1974), 277, where Moltmann argues that "a trinitarian theology of the cross perceives God in the negative element and therefore the negative element in God, and in this dialectical way is panentheistic."
[72]Moltmann, *Creating a Just Future*, 15.
[73]Moltmann, *God in Creation*, 17. See also, e.g., *Creating a Just Future*, 59 where Moltmann affirms that "God is in the world and the world is in God."
[74]Moltmann, *God in Creation*, 13-14.
[75]Ibid., 13.

God's *immanence* in the world"--an approach which "does not mean departing from the biblical traditions."[76]

While clearly emphasizing divine immanence, Moltmann is nevertheless equally clear in his determination to preserve divine transcendence. For example, he argues that *creatio originalis* and *creatio ex nihilo* indicate God's self-distinction from the world and entail "that the world is not in itself divine" nor "an emanation from God's eternal being."[77] For Moltmann, "the truth that God is all in all," derived from much quoted and debated 1 Corinthians 15:28, "does not imply a pantheistic dissolution of creation in God."[78] Even in the new creation, "when the Creator's distance from those he has created will be ended through his own indwelling in his creation"--even then "the difference between Creator and creature will not disappear."[79] Some distinction between God and creation is fundamental.

Moltmann illustrates this point in a number of ways. For example, he argues that process theology fails "to preserve the fundamental distinction (*die fundamentale Unterscheidung*) between creation and Creator" since "it is conversant only with a doctrine about the preservation and ordering of the world."[80] Because in process theology *creatio ex nihilo* is rejected and God is viewed as only an orderer, "God and nature are fused into a unified world process."[81] Or Moltmann claims, with respect to Tillich, that "if the eternally divine life and the divine creativity are one and the same, it becomes difficult to distinguish between God's creatures and God's eternal creation of himself;" thus "by identifying the divine creativity with the divine life itself, Tillich is really abolishing God's self-differentiation from the world which he has created."[82]

Moltmann thus intends with his panentheism to retain an emphasis on *both* divine transcendence and immanence. The

---

[76]Ibid., 14.
[77]Ibid., 72.
[78]Ibid., 89.
[79]Ibid., 64.
[80]Ibid., 79.
[81]Ibid., 78.
[82]Ibid., 84.

relation between God and that which is not-God, he says, is best characterized by "a dialectical structure of transcendence and immanence."[83] Speaking of creation in the context of evolution, Moltmann argues:

> It is therefore impossible to think of this world-transcendence of God unless we think simultaneously of his world-immanence; and it is equally impossible to conceive of God's evolutive immanence in the world without his world-transcendence. The two are mutually related (*Beide sind wechselseitig aufeinander bezogen*). It is only if we perceive the this-worldliness of God that we can usefully talk about a divine presence beyond the world; and the reverse is equally true (*Nur dann lässt sich sinnvoll von einem göttlichen Jenseits der Welt sprechen, wenn das göttlichen Diesseits in der Welt wahrgenommen wird und umgekehrt*).[84]

We must, therefore, speak of "an immanent transcendence" and "a transcendent immanence."[85] Concludes Moltmann:

> The one-sided stress on God's transcendence in relation to the world led to deism, as with Newton. The one-sided stress on God's immanence in the world led to pantheism, as with Spinoza. The trinitarian concept of creation integrates the elements of truth in monotheism and pantheism. In the panentheistic view, God, having created the world, also dwells in it, and conversely the world which he created exists in him.[86]

Moltmann develops his "panentheistic view" with the use and adaptation of Isaac Luria's concept of *zimzum* or divine self-limitation. Moltmann argues that if God is omnipresent, and if God created all things ex nihilo, then there must in some sense be "a 'within' and a 'without' for God."[87] In other words, in order for there to be *opera trinitatis ad extra* there must be an *extra Deum*. As Moltmann posits: "In order to create something outside himself, the infinite God must have made room for this finitude beforehand, 'in himself.' But does not creation as *opera ad extra* then presuppose an inversion of God which releases that *extra* in the

---

[83]Ibid., 182.
[84]Ibid., 206. See also, Moltmann, *The Crucified God*, 252, 255.
[85]Moltmann, *God in Creation*, 318.
[86]Ibid., 98; cf. 9.
[87]Moltmann, *The Trinity and the Kingdom*, 109.

first place?"[88] The *extra Deum* implies "a *self-limitation* of the infinite, omnipresent God, preceding his creation."[89]

Thus Moltmann argues that "it is only God's withdrawal into himself which gives that *nihil* the space in which God then becomes creatively active."[90] There is a contraction or shrinkage in God which makes creation possible. But if this is true, then we must affirm that "this 'creation outside of God' exists simultaneously *in* God, in the space which God has made for it in his omnipresence."[91] Hence creation must be viewed as "God's act in God and out of God."[92] In short, according to Moltmann "the basic idea of this doctrine [*zimzum*] gives us the chance to think of *the world in God* without falling victims to pantheism."[93] If we view creation as necessarily involving this kind of divine self-limitation, then creation can be in God without God being identical with or exhausted in creation.

Moltmann's conception of the the relationship between God and the world is perhaps best understood in terms of his notion of "trinitarian creation." In wrestling with how best to explain "the creation of the world out of God in God (*aus Gott in Gott*)," Moltmann argues that because the Father loves the Son, his like, the Father becomes creator, since "his self-communicating love for the one like himself opens itself to the Other and becomes creative."[94] Hence "the Father creates the one who is his Other [creation] by virtue of his love for the Son" and so "creation does not only correspond (*entspricht*) to God's will" but "it corresponds to his eternal love as well."[95] Furthermore, the Father "creates through the operation of *the Holy Spirit*."[96] This means that it is "the powers and the energies of the Holy Spirit that bridge the difference between Creator and creature...a difference which

---

[88]Ibid.

[89]Ibid.

[90]Ibid.

[91]Ibid.

[92]Ibid.

[93]Ibid., 110. The same argument can be found in Moltmann, *God in Creation*, 86ff.

[94]Moltmann, *The Trinity and the Kingdom*, 111-112.

[95]Ibid., 112.

[96]Ibid., 113.

otherwise seems to be unbridged by any relation at all (*wird die sonst beziehungslos erscheinende Differenz von Schöpfer und Geschöpf...überbrückt*)."[97] The Holy Spirit is the ontological bond, as it were, between God and creation. God and creation are connected via the Spirit.

Thus Moltmann argues that "the Christian doctrine of creation takes its impress from the revelation of Christ and the experience of the Spirit."[98] Any specifically Christian, i.e., messianic, doctrine of creation must view creation as a "trinitarian process" in which "the Father creates through the Son and in the Holy Spirit;" hence the world is "created 'by God,' formed 'through God,' and exists 'in God.'"[99] Or, to use other words, Moltmann maintains:

> The One who sends the Son and the Spirit is the Creator--the Father. The One who gathers the world under his liberating leadership, and redeems it, is the Word of creation--the Son. The One who gives life to the world and allows it to participate in God's eternal life is the creative Energy--the Spirit. The Father is the creating origin of creation, the Son its shaping origin, and the Spirit its life-giving origin. Creation exists in the Spirit, is moulded by the Son and is created by the Father. It is therefore from God, through God and in God.[100]

In short, Moltmann argues that "the trinitarian concept of creation binds together God's transcendence and his immanence."[101]

The Divine Perichoresis

The above discussion raises the issue of how best to envision the works of God not *ad extra* but *ad intra*--not with respect to creation but with regard to the inter-relationships within God. For Moltmann this issue of how to conceive of the relations in God is absolutely crucial since he holds that there is an analogy between the relationships *within* God and the relationship *between* God

---

[97]Ibid.
[98]Moltmann, *God in Creation*, 97.
[99]Ibid., 9.
[100]Ibid., 97-98.
[101]Ibid., 98.

and the world. That is, if God is viewed in a certain way, then certain conclusions follow, if not necessarily then more easily, for how to view the relation between God and creation.

In this regard one of Moltmann's central claims is that "a social doctrine of the Trinity" necessarily implies or entails "the corresponding ecological doctrine of creation."[102] In other words, argues Moltmann:

> If we cease to understand God monotheistically as the one, absolute subject, but instead see him in a trinitarian sense as the unity of the Father, the Son, and the Spirit, we can then no longer, either, conceive his relationship to the world he has created as a one-sided relationship of domination. We are bound to understand it as an intricate relationship of community (*Gemeinschaftverhältnis*).[103]

A genuinely social Trinity, Moltmann asserts, implies that God is intrinsically relational--constituted by relations of community and fellowship. And if God is constituted by such relationships, then *all* of God's relationships must be of such a character, including God's relation to the world. For Moltmann, "the archetype of this dialectical movement [between God and creation] is to be found in the Godhead itself."[104] In short, if *Gemeinschaft ad intra*, then *Gemeinschaft ad extra*. The inner-trinitarian *perichoresis* is the pattern for the relation between God and the world.

Before building his case for a fully social Trinity, Moltmann first criticizes some traditional views of God. For example, he rejects two popular ways of conceiving of God: God as supreme substance and God as absolute subject. In both cases--whether the Aristotelian-Thomist tradition or the Cartesian-Hegelian line of development--Moltmann argues that there is a "reduction of the doctrine of the Trinity to monotheism."[105] That is to say, in each case there is "undue stress on the unity of the triune God" which leads "unintentionally but inescapably to the disintegration of the

---

102Ibid., 1.

103Ibid., 2.

104Ibid., 16.

105Moltmann, *The Trinity and the Kingdom*, 18; cf. Moltmann, *God in Creation*, 83.

doctrine of the Trinity in abstract monotheism."[106] There is, in both cases, no genuine self-differentiation within God. Divine threeness is dissolved in divine oneness.

More specifically, Moltmann opposes any "Christian monotheism," i.e., any view which posits that "the One is the principle and the point of integration for the many."[107] Moltmann's main argument is that in any such perspective "faith in Christ is threatened: Christ must either recede into the series of prophets, giving way to the One God, or he must disappear into the One God as one of his manifestations."[108] In either case, "the strict notion of the One God really makes theological christology impossible" since it "obliges us to think of God without Christ" and "Christ without God as well."[109] In contrast, Moltmann insists that if "trinitarian dogma maintains the unity of essence between Christ and God, then not only is Christ understood in divine terms; God is also understood in Christian ones."[110] Hence the doctrine of the Trinity implies "not only the deification of Christ," but "even more the Christianization of the concept of God."[111] In short, "Christian monotheism" violates one of Moltmann's central theological maxims, namely, that "God cannot be comprehended without Christ, and Christ cannot be understood without God."[112] Divine simplicity must be conceived in those terms.

In light of this basic maxim, therefore, both the "monotheistic Christianity" of Arianism and the "Christian monotheism" of Sabellianism must be firmly rejected.[113] Moltmann also criticizes Tertullian for viewing God in trinitarian terms only with respect to the economy of salvation. God must, insists Moltmann, be thought of in trinitarian terms not only "where his creative and redemptive self-communication is concerned" but also "for his own sake."[114] On

---

[106]Moltmann, *The Trinity and the Kingdom*, 17.
[107]Ibid., 130.
[108]Ibid., 131.
[109]Ibid.
[110]Ibid.
[111]Ibid., 132.
[112]Ibid. See also, Moltmann, *The Crucified God*, 236, 245 for a statement of this with respect to the crucified Jesus.
[113]Moltmann, *The Trinity and the Kingdom*, 132-137.
[114]Ibid., 138.

similar grounds Moltmann criticizes both Barth and Rahner. For example, Moltmann argues that Barth's view of the Trinity as a *repetitio aeternitatis in aeternitate* "does not yet mean thinking in trinitarian terms" since "the doctrine of the Trinity cannot be a matter of establishing the same thing three times."[115] Furthermore, for Barth the Spirit is "an energy but not a Person" and "a relationship but not a subject"--an unacceptable position if the Spirit is genuinely personal.[116] Moltmann claims that Rahner's view of God, with its emphasis on a single divine subject, also is a form of modalism. Hence, in Moltmann's opinion, "Rahner's reinterpretation of the doctrine of the Trinity ends in the mystic solitariness of God."[117]

In light of the above, Moltmann poses a key question: in what *precisely* does divine unity lie? With respect to the early creeds, for example, does the unity consist of a "unity of substance" between the persons of the Trinity, as suggested by the term *homousios* in the Nicene Creed; or does the unity consist in the "identity of the one divine subject," as suggested by the phrase *unus Deus* in the Athanasian Creed?[118] As Moltmann puts it:

> So are Father, Son, and Spirit *one* in their possession of the same divine substance, or *one and the same*, in being the same divine subject? Can the unity of the three distinct Persons lie in the homogeneity of the divine substance, which is common to them all, or does it have to consist in the sameness and identity of the one divine subject?[119]

Is divine oneness best construed as having the same substance, or being the same subject; as tri-unity (*Drei-einigkeit*), or three-fold-ness (*Dreifaltigkeit*); as unity of essence or numerical unity?[120]

Moltmann rejects both of these alternatives. The unity of God must not be conceived of as either "homogeneity of divine substance" or "identity of the absolute subject" since neither

---

[115]Ibid., 141.
[116]Ibid., 142.
[117]Ibid., 148.
[118]Ibid., 149.
[119]Ibid.
[120]Ibid.

conception allows divine unity to be   "understood as a *communicable* unity and as an *open, inviting unity, capable of integration*;" therefore "we must dispense with both the concept of the one substance and the concept of the identical subject."[121] The only option available, states Moltmann, is to understand divine unity as "the unitedness, the at-oneness of the three persons with one another, or: the unitedness, the at-oneness, of the triune God (*die Einigkeit der drei Personen untereinander, oder: die Einigkeit des drei-einigen Gottes*)" because "only the concept of unitedness (*Einigkeit*) is the concept of a unity that can be communicated and is open."[122] The unity of God thus means that "the one God is a God *at one* with himself (*Der eine Gott ist ein einiger Gott*)."[123] In short, divine unity means at-one-with-ness. Hence Moltmann concludes that

> the concept of God's unity cannot in the trinitarian sense be fitted into the homogeneity of the one divine substance, or into the identity of the absolute subject either; and least of all into one of the three persons of the Trinity. It must be perceived in the *perichoresis* of the divine persons. If the unity of God is not perceived in the at-oneness of the triune God (*in der Einigkeit des dreienigen Gottes*), and therefore as a *perichoretic* unity, then Arianism and Sabellianism remain inescapable threats to Christian theology.[124]

Like the Cappadocians, Moltmann consciously employs "the category of community" to understand and articulate "*the sociality* of the three divine persons."[125] In other words, he affirms that "in distinction to the trinity of substance and to the trinity of subject we shall be attempting to develop a social doctrine of the Trinity."[126] In so doing Moltmann expressly emphasizes the threeness of God and consciously chooses "to make the unity of the three divine Persons the problem."[127] And so while the Western tradition typically begins

---

[121]Ibid., 149-150.

[122]Ibid., 150.

[123]Ibid.

[124]Ibid.

[125]Ibid., 198. See also Jürgen Moltmann and Elisabeth Moltmann-Wendel, *Humanity in God* (London: SCM, 1983), 94ff.

[126]Moltmann, *The Trinity and the Kingdom*, 19; cf. xvi.

[127]Ibid., 149.

with God's unity and then asks about the trinity, Moltmann states that like Eastern theology "we are beginning with the trinity of the Persons and shall then go on to ask about the unity."[128] Only in this way can one adequately express the community God is.

Thus in his doctrine of the Trinity Moltmann explicitly rejects psychological or intra-personal models in favor of *inter*-personal models of the Trinity. As he asserts: "In contrast to the psychological doctrine of the Trinity, we are therefore developing a social doctrine of the Trinity."[129] In fact, Moltmann draws upon the particular inter-personal model of the *family* to develop this social view of the Trinity.[130] Citing an analogy put forth by Gregory of Nazianzus, Moltmann argues:

> Just as the three divine hypostases form a unity, by virtue of their common Being, so these three human persons (Adam, Eve, and Seth) also share the same flesh and blood, and form a single family. In the primal human community of husband, wife, and child, the Trinity sees itself reflected and appears on earth.[131]

Thus the Trinity, in Moltmann's view, is not only a community of persons, but in some sense like that particular type of community known as family.

While he speaks of the Trinity in the ways delineated above, e.g., as community and family, Moltmann's favorite way of describing the Trinity is in terms of *perichoresis*. For example, Moltmann claims that the unity of God "must be perceived in the *perichoresis* of the divine Persons."[132] This means that "if this uniting at-oneness (*vereinigende Einigkeit*) of the triune God is the quintessence of salvation, then its 'transcendent primal ground' cannot be seen to lie in the one, single, homogeneous divine essence (*substantia*), or in the one identical, absolute subject;" rather the ground of salvation must lie "in the eternal *perichoresis* of the

---

128Ibid., 19. On p. 140 Moltmann claims that such an approach "is of decisive importance for the doctrine of God" since only then can the sovereignty of God be properly understood.
129Ibid., 157; cf. 189. See also, Moltmann, *Humanity in God*, 100ff; and *God in Creation*, 234.
130Moltmann, *The Trinity and the Kingdom*, 199, 202.
131Moltmann, *God in Creation*, 235.
132Moltmann, *The Trinity and the Kingdom*, 150, cf. 95.

Father, the Son and the Spirit."[133] All three divine persons and their various inter-relationships form the basis of salvation.

Moltmann explains his understanding of *perichoresis* by retrieving the concept from John of Damascus, since "this concept grasps the circulatory character of the eternal divine life."[134] States Moltmann:

> The Father exists in the Son, the Son in the Father, and both of them in the Spirit, just as the Spirit exists in both the Father and the Son. By virtue of their eternal ove they live in one another to such an extent, and dwell in one another to such an extent, that they are one. It is a process of most perfect and intense empathy. Precisely through the personal characteristics that distinguish them from one another, the Father, the Son and the Spirit dwell in one another and communicate eternal life to one another. In the perichoresis, the very thing that divides them becomes that which binds them together.[135]

Perichoresis means circumincession or coinherence. Therefore Moltmann insists that "the trinitarian persons are not to be understood as three different individuals, who only subsequently enter into relationship with one another," as in tritheism; nor are they "three modes of being or three repetitions of the One God," as in modalism; rather "the doctrine of perichoresis links together in a brilliant way the threeness and the unity, without reducing the threeness to unity, or the dissolving the unity in the threeness."[136] With this concept of *perichoresis*, there is genuine unity in difference and authentic difference in unity.

As stated previously, Moltmann argues that this divine *perichoresis* or mutual interpenetration provides the "archetype" for properly understanding the relation between God and creation. If within God "there is no one-sided relationship of superiority and subordination, command and obedience, master and servant" but is rather "the mutuality and the reciprocity of love," then the relation between God and creation must be characterized in terms of

---

[133]Ibid., 157.
[134]Ibid., 174.
[135]Ibid., 175.
[136]Ibid.

mutuality and reciprocity.[137] If God is seen in terms of "a relationship of fellowship, of mutual need and mutual interpenetration (*ein Gemeinschaftsverhältnis wechselseitiger Bedürftigkeit und wechselseitiger Durchdringung*)," then the relationship between God and creation shares the same features.[138] In other words, since there is an analogy between the relations *within* God and the relation *between* God and the world, and because the inner-trinitarian relation is a perichoretic "relationship of fellowship (*Gemeinschaftsverhältnis*)," the relationship between God and the world "must also be viewed as a perichoretic relationship" rather than a "one-sided relationship of domination."[139] As Moltmann puts it:

> Our starting point here is that all relationships which are analogous to God reflect the primal, reciprocal indwelling and mutual interpenetration (*wechselseitige Einwohnung und gegenseitige Durchdringung*) of the trinitarian perichoresis: God *in* the world and the world *in* God."[140]

The Indwelling Spirit

As stated previously, Moltmann affirms that creation is a trinitarian process. As he puts it, "the Father creates through the Son in the Holy Spirit" and therefore the world is "created 'by God', formed 'through God' and exists 'in God'."[141] This last phrase refers particularly to the Holy Spirit and points to one of the "guiding ideas" of Moltmann's doctrine of creation, namely, "creation in the Spirit."[142] In contrast to theologies which stress the role of God the Father as Creator and also those which attempt to develop a christological doctrine of creation, Moltmann states that he will "proceed differently" and "present the trinitarian understanding of creation by developing the third aspect, creation

---

[137]Moltmann, *God in Creation*, 16-17.
[138]Ibid., 258. See also p. 307 where Moltmann states that "the eternal perichoresis of the Trinity might also be described as an eternal round danced by the triune God."
[139]Ibid.
[140]Ibid., 17.
[141]Ibid., 9; cf. 98.
[142]Ibid.

in the Spirit."[143] Moltmann proceeds in this fashion because such an approach, he believes, retrieves and emphasizes an important but often neglected part of the Christian tradition, viz., the immanence of God the Spirit. Moltmann claims, for example, that "John Calvin was one of the few people to take up and maintain this conception: '*Spiritus Sanctus enim est, qui ubique diffusus omnia sustinet, vegetat et vivificat*'."[144] Given the failure to develop this concept of an omnipresent Spirit who sustains and enlivens all things, Moltmann argues that "the concept of creation in the Spirit" is "still awaiting theological development even today."[145] Furthermore, Moltmann emphatically insists that affirming "the immanence of God the Spirit in creation" is especially crucial in our age of ecological crises. In what is one of his major claims in *God in Creation* Moltmann states:

> Creation in the Spirit is the theological concept which corresponds best to the ecological doctrine of creation which we are looking for and need today. With this concept we are cutting loose the theological doctrine of creation from the age of subjectivity and the mechanistic domination of the world, and are leading it in the direction in which we have to look for the future of an ecological world-community (*Weltgemeinschaft*).[146]

In explicating his doctrine of creation in the Spirit, Moltmann makes a number of important distinctions.[147] First, he distinguishes between three different aspects of the *indwelling* of the Spirit: cosmic, reconciling, and redeeming presence. Second, he differentiates between three *modes of self-manifestation*: the Spirit as subject, as energy (*Kraft*), and as potentiality. Third and last, Moltmann distinguishes between different types of divine *efficacy* (*Wirkung*): creating activity, preserving activity, renewing activity, and consummating activity. These categories form an implicit if not explicit framework for his pneumatology.

---

[143]Ibid.
[144]Ibid., 11.
[145]Ibid., 10.
[146]Ibid., 12.
[147]Ibid.

With respect to the modes of the Spirit's self-manifestation, one of Moltmann's favorite ways of speaking about the Spirit is in terms of energy. For example, Moltmann asserts that "we have to understand the Spirit as *the creative energy* (*die Schöpferkraft*) of God and the *vital energy* (*die Lebenskraft*) of everything that lives."[148] Elsewhere he maintains that "the divine energy (*Kraft Gottes*) which the experience of believers calls the Holy Spirit is the Spirit of creation and the Spirit of the new creation of nature."[149] As Moltmann acknowledges with respect to the testimony of the New Testament, "in most passages the mode of efficacy (*die Wirkungsweise*) of the Spirit is described as the operation of a divine energy (*wie die Wirkungsweise einer göttlichen Kraft*)."[150]

Moltmann often links the energies of the Spirit with the potentialities of the Spirit. For example, he argues that "we have to understand every created reality in terms of energy, grasping it as the realized potentiality (*als verwirklichte Möglichkeit*) of the divine Spirit."[151] Therefore, Moltmann continues, "through the energies (*Energien*) and potentialities of the Spirit, the Creator is himself present in his creation."[152] Since God is "a Being open to the world (*ein weltoffenes Wesen*)," God "encompasses the world with the possibilities of his Being, and interpenetrates it with the powers of his Spirit. Through the energies (*Energien*) of the Spirit, he is present in the world and immanent in each individual system."[153] These two modes of divine self-manifestation are obviously, for Moltmann, closely related. Whatever the nuances in each case, Moltmann's main point is that through the Spirit God is present in, with, and under creation.

Above all, however, Moltmann argues that the Spirit is a subject. While, as noted above, Moltmann acknowledges that the New Testament most often speaks of the Spirit as an energy, in the very same passage he also maintains:

148Moltmann, *The Way of Jesus Christ*, 91.
149Ibid., 253-254.
150Moltmann, *God in Creation*, 97.
151Ibid., 9.
152Ibid.
153Ibid., 206.

But what is special about the efficacy of the Spirit cannot be assigned to the attributes or powers (*Kräfte*) of God. The Spirit also acts as an independent subject (*Der Geist wirkt auch als ein Subjekt*), and he does so not merely towards men and women; in the glorification of the Son and the Father, he acts on the Son and the Father as well. We have to see the Holy Spirit as a divine subject (*göttlichen Subjekt*) wherever he is named together with the divine subjects of the Father and the Son but is distinguished from them, as is the case in the benedictory and baptismal formulas.[154]

Moltmann argues that a dynamistic view of the Spirit as energy fails to secure adequately the personal character of the Spirit. For example, he claims that the phrases "the Spirit of God" and "the Spirit of Christ" imply "an energy or power (*eine Kraft oder eine Macht*) whose subject is God or Christ."[155] The Holy Spirit, however, is "the independent subject of his own acts (*eines selbständigen Subjektes von Handlungen*)" and thus a "divine person."[156] Indeed, with respect to the Spirit as "the glorifying God," Moltmann maintains that "the Spirit is not an energy (*Kraft*) proceeding from the Father or from the Son" but "a subject from whose activity the Son and the Father receive their glory and their union."[157] In short, the Holy Spirit is more than an energy; the Spirit is a subject or person or agent.

As indicated above Moltmann distinguishes between four different types of efficacy of the Spirit. His basic distinction, however, is between the creating and preserving Spirit, on the one hand, and the renewing and consummating Spirit, on the other. For example, Moltmann claims that "when we are considering the Spirit of creation, preservation and development" we must call this Spirit "the Spirit of God and the presence of God in the creature he has made;" however, he argues that "according to biblical usage,

---

[154]Ibid., 97. See also *The Trinity and the Kingdom*, 168, where Moltmann admits that "it is not always clear from the New Testament that the Holy Spirit is not merely a divine energy, but a divine subject too."

[155]Moltmann, *The Trinity and the Kingdom*, 125.

[156]Ibid.

[157]Ibid., 126. On p. 142 Moltmann criticizes Barth for precisely this reason, namely, that he fails to affirm that the Spirit is a person or subject. For Barth, "he [the Spirit] is then an energy but not a Person. He is then a relationship but not a subject."

this is not the Holy Spirit" since "the Holy Spirit is the name given to the Spirit of the redeeming and newly creating God."[158] But, maintains Moltmann, "'the Holy Spirit' does not supersede (*verdrängt*) the Spirit of creation but transforms it."[159] Moltmann thus clearly distinguishes between different works of the Spirit.

With respect to this category of efficacy, Moltmann often speaks of the "creative Spirit." With this term, however, he refers not to the Spirit's creating and preserving efficacy, but rather to the renewing and consummating efficacy of the Spirit. States Moltmann:

> Here it cannot be forgotten that in the whole of the New Testament the Spirit is understood eschatologically. He is the power (*Macht*) of the new creation. He is the power (*Kraft*) of the resurrection. He is the earnest and pledge of glory. His present efficacy (*Wirkung*) is the rebirth of men and women. His future goal is the raising up of the kingdom of glory.[160]

While the Spirit plays an important role in the sending, delivering up and resurrection of Christ, as well as in the lordship of Christ, only in the "eschatological consummation and glorification" is the Spirit actually an agent within the Trinity.[161] As Moltmann affirms, in eschatology not only is the Son the actor, "but in eschatology the Holy Spirit is the actor (*der Handelnde*) equally" while "the Father is the One who receives."[162]

The primary task, then, of the Spirit is the transformation of the world. The New Testament writings, asserts Moltmann, "testify to the experience of the Holy Spirit, and the hope that through him *the world will be transfigured*, transformed into God's world, which means into God's own home (*und die Hoffnung auf die Verklärung der Welt durch ihn zur Welt--d.h. zur Heimat--Gottes*)."[163] The energies of the Spirit are therefore "the

---

[158]Moltmann, *God in Creation*, 263.
[159]Ibid.; cf. Moltmann, *The Way of Jesus Christ*, 253.
[160]Moltmann, *The Trinity and the Kingdom*, 89.
[161]Ibid., 94.
[162]Ibid.
[163]Ibid., 104; cf. 98.

energies of the new creation of all things."[164] Furthermore, this new creation has begun. As Moltmann insists:

> In the Spirit people already experience now what is still to come. In the Spirit is anticipated what will be in the future. With the Spirit the End-time begins. *The messianic era* commences where the forces and energies (*die Kräfte und Energien*) of the divine Spirit descend on all flesh, making it alive forever more. In the activity of the Spirit (*Im Wirken des Geistes*), consequently, the renewal of life, the new obedience and the new fellowship of men and women (*Gemeinschaft der Menschen*) is experienced.[165]

In short, the efficacy of the Spirit is concentrated on the renewal and consummation rather than the creation and preservation of the created order.

Finally, with respect to the category of presence or indwelling, Moltmann emphasizes the cosmic presence of the Spirit. For example, employing some of the terms already explicated, he affirms that "everything that is, exists and lives in the unceasing inflow of the energies and potentialities of the cosmic Spirit (*vom andauernden Zufluss der Energien und Möglichkeiten des kosmischen Geistes*)."[166] In fact, Moltmann delineates a number of "ways in which the cosmic Spirit operates in nature (*Wirkungsweisen des kosmischen Geistes in der Natur*)."[167] The Spirit "is the principle of creativity on all levels of matter and life;" the Spirit "is the holistic principle" which "at every evolutionary stage" creates a "life of co-operation and community;" the Spirit "is the principle of individuation" which differentiates matter and life into various levels; and the Spirit is "the principle of intentionality" which directs all things "towards their common future."[168] In each of these ways the cosmic Spirit is present in creation.

As intimated above, Moltmann emphasizes the reconciling and unifying presence of the Spirit. The Spirit is the "holistic principle" which creates "harmony" and "mutual perichoreses" and

---

[164]Ibid.
[165]Ibid., 124.
[166]Moltmann, *God in Creation*, 9.
[167]Ibid., 100.
[168]Ibid.

hence "community" among the individual existents of creation.[169] The cosmic Spirit is "the common bond which holds things together" and "works to bring unity" to creation.[170] In this regard Moltmann speaks of creation through the Spirit and the Word. "All things," contends Moltmann, "have their genesis in a fundamental underlying unity (*entstehen aus ihrer zugrundeliegenden Einheit*), which is called God's Wisdom, Spirit or Word."[171] More exactly, he argues that according to the biblical images "the Creator differentiates his creatures through his creative Word and joins them through his Spirit."[172] Thus, according to Moltmann:

> In the unity of created things, Word and Spirit complement one another. The Word specifies and differentiates through its efficacy; the Spirit binds and creates symmetries, harmonies and concord through its presence (*Da Wort spezifiziert und differenziert durch seine Wirkung, der Geist verbindet und schafft Übereinstimmung, Einklang und Gemeinschaft durch seine Gegenwart*).[173]

The Spirit's presence is a unifying presence. It is the bond which unifies the world.

Furthermore, Moltmann posits that the Spirit is not only the bond between the existents in the world, but also the bridge between God and the world as a whole. While he accepts the belief that God creates *ex nihilo*, Moltmann also affirms that God "creates out of the powers and energies (*aus den Kräften und Energien*) of his own Spirit."[174] As Moltmann asserts:

> It is the powers and the energies of the Holy Spirit that bridge the difference between Creator and creature, the actor and the act, the master and the work--a difference which otherwise seems to be unbridged by any relation at all (*Durch die Kräfte und Energien des Heiligen Geistes wird die sonst beziehungslos erscheinende Differenz von Schöpfer und Geschöpf, Täter und Tat, Meister und Werk überbrückt*).[175]

---

[169]Ibid.
[170]Moltmann, *Creating a Just Future*, 58.
[171]Moltmann, *The Way of Jesus Christ*, 288.
[172]Ibid., 289.
[173]Ibid.
[174]Moltmann, *The Trinity and the Kingdom*, 113.
[175]Ibid.

With this idea, Moltmann claims that his "trinitarian doctrine of creation is able to absorb the elements of truth in the idea of creation as God's 'work' and in the notion of creation as a divine overflowing or 'emanation'."[176] In other words, while Moltmann affirms *creatio ex nihilo*, i.e., the belief that God creates the world out of no prior *substance*, he also insists that God creates *out of* the powers and energies of the Spirit. And while Moltmann affirms that "the metaphor of emanation belongs to the language of pneumatology," since creation is a kind of outpouring of the Spirit, he also maintains that "the world is not 'begotten' by God, as is the Son," and therefore is not divine.[177] In short, creation is not God but creation is intimately related to God since the Spirit is the bond or bridge between God and creation. The Spirit is "the immanent transcendence in all things" and as such "the ground and source" of all that is contingent.[178]

Finally, Moltmann speaks of the redeeming presence of the Spirit. As indicated previously with respect to the renewing and consummating efficacy of the Spirit, Moltmann views the Spirit as crucial in the redeeming transformation and transfiguration of creation into the home of God. In the great visions of the eschaton, he affirms, "the whole world will become God's home" and the "whole creation will be transfigured through the indwelling of God's glory."[179] When the world is transformed and glorified through the Spirit--when, to use one of Moltmann's favorite texts, God will be "all in all" (1 Corinth. 15:28)--then the world will be "*the home of the Trinity*."[180] As Moltmann states:"In the gift and through the powers (*die Kräfte*) of the Holy Spirit a new divine presence (*eine neue Präsenz Gottes*) is experienced in creation. God the Creator takes up his dwelling in his creation and makes it his home."[181] The Spirit is the divine means of achieving God's *telos* for creation.

---

[176]Ibid.
[177]Ibid.
[178]Moltmann, *Creating a Just Future*, 58.
[179]Moltmann, *The Trinity and the Kingdom*, 104-105.
[180]Ibid., 105.
[181]Moltmann, *God in Creation*, 96.

> In the life-giving operations of the Spirit and in his indwelling
> influence (*In dem lebendigmachenden Wirken und in der
> einwohnenden Wirkung des Geistes*), the whole trinitarian efficacy
> of God (*Wirken Gottes*) finds full expression. The presence and the
> efficacy of the Spirit (*Gegenwart und Wirken des Geistes*) is the
> eschatological goal of creation and reconciliation. All the works of
> God end in the presence of the Spirit.[182]

The indwelling of the Spirit will redeem all creation and transform
it into the permanent dwelling of God.

Hence, according to Moltmann, the doctrine of creation must
take "as its starting point the indwelling divine Spirit of
creation."[183] Such a "pneumatological doctrine of creation," claims
Moltmann, is also "an *ecological doctrine*" since the indwelling of
the Spirit takes place in the *oikos* or dwelling that is creation.[184] In
other words,

> if we understand the Creator, his creation and the goal of that
> creation in a trinitarian sense, then the Creator, through his Spirit,
> *dwells in* his creation as a whole, and in every individual created
> being, by virtue of his Spirit holding them together and keeping
> them in life. The inner secret of creation is this *indwelling of God*
> (*Einwohnung Gottes*).[185]

In sum, creation is God's dwelling--God's residence and God's
home--because of the presence and action of the Holy Spirit. As
Moltmann insists: "Through his Spirit God himself is present in his
creation. The whole creation is a fabric woven and shot through by
the efficacies of the Spirit (*Die ganze Schöpfung ist
geistgewirkt*)."[186]

---

[182]Ibid.
[183]Ibid., xii.
[184]Ibid.
[185]Ibid.
[186]Ibid., 212.

CHAPTER 5

THE CHALLENGE OF RUETHER'S ECOFEMINISM: A CRITICAL APPRAISAL

An ecological-feminist theology of nature must rethink the whole Western theological tradition of the hierarchical chain of being and chain of command. This theology must question the hierarchy of human over nonhuman nature as a relationship of ontological and moral value.[1]

Rosemary Radford Ruether

As indicated in the introductory chapter, this analysis and critique is divided into three parts: anthropology, ontology, and theology proper. We first explore Ruether's views concerning the nature of humankind and its place in the world, then investigate how Ruether understands the basic nature of reality, and finally inquire into how Ruether construes the being and action of God. In this way I intend to identify both the main claims and the central arguments of Ruether's thought and also critically evaluate her views and ultimately assess her contributions to a Christian ecological theology.

Hence analysis of Ruether's thought is intermixed with evaluation. That is, at appropriate points in the analysis I raise critical questions which highlight both the strengths and the weaknesses of Ruether's theology. While her theology evinces many strengths and thus offers considerable resources, especially with regard to the doctrine of God, there also are a number of ambiguities, unanswered questions, and significant problems. In short, from Ruether there is much to learn--about both what is helpful and what is not helpful--in developing a Christian ecological theology.

---

[1]Ruether, *Sexism and God-Talk*, 85.

Anthropology

Body and Soul

The issue of the composition of the human provides an excellent entry point into Ruether's anthropology. In response to this question of what the human is made of, Ruether very clearly repudiates any soul/body or mind/body dualism. The human person is unitary. Indeed, spirit and matter are, as she says, two sides of the same coin--the same reality viewed from different perspectives--a claim she backs both with appeals to the Old Testament and to modern science.[2]

This affirmation of the unity of the human person is important because Ruether argues that the split between spirit and matter, viewed anthropologically as the dualism between soul and body, is largely responsible for the world-negating worldview that has contributed so mightily to the ecological crisis. More precisely, Ruether argues that a dualism between body and soul inevitably leads to the domination of the earth because: 1) the soul or spirit is always viewed not merely as different than but of higher value than the body; 2) the body represents matter and the earth; 3) therefore that which is identified with the body--the earth--is of lesser value than things spiritual and may be used (and abused).

Ruether contends, furthermore, that this dualism of body and soul is rooted in "the male ideology of transcendent dualism" the primary characteristic of which is the inability to treat any "other" as subject rather than object.[3] The dualisms of soul/body, spirit/matter, and culture/nature are themselves based on the male attempt to control and conquer the body, matter, nature. This attempt itself assumes a dualism between male and female--an alienation of men from women. And it is this "subjugation of the female by the male" which is "the primary psychic model" for other forms of oppression.[4]

---

[2]See, e.g., Ruether, *New Woman/New Earth*, 188; and *Sexism and God-Talk*, 85.

[3]Ruether, *New Woman/New Earth*, 195.

[4]Ruether, *Liberation Theology*, 118.

Peeling back the explanatory layers ever farther, Ruether claims that this dualism of male and female itself derives from fear of the body, and the finitude and ultimately death that the body represents. Hence the attempt to flee the body through the positing of "a one-sided expression of the ego" as "transcendent consciousness" or "transcendent mind" or "transcendent Spirit" psychologically grounds anti-ecological spirituality, especially in Christianity.[5] And so a more ecologically affirming theology is possible only if bodiliness and finitude are affirmed. And they can be fully affirmed only if some kind of unitary anthropology is adopted. In sum, Ruether believes that, whatever we are, we are unitary beings, and the failure to acknowledge this has contributed to ecological degradation.

Ruether here raises the important issue of the connection between anthropology and ethics, specifically how a particular kind of anthropological dualism can foster the devaluation and thus exploitation of the earth. However, there are different kinds of anthropological dualisms and Ruether's argument lacks precision precisely at the point where it needs it most.[6] While it is somewhat clear what Ruether is rejecting, it is not clear what she is affirming and proposing as an alternative. Merely asserting that spirit and matter are two sides of the same coin is insufficient. What *exactly* is being affirmed in the claim that a more unitary anthropology must be accepted? I too wish to affirm a more holistic and unified anthropology, but more specific and detailed help is needed from Ruether on this important issue before an adequate anthropology can be developed.

Furthermore, Ruether's claim that the dualism between male and female is "the primary psychic model" for other dualisms, e.g., the dualism between culture and nature, conflicts with her acceptance of the influential thesis of Sherry Ortner. Ortner's argument is that the dualism of culture over nature is symbolically primary, and since women are identified with the lower realm of nature, they like nature are dominated. In other words, if culture is

---

[5]Ibid., 122, and Ruether, *Sexism and God-Talk*, 79, 54. See also, Ruether, *To Change The World*, 60-61.

[6]See, e.g., John Cooper, *Body, Soul, and Life Everlasting* (Grand Rapids: Eerdmans, 1989) for a recent examination of this topic.

seen as superior to nature, and if male is to female as culture is to nature, then women will be devalued and subjugated. For Ortner, humanocentrism is more basic than sexism. Ruether accepts this, yet argues in various places for the converse. That is to say, in accepting Ortner's hypothesis of the de facto universal devaluation of women, Ruether also accepts a reversal of the relationship between androcentrism and anthropocentrism, and thus Ruether contradicts her claim that *sexism* is the foundational model for other forms of oppression. There is, at best, some lack of clarity here, and, at worst, a contradiction about which premise is most basic in her argument.

In any event, whether androcentrism or anthropocentrism is primary, Ruether perceptively concludes that these forms of domination are linked and thus "we cannot criticize the hierarchy of male over female without ultimately criticizing and overcoming the hierarchy of humans over nature."[7] Sexism and humano-centrism are interconnected forms of oppression and hence the liberation of women--indeed the liberation of all oppressed humans--must be tied with the renewal of the earth. Few have argued this with as much insight, energy, and passion as Ruether. Indeed, this recognition of the profound connections between ecology and social justice--between the concerns of the environmental movement and the goals of the various movements for human liberation--is one of Ruether's major achievments and contributions for an ecological theology. As she rightly insists again and again, ecology and justice must be seen as aspects of the *single* concept of ecojustice. The proper care of creation and the liberation of women and all oppressed groups are necessarily interconnected.

Human Uniqueness

Another facet of Ruether's argument can be seen in what she takes to be the property which differentiates humans from other beings. In her reading, the Greek inspired tradition that strongly emphasizes reason as that which distinguishes humans from nonhumans, and which has been so influential in much of the

---

[7]Ruether, *Sexism and God-Talk*, 20.

Christian tradition, is largely to blame for the current ecological crisis since that Greek tradition accentuated an understanding of reason which separated rationality from bodiliness and devalued relationality. For example, the belief that reason is what makes us different from other creatures, avers Ruether, has fostered both the view that animals are mere "brutes" and the belief that women are second-class citizens. What lacks reason lacks value and thus may be subjugated by those who are believed to be rationally superior, i.e., humans in the first case and men in the second.

Ruether nevertheless claims that human intelligence is "a special, intense form of this radial energy" of matter--"the self-conscious or 'thinking dimension.'"[8] Indeed, she argues that "the human capacity for technological rationality is itself the highest gift of nature."[9] Thus Ruether argues that, in an important sense, reason *is* a distinguishing feature of human being and therefore should not be repudiated. She further argues, however, that in place of "left-brain linear thought" we must seek "a different kind of rationality" that integrates left-brain linear thought with right-brain spatial and relational thought.[10] For both men and women both left and right brain thought should be integrated. And the fact that humans are different from other creatures in this way, she argues, in no way gives humans license for exploitation. Indeed, this human uniqueness is not an opportunity for domination but a summons to responsibility. As the most complex and intelligent form of evolutionary consciousness, we have "the responsibility and the necessity to convert our intelligence to the earth."[11] Since humans are, due to their reflective consciousness, "the 'mind' of the universe, the place where the universe becomes conscious of itself," humans are called to be the caretakers of the earth.[12]

In sum, Ruether claims that it is *improper* to view reason as that property which distinguishes humans from non-humans, and yet also claims that intelligence or reflective consciousness in fact *is*

---

[8]Ibid., 87. See also, *Gaia and God*, 245, where Ruether states that "mind is the interiority of matter."

[9]Ruether, *New Woman/New Earth*, 205.

[10]Ruether, *Sexism and God-Talk*, 113.

[11]Ibid., 89.

[12]Ruether, *Gaia and God*, 249.

that property which distinguishes humans from other beings. She attempts to escape the apparent tension in this position by arguing for a different concept of human rationality. She rightly repudiates the rationalist tendencies of the Greek influenced Western tradition, which have contributed to the ecological crisis, and helpfully points in the direction of a more inclusive and integrated view of human rationality. However, it is unclear whether this tension in her anthropology can that easily be resolved. If intelligence is the distinguishing feature of human being, and if it is believed that what lacks reason lacks value and may therefore be subjugated, then even a radically reformulated view of reason will not overcome the ecologically deleterious consequences of such a belief. While her intention is plain--that however we distinguish humans from other beings we must do so in such a way that our responsibility as earthkeepers is accepted--it is unclear whether she can successfully realize that intention.

Ruether's views with respect to these issues give greater insight into what is probably her primary contention with respect to anthropology, namely, that there is no dualism between culture or history and nature. Again and again she disavows any separation and opposition between human history and the workings of the natural world.[13] Whether inspired by Greek rationalism, Enlightenment humanism, or theological notions of a covenant with only humans, a view of humanity which separates it from and places it over against the natural world inexorably but falsely elevates humanity and devalues nonhuman creatures.

Ruether's grounds for this repudiation are that a dualism between history and nature: 1) is in fact false since the natural world itself is continually changing and thus is historical in its own right; 2) is in fact false since the natural world has become pervasively and indelibly affected by human action and so is an inescapable part of human history; 3) is in fact false because humans are inextricably embedded in the natural world; 4) inevitably sanctions the exploitation of nonhuman creatures and

---

[13]For example, Ruether, *Liberation Theology*, 116; *New Woman/New Earth*, 195; "The Biblical Vision," 1131; *To Change The World*, 68; *Sexism and God-Talk*, 86; *Gaia and God*, 207.

anything that is identified with "nature", e.g., women; and 5) runs counter to the biblical idea of a single covenant embracing both human and nonhuman creatures. Thus whether on scientific, anthropological, pragmatic, or explicitly theological grounds, the typical dualism between history and nature is highly problematic and must be rejected.

Given the truth of Holmes Rolston's maxim "value generates duty," derived from his Augustinian aphorism that "we follow what we love,"[14] and given the fact that the inverse of the maxim is also usually regarded as true, i.e., that lack of value implies no or fewer duties, and thus given that value is both a necessary and sufficient condition for ethical obligation, Ruether's claim regarding the deleterious consequences of a culture/nature dualism can be seen in new terms. For if the above maxim is true, then any perspective which denies value, especially intrinsic value, to the natural world cannot provide any solid basis for affirming ethical duties toward creation. In other words, insofar as a culture/nature dualism leads people to see the earth as value-less, or as having instrumental value only, then to that degree humans will see themselves as being free from ethical obligations to nonhuman creatures and hence find it ethically permissible to rape, pillage, and plunder the earth. Ruether's vigorous claim that any such dualism be rejected can thus be interpreted both as a claim for what must be denied and what must be affirmed. We must deny that the natural world has no value and can therefore be wantonly exploited. We must, rather, affirm that because it has value, we have obligations to care for wolves and alpine asters and golden eagles and the Adirondacks.

This persistent criticism of a dualism between nature and history is perhaps Ruether's central insight and most important contribution to a Christian ecological theology. Especially since Kant, "nature" has been seen as having only instrumental value, with the consequence that an ontological and moral dualism between history or culture and nature has been assumed in much theology and philosophy. On a number of grounds Ruether correctly challenges this harmful dualism. The natural world does

---

[14]Rolston, *Environmental Ethics*, 41.

have its own history and is thus historical. And with the pervasive impact of humanity, human action and the events of the nonhuman world are intermixed and hence inseparable, even in the remotest places of the world.[15] Humans are in fact creatures, having much in common with nonhuman creatures. And though often ignored, the biblical drama speaks of a single comprehensive covenant that embraces both humans and the natural world.

But while she, again, is clear about what she rejects, Ruether is somewhat unclear about what she affirms. Does her rejection of a dualism between history and nature imply that there is *no* valid distinction between human action and the events of the natural world? Certainly *some* distinction is warranted. A distinction does not necessarily imply a dualism. Ruether herself suggests some such distinction when she asserts: "Humans alone perpetuate their evolutionary advances primarily through cultural-social means. We don't grow our clothes on our backs or our tools in the nails at the ends of our hands; we create these as artifacts."[16] In other words, only humans have the capacity to create culture. And some type of distinction is implied by her claim that "humans alone, amid all the earth creatures and on all the planets of these vast galaxies, are capable of reflective consciousness."[17] However, this legitimate difference between human and non-human activity is not clearly or sufficiently worked out. What are the individually necessary and jointly sufficient conditions for human action? What are the properties that *all* humans and *only* humans have, at least in a distinctively human way, that allow us to distinguish between human action and the events of the natural world? Answers to these admittedly difficult questions would go a long way toward clarifying the relationship between what we call "history" and what we call "nature" and thus move forward the development of an adequate ecological theology.

---

[15]See, e.g., Bill McKibben, *The End of Nature.*

[16]Ruether, *Sexism and God-Talk*, 88.

[17]Ruether, *Gaia and God*, 249. Ruether also addresses this topic on p. 5 when she delineates different concepts of nature, but she still does not give this issue adequate attention.

Life and Death

Further insight into Ruether's thought can be gained by exploring her views on the end or final state of human existence. For Ruether, even to ask about human destiny is to risk being sidetracked from our proper concern for *this* time and *this* place, and thus is a threat to an ecological theology, since such a question all too often allows us to ignore that fact that "our responsibility is to use our temporal life span to create a just and good community for our generation and for our children."[18] Ruether contends that religion should not make concern about immortality the focus of its message since such a concern too easily allows religion to become an opiate that drugs its adherents into passive social conformity and inactivity. Concern for justice and peace in our *present* temporal existence, rather than "flight into the unrealizable future," is the proper subject of Christian eschatology.[19]

While one can appreciate Ruether's anxiety that preoccupation with eschatology *can* subvert proper concern for social justice and ecological wholeness, especially given obvious cases of this in the past, it is altogether unclear why this *has* to be the case. Possibility is, after all, not necessity. Why is it the case that the only alternative to an other-worldly eschatology is to reduce the importance of eschatology per se? Certainly another option is to formulate a *different*, more creation-affirming eschatology. Ruether seems to assume an unwarranted dualism between history and eschatology. Why is eschatology necessarily interpreted to be about only "last things," rather than about *all* time and history-- past, present, and future? And even if one grants her assumption that eschatology is about a future time, certainly there are *other* cogent theological reasons for being concerned with this life in this place, e.g., the doctrines of creation and incarnation.

Ruether does, however, offer opinions about matters eschatological. For example, she denies any individual existence after death, or at least has in the past. For example, in 1972 she remarked that death is "a friend that completes the proper cycle of

---

[18]Ibid., 258.
[19]Ibid., 255-256.

the human soul."[20] This seems to be her view in 1975 as well when she maintained that the earth is that "out of whose womb we arise at birth and into whose womb we are content to return at death."[21] By 1983 her views are more ambiguous. In answer to the question of whether people's achievements in life are merely "fading memories" or whether there is "some larger realm where the meaning of their lives is preserved," she now admits "an agnosticism."[22] As before, however, she asserts:

> Death is the cessation of the life process that holds our organism together. Consciousness ceases and the organism itself gradually disintegrates. This consciousness is the interiority of that life process that holds the organism together. There is no reason to think of the two as separable, in the sense that one can exist without the other.[23]

There are no individual centers of being after death; rather "our existence ceases as individuated ego/organism and dissolves back into the cosmic matrix of matter/energy"--into "the great organism of the universe itself."[24] We are recycled just like every other form of life, our component parts becoming food for other beings. The earth is our home, even in death, and refusal to accept this fact lies at the very heart of the attempt to escape or to dominate the earth. In sum, in response to the question of destiny, Ruether insists that, as Genesis 3:19 puts it, "you are dust, and to dust you shall return."

It is entirely unclear, however, why such a position as this is necessary for an ecological theology. Why is the belief that there is no individual existence after death--that we completely dissolve "back into the cosmic matrix of matter/energy"--more in harmony with an ecological perspective than one which denies this claim? Why cannot an eschatology that insists not only on individual but personal existence after death be as creation-affirming as one that does not make that claim? For example, rightly interpreted, texts like Matthew 24 and 2 Peter 3 affirm the essential *continuity* of this earth with the next. So traditional Christian ideas about "the

---

[20]Ruether, *Liberation Theology*, 125.
[21]Ruether, *New Woman/New Earth*, 211.
[22]Ruether, *Sexism and God-Talk*, 257.
[23]Ibid.
[24]Ibid., 257-258.

resurrection of the body" and "life everlasting" can go hand in hand with a vigorous belief that the earth is our home. In short, there are no compelling reasons why an eschatology like that which Ruether espouses is necessary for an ecological theology. Our relatedness to the earth can be affirmed in ways that do *not* require the abandonment of the classic Christian belief in life after death.

Ruether herself illustrates this point. As intimated above, Ruether seems to have changed her mind on this matter of personal existence after death. For example, in her 1985 feminist reader she asks: "Is it possible to hope for immortal life without tending to despise and therefore fail to value and cultivate those very life processes by which the cosmos and human beings are sustained from generation to generation?"[25] She answers: "Perhaps immortal life, if it is possible, can be safely left in the hands of God/ess from which all reality came forth in the beginning?"[26] What was once an absolute impossibility is now a real possibility engendering genuine hope. This change of perspective is even more evident in Ruether's liturgical guide for women-church. In the suggestions for a funeral she advises that "the prayers at the grave should indicate both an acceptance of the mortal aspects of our human being, as well as a trust in the mystery of the transcendence of mortality."[27] In commenting on 1 Corinthians 15, Ruether states that "our perishable bodies contain also the mystery of imperishable life" and so "our human spirits must let go of their perishable form to be transformed into imperishable spirit."[28] "This," says Ruether, "is a great mystery which we do not pretend to understand."[29] Ruether here apparently believes that mortality can, in some sense, be transcended in the mystery of eternal life. And as she rightly suggests, such belief in immortal life need *not* necessarily entail a failure to value the earth. A creation-affirming theology is fully comportable with belief in "imperishable life" or life after death.

---

[25]Rosemary Radford Ruether, *Womanguides: Readings Toward a Feminist Theology* (Boston: Beacon, 1985), 224.

[26]Ibid.

[27]Rosemary Radford Ruether, *Women-Church: Theology and Practice* (San Francisco: Harper and Row, 1986), 212.

[28]Ibid., 213.

[29]Ibid.

In her most recent work, *Gaia and God*, Ruether seems to have returned to her previous position, though even here her precise view is somewhat unclear. She maintains that we must accept the transience of the self. When our bodily organism dies, "the light of consciousness goes out, and with it our 'self'."[30] Indeed, one of the three basic premises on which an ecological spirituality must be built, Ruether contends, is "the transience of selves."[31] When we die, our bodies "enter the cycle of decomposition and recomposition as other entities" and "the personal center of each being" is, at best, only remembered in the mind of God.[32] However, in answer to an apparently rhetorical question about whether there is "a consciousness," i.e., God, who "remembers and envisions and reconciles all things," Ruether responds: "Surely, if we are kin to all things and offspring of the universe, then what has flowered in us as consciousness must also be reflected in that universe as well, in the ongoing creative Matrix of the whole."[33] That is, insofar as our human consciousness is "reflected" in that larger consciousness that is Gaia/God, there is some continuity of existence after death. But the unique personal centers of being and identity that constitute who we are do not perdure beyond biological death. What remains is only some cosmic energy or life-force which takes a different form in new beings. Once again, it is unclear why this position is necessary for an adequate Christian ecological theology.

The Good Life

Additional insight can be gained into Ruether's contributions to a an ecological theology by exploring her views on the authentic goal of human existence. This issue is often approached in terms of some description of both the good life of an individual and the good life of a community or society, e.g., Aristotle's treatment of these two topics in his *Nicomachean Ethics* and *Politics*. In other words,

---

[30]Ruether, *Gaia and God*, 251.
[31]Ibid.
[32]Ibid., 252-253.
[33]Ibid., 253.

discussion of the purpose of human life inevitably involves, among other things, some treatment of ethics and politics.

With respect to this issue, Ruether has much to say. However, like most of us she rarely speaks the language of moral philosophy and moral obligation. Rather, her shoulds, oughts, and musts come partly between the lines of her historical analysis, partly from her metaphors, and mostly from her unconcealed and unapologetic commitment to a feminist critical principle, namely, "the promotion of the full humanity of women."[34] This principle implies "a continually expanding definition of inclusive humanity" which in the end rejects not only androcentrism and other related forms of human chauvinism, but rejects "humanocentrism" as well.[35] This critical principle ultimately provides the basis for her advocacy of typical moral norms like justice, equality, and community.

For example, Ruether criticizes both the ecology movement and the liberation movement for having truncated understandings of inclusivity and community and calls upon the women's movement to provide leadership in moving toward a new cooperative social order characterized by mutuality between people and harmony with the earth.[36] Ruether claims that women must unite the demands of the women's movement with those of the ecological movement if the norms of mutuality, reciprocity, and solidarity are to be socially embodied. Such a task involves nothing less than "a radical reshaping of the basic socioeconomic relations and the underlying values of society."[37] Ruether is, in short, no mere reformist. Her critique and alternative vision of authentic human life is, as one commentator says, one of the "*radical* critiques, which raise questions concerning the very philosophical foundations of Western industrial society."[38] Indeed, Ruether moves beyond the usual forms of feminism--liberal, Marxist,

---

[34]Ruether, *Sexism and God-Talk,* 18. See also Ruether's essay "Feminist Interpretation: A Method of Correlation," in *Feminist Interpretation of the Bible,* ed. Letty Russell (Philadelphia: Westminster, 1985), 115.

[35]Ruether, *Sexism and God-Talk,* 20.

[36]Ruether, *Liberation Theology,* 124-125.

[37]Ruether, *New Woman/New Earth,* 204.

[38]Mary Ann Hinsdale, "Ecology, Feminism, and Theology," *Word and World* 11 (Spring 1991): 157.

romantic, radical feminism--to a form of "socialist feminism."[39] Ruether's vision of normative human existence entails the radical restructuring of society.

As indicated previously, Ruether provides some specific proposals of her "democratic socialism" or "communitarian socialism," e.g., changes in the transportation system, restructuring of the relationship between home and work. She outlines three principles of an "ecological-libertarian worldview" that emphasizes harmony, balance, justice, and interdependence: acceptance of limits and finitude, construction of an ethic of ecojustice, and replacement of a linear model of history with a view of periodic revolutionary conversion.[40] And in her treatment of "socio-economic redemption from sexism," Ruether presents an integrative vision of a society which affirms equality, dismantles all hierarchical patterns of relationship, builds "organic community," and produces "harmonious and mutually supportive" relations between humans and the earth.[41] In sum, terms such as equality, equity, solidarity, harmony, mutuality, reciprocity, integrity, responsibility, and justice figure prominently in Ruether's vision of the good life, functioning as norms for the transformation of society and of our relationship to the earth and its creatures.

Ruether's vision of the authentic goal of human existence--a vision which illuminates both her theology of nature and her theology of human liberation--is surely a much-needed move is the right direction. With respect to both the natural and human worlds, she rightly emphasizes the norms of community, mutuality, harmony, responsibility, justice, and equality. The cries of the hungry, the poor, and the homeless daily ring out for the

---

[39]Kathyrn Allen Rabuzzi, "The Socialist Feminist Vision of Rosemary Radford Ruether," 5. For an explication of the various types of feminism, see Alison Jaggar, "Human Biology in Feminist Theory: Sexual Equality Reconsidered," in *Beyond Domination*. A short, but helpful overview is provided by Mary Ann Hinsdale in "Ecology, Feminism, and Theology." Ruether herself uses these categories and, true to her dialectical method, both denies and affirms various aspects of each type of feminism in the attempt to arrive at a more adequate synthesis. For example, see *Sexism and God-Talk*, 214ff.

[40]Ruether, *To Change The World*, 66ff.

[41]Ruether, *Sexism and God-Talk*, 232-233.

realization of a social vision that takes such norms seriously, e.g., by recognizing sustenance rights and the criterion of need in matters of distributive justice. And likewise the cries of the earth--acidified lakes, ravaged mountains, oil-stained loons--daily remind us of the pressing need for a vision of shalom for all God's creatures--nonhuman as well as human

In particular, Ruether's insistence on a more communal perspective properly criticizes and thereby undercuts the individualism pervasive in much of Western culture, especially in the United States where the "Marlboro man mystique" continues seemingly unabated.[42] Her critique is necessarily radical in raising profound questions about the very intellectual and social foundations of modernity, especially on the issue of community.[43] This communitarian perspective pushes Ruether beyond the typical plea for individual change to call for structural, i.e., systemic, socio-cultural change. Indeed, Ruether advocates an entirely new social-political-economic order based not on classic liberalism but on a form of democratic socialism. Whether one agrees with all the specific proposals for such a democratic socialism, Ruether incorporates liberal ideals like equality, liberty, and justice into a vision of the good society that emphasizes mutuality and community, and in so doing articulates a more inclusive social vision than most political theorists.[44]

However, is it true that such an egalitarian vision of the good life and the good society--of the authentic goal of human life--necessarily dismantles *all* hierarchical patterns of relationship, or even that it *should* do so? For example, does it follow that since the hierarchy of male over female is morally impermissible that there should be no relation of super and subordination between a parent and child? Is hierarchy *per se* a bad thing, or is only hierarchy *in certain respects* objectionable? Much depends upon how hierarchy

---

[42]For example, see Robert Bellah et. al. *Habits of the Heart: Individualism and Commitment in American Life* (New York: Harper and Row, 1985).

[43]See also, e.g., Goudzewaard, *Capitalism and Progress*.

[44]For a helpful typology of concepts of justice and visons of the social good, see Douglas Sturm, "The Prism of Justice: E Pluribus Unum?" *The Annual of the Society of Christian Ethics 1981*.

is defined and whether the connotations of imperialism and domination that often accompany the term are intrinsic to the term itself. Whether this term is used or not, it seems inescapable that one acknowledge that there are relationships which necessarily and legitimately involve something like hierarchy not only in the human world, e.g., between employer and employee, parent and child, but also in the natural world, e.g., food chains, social patterns of animals. Indeed, community itself, whether human or natural, seems to *require* certain relationships of this kind. Thus Ruether's claim that *all* hierarchy is wrong seems misguided. A more modest but defensible claim is that not hierarchy in general but certain *forms* of hierarchy must be repudiated: male over female, white over non-white, rich over poor.

The Human Condition

William James insists that there are two parts to every religion: "an uneasiness" or "a sense that there is *something wrong about us* as we naturally stand," and "its solution" or "a sense that *we are saved from the wrongness* by making proper connection with the higher powers."[45] There is, in other words, in every religion--indeed in every worldview, "religious" or not--a diagnosis of illness and a prescription for health. In theological terms, there is a hamartiology and a related soteriology.[46] Ruether, too, perceives there to be something wrong with the human condition and she offers both a diagnosis of human fault and a prescription for renewal. Further insight into Ruether's contributions to a Christian ecological theology can be gained by attending to her views concerning this issue of the current condition of human being.

---

[45]William James, *The Varieties of Religious Experience* (New York: New American Library, 1958), 383.

[46]The literature on worldview is large and growing, but for representative and clear accounts of the basic questions at the heart of every worldview, see Leslie Stevenson, *Seven Theories of Human Nature* (New York: Oxford, 1974); Brian Walsh and Richard Middleton, *The Transforming Vision: Shaping A Christian Worldview* (Downers Grove: Intervarsity, 1984); and Arthur Holmes, *Contours of a Worldview* (Grand Rapids: Eerdmans, 1983).

Ruether typically finds that wrongness or fault to lie in the basic human sin of sexism.[47] Evil is real, and manifests itself in "the fundamental distortion and corruption of human relationality" that names men as superior to women.[48] As a result of this superiority complex, men and women are alienated from each other. This "primary alienation and distortion of human relationality is reflected in all dimensions of alienation: from one's self as body, from the other as different from oneself, from nonhuman nature, and from God/ess."[49] Lest some romantic notion of the untainted female insinuate itself here, Ruether also asserts that "both males and females, as human persons, have the capacity to do evil. Historically, however, women, as well as subjugated men, have not had the same *opportunities* to do so."[50] Rightly critical of any simple reversal of sexism that would posit men only as sinners, Ruether acknowledges both the possibility and actuality of sin in the lives of all people, regardless of sex. She maintains, however, that with the monopolization of power comes greater opportunity for sin and more harmful effects of sin. Thus men, having greater power, are more blameworthy.

Furthermore, Ruether argues that men and women sin in different ways. Males sin by dominating others, while "women sin by cooperating in their own subjugation, by lateral violence to other women who seek emancipation, and by oppressing groups of people such as children and domestic servants under their control."[51] Others have suggested a similar analysis of the different types of sin according to gender. Mary Stewart VanLeeuwen, for example, posits that the distinctively male sin is that "dominion becomes domination," while the distinctive sin for women is that "sociability becomes social enmeshment."[52] Ruether reminds us, however, that "these forms of female evil cooperate with and help to perpetuate an overall system of distorted humanity in which

---

[47]Ruether, *Liberation Theology*, 115ff. See also, Ruether, *Sexism and God-Talk*, 173ff.

[48]Ruether, *Sexism and God-Talk*, 163.

[49]Ibid., 161.

[50]Ibid., 180.

[51]Ibid.

[52]Mary Stewart VanLeeuwen, *Gender and Grace* (Downers Grove: Intervarsity, 1990), 44-45.

ruling-class males are the apex."[53] While both men and women perpetuate evil, they do so within a sexist socio-cultural system that puts men at the top of the hierarchy, above both women and nature. In short, while "we are all products of the original sin of sexism," the original sin is still *sexism*.[54]

Ruether's response to this issue of human sin sheds light on her theology of nature. In short, Ruether claims that we are not what God intended us to be, and therefore neither is the nonhuman world. Our current condition and that of the natural world are gross distortions of God's intentions. Relationships of mutuality and harmony have been supplanted by relationships of domination and antagonism. Creation is not now what it could be and what it should be. This affirmation is in accord with one of the central insights of the Christian tradition, namely, that evil is a perversion of God's intentions. Ruether also rightly acknowledges the pervasity of human sin and perceptively resists any simple reversal of sexism that would exempt women from the community of sinners. And as usual she notes the distorted socio-cultural system within which human action takes place.

However, a number of questions arise as a result of Ruether's response to this issue of human disposition. Is it the case, for example, that *sexism* is the *original* sin? Is the alienation of men and women the "fundamental distortion and corruption of human relationality"? Certainly sexism is both a profound and a pervasive distortion. But is it the "primary alienation" which is "reflected in all dimensions of alienation"? Or is alienation *from God* more primary, as both scripture and Christian tradition suggest? A more theocentric perspective maintains that the desire to be God is the foundational and original sin. Denial of finitude and creatureliness is the most basic sin, not sexism. Sexism, like other "isms," is a manifestation of this more basic problem. Ruether is closer to this theocentric understanding of original sin when she speaks of the human fear of finitude than when she speaks of sexism.

Another advantage of this theocentric approach is that it is better able to ground an account of the responsiveness and

---

[53]Ruether, *Sexism and God-Talk*, 180-181.
[54]Ibid., 182.

distortion of *all* creation. In other words, by focusing on the Creator-creature relationship rather than the male-female relationship, a view of original sin as fundamentally a broken relationship with God is able to give a more adequate explanation of both the profoundity and the pervasity of human fault and human responsibility. A perspective which posits that the desire to be God--with its correlative denial of creatureliness--is the primary sin is better able to account for the sin of sexism as well as various other distortions of relationality, e.g., self-alienation, alienation between human and nonhuman creatures.

Ruether's most recent work displays this more adequate understanding of sin. In *Gaia and God*, sin is most fundamentally not sexism but broken relationship, one form of which is sexism. As Ruether puts it:

> The central issue of 'sin' as distinct from finitude is the misuse of freedom to exploit other humans and the earth and thus to violate the basic relations that sustain life. Life is sustained by biotic relationality, in which the whole attains a plenitude through mutual limits in interdependency.[55]

Thus sin is, in this understanding, the denial of finitude through the misuse of freedom and a grasping at power which exploits the other and breaks relationship--whether between men and women, or among people in general, or between humans and non-humans, or between humans and God. Sin, asserts Ruether, "lies in distortion of relationship, the absolutizing of the rights to life and power of one side of a relation against the other parts with which it is, in fact, interdependent."[56]

Ruether's understanding of original sin points to a larger problem. As will be evident when we examine her ontology and theology, Ruether tends to engage in an *unargued* historicistic reductionism in which God's action is reduced to action explainable entirely in terms of the world. In other words, Ruether seems to begin with the naturalistic assumption that God's being and action can be *fully* explained without remainder in purely human terms.

---

[55]Ruether, *Gaia and God*, 141.
[56]Ibid., 142. See also p. 256.

For example, her crucial concept of conversion is articulated in terms of "conversion to the center, conversion to the earth and to each other."[57] Here God is noticable by her absence, or perhaps reference to the center or the earth is a cipher for God. In any case, it seems that God is radically if not exclusively immanent, but at the cost of God's transcendence--a contention which directly conflicts with Ruether's own assertion that God must be viewed as *both* immanent and transcendent. This apparent naturalism gives away too much of the tradition and, moreover, goes entirely unargued. There is no argument given for either the necessity or desirability of such an approach. It is merely assumed. But such a position is *not* required for an adequate Christian ecological theology; in fact it has the untoward consequence of undermining certain crucial claims, e.g., the belief that God created the world *ex nihilo*.

Ontology

Ruether nowhere explicitly sets forth an ontology. This fact alone is no reason for criticism since such a strictly philosophical task lies beyond the purview of her historically oriented theological endeavors. However, like everyone, Ruether makes certain ontological assumptions. Ferreting out these assumptions, inchoate and inarticulate as they may be, can go a long way toward coming to a better understanding of her theology, especially her views on creation.

The Coherence of Creation

Ruether's emphasis on a single unified covenant of creation-- "a cosmic covenant"--points to her belief in the fundamental unity of creation.[58] Whether she points to the pre-exilic heritage of Hebrew religion, in which there is a unified vision of a single community of life, exemplified in a text like Isaiah 24, or to the pivotal importance of the concept of ecojustice, which ties together the norms of ecological harmony and social justice, Ruether

---

[57]Ibid., 255-256.
[58]Ruether, "The Biblical Vision," 31.

emphasizes the unity and coherence of creation.[59] There is no dualism between nature and history, or any split between matter and spirit.[60] Creation is unitary and it hangs together.

This emphasis on the coherent oneness of creation is also evident in her stress not just on the interrelationship between but the interdependence of the various aspects of creation. Our vision must be of "the interdependence of all living things in a global community"--a vision of "reciprocal interdependence" rooted in "our actual solidarity with all others and with our mother, the earth, which is the actual ground of our being."[61] Indeed, as we have seen, Ruether refers to the earth as the generating matrix from which we come and into which we go upon death. We inescapably depend upon the earth, just as it now depends upon us to be its responsible caretakers. Creation exists only in the mutual interdependence of its constituent parts.

This emphasis on the interdependent oneness of the cosmos-- on the "fellowship of life" in which the earth is "our sister"[62]--is further developed in Ruether's non-hierarchical model of reality. In Ruether's ontological paradigm, reality is not just a coherent unity, and not just interdependent, but a whole in which each part has *equal* ontological and moral value. Her vision is of a democracy of being in which there is no up and down, higher and lower, better and worse. According to Ruether:

> Conversion means the interconnectedness of all parts of the community of creation so that no part can long flourish if the other parts are being injured or destroyed. In a system of interdependence, no part is intrinsically 'higher' or 'lower.' Plants are not 'lower' than humans because they don't think or move. Rather, their photosynthesis is the vital process that underlies the very existence of the animal and human world. We could not exist without them, whereas they could exist very well without us. Who, then, is more 'important'?

---

[59]Ruether, "Paradoxes of Human Hope," 235ff; *New Woman/New Earth*, 187ff; "The Biblical Vision," 1130ff; *To Change The World*, 68; *Gaia and God*, 48ff.

[60]Ruether, *Sexism and God-Talk*, 85ff.

[61]Ruether, "Paradoxes of Human Hope," 241; and *New Woman/New Earth*, 211.

[62]Ruether, *New Woman/New Earth*, 31, 83.

> The hierarchical model of reality is misleading. Ecological harmony
> is based on diversity in which each part has an equally vital part to
> play in maintaining the renewed harmony and balance of the
> whole. We must start thinking of reality as the connecting links of a
> dance in which each part is equally vital to the whole, rather than
> the linear competitive model in which the above prospers by
> defeating and suppressing what is below.[63]

We must, concludes Ruether, rethink "the whole Western
theological tradition of the hierarchical chain of being and chain of
command."[64] The chain of being ontology, with its graded levels of
being and value, is misguided and must be rejected. The proper
spatial metaphor is not a pyramid, but rather a circle. For Ruether,
reality is most like a dance.

While all of the above considerations point toward an
ontology which stresses that reality as a whole is coherent and
unitary, perhaps the clearest pointer in that direction is Ruether's
use of the analogy of organism, since the most relevant aspects of
this analogy imply unity and coherence (not to mention growth and
development). While she refers to the organic harmonies of nature
and the organic systems of animal and plant, earth and sky,
Ruether's most revealing reference is to the cosmos as "the great
organism of the universe itself."[65] Indeed, Ruether's use of Gaia to
refer to the earth is directly and explicitly designed to emphasize
the interdependent, self-sustaining, and self-conscious character of
the earth and its various systems.[66] There is a coherence to the
world that allows it to be spoken of as an organism. The cosmos is
more than merely an aggregation of disparate elements. It is a
Gestalt--a coherent unity the whole of which is greater than the
sum of its parts. Ruether's many references to harmony, mutuality,
integrity, and balance stem from this basic analogy of organism.[67]
Indeed, such terms function as important norms in Ruether's moral
vocabulary--a vocabulary which strongly resembles that of Aldo

---

[63]Ruether, *To Change The World*, 67.

[64]Ruether, *Sexism and God-Talk*, 85.

[65]Ibid., 258; cf. 232. See, e.g., Ruether, *Liberation Theology*, 125, and
"Paradoxes of Human Hope," 241 for other references to organic metaphors.

[66]Ruether, *Gaia and God*, 4-5, 42ff, 243ff.

[67]See, e.g., Ruether, *New Woman/New Earth* 205; *To Change The
World*, 67, 69; *Sexism and God-Talk*, 89, 91-92, 232-233.

Leopold in his famous description of the land ethic: "A thing is right when it tends to preserve the integrity, stability, and beauty of the biotic community. It is wrong when it tends otherwise."[68]

Much of the above is definitely a step in the right direction with respect to an ecological theology. Emphasis on the unity, coherence, and interdependence of creation is in harmony not only with modern science, but also the best of the Christian scripture and tradition. There are good grounds for claiming that the world is, in significant respects, a unitary and interdependent whole--a claim, it should be noted, about the basic organization of reality and the relationships between its constituent parts, rather than a claim about the basic stuff of reality or what those parts have in common. As one of the central tenets of ecology puts it: everything is related to everything else. Or to use the words of John Muir: "When we try to pick out anything by itself, we find it hitched to everything else in the universe."[69] Ruether does a great service to stress these features of the natural and human worlds.

As suggested previously, however, Ruether's absolutely non-hierarchical model of reality runs aground on reality itself. It is simply not the case that each part of reality has the same or should have the same ontological and moral value. One can grant her contention that "photosynthesis is the vital process that underlies the very existence of the animal and human world" *without* accepting the conclusion that therefore every part of reality has equal value. It is a *non sequitur* to claim that all talk of levels of reality must be banished because the world is interdependent. Furthermore, with respect to ethics, it may be the case that not only animals and plants but also endangered species and ecosystems have not only instrumental but intrinsic value; but this in itself does not answer the question of moral obligation and does not erase the fact of or need for hierarchies of value. For example, something may have intrinsic value and yet not be a moral patient, i.e., not be morally considerable. Or something may have intrinsic value and also be a moral beneficiary, but have its rights trumped by some

---

[68]Aldo Leopold, *Sand County Almanac* (New York: Ballentine, 1970), 224-225.

[69]See, e.g., Muir, *My First Summer in the Sierra*, 110.

more compelling obligation, perhaps on the basis of some morally appropriate hierarchy of value.[70] In short, while *some* hierarchies should certainly be rejected, it is *not* clear that *all* hierarchies should be dismissed.

The Mutability of Creation

In addition to this emphasis on the fundamental unity, coherence, and interdependence of creation, Ruether also stresses change and becoming. For example, Ruether's affirmation of the historicity of nature--of its temporal becoming--points in this direction. Not just human but nonhuman creatures too are in process. Indeed, for Ruether the being of nature is in becoming.[71] Mutability is of the essence of creaturely existence, affirms Ruether, a claim made evident by, among other things, the "mortal limits of covenantal existence" imposed by death.[72]

Ruether's emphasis on becoming is also evident in her reflections on the development of human self-consciousness. Invoking both the new physics and Teilhard de Chardin, Ruether speaks of consciousness as "the most intense and complex form of the inwardness of material energy itself as it bursts forth at that evolutionary level where matter is organized in the most complex and intensive way," i.e., the human brain.[73] All of reality is continually evolving, including human consciousness. Putatively abiding structures themselves change.

Ruether's use of organic analogies, referred to above, is yet another reason to view becoming as most basic in her theology, since in addition to the unity implied by the organic metaphor, process, change and development are also implied by this image. In his discussion of "organicism" Stephen Pepper states that not only does this root metaphor connote the "integration" or unity of the

---

[70]See, e.g., Rolston, *Environmental Ethics*, especially chap. 6 for an excellent discussion of these issues.

[71]Ruether, *Sexism and God-Talk*, 86ff.

[72]Ruether, *To Change The World*, 69.

[73]Ruether, *Sexism and God-Talk*, 86.

world, but also the world's fundamental nature as "process."[74] Calling the universe an organism, or Gaia, as Ruether does, fosters the idea that the cosmos is not only a unified whole, but also in process and evolving rather than static or fixed.

Ruether's ontological model can perhaps best be illustrated by comparing in her own words the two worldviews that she sees competing for allegiance today.

The traditional worldview	The ecological-feminist worldview
competition	cooperation
hierarchy	mutuality
conflict	harmony
domination	reciprocity
individualism	interdependence
separation	solidarity
quest for immortality	acceptance of finitude
earth as alien	earth as home
God as Father	God as Primal Matrix
cosmos as machine	cosmos as organism

This last contrast, between cosmos as machine and cosmos as organism, perhaps best summarizes the underlying ontological metaphor in Ruether's thought. Reality is like (or is) an organism: unified, coherent, interdependent, developing, growing, changing. As indicated previously, the organismic and wholistic language of ecology seems to provide the basis for much of her ecological-feminist worldview.[75] In short, with respect to ontology, Ruether emphasizes the unitary and developing character of the world. Creation is in process and continually evolving as well as coherent and interdependent.

As indicated previously, Ruether's ontological model offers much assistance to those developing an ecological theology. Her emphasis on the unity, coherence, and interdependence of creation

---

[74]Stephen Pepper, *World Hypotheses*, 280-281. Pepper also criticizes the root metaphor of organicism for its "internal contradiction" between "ideal" and "progressive" categories.

[75]See, e.g., Ruether, *New Woman/New Earth*, 206ff; *To Change the World*, 66ff; and *Sexism and God-Talk*, 85ff, 233, 253, 258.

is a more scientifically and theologically accurate alternative to the once dominant and still influential atomistic and dualistic world-picture. Ruether's stress on change and process rightly displaces the overly static image of the world conveyed by the once pervasive metaphor of world as machine. And the general ecological tenor of her thought--for example her many references to the harmony, balance, and integrity of the natural world--lends itself well to the project of formulating an ecological theology. All in all, there is much to commend.

There are, however, various problems with Ruether's ontology. For example, her evolutionary ontology, with its talk of consciousness as "the most intense and complex form of the inwardness of material energy itself as it bursts forth at that evolutionary level where matter is organized in the most complex and intensive way," is unclear at best. It is unclear because Ruether never spells out exactly what she means here. For example, what precisely is meant by "the inwardness of material energy itself"? Even in her more recent work, where she presents in somewhat greater detail her ontological musings, there remains much left unexplained. Concepts like "the dancing void of energy patterns" and "this matrix of dancing energy" need further explanation, and claims like "consciousness is where this dance of energy organizes itself in increasingly unified ways, until it reflects back upon itself in self-awareness" need both greater explanation and defense.[76] While one may be sympathetic to this aspect of Ruether's ontology, much more work is needed to elucidate precisely what such concepts mean and much more careful argumentation is necessary before her ontological perspective can function as an adequate basis for a more ecologically informed theology.

Moreover, Ruether's references to humankind as the most complex and intelligent form of evolutionary existence appear to contradict or at least be tension with her own contentions about the non-hierarchical and egalitarian nature of reality. That is to say, if humans are the most complex and intelligent form of life, and if being complex or having intelligence confers greater moral if not ontological value, then in *that* respect at least all forms of life are

---

[76]Ruether, *Gaia and God*, 248-250.

not equal, and hence it is a mistake to insist on a radically egalitarian ontology. Ruether wants to deny the second premise in the above argument; however, our common moral intuitions about the relatively greater value of human life--in contrast, for example, to the life of a ladyslipper or a marmot--are *prima facie* evidence in support of that premise. If all Ruether really intends to claim is that the flourishing of lady slippers and marmots and wolves is dependent on the flourishing of Sequoias and peregrine falcons and humans, and conversely, then her claim more easily stands. But in order to back that claim she need not further argue that only a radically egalitarian ontology is sufficient. Some sort of moral if not ontological scale of value is both necessary and legitimate. And this scale of value need not necessarily entail an ethic of domination. In short, Ruether's view of humans as superior in intellect and evolutionary complexity appears to be in tension with her claim about the thoroughly egalitarian nature of reality.

In addition, behind Ruether's ecological-feminist worldview, as outlined previously, lies an organic metaphor, with its presumption of a hidden harmony or natural balance in the cosmos. However, Ruether acknowledges that since nature "is a product not only of natural evolution but of human historical development," and thus "partakes of the evils and distortions of human development," it is "fallen."[77] If this is the case, then on what basis does Ruether claim that there is a hidden harmony or balance to nature? For example, if she argues on the basis of an organic model drawn from ecology that a harmony is evident in the natural world itself, and that one gains such knowledge by careful observation of ecosystems, then in what sense is nature fallen? Could it not be argued that the harmony is a result not of natural but of human development, or of some combination of natural and human evolution, or even of the fall, and that *dis*harmony is the true character of the natural world? In other words, Ruether's presumption of harmony in creation has difficulty overcoming the epistemological problem involved in acknowledging that in some sense creation is fallen.

---

[77]Ibid., 91.

Theology

Discussion of ontology inevitably leads to theology, at least for theists. That is to say, inquiry into being as such necessarily leads to inquiry concerning God's being and God's activity. Mention of God's being and activity points to the two *basic* theological issues under consideration here: the question of the attributes of God and the question of the action of God. These questions are interrelated since how one describes the character of God influences what one thinks about the conduct of God, and how one construes divine action determines to some extent one's concept of divine being. Hence the analysis and critique which follow address both of these issues simultaneously.

Questions concerning both the attributes and action of God are bound up with what is probably for theists the central metaphysical and theological issue in the history of Western thought, namely, the question of how God and the world relate. Limiting oneself to just the Christian tradition, from Origen and Augustine to John Scotus Eriugena and Aquinas, from Calvin and Scheiermacher to Barth and Rahner, the question of the God-world relation looms large. Robert Neville observes that the question of the relation between God and world "has been a central issue of the Western speculative tradition since the earliest days."[78] This "metaphysical, epistemological, and religious" question usually is presented in terms of "the speculative problem of the transcendence and presence (or immanence) of God."[79] Langdon Gilkey confirms this observation when he says that

> as always, the central problem for the doctrine of God is how to unite intelligibly the *absoluteness* of God as the unconditioned source of our total being with the dynamic *relatedness* and the *reciprocal activity* of God as the ground, guide, dialogical partner and redeemer of our freedom.[80]

---

[78]Robert Neville, *God the Creator: On the Transcendence and Presence of God* (Chicago: University of Chicago, 1968), 1; cf. 11.

[79]Ibid., 2.

[80]Langdon Gilkey, "God," in *Christian Theology: An Introduction to its Tasks and Traditions*, rev. ed., eds. Peter Hodgson and Robert King, 108; cf. also 94.

As stated above, one way of looking at this issue is in terms of the classical categories of transcendence and immanence, or, to use the language of Gilkey, absoluteness and relatedness. Does God transcend the world? If so, then to what degree and in what respect? If God is transcendent and if God is also immanent, then how is that relatedness best expressed? If God is not transcendent, then is it meaningful to talk of a distinction between God and the world, and if so, then how exactly? Often the assumption is that insofar as stress is placed on the absoluteness of God, to that degree God's relatedness necessarily suffers, and to the extent that emphasis is put on divine immanence, divine transcendence is necessarily minimized.

Obviously there are a number of possible responses to this perennial issue. For example, God can be seen as identical and coextensive with the world, e.g., pantheism. Or God can be envisioned as including but not exhausted in the world, e.g., panentheism. Or God can be viewed as utterly distinct from the world as its creator (but not as its sustainer), e.g., deism. Or God can be seen as both distinct from the world and also related to the world--as its creator, sustainer, and ultimately its redeemer, e.g., classic Christian theism. All of these views have at one time been adopted by thinkers in the Western tradition.

Like Gilkey, Bernard McGinn affirms that for Christians the crucial requirement is that "every Christian theology of creation has to insist not only that God is absolutely different from creation, but also that he is related to it in an essential way."[81] An adequate Christian ecological theology must, in other words, articulate "how God is both transcendent and immanent."[82] So also Robert Neville argues on philosophical grounds as well as on the basis of the classic Christian affirmation of *creatio ex nihilo* that "the creator both transcends and is present in his creation."[83] Thus, at a

---

[81]Bernard McGinn, "Do Christian Platonists Really Believe in Creation?" in *God and Creation: An Ecumenical Symposium*, eds. David Burrell and Bernard McGinn (Notre Dame: University of Notre Dame, 1990), 210.

[82]Ibid., 211.

[83]Neville, *God the Creator*, 13.

minimum, both pantheism and deism are ruled out as acceptable positions for any authentically Christian ecological theology.

God/ess as Primal Matrix

Ruether is keenly aware that these theological questions and this central issue lie at the heart of her project. As indicated previously, she concludes that sexism will not be exorcized unless and until we transform all relations of domination, including "our model of God in relation to creation."[84] The traditional hierarchical chain of being ontology that puts God on top and matter on the bottom, with men above women above nature in the middle, must unequivocally be replaced. In her words, "the unfinished effort of classical Christian theology is to synthesize the world-affirming and world-negating traditions of religious hope"--the hope "which combines the myth of the world-renewing Ba'al with the world-transcending Yahweh-Christ."[85] In similar language Ruether argues that we must combine "the values of the world-transcending Yahweh with those of the world-renewing Ba'al in a post-technological religion of reconciliation with the body, the woman, and the world."[86] Thus Ruether explicitly and rightly asserts that God must be conceived *both* in terms of transcendence and of immanence. She furthermore proposes a synthesis of two religious traditions as the way to achieve this objective.

While Ruether rightly wishes to conceive of God in such a way as to affirm adequately both divine transcendence and immanence, it is not clear that her particular proposal is able to do so. She asserts that we must "synthesize" two different traditions--"the world-renewing Ba'al with the world-transcending Yahweh-Christ;" but is it possible to combine these two views of God--views which seem quite unsynthesizable? And if it is possible, *how exactly* is it to be done? Ruether speaks as if it is a relatively easy task to synthesize these two traditions. But it is unclear how Canaanite fertility religions and Hebrew Yahwehism can easily be reconciled.

---

[84]Ruether, *New Woman/New Earth*, 83; cf. Ruether, *Sexism and God-Talk*, 85.
[85]Ruether, "Paradoxes of Human Hope," 251.
[86]Ruether, *Liberation Theology*, 125.

Moreover, to accomplish what Ruether intends it is questionable whether she *needs* to adopt such an approach. That is, in order to emphasize the immanence of God it is not necessary to retrieve ancient Canaanite religions since there are other ways to envision God as both satisfactorily transcendent and immanent--ways which are more in line with the classical Christian tradition. In sum, it is not clear whether it is either possible or necessary to accept Ruether's proposal that the religions of Ba'al and Yahweh be combined.

In light of a perceived emphasis on divine transcendence within the classical Christian tradition, Ruether appropriately places greater stress on divine immanence. For example, over against the dualism of history and nature, which virtually evacuates the natural world of God's action and concern and so limits God's presence to history, she draws upon prophetic texts like Isaiah 24 which speak of the natural world both as filled with God's presence and as a vehicle of God's judgement. This is not, Ruether insists, romanticism or neoanimism--views in which nature is divinized--but rather the proper but long overdue recognition of the presence of God in all of reality. Such an acknowledgment of God's presence serves as a necessary corrective to views which emphasize divine transcendence in such a way that divine immanence is slighted.

Ruether's most important and pervasive move to recapture divine immanence or relatedness is to reconceive God as God/ess, the primal matrix. Borrowing from the religions of the ancient Near East, Ruether describes God/ess as "the Primal Matrix, the great womb within which all things...are generated."[87] God/ess is not the radically transcendent other, but that within which all creation comes to be. Waxing Tillichean, Ruether speaks of God as the ground of our being--the simultaneous foundation of being and new being. God/ess as matrix is the all-encompassing womb which enfolds the entire range of being, from matter to spirit, within its embrace. Ruether further claims that this alternative construal of God more adequately expresses divine relatedness while not sacrificing divine absoluteness. As she maintains: "God/ess who is

[87]Ruether, *Sexism and God-Talk*, 48; see also *Gaia and God*, 253.

primal matrix, ground of being-new being, is neither stifling immanence nor rootless transcendence."[88] Reconceiving God as God/ess holds divine transcendence and immanence together. It is at this point that Ruether finds fault with patriarchal liberation theologies for failing to make this connection between being and new being. Ruether rightly insists that God the Liberator must *also* be God the Matrix. Thus liberation properly construed is not "out of or against nature into spirit," but *back into* a proper relationship with nature, since the God who liberates is the author of being as well as new being and is him/herself rooted in the very foundations of being.[89] Liberation, rightly conceived, reconnects us with the natural world. The divine liberator heals our broken relationships not only with other people, but also with nature. To use traditional language, Ruether affirms that our Redeemer is our Creator. Creation and redemption, being and new being, are theologically joined. God's action in redemption must be seen as congruent with God's action in creation. Creation is not something from which we must escape but that to which we are restored in a right relationship. In an age which has seen "the eclipse of creation," Ruether's insistence on this inner connection between God the Creator/Matrix and God the Redeemer/Liberator is a welcome and much-needed alternative.[90]

To speak of God's action as Ruether does, however, is problematic since it is unclear whether God/ess is a personal agent. On the one hand, Ruether describes the being of God in ways that assume personal agency. For example, we can appropriately speak of God as the king above all kings and as both mother and father.[91] God is like a liberating sovereign who champions the cause of the oppressed and marginalized. God is like a mother or father who cares for her or his children and parents them into responsible adulthood. God is creator and redeemer, mother and sister. On the other hand, however, Ruether also tends to identify God/ess with the cosmos in a way that casts doubt on whether it is meaningful to speak of God as an agent. For example, she identifies "the great

---

[88]Ibid., 85.
[89]Ibid., 70.
[90]See, e.g., Per Lønning, *Creation--An Ecumenical Challenge?*, 5.
[91]Ruether, *Sexism and God-Talk*, 65, 69.

matrix of being" with "the great organism of the universe itself" which is "the Holy Being" and "Holy Wisdom."[92] She also refers to this "great matrix" as "that great collective personhood." It is unclear, however, what personhood here means. Is this collective personhood a *person*, an agent? Is this God/ess, this Holy Being, capable of action? Elsewhere Ruether speaks of God as "the ongoing creative Matrix of the whole" and "the great Thou, the personal center of the universal process."[93] But this "personal center" seems not to be a person or agent, but rather merely the principle of creativity and order for the cosmic process. The Matrix--God/Gaia--is simply "the wellspring of life and creativity" rather than an agent capable of intending actions.[94] On this question of divine agency, then, Ruether is ambiguous. She both affirms God's agency and yet calls it into question.

This ambiguity regarding divine agency leads to the question of how God is seen with respect to Ruether's implicit ontology. At times, especially in speaking of God as all-inclusive matrix, Ruether suggests that God is part of the cosmos. As cosmic womb God is identified or merged with the world. Not just the world but all that has being, including God, is encompassed within the unitary structure of being. There appears to be no fundamental ontological distinction between God and creation, and therefore divine transcendence is engulfed by divine immanence. Her attempt to avoid a "stifling immanence" seems to have failed. Given Ruether's insistence that a proper view of God must include adequate attention to *both* transcendence and immanence, there obviously is some tension, if not a contradiction, in her view of God. Ruether does insist that God be viewed as transcendent. We need a "world-transcending" as well as a "world-renewing" God. Rightly understood her concern is not to repudiate transcendence *per se*, but only a "rootless transcendence." For Ruether divine transcendence must necessarily involve divine relatedness. However, the exact relation between these two attributes of God is, at best, unclear.

---

[92]Ibid., 258.
[93]Ruether, *Gaia and God*, 253; see also p. 249.
[94]Ibid.

The most plausible interpretation of Ruether's position is that she advocates a form of panentheism. God and the world, while distinct in one respect, are necessarily non-distinct in another respect. The being of God in some sense includes the world, but is not exhausted by the world. For example, Ruether's claim that "God/ess...embraces both the roots of the material substratum of our existence (matter) and also the endlessly new creative potential (spirit)" could be construed to mean that the being of God includes the human spirit and at least the roots of the material substratum of human being (whatever that means), but extends beyond that to include also some greater collective whole--"that great collective personhood [which] is the Holy Being."[95] But if this is the case, it is still quite unclear *exactly* how God is related to the world and whether this God is a personal agent. Furthermore, it is unclear whether this form of panentheism can retain a sufficiently strong distinction between God and the world. Or when Ruether states that "the small selves and the Great Self are finally one," divine transcendence seems to have completely evaporated into divine immanence.[96] As stated previously by Bernard McGinn, in Christian theology God must be viewed as "absolutely different from creation" as well as "related to it in an essential way." Whether Ruether can retain this absolute difference remains an open question.

With respect to the question of whether God is in process, a similar ambiguity is evident. It is unclear whether Ruether includes God within the development and evolution of the universe, though it appears with her recent work that Ruether does conceive of God/Gaia as in process. For example, she speaks of the divine consciousness as "the ongoing creative Matrix of the whole."[97] And while she perceptively criticizes the views of both Matthew Fox and Teilhard de Chardin, she offers no criticism of process theology, presumably because she finds that view of God in process congenial.[98] If divine immanence is given precedence over divine transcendence such that the very being of God is constituted by

---

95Ruether, *Sexism and God-Talk*, 71, 258.
96Ruether, *Gaia and God*, 253.
97Ibid.
98Ibid., 246-247.

being in relationship with creation, and if creation is in process, then it follows that God too is in process. In other words, if Ruether denies any fundamental ontological distinction between God and the world, and if the being of the world is constituted by becoming, then God too must become. The relevant question then becomes: in what precise respect(s) does God become? With regard to which attributes or aspects of being does God change? Unfortunately these questions are not addressed, and so the answer to the question of how God changes, if God changes, is left unclear. Much more work is needed in order to clarify these important issues.

God as Mother

Despite the above-mentioned ambiguities, in a number of ways Ruether's reconception of God provides an important service for a Christian ecological theology. First of all, with her talk of God as mother as well as father Ruether retrieves an important, more inclusive view of God found within the Christian scriptures and tradition, e.g., in Proverbs 8 and with Julian of Norwich, and so moves beyond *exclusively* male imagery of God. This recovery of lost and suppressed elements of the tradition and affirmation of both female and male images for God is important because, as Ruether painfully notes, "male monotheism" has alienated many people, especially women, from the Christian faith. And thus if Christianity is to be a religion of wholeness and healing for *all* people, as well as if it is to be true to its own scriptures and traditions, then there must be some modification of the concept of God along more gender inclusive lines. God is like a father but *not only* like a father. God is, as Ruether insists, also like a mother.

This is significant for developing a Christian ecological theology because exclusively male imagery of and language for God all too often connotes distance and lack of relationality--traditionally "male" or "masculine" traits that emphasize transcendence at the cost of relatedness. For example, if God is seen only as a distant monarch, whose relationship with and care for creation is ambiguous at best, then it is relatively difficult to develop an adequate ecological theology. In other words, if God is seen as male, and if male usually implies distance, then God's transcendence will be emphasized and God's presence in and with the world will be correlatively minimized. And if God's presence in and with the world is minimized, then an ethic of exploitation is more easily sanctioned--implicitly, if not explicitly. Reference to God only as Father will thus continue to underwrite a view of God's relationship with creation which underplays divine presence and so perpetuates an ethic of domination. A more inclusive view of God as mother as well as father, on the other hand, is better able to emphasize the relatedness of God to creation and thereby foster a more ecologically sound ethic. And as Ruether correctly maintains, an affirmation of divine presence does not necessarily entail an animistic reenchantment of the world. It simply means giving proper attention to God's intimate relation to and loving care for creation.

Ruether perceptively observes that while the strategy of envisioning God as mother as well as father is helpful in portraying the fullness of God, especially God's relatedness to creation, nevertheless it can subtly reinforce harmful gender stereotypes since this approach assumes that maleness means distance and that femaleness means relatedness. Such assumptions feed the very stereotypes which have in part created a problematic view of God in the first place. Hence Ruether argues that until stereotypes of gender roles change and there is a new model of full *human* personhood that incorporates *both* "masculine" and "feminine" traits, viewing God as mother as well as father, while helpful, will still not offer the kind of solution to language about God that is required. Like proposals for speaking of the androgyny of God, in which God has "masculine" as well as "feminine" characteristics, an alternative construal of God as mother as well as father continues to assume typical gender roles and thus is an ultimately inadequate response to the need to have more inclusive language and images for God.

In her reflections on God-language Ruether maintains something like the classic view of analogical predication. Drawing upon the biblical proscription against idolatry Ruether argues that "verbal pictures" as well as pictures of the more traditional sort must be included within the purview of this prohibition and therefore any term which is taken as literally referring to God is idolatrous.[99] Hence "all names for God are analogies."[100] This implies, states Ruether, that "God is both male and female and neither male and female."[101] God is in some respects like men and women and in other respects unlike men and women.

But Ruether emphasizes the *dis*similar or *dis*analogous character of language about God. In keeping with the tradition of apophatic theology, which she explicitly mentions and relies upon, Ruether "emphasizes the unlikeness between God and human words for God."[102] Given this emphasis on "unlikeness," however, it is unclear how Ruether grounds her claim for gaining genuine knowledge via analogical language. Unlike Aquinas there is no *analogia entis* to provide some understanding of how humans are able to speak appropriately of God. While Ruether need not adopt Aquinas' ontology in order to advocate analogical predication, some greater clarity on this matter is necessary. In short, how exactly is analogical predication possible? Furthermore, if as Ruether claims God is "the great matrix of being" and "the great organism of the universe itself," then why does she so emphasize the "unlikeness" of God and language about God? If Ruether advocates some sort of panentheism, then how precisely is God so unlike creation? Further attention must be given to these admittedly complex issues of theology and religious language.

Finally, while vigorously affirming the legitimacy and necessity of speaking of God as mother, as well as father, Ruether argues that parental language for God is inadequate. She asserts that "the parent model for the divine has negative resonance" since "it suggests a kind of permanent parent-child relationship to God."[103] In this model, insists Ruether, "God becomes a neurotic parent who does not want us to grow up" and so "to become autonomous and responsible for our own lives is the gravest sin against God."[104] As stated in chapter two, Ruether claims that the use of parental language to refer to God prolongs "spiritual

---

[99]Ruether, *Sexism and God-Talk*, 66.
[100]Ibid., 67.
[101]Ibid.
[102]Ibid.
[103]Ibid., 69.
[104]Ibid.

infantilism as virtue" and makes "autonomy and assertion of free will a sin." With these claims, however, Ruether calls into question her whole thesis that we must refer to God as mother. If all parental language for God is unsatisfactory, then how can speaking of God as mother be acceptable? Should we or should we not refer to God as mother? Furthermore, it does not necessarily follow that using parental language with respect to God means that God is viewed as "a neurotic parent who does not want us to grow up." It is a *non sequitur* to suggest that personal responsibility is incompatible with viewing God as a parent. In addition, Ruether assumes that "autonomy and assertion of free will" are the characteristic features of maturity. But how does this comport with her critique of such "male" traits and advocacy of values like interdependence and community? In short, there are numerous problems with Ruether's claims regarding language for God.

In summary, Ruether offers a number of necessary and helpful revisions to theology and traditional language about God, especially with respect to developing a more adequate Christian ecological theology. For example, her insistence that God be envisioned as mother as well as father is an important correction to patriarchal views of God that tend to legitimate ecological degradation. Her views are also in some respects unclear and contradictory. For example, it is unclear how speaking of God as a God of peace, justice, and compassion who acts in ways consonant with that character fits with talk of the being of God which is non-personal. It is unclear how her emphasis on divine relatedness can also retain a necessary concern for divine absoluteness. Despite these problems, however, Ruether has much to offer those seeking to develop a more earth-friendly Christian theology.

Conclusion

There are both assets and liabilities in Ruether's theology. As clearly shown by this exploration into her anthropology, ontology, and theology, Ruether's thought both displays certain features that should be incorporated into an adequate Christian ecological theology and suffers from a number of problems. Further attention is given in chapter eight to both these strengths and weaknesses.

The above negative remarks should not detract from the previous positive comments, nor should they in any way deny the impressive and provocative, the learned and creative work of Rosemary Radford Ruether. Whether one agrees with all of her analyses and positions or not, reading her works forces an engagement with the fundamental issues pertaining to Christian theology. As Kathryn Allen Rabuzzi says, Ruether "touches her reader in such a deep way that nonresponse is impossible."[105] Indeed, "the *power* her writing exerts on the attentive reader" evokes not just thoughts, but feelings of discomfort, guilt, anger.[106] This also is an important--nay indispensable--service with regard to an ecological theology, since, as Aristotle reminds us, if we fail to *feel* the appropriate emotions at the appropriate times, we will despite all our reflections fail to *act* in morally excellent ways.

---

[105]Rabuzzi, "The Socialist Feminist Vision of Rosemary Radford Ruether," 7.
[106]Ibid.

CHAPTER 6

THE CHALLENGE OF SITTLER'S HOLY NATURALISM: A CRITICAL APPRAISAL

The largest, most insistent, most delicate task awaiting Christian theology is to articulate such a theology for nature as shall do justice to the vitalities of earth and hence correct a current theological naturalism which succeeds in speaking meaningfully of earth only at the cost of repudiating specifically Christian categories. Christian theology cannot advance this work along the line of an orthodoxy--neo or old--which celebrates the love of heaven in complete separation from man's loves in earth, abstracts commitment to Christ from relevancy to those loyalties of earth which are elemental to being. Any faith in God which shall be redemptive and regenerative in actuality dare not be alien to the felt ambiguities of earth or remain wordless in the resounding torments of history and culture.[1]

Joseph Sittler

As in the previous chapter, the analysis and evaluation here fall under the three headings of anthropology, ontology, and theology. Thus with respect to Sittler's thought we first examine his views concerning the nature of the human, then analyze his beliefs about the basic character of reality, and finally seek to understand better his views on God. The intention here is to identify and assess the main claims and crucial arguments of Sittler's thought with respect to a Christian ecological theology.

As before evaluation is combined with analysis and so critical questions are posed which highlight the strengths and weaknesses of Sittler's theology. Like Ruether, Sittler offers considerable resources for developing a Christian ecological theology, particularly with regard to christology. However, with Sittler's theology there are some unanswered questions and significant problems which must be acknowledged and addressed.

---

[1]Sittler, "A Theology for Earth," 373-374.

Anthropology

Body and Soul

As with Ruether the issue of the composition of the human provides a useful entrée into Sittler's anthropology. In arguing that the human person is unitary Sittler disavows any typical dualism of body and soul. One of the ways he warrants this claim is by arguing that the different terms used in scripture point to the unity of the human person. For example, with respect to Hebrew anthropology he states: "There is no soul, as one slice of the pie of personhood, in Hebrew thought, as there is in that notion of the immortality of the soul in the Greek philosophers. The soul means the whole life of the whole person in corporate identity with the life of all of Israel."[2] Sittler makes a similar claim with respect to the terms used in the New Testament. For example, he renders Paul's use of *sôma*-- usually translated body--in Romans 12:1 as "entire personality."[3] Sittler thus affirms that "at the heart of the Christian and Judaic tradition there does indeed lie an organic and holistic way of regarding man in the world."[4]

One of Sittler's primary ways of describing the human is in terms of rootedness in the natural order, a claim he backs with appeals to scripture. For example, the fact that Genesis portrays God as making the first humans "not out of angelic substance or out of sheer gas or wind but out of the dust of the earth," says Sittler, "is a symbolic and powerful way of saying that the human race belongs to the biological order. We are part of nature. We cannot lay aside our natural beginning, our rootedness in the ecological system that characterizes the natural world."[5] Or as Sittler insists with respect to Romans 8, Paul "enlarges his language of redemption to include man's irreversible rootedness in the natural world."[6] And so in response to the "strange assertion"

2Sittler, "Speeches," 50.
3Sittler, *Structure*, 9.
4Sittler, "Perils," 76.
5Sittler, *Gravity and Grace*, 12.
6Sittler, "Speeches," 38.

that "God is concerned to save men's souls" Sittler remarks: "I know no soul save an embodied soul, I have no body save this one born of other bodies, and there is no such thing as a man outside the created context of other men."[7] "God," says Sittler, "is an undeviating materialist."[8] Humans are by divine design part of the biological order.

Sittler also provides warrant for his argument that humans are rooted in the natural world by appealing to modern science. Largely on the basis of his knowledge of ecology, Sittler again and again refers to "man's embeddedness in the web of nature."[9] Questioning views which abstract the human out of its inescapable embeddedness in nature, Sittler rhetorically asks: "Does it mean nothing for our reality as persons that the natural world which is not human is yet *to* the human a life-sustaining placenta of self-consciousness?"[10] As Sittler asserts regarding human self-identity: "I am what I am not only as one with, among, and in self-forming transactions with men; I am who I am in relation to the web, structure, process and placenta of nature."[11] He concludes: "There is a mass of evidence--to which the professional theological community has not seriously attended--which attests the force of man's sheer animal fixedness within the natural world of the not-self as profoundly constitutive of his sense of identity."[12] Thus on both biblical and scientific grounds Sittler argues that humans are inextricably embedded in the natural world. It is not peripheral to but rather constitutive of human being and human self-identity.

Sittler's claim regarding the "organic and holistic" anthropological language of the Bible is well founded. A host of biblical scholars support Sittler's contention that both the Old and New Testaments demand a more unitary anthropology.[13] And

---

[7]Sittler, "A Theology for Earth," 373.

[8]Ibid.

[9]Sittler, "Speeches," 44. See also, Sittler, *Essays*, 2.

[10]Sittler, *Essays*, 108. See also "The Presence and Acts," 132, where Sittler states that nature is "the immemorial placenta of his [the human's] personal being."

[11]Sittler, "Scope," 333.

[12]Ibid.

[13]For illustrative biblical scholarship, see. e.g., Hans Walter Wolff, *Anthropology of the Old Testament* (Philadelphia: Fortrtess, 1974); Herman

Sittler's claims about the rootedness of the human in the natural world are also well founded. Both scripture and modern science readily attest to the embeddedness of humanity in the web of nature. Whether with respect to genetic inheritance, evolutionary kinship, human bodiliness, or the influence of geography, to mention only a few such factors, in a variety of ways "nature" is indeed constitutive of human being and identity.[14] Sittler's observation that the "force of man's sheer animal fixedness within the natural world" has not been attended to by many within the Christian community is also on target. The dichotomies between nature and history, matter and spirit, still pervade much theology, usually leading to ecologically disastrous consequences.

However, some of Sittler's arguments are unclear or downright fallacious. For example, Sittler seems to argue that "man's embeddedness in the web of nature" *necessarily* implies an "organic and holistic way of regarding man in the world." That is, he seems to argue that humans are rooted in the natural world *only if* they are unitary beings. But surely that is not the case, since it could be claimed that the human person consists of soul and body, with (only) the latter embedded in nature. Even Descartes' sharp dualism of mind and matter would seem to serve as a counter-example to Sittler's argument. In other words, being a unitary being is *not* a necessary condition for having the property of being rooted in the natural order. If Sittler does offer this argument, more is required for it to work. Some additional premise like "if any part of the human person is rooted in nature, then all of the human person is rooted in nature" is necessary.

On the basis of the fact of human rootedness in the bio-physical world Sittler rightly concludes that the typical dualism between nature and history is false and misleading. Human "embeddedness in nature," which is "the truth of man's

---

Ridderbos, *Paul: An Outline of his Theology* (Grand Rapids: Eerdmans, 1975); G.C. Berkouwer, *Man: The Image of God* (Grand Rapids: Eerdmans, 1962). For a thorough recent review of much of this literature, see John Cooper, *Body, Soul, and Life Everlasting.*

[14]Many works could be mentioned here, but with respect to the influence of geography on human self-identity, and spirituality in particular, see Beldon Lane, *Landscapes of the Sacred: Geography and Narrative in American Spirituality* (New York: Paulist, 1988).

evolutionary identity," precludes any dualism between nature and history.[15] "Man's placement in nature," says Sittler, "is as fundamental to his self-hood as his placement in history with the fellow creature."[16] Humans are inextricably related to and in fact constituted by the natural world and thus there can be no sharp separation between nature and history. Thus Sittler declares: "History and nature, man and his life as an animal in the world of nature, as well as man in the elevation of a potentially dreaming angel, are all of a piece."[17] One should not speak of nature and history as if they were separate realms of existence; rather one should more properly speak of "the world-as-nature" and "the world-as-history."[18]

Sittler perceptively notes, however, that Christians especially are tempted to set "nature" over against "history." Largely because "Christianity proudly presents itself as a historical religion," the *distinction* between world-as-nature and world-as-history is turned into a *dualism*.[19]

> The Christian believer is liable, therefore, to make an *opposition*, not just a distinction, between man-as-nature and man-as-history. This is the fateful separation which marks the post-Enlightenment community particularly. We suppose that redemption is a historical drama which leaves untouched and has no meaning for and cannot be celebrated in terms of care of the Creation. This is a fundamental misunderstanding.[20]

In response to this mistake, Sittler declares that "we must somehow bring under question the notion that man in his historical entity, his individual selfhood, is so set apart from the rest of God's Creation that he can deal with it with Olympian arrogance as if it has no selfhood of its own by virtue of the Creation."[21] This acknowledgment of and emphasis on human embeddedness in the

---

[15]Sittler, *Essays*, 69.

[16]Sittler, "Nature and Grace," 254.

[17]Sittler, "Perils," 77.

[18]Ibid., 76. These terms occur throughout Sittler's writings; see also Bakken, "The Ecology of Grace," 258.

[19]Sittler, "Ecological Commitment," 176.

[20]Ibid., 175-177.

[21]Ibid., 175.

natural world is one of Sittler's primary means of questioning the notion of human separateness and its resulting *hubris*.

Sittler also provides another argument against any dualism between nature and history. He argues that history and nature in fact include each other. As Sittler states:

> The huge categories, nature and history, are no longer clearly defined or capable of being cleanly set over against each other. If by history we mean most simply the realm of human action, and if by nature we mean the not-self as the given theatre within which such actions occur, then it is clear that as historical life witnesses broad and deep advances in knowledge about and interference with natural life the interpenetrative and modifying energies of this transaction will present an ever more subtle situation. And the appropriateness of the relatively distinct older use of the theological categories of nature and grace will have to follow facts and reformulate their meanings.[22]

With the pervasive effects of human action it is no longer clear what is "natural" and what is "historical" or "cultural," and thus the categories of nature and culture must be reformulated. In short, because of both human embeddedness in and interaction with the world-as-nature, there can properly be no dichotomy between nature and history.

Here too Sittler's argument is persuasive. With the pervasive impact of humanity, human action and natural event interpenetrate, the conceptual boundaries become fuzzy, and the traditional categories of nature and history stand in need of reformulation. Nature not only has its own history, but is pervasively and indelibly affected by human action. For example, as many earthwatchers now point out, we have radically changed the atmosphere. The weather is no longer something "natural"--it is no longer hot or cold, windy or calm, dry or wet irrespective of human action in the world. "Pristine wilderness" is now an oxymoron. Indeed, even the wind in the Arctic bears human

---

[22]Sittler, *Essays*, 97-98. On p. 114 Sittler contends that "the life of nature has been so drawn up into the energies of history in virtue of man's science-based manipulations of nature, that these categories...are no longer of the same categorical efficiency." Bill McKibben persuasively and with understandable lament makes this same argument in *The End of Nature*.

footprints. Insofar as anthropocentric "Olympian arrogance" is based on this assumption that there is a radical separation between the human and the natural worlds, Sittler is correct in pointing to the flimsy foundations of such a harmful anthropocentrism.

In addition to being constituted by our embeddedness in and relationship to the natural world, Sittler also insists that the human is constituted by relationships with other humans. In commenting on the Genesis 1 creation story Sittler remarks:

> We humans are made for each other. The meaning of the Adam and Eve story, in particular the introduction of the figure of Eve, is not simply to say that it takes two to tango. But the Eve story communicates to all of us the meaning of the German proverb, "*Ein Mensch ist kein Mensch.*" A solitary person is no person; personhood is relation and presupposes another for its actualization.[23]

As Sittler succinctly and simply puts it: "Without community there is no person....Personhood is a social state."[24] Indeed, as Sittler insists, "the very notion of personhood is not a possibility save in the presence of the other in whom and by whom a person is postulated into reality."[25] In sum, the very concept of person is intrinsically relational.

In this anthropological affirmation Sittler captures an important and much-needed aspect of the pre-modern notion of person. Despite other differences in meaning, from Tertullian and Boethius through Aquinas, Calvin, and the Protestant Scholastics, the concept of person necessarily implies relationality and thus should be distinguished from the concept of the modern individual. Sittler's insistence on a relational and thus more communal understanding of human being-in-the-world properly criticizes and undermines the anthropological assumptions backing the community-destroying individualism pervasive in Western culture. Hence Sittler gives important theological grounds for affirming that humans are constituted by relationships.

---

[23]Sittler, *Gravity and Grace*, 42.
[24]Sittler, *Grace Notes*, 98; cf. p. 13 where Sittler states that "the self is constituted by its relationships." See also, Sittler, *Gravity and Grace*, 68.
[25]Sittler, "The Presence and Acts," 97.

Thus according to Sittler the human is constituted by relationships with *both* the human and the natural worlds. States Sittler: "I am constituted by my relationships [with the human world]....But I am also constituted by my encounters with the non-human world."[26] In yet other words, in addition to seeing the "self in communion with selves," another "contextual matrix for the achievement of identity must be grasped with equal resolution and insight," namely, "the natural world" which is a "self-constituting datum operative in deep and steady interiority."[27] In short, not only is the social world constitutive for human being and identity, but "the world of nature...is also a self-constituting datum" of human existence.[28] We are what we are only in relationship, including our (often unnoticed or unacknowledged) relationships with the earth and its plethora of creatures.

Sittler nicely summarizes the various relationships which he sees as constitutive for human being when he states that humans are created by and dependent upon God, made to exist among and in communion with other humans, and are made "out of, within, and absolutely dependent upon the *whole* world that he [God] has made."[29] Hence, declares Sittler, "I am stuck with God, stuck with my neighbor, and stuck with nature (the 'garden'), within which and out of the stuff of which I am made."[30] Humans are thoroughly relational, in Sittler's view, inextricably related to and bound up with not only God, and not only other human beings, but also the animals and plants and oceans and mountains of this exquisitely complex and beautiful blue-green earth.

This triad of God, humanity, and nature is a pervasive theme in Sittler's theology.[31] As Sittler succinctly puts it: "Created life is a triad of God, and man, and nature."[32] With this triad Sittler nicely captures the more complete range of relationships which in fact

---

[26]Sittler, "Speeches," 45.

[27]Sittler, *Essays*, 107; cf. 17 where Sittler says that the human person "lives in a nexus of human relations and nature relations."

[28]Sittler, "The Presence and Acts," 131.

[29]Sittler, "Evangelism and the Care of the Earth," 101-102.

[30]Ibid., 102.

[31]See, e.g., Sittler, *Structure*, 3; *Anguish*, 62; *Essays*, 75; "A Theology for Earth," 373.

[32]Sittler, "Called to Unity," 14.

shape who we are as humans. Often in Christian theology only the first two members of the triad--God and humans--are actually considered or taken seriously. The world is assumed to be a mere stage upon which the real actors interact. Not surprisingly, given his "love affair with the natural world," Sittler reminds us that non-human creation is a constitutive dimension of human being, and important and valuable in its own right, and hence must be taken seriously in any adequate Christian theology.

However, beyond his various critiques Sittler gives little specific direction as to how precisely to proceed on this issue of anthropology. More is needed than a mere affirmation that there is "an organic and holistic way of regarding man in the world." What *exactly* does it mean to describe humanity in terms of "man and his life as an animal in the world of nature as well as man in the elevation of a potentially dreaming angel"? Also, while a repudiation of a dualism between nature and history is necessary and helpful, much more is required for the task of theological construction. Sittler does offer the suggestive alternative of envisioning the earth as our sibling, but here too he fails to work out the needed details of such a vision.[33]

The Good Life

Further insight into Sittler's anthropology can be gained by examining his views on the purpose of human life. For Sittler the authentic goal of human existence derives from the fundamentally relational character of human being. Given that God, neighbor, and nature are constitutive of what it means to be human, the purpose of human life lies in being in proper relationship to each member of that triad.

This is especially the case with respect to God since, with reference to Augustine, Sittler affirms that "the human is created for transcendence."[34] States Sittler:

---

[33]See Bakken, "The Ecology of Grace," 301-308 for a helpful explication of this theme in Sittler's writings.

[34]Sittler, *Gravity and Grace*, 27.

> We are formed for God; we are formed to be in relation to that which was before we were, from which we proceed, and in which we will ultimately end. Faith is a longing. Humankind is created to grasp more than we can grab, to probe for more than we can ever handle or manage.[35]

In Sittler's view, "man is what he is because he is related to that one [God]."[36] Indeed, "the fundamental term *imago Dei* is not a term that points to a substance, an attribute, or a specifiable quality, but one which specifies a relation," namely, the relation of humanity with God.[37] In language strikingly similar to the first question of the Heidelberg Catechism, which itself is indebted to the opening lines of Calvin's *Institutes,* Sittler affirms: "Knowing *who* we are is a reality that depends finally on *whose* we are."[38] As Sittler asserts: "He [the human] is *relational* in his structure; and the ultimate relation is [with] a Creator."[39]

Sittler's emphasis not only on the relational nature of human being, but on the centrality of and relationship to God is an important contribution to a Christian ecological theology. Such a theocentric orientation well captures one of the major themes of the Bible and clearly articulates a dominant strand of the Christian tradition--from Augustine's longing heart to Calvin's *sensus divinitatis* to the recent work of James Gustafson. And as both Sittler and Gustafson argue, such an assertion also comports well with modern science, e.g., the displacment of humankind in both time and space from the center of the universe. Anthropocentrism in its usual guises is no longer viable. As Gustafson puts it, while humankind is no doubt the measur*er* of all things, pace Protagoras, "there are some good reasons for asking in our time and in light of the Western religious tradition whether the apparent assumption

---

[35]Ibid.

[36]Sittler, "Ecological Commitment," 174.

[37]Ibid.

[38]Sittler, *Grace Notes,* 113; cf. Sittler, *Structure,* 5.

[39]Joseph Sittler, "In the Light of Our Biblical Tradition," in *What is the Nature of Man?: Images of Man in Our American Culture,* no editor (Philadelphia: The Christian Education Press, 1959), 188. As Sittler says on p. 12 of *Gravity and Grace*: "Our God relationship is the first building block of this structure" of constitutive forces.

that man is the moral measure of all things can be sustained."[40] Or as Holmes Rolston argues: "Man may be (in some advanced senses) the only *measurer* of things, but it does not follow that man is the only *measure* of things."[41] As Gustafson rightly concludes: "God does not exist simply for the service of man; man exists for the service of God."[42] Sittler's theocentrism is an important reminder that humans are creatures who find their being and identity ultimately in God.

For Sittler, being in right relationship with God means many things, but perhaps most centrally and not surprisingly it involves the acceptance of divine grace. Again following Augustine, Sittler affirms that humans are faulted and incapable of saving themselves and so in need of help. God, whose reality and essence is grace, accepts and remolds sin-plagued humans in order that they might be healing balms of love in a sin-sick world. As Sittler insists:

> Our acceptance of God does not imply mutuality. It [God's acceptance of us] is a word spoken to us--and it is incredible....What marks the words *acceptance by God* is the unconditional fact that God accepts precisely the unacceptable. The holy accepts, goes after, and loves the sinner....That God accepts me is crazy.[43]

Sittler here describes, to use Augustine's term, prevenient grace. He further claims that "the miracle of the divine acceptance, the amazing grace of it, can open us up and make us more generous, charitable, just, and accepting."[44] Hence the purpose of human life, whatever else it means for Sittler, involves a relationship with God, made possible by divine grace, which engenders more Christ-like action. Using terms from my own tradition, Christians, having acknowledged their guilt and accepted the grace of God, are

---

[40]James Gustafson, *Ethics from a Theocentric Perspective: Theology and Ethics* (Chicago: University of Chicago, 1981), 91.

[41]Rolston, *Environmental Ethics*, 32.

[42]Gustafson, *Ethics*, 342. See also, more recently, James Gustafson, *A Sense of the Divine: The Natural Environment from a Theocentric Perspective* (Cleveland: Pilgrim, 1994).

[43]Sittler, *Grace Notes*, 111.

[44]Ibid.

empowered to live lives of gratitude to God, attempting to be agents of shalom in a troubled world.

This aspect of Sittler's theology of grace also is necessary ingredient in a Christian ecological theology. Sittler's large view of grace presupposes an equally expansive and profound view of sin. As recent ecological disasters all too readily illustrate, there seem to be few bounds to either the depth or the intractability of human perversity. As Sittler remarks: "I have no great hope that human cussedness will somehow be quickly modified."[45] Yet because of who God is and what God does--because God is a God of unbounded grace, Sittler declares, "I still go around planting trees on the campus."[46] Both the necessity and prevenience of grace must be acknowledged in any Christian theology consonant with Christian tradition and human experience and able to inspire credible hope for our common future.

An important implication of Sittler's expansive doctrine of grace is the shattering of "the false separation of sacred and secular."[47] If grace is as wide and deep as Sittler says it is--if, to use Peter Bakken's language, there is "cosmological and ecological breadth as well as existential depth" to grace[48]--then the belief that some activities or social spheres or aspects of life are outside the scope of grace is false. Being agents of shalom cannot properly be confined, for example, to private affairs, or personal ethics, or so-called religious life. As Sittler observes in his famous New Delhi speech:

> Our vocabulary of praise has become personal, pastoral, too purely spiritual, static. We have not affirmed as inherent in Christ...the world-political, the world economical, the world asethetic, and all the other commanded orderings of actuality which flow from the ancient summons to tend the garden of the Lord.[49]

Sittler rightly reminds Christians that "God is interested in a lot of things besides religion. God is the Lord and Creator of all life, and

---

[45]Sittler, "Speeches," 41.
[46]Ibid.
[47]Sittler, *Structure*, 80.
[48]Bakken, "The Ecology of Grace," 203.
[49]Sittler, "Called to Unity," 12.

there are manifestations of the holy in its celebration or in its repudiation--in every aspect of the common life."[50] Or, with respect to the Apostles' Creed, Sittler affirms:

> We must expand our doctrine of God to acknowledge that he is not only the Lord to whom I flee in times of trouble, but he is also the maker of heaven and earth--God of all that is. When we say, "I believe in the Holy Spirit, the Lord and giver of life," the reference is not just to religious life, devotional life, prayer-book life. It means all of life.[51]

In sum, if the scope of grace is as wide and deep as creation itself, then *nothing* lies beyond the bounds of God's love or should lie outside the borders of Christian concern. Service to God and to neighbor cannot be delimited to certain typically religious activities.

Mention of service to neighbor points to the second item in the triad God, neighbor, nature. For Sittler, the authentic goal of human existence also necessarily involves a vision of right relationships with other humans. One of Sittler's favorite ways of expressing this is to speak of faith active in love: "Love and faith are not, in the New Testament, alternative or opposing terms. Faith is the name for the new God-relationship whereby the will of God who himself establishes the relationship is made actual. And that will is love. Faith active in love is alone faith."[52] Like Martin Luther in his treatise *The Freedom of a Christian,* who despite his portrayal of the book of James as an "epistle full of straw" was following its message that faith without works is dead, Sittler insists that faith must "work where love reveals need."[53] The Christian is free from sin through faith in God yet bound by love to serve the neighbor in need. Faith frees us not only from sin but for service--a service which finds the needy through the eyes of love.

---

[50]Sittler, *Gravity and Grace,* 95.

[51]Ibid., 35. On p. 205 of "The Necessity of Faith," *The Christian Scholar* 38 (September 1955), Sittler states that "the faith-relationship...creates an existence for the individual which colors everything that he touches, everything that he knows."

[52]Joseph Sittler, "Ethics and the New Testament Style," *Union Seminary Quarterly Review* 13 (May 1958): 35.

[53]Ibid., 36.

Contrary to much of contemporary culture, Sittler perceptively contends that "love is not merely an affection" since affections cannot be commanded and yet in the New Testament love is commanded.[54] To account for the multivalent character of love, Sittler distinguishes between liking and loving one's neighbor. He then argues that "though I cannot will myself to feel an oceanic affection for all people, I can acknowledge my bond with the whole of creation."[55] This acknowledgment is the basis for a sense of concern and obligation which extends beyond affections. As Sittler affirms in explicating the relationship between love and justice: "In the broad context of human solidarity the exercise of love is realized in transaffectional justice. Real love grasps the hand that need holds out. Needs cry out from millions I will never met. Justice is love operating at a distance."[56] Justice is love actualized in cases where the feeling of affection is less strong and does not easily compel one to appropriate action.

However, Sittler's conception of the relationship between love and justice is somewhat problematic, or at least unclear. Unlike those who see love and justice as different and unrelated, e.g., some readings of Luther, or different and opposed, e.g., Nygren, Sittler suggests that love and justice are different yet positively related-- similar, for example, to the views of Augustine or Reinhold Niebuhr. More exactly, while Sittler argues that we should "seek justice without identifying justice and love,"[57] he also claims that justice extends the reach of love to include distant neighbors in need.

So Sittler seems to hold that love and justice are in some sense dialectically related. But the precise nature of this relationship is unclear. Is justice necessarily or always a form of love? Is love always realized merely in acts of justice? If justice is respect for people's rights and love is care for people's needs, then can their interrelationship be construed in the ways Sittler suggests? Finally, what precise kind of love and what precise type of justice is being spoken of here? Traditionally at least four types

---

[54]Sittler, *Gravity and Grace*, 116.
[55]Ibid.
[56]Ibid.
[57]Sittler, "Ethics and the New Testament Style," 36.

of justice--contractural, retributive, distributive, and substantive--
and four kinds of love--*erôs, storgê, philia,* and *agapê*--are
distinguished. Sittler distinguishes between liking and loving--akin
to the distinction between *philia* and *agapê,* but further distinctions
are needed if greater clarity is to be achieved.

Thirdly and finally, for Sittler the authentic goal of human
existence necessarily entails right relationships with our non-
human neighbors. This theme is more fully addressed later in this
chapter; however, it is important here to note Sittler's distinction
between looking and beholding. Proper relationships with the
natural world, Sittler rightly reminds us, will not occur without the
acquisition of a "sense for the world." And this "sense for the
world" can be gained only if a different kind of attending to the
world is adopted. As Sittler correctly observes:

> The word "behold" lies upon that which is beheld with a kind of
> tenderness which suggests that things in themselves have their
> own wondrous authenticity and integrity. I am called upon in such
> a saying ["Behold the lilies of the field"] not simply to "look" at the
> nonself but to "regard" things with a kind of spiritual honoring of
> the immaculate integrity of things which are not myself.[58]

Only if humans move beyond mere looking to a wonder-full
beholding of the other in "its infinite preciousness, irreplaceability,
and beauty" will they be moved to act responsibly and so enter into
the kind of relationship that is necessary for the flourishing of all
creation. And, in the words of Aldo Leopold, this kind of perception
"cannot be purchased with either learned degrees or dollars."[59]

One necessary condition for such a conversion in perspective,
as indicated by Sittler's language in the quote above, is the
acknowledgment of the integrity of the other--in this case the
natural world. There is, declares Sittler, "a given integrity built into
the variety that issues forth from the fountain of life."[60] We must
not only acknowledge but also honor this integrity--"the integrity
in the thingliness of the thing itself."[61] One way of honoring this

---

[58]Sittler, "Ecological Commitment," 175.
[59]Leopold, *Sand County Almanac,* 292.
[60]Sittler, "Ecological Commitment," 176.
[61]Ibid.

creaturely integrity, states Sittler, is to distinguish between proper
and improper use. Employing Augustine's distinction between use
and enjoyment, Sittler argues: "To enjoy means to let a thing be
itself and rejoice in it. So the first relation we have to the earth is to
enjoy it, that is, understand its strangeness, its structure, its utility,
its beauty because, says Augustine, if you enjoy a thing, you will not
abuse it."[62] Sittler maintains that this "doesn't mean that the
natural world is not to be used; it is made for use. A forest has a
lifetime; it should be harvested."[63] But he argues that "if you understand and enjoy forests, then you will use them in relationship to
their integrity, their own quality and nature."[64] Being in proper
relationship with nature does not preclude appropriate use, but it
does preclude abuse or "use without grace."[65]

In this regard Sittler, like Ruether, perceptively and properly
recognises the interconnections between the abuse of persons and
the abuse of nonhuman creatures. In response to a book by Richard
Neuhaus which severely criticizes the ecological movement, Sittler
eloquently argues that

> Mr. Neuhaus knows very well that the human brutality he records
> is of a piece with the less dramatic and quieter fault to which
> attention is called in these essays [*Essays on Nature and Grace*]: i.e.,
> that all abuse is a distortion of right use, for persons as for all things.
> What is not regarded as a grace will be disgraced into use without
> care.[66]

The domination of women, African-Americans, and the poor is "of
a piece with" the domination of California condors, giant sequoias,
and Canadian Shield lakes. All abuse, whether of human or of non-
humans neighbors, is linked. As Peter Bakken correctly notes:
"Sittler therefore believed that ecological degradation and social
injustice shared a common root."[67] So also, Sittler rightly, if only
implicitly, affirms that only a concept like ecojustice, which links

---

[62]Sittler, "Speeches," 21.
[63]Ibid.
[64]Ibid.
[65]Ibid.
[66]Sittler, *Essays*, 133; cf. 119.
[67]Bakken, "The Ecology of Grace," 300; cf. 308, 333.

ecological harmony and social justice, is adequate to describe the comprehensive vision of creaturely flourishing to which humans everywhere should aspire. In sum, Sittler's vision of the purpose or the authentic goal of human life, whatever else it entails, involves right relationships not only with God and human neighbors, but also with the nonhuman creatures of the earth.

Ontology

Like Ruether, Sittler does not explicitly present an ontology. And as with Ruether, this in itself is no reason for criticism since such a task is not Sittler's primary concern as a theologian, especially a theologian who admits that "my way of reflection is too impressionistic to deserve the adjective 'systematic.'"[68] However, Sittler does have an implicit, and at times explicitly articulated, ontology. Teasing out Sittler's ontological assumptions provides further insight into his contributions to a Christian ecological theology.

The Coherence of Creation

With his many references to ecology Sittler clearly emphasizes the coherent unity of creation. As indicated previously, Sittler constantly speaks of the "ecologically intricate structure" and "ecologically integrated structure" of the ecosystems of the earth. Everything is related to everything else to such an extent that, like a fine piece of cloth, "you pull a thread here, and it vibrates throughout the whole fabric."[69] Indeed, for Sittler, echoing the words of Aldo Leopold, "the environment is not just a dumb resource, but it is a living organism," and so there is a Gestalt-like wholeness to creation.[70] Creation is more than simply an aggregate of elements. One can properly speak of creation as a whole as well as the whole of creation. Creation has a oneness, an integrity, a unity of being.

---

[68]Sittler, "Speeches," 20; cf. Sittler, *Grace Notes*, 24.

[69]Sittler, *Gravity and Grace*, 22.

[70]Sittler, "Speeches," 37. For an excellent comparison of Sittler and Leopold, see Bakken, "The Ecology of Grace."

Furthermore, creation is not just a unified whole, but an interdependent whole. The various non-human creatures are dependent upon each other and humanity is equally dependent upon "the entire vast, cosmic, all-engendering, and all-enfolding matrix."[71] As stated in chapter three, according to Sittler the natural world is "an interlaced web of origin and sustenance." It is the "life-sustaining placenta" of human existence. Interdependence is indeed an essential feature of existence, exemplified in countless ways: food chains, the hydrological cycle, the exchange of energy, the recycling of waste , and so on.

This physics of an interdependent, coherent, and unified creation, contends Sittler, necessarily implies a metaphysics of relations--more specifically, an "ontology of relations." Espousing a view similar to William James' radical empiricism, with its emphasis on ontic relations, or perhaps closer to the process metaphysics of Whitehead, whom he approvingly quotes,[72] Sittler claims, as mentioned previously, that "there is no ontology of isolated entities, or instances, of forms, of processes, whether we are reflecting about God or man or society or the cosmos." Given what we know from both the Bible and modern science, the only possible Christian ontology is "an ontology of community, of communion, of ecology." Posits Sittler: "'Being itself' may be a relation, not an entitative thing."[73] Reality is relational--a unified, coherent, interdependent whole.

Such an ontology is a considerable advance over much of the metaphysics of Western thought. Having listened to and learned from both the ancient scriptures and modern science, Sittler's "ontology of community" accurately captures certain key properties of reality that are ignored or minimized in other ontologies. In so doing such an ontology provides not only a more adequate foundation for an ecological theology, but also a more solid basis for an ecological ethic. As Aldo Leopold succinctly puts it: "All ethics rest upon a single premise: that the individual is a member of a

---

[71]Sittler, *Essays*, 109.

[72]Sittler, "A Christology of Function," 123.

[73]Sittler, "Ecological Commitment," 174. For references to a "Christian ontology," see Sittler, *Essays*, 59, and "The Presence and Acts," 121.

community of interdependent parts."[74] If such a claim is true, then an ontology which conceptualizes being in terms of community will more firmly ground an ethic of ecojustice.

One major problem, however, with Sittler's ontological musings is that that is precisely what they are--musings. Sittler's articulation of an "ontology of relations" is more of a promissory note than a programmatic statement. Sittler intimates a direction to be pursued rather than an agenda to be followed. As Peter Bakken observes, Sittler "never developed this striking proposal [of a relational ontology] into a metaphysical system of his own."[75] Yet as Bakken also notes, "while Sittler's main interests might be categorized as rhetorical, phenomenological, and proclamatory or pastoral, he seems to have presupposed a certain kind of ontological backing for his proposals in those genres."[76] Now it is Sittler's extraordinary gift that these musings were so eloquent and so timely, and hence it would be unfair to hold him accountable for something not central to his own theological project. However, his failure to develop further the "ontological backing" for his more strictly theological proposals points to the need to develop in sufficient detail an ontology faithful to scripture and tradition and informed by the best of modern science.

Despite the limitations of his reflections on ontology, and in addition to the assets of his perspective mentioned above, Sittler provides a number of important reminders and creative suggestions. For example, he perceptively cautions against thinking that, because of the contemporary fascination with and knowledge about "nature", there is a proper understanding of *creation*. Just because we live in a scientific culture in many ways enamored with the exploration of the natural world does not necessarily mean that we speak about or know of creation. While most people use the terms creation and nature interchangeably, there is a significant difference. Insists Sittler:

---

[74]Leopold, *A Sand County Almanac*, 203.
[75]Bakken, "The Ecology of Grace," 248. Creede also notes the unfinished nature of Sittler's thought, e.g., on p. 426 of "Logos and Lord."
[76]Bakken, "The Ecology of Grace," 249.

> It is a fallacy to suppose that because we know about and think about atoms, genes, astrophysical space and organization we are thereby thinking about the creation. That fallacy arose out of the ironical fact that human exuberance about the knowledge of and control of aspects of nature has really little to do with nature-as-creation. *Creation* is a religious and philosophical term; it is not a term whose proper reference is simply the fact of, or the possible structure and process of, the world. The term "creation" contains and requires a God-postulation. Until we get this through our heads, and admit nature as the *creation* into our reflective nexus, and permit nature there to retain its intransigent reality, we shall neither theologize soberly nor be theologically guided to act constructively.[77]

As Robert Quam similarly argues, it makes a difference whether the natural world is spoken of as creation or as nature. Besides being more faithful to the language of the Bible, speaking of the natural world as creation has the advantage that it implies the solidarity of all creatures before God the Creator, thereby contravening the typical nature/history dualism. Furthermore, envisioning the natural order as creation emphasizes that "human redemption and the redemption of all creation are of a piece."[78]

Since from a Christian perspective "nature" should be construed as *creation*, Sittler appropriately argues that the modern idea of autonomous nature must be repudiated. The natural world is not somehow detached or separate from God--a law unto itself. "Nature is not," says Sittler, "an entity or a process set alongside God having its own autonomy, its own 'insides,' its 'laws.' It is, rather, continuous with the reality of God as Creator."[79] Hence he concludes that "our modern view of nature as by definition not having anything to do with the divine is in complete hiatus with the Old Testament view. There nature comes from God, cannot be apart from God, and is capable of bearing the 'glory' of God."[80] Over against certain forms of naturalism Sittler maintains that "the universe is not closed to God's agency."[81] While the universe is

---

[77]Sittler, *Essays*, 99.

[78]Robert Quam, "Creation or Nature?: A Manner of Speaking," *Word and World* 11 (Spring 1991): 134-136.

[79]Sittler, *Essays*, 24.

[80]Ibid., 37.

[81]Ibid., 95.

closed in the ecological sense of being a closed system of energy and matter, it is not a closed system with respect to divine action.

If nature is not autonomous, neither is it divine. As Sittler asserts: "The world is not God, but it is God's." The world is not God, hence pantheism is ruled out. But the world is God's, therefore naturalism, at least in its atheistic forms, is precluded. And since Sittler affirms that this God is not an absentee landlord, but the creator and sustainer of the world, deism also is not a live option. In a culture in which the rejection of the autonomy of nature often leads to the divinization of nature, Sittler's firm rejection of *both* naturalism and pantheism, combined with his articulation of an alternative perspective which preserves the distinction between God and the cosmos while yet strongly emphasizing their intimate relatedness, is a noteworthy feature of his theology.

Furthermore, Sittler is surely right to argue that if the natural world is more properly seen as creation, and if such a claim implies the solidarity of all creatures *coram Deo*, then it is fitting to speak of nonhuman creatures as siblings. "Nature," says Sittler, "is God's other creation who stands alongside of us with her own individuality, integrity, vitality."[82] The earth is our sister, sharer of our sorrows and joys who, to employ Sittler's eloquence again, "unquenchably sings out her violated wholeness, and in groaning and travail awaits with man the restoration of all things."[83] Paul Santmire employs the same image when he speaks of the world as "brother earth."[84] Nature is not our mother; the Church is our mother. But nonhuman creatures are our siblings, standing not beneath us but "alongside of us" as kin of the same parent. The earth also asks that its individuality and integrity be respected. It too awaits the redemption of all things. Humans and non-humans alike are fellow creatures--relatives--before the creator God.

The image of nonhuman creatures as siblings is also one way Sittler suggests that the natural world is much more responsive than usually thought. Without re-enchanting the natural order

---

[82]Sittler, "Speeches," 38.
[83]Sittler, "A Theology for Earth," 370.
[84]H. Paul Santmire, *Brother Earth* (New York: Thomas Nelson, 1970).

with quasi-divine status or attributing human-like agency to birches and bears, Sittler nonetheless rightly speaks of a kind of response-ability appropriate to non-human creatures. For example, Sittler affirms:

> Man is not alone in this world, not even when his aloneness is unalleviated by the companionship of the fellowman. The creation is a community of abounding life--from the invisible microbes to the highly visible elephants, the vastness of mountains, the sweep of the seas, the expanse of land. These companions of our creaturehood are not only *there*: they are there as things without which I cannot be at all! They surround, support, nourish, delight, allure, challenge, and talk back to us.[85]

If our non-human companions can "talk back to us" and are our fellow creatures with whom we are in solidarity, then the common view of the natural world as an enemy to be vanquished is wrongheaded. As Sittler with justified indignation exclaims, such an adversarial perspective illustrates "the depth of the perversion that popularly prevails as regards man's living bond to nature" and displays the "stupor of mind" all too prevalent in today's world.[86]

The responsiveness of creation and the possibility of creature-specific forms of agency has been explored by others besides Sittler. For example, Brian Walsh, Marianne Karsh, and Nik Ansell claim that both a careful reading of the Bible and a creational listening to the earth lead to the conclusion that trees, for example, have their own peculiar kind of responsiveness.[87] Similarly, Paul Santmire argues that because of "a certain *mysterious activity*" of non-human creatures, "man properly can and occasionally does exist in a relation to his material-vital world which is neither an I-Thou relation as such nor an I-It relation."[88] We must, therefore, "speak of a third type of relation, which for the

---

[85]Sittler, "Evangelism and the Care of the Earth," 102.

[86]Sittler, *Essays*, 126.

[87]This claim is found in the stimulating (but yet unpublished) paper "Trees, Forestry, and the Responsiveness of Creation," by Brian Walsh, Marianne Karsh, and Nik Ansell of the Institute for Christian Studies in Toronto.

[88]Santmire, "I-Thou, I-It, and I-Ens," 266.

lack of better terminology can be called the *I-Ens relation.*"[89] That the natural world exhibits this kind of responsiveness is a claim often ignored or ridiculed as "unscientific." However, Sittler rightly insists that such a claim must be taken seriously and categories developed which express the possibility of this kind of relation. His insistence must be heeded by those articulating a Christian ecological theology.

The Mutability of Creation

In addition to his emphasis on the unity, coherence, interdependence, and responsiveness of creation, Sittler also points to the dynamic character of creation. As previously mentioned, Sittler insists that because we live in "an evolutionary ecosystem" and "evolving world-process" we must understand "creation as continuous" and "life as dynamic, in-motion, developmental." As Sittler concludes: "There is no such thing as a steady-state."[90] Indeed, as Sittler puts it in a memorable aphorism: "The history of nature is the context for the nature of history." And this dynamism of both the historical and the natural worlds, Sittler rightly acknowledges, is "terrifying." As Langdon Gilkey astutely observes, like the experience of contingency, the experience of relativity and temporality--of potential meaninglessness and uncontrollable temporal passage--can be occasions for profound anxiety.[91]

Sittler's emphasis on the dynamic and evolutionary nature of creation provide him with another basis for criticizing anthropocentrism since the greatly expanded sense of space and time provided by an evolutionary perspective relativizes the place of the human in the life of the cosmos. As Sittler argues, given "the finitude, the limitedness, the miniscule facticity of man, the notion of the illimitability of space tends to reduce the human in such a way that he is a very bad second to the space of the cosmos."[92] So

---

[89]Ibid., 269, 266. Other advocates of such a view of creaturely responsiveness include John Muir and Barbara McClintock.

[90]Sittler, "The Presence and Acts," 123.

[91]Langdon Gilkey, *Naming the Whirlwind* (Indianapolis: Bobbs-Merrill, 1969), part II, chap. 3.

[92]Sittler, "Speeches," 32.

also, "just as the dimension of space now has an infinite quantity, so the dimension of time has been equally exploded."[93] If the evolutionary character of creation points to the virtual illimitability of both space and time, then the significance of the human as well as the value of the non-human must be radically reassessed. Peter Bakken nicely summarizes the conclusions Sittler draws from his reflections on contemporary cosmology:

> The meaning of nature cannot rest solely on the meaning of human history; the value and destiny of the rest of the universe is not reducible to the needs, interests, activities and projects of human beings. The meaning of human being itself must be rethought within the context of a natural world with trans-human meaning.[94]

Sittler reaches this same conclusion via his expansive doctrine of grace. More exactly, Sittler argues that because of God's common grace, the world in all its fullness--especially the non-human world--has meaning and value. As mentioned previously, Sittler describes common or created grace as "that grace which is a power and gift of God the Creator and with which he endows his creation." It is the grace which is inherent in, with, and under creation. Common grace "is exactly the grace that inheres in the world by virtue of the fact that it is a creation of a gracious God." This means that in addition to being "a term wherewith to specify the incarnated presence and historical focus of that Light which is God," grace is also a term for "the created goodness of all reality."[95] There is grace *in* nature and nature exists *as* grace. It follows, argues Sittler, that if there is grace in the natural world, then the natural world has intrinsic or "trans-human value."

Therefore, Sittler asserts, nonhuman creatures have intrinsic value. The natural world and its plethora of creatures have value over and above any instrumental or use value that they may also have. As he argues:

93Ibid.
94Bakken, "The Ecology of Grace," 232.
95Sittler, *Essays*, 64.

> If things cannot continue to be at all except men deal with them
> with due regard for their given structure and need, then there is
> certainly rational warrant that assessment of things according to
> their transutilitarian "good" is an appropriate recognition of an
> intrinsic "good" in things that are.[96]

In other words, if the very existence of things natural is contingent upon respect by humans for their creaturely integrity, then one is rationally justified is believing that such things have value irrespective of any use to humans. Analogous to Kant's third form of the categorical imperative in the *Grundlegung*, Sittler argues that humans should act so that they treat *all creatures* always as an end and never as a means *only*, since not only rational agents but *all beings* have value as ends in themselves. Humans are morally obligated to consider the transutilitarian value of trees, rivers, and mountains. As Sittler acknowledges, this does not necessarily entail that the natural world should not be used. But recognition of the intrinsic value of the natural world does entail that it is a moral patient and so should *at least be considered* in making moral judgements. Sittler concludes that "to evaluate the gift of the world at a sufficient elevation to deal with it sustainingly requires nothing less than a trans-pragmatic evaluation and use."[97] If creation has intrinsic value, then the traditional approach in ethics will not do.

But Sittler argues not just that humans are morally obligated to *consider* the value of the natural world when making ethical decisions, but that humans *actually have* moral duties and obligations toward things non-human. We have an undeniable responsibility to care for the earth. As Sittler claims: "Nature is never, for Jesus, simply a resource out of which we are to dig iron and copper and zinc, and pump oil; it is the theatre of human life-- the garden of our life--which it is our obligation to care for."[98] The natural world is the garden which humankind "is to tend as God's other creation--not to use as a godless warehouse or to rape as a

---

[96]Ibid., 121; cf. Sittler, *Grace Notes*, 90.

[97]Sittler, "The Presence and Acts," 134.

[98]Sittler, *Gravity and Grace*, 13; cf. 21. See also *Grace Notes*, 96, where Sittler speaks of "the Christian responsibility for the care of the earth," and p. 88, where Sittler claims that "the care of the earth is rational, necessary, aesthetic."

tyrant."[99] That there is grace in creation also implies that humans must respect and care for creation. Affirms Sittler: "We must respect, care for, learn from that residency of the grace of the Creator which lies in all that has been created--learn from it, enjoy the difference, and honor its created right to be."[100] In this context Sittler not only argues against the traditional interpretation of dominion as domination in Gen. 1:26-28, but also rightly points to Gen. 2:15. In this neglected but important text humans are commanded to till and keep--or more faithful to the Hebrew, serve and protect--the garden that is the earth.[101] Hence Sittler claims that "the Christian is called, commanded, interiorly obligated to care for the earth as part of *being a Christian*."[102] Care for creation is an essential part of authentic Christian discipleship.

Sittler's reflections on the dynamic character of creation contain many important insights. For example, he surely is right to speak of the need to understand the processual or developmental character of creation. The history of "nature" is indeed the context for the nature of history and thus any dualism between nature and history is misguided. Furthermore, the quite late arrival of humanity in the evolutionary scheme and the vastness of the cosmos do undercut certain kinds of anthropocentrism, thus fostering a healthy theocentrism which displaces us from the center of the universe.The natural world does have trans-human value-- witness the Leviathan is Psalm 104. And all humans are called to care for the earth. Christians especially are called to care for creation as part of what it means to be faithful disciples.

Perhaps most importantly from a strictly theological point of view, Sittler rightly affirms that creation is *intrinsically* grace. Grace is not some later addition, but is constitutive of creation. Grace is an essential and not merely accidental property. Peter Bakken nicely summarizes Sittler's main claim:

---

[99]Sittler, "A Theology for Earth," 372.

[100]Sittler, "Perils," 77.

[101]See, e.g., Sittler, "Speeches," 37-38; "Evangelism," 103; *Gravity and Grace*, 18.

[102]Sittler, "Evangelism," 101. One of Sittler's sermons well captures his message: "The Care of the Earth." See chapter 7 of Joseph Sittler, *The Care of the Earth and Other University Sermons* (Philadelphia: Fortress, 1964).

The relationship between grace and creation is not extrinsic but intrinsic. Nature does not become a bearer of grace by an arbitrary divine *fiat* that supervenes on the prior fact of creation as a concession to humanity's physicality. Rather, as created, loved, and incarnationally entered by a gracious God, it cannot but be a theatre of grace. It is not a reality that exists apart from grace that is then arbitrarily employed by God to communicate grace; its graced character is given to it together with its original being and integrity.[103]

Thus while there may be grace apart from creation, e.g., in the Trinity, there is no creation apart from grace. In other words, assuming the *ex nihilo* character of creation, grace is a necessary but not sufficient condition for creation.

There are, however, a number of problems with certain of Sittler's claims and arguments. For example, while Sittler speaks of the need to understand creation as continuous, it is unclear precisely what this claim means since there are at least two different senses of *creatio continua*. Does Sittler mean the continual creation of absolutely new things *de novo*, or does he mean the continual process of changing already existing things into relatively new things, or both? The unfinished and impressionistic nature of Sittler's theological reflections again leaves some important matters unclear.

Furthermore, with Sittler's emphasis on process it is unclear how exactly creation is ordered and structured. Sittler admits that all is not absolute flux, yet he fails to specify how it is that creation is in some respects stable and relatively unchanging. Sittler alludes to the role of the divine Word in the creation and ordering of the cosmos and refers to the Torah as "the structure of all things as God intends them."[104] However, it is unclear why and how creation exhibits the orderliness that it does. Perhaps this request for greater clarity is asking too much from Sittler. This important issue, however, must be addressed. If the cosmos is fundamentally characterized by change, how is constancy best accounted for? Given the developmental nature of the created world, what does it

---

[103]Bakken, "The Ecology of Grace," 295; cf. 317.
[104]Sittler, "Speeches," 17, 36.

mean also to affirm that development is often not chaotic but ordered, not to mention, as many Christians would wish to further claim, purposefully ordered? These questions of ontology merit more attention than Sittler is able or willing to give them.

Theology

As in chapter five, there are here two basic theological issues under consideration, namely, the being and the action of God, both of which are again addressed at the same time. And as stated before, these issues are very closely related to the question of the relationship between God and the world. How one construes the being and action of God involves decisions about divine transcendence and immanence, and conversely, beliefs about the absoluteness and relatedness of God vis-a-vis creation are implied by beliefs regarding divine attributes and agency.

Also as indicated previously, thinkers such as McGinn, Neville, and Gilkey all argue that any adequate Christian theology must articulate how God is both transcendent and immanent. God must be not envisioned as so distinct from the world as to be unrelated to the world. Nor must God be envisioned as so related to the cosmos that there is no significant difference between God and the cosmos. In short, *both* transcendence and immanence are necessary features of an adequate Christian ecological theology.

The Triune God of Grace

Sittler is not only very aware of the centrality of these issues, but he articulates a theology which meets the conditions specified above. For example, Sittler explicitly affirms all four of the basic constituents of the Christian creation tradition--what Bernard McGinn calls "the four D's": dependence, distinction, decision, and duration.[105] According to Sittler, "God is the fountain of all livingness"--that one from whom all things flow. God is the

---

[105]McGinn, "Do Christian Platonists Really Believe in Creation?" 209-210. In addition to those criteria listed by McGinn, for any Christian doctrine of creation one must add three additional D's: design, defect, and delight.

necessary ground of creation upon which creation depends for its existence. God is also "the maker of heaven and earth" and thus "God is not the same as the world." God is the unconditioned other distinct from creation. In addition, God is not compelled to create at all or forced to create a certain thing in a certain way, but creates in freedom--"the freedom of God in his grace" being "a right designation of the central substance of the Christian confession." God is a genuinely free agent. And God exhibits an "eternal livingness." God is an eternal being. In short, there is, says Sittler, "a Creator-creature structure of existence" in which God is "the holy Source of all that is."[106]

These affirmations about the being and action of God, however, while necessary are not yet sufficient for a fully adequate Christian theology since they can be taken as affirming only the transcendence and not the immanence of God. That God is posited to be the eternal, free, distinct ground upon which creation depends does not necessarily imply that God is integrally related to creation. While such an affirmation does suggest that creation is inextricably related to God and that God is related to creation in certain respects, it does *not* yet affirm that the relatedness of God to creation is as intimate and profound as the biblical narrative often suggests.

Sittler recognizes that more is needed than merely an affirmation of "the four D's," and properly and clearly insists that while God is distinct from creation, God is also intimately and profoundly related to creation. As mentioned previously, he claims that "God is not identical with but is present in" what God creates, redeems, and restores. God, says Sittler, is integrally related to "chipmunks, squirrels, hippopotamuses, galaxies, and light years." As Sittler nicely puts it in an already quoted aphorism: "God is not identified with the world, for he *made* it; but God is not separate from his world, either. For *He* made it." God is not identical with the world because God is the creator of the world. But God is not separate from the world because the maker of heaven and earth is, as the emphasis on "He" implies, a certain kind of God.

---

[106]Sittler, *Structure*, 70.

The assumption in the second part of the statement above is that God is not aloof or uncaring, fickle or undependable. The God of the Bible, says Sittler, is a covenant-keeping God characterized by "faithfulness in mercy and judgment."[107] The maker of heaven and earth is "the Giver and Promiser who does not abandon what he has given or renounce his promises."[108] Despite admitting that "I have no great expectation that...humanity's care of the earth will improve much," Sittler also acknowledges, as mentioned above, that the God who will not abandon creation gives sufficient hope to allow him to "go around planting trees on the campus." In the end for Sittler, God is faithful since God's will is "a loving will."[109] Sittler here affirms one of the basic beliefs of the Christian faith: God can be trusted because God is loving and faithful.

With his contention that grace is perhaps the single most comprehensive term to describe the being and action of God Sittler rightly emphasizes the loving and faithful character of God. God can be trusted, states Sittler, precisely because God is a God of grace and "the God of grace *is* a God of grace in the fullness of his being." As Sittler reminds us, grace characterizes *all* three persons of the Trinity since it is the "fundamental reality of God." Hence *all* of God's actions, not only as redeemer but also as creator and sanctifier, exhibit the grace that God is. Given the implicit tendency in the various practices of the Church to associate the grace of God with the work of Christ and thus with only the second person of the Trinity, Sittler's stress on the fullness of grace is a needed corrective, serving as a reminder that the creation and sustenance of the world are equally acts of grace by a gracious God.

However, one of the assets of Sittler's view of grace, namely, its expansiveness and scope, is also a liability. While Sittler makes a number of necessary and important distinctions, the concept of grace tends nevertheless to grow fuzzy. If grace becomes a term for almost everything, then it can easily become a term for virtually nothing. For example, Sittler posits that grace is "the elemental character of God" both in relation to all that is not-God and within

---

[107]Sittler, "The Presence and Acts," 100; cf. *Essays*, 24-25 where Sittler discusses terms like *hesed*.

[108]Sittler, *Essays*, 119; cf. Sittler, *Grace Notes*, 88.

[109]Sittler, *Structure*, 28.

the Trinity itself. Grace "is that particular 'attribute' or reality, or energy, essence, or substance" of God.[110] Grace is also a "term for the created goodness of all reality." Grace is, as it were, built into the structure of being. And on a phenomenological level, grace expresses the "sheer *givenness*-character of life." It is the need-not-have-been character of being.

But even if one agrees with the substance of these various claims, they invite numerous questions. For example, is grace a substance such that one can talk of grace *in* creation? Or is it better to speak of creation as *graced* or an expression of divine grace? In what precise sense is grace "the whole giftedness of life"? In response to questions about the contingency of existence, is grace most appropriately a feature of creation or the creator? And if "the fundamental meaning of grace is the goodness and lovingkindness of God,"[111] then how do these other senses of grace cohere with this basic one? These questions point to certain ambiguities in Sittler's concept of grace.

Sittler's affirmation that grace characterizes all three persons of the Trinity and therefore all of God's actions illustrates that, while critical of the traditional language of Nicea and Chalcedon, Sittler articulates his doctrine of the Trinity along fairly traditional lines. What is rather unique is Sittler's combination of Western and Eastern trinitarian terms and concepts in a single perspective. For example, by employing the language of divine energy, a typically Eastern concept, Sittler emphasizes the unity of divine action, a typically Western concern. The doctrine of the Trinity affirms "that the life and energy of each person of the Trinity is the function of all."[112] As Sittler puts it: "God as the all-engendering Father, God as the absolutely obedient Son, God as the illuminating and empowering Spirit constitute one action."[113] Commenting on the often repeated benediction of St. Paul found in 2 Corinthians, Sittler says:

---

[110]Sittler, *Essays*, 82.
[111]Ibid., 24.
[112]Sittler, "The Presence and Acts," 128.
[113]Ibid., 105; cf. 103.

You know the benedictory words in Paul's letter, "Now may the grace of our Lord Jesus Christ and the love of God and the communion of the Holy Spirit" and so forth--this also invites the mind to suppose that God is love but Jesus is grace and the fellowship belongs to the third person of the Trinity (he creates the community). There is a legitimacy to dividing things up that way. But we forget, if I may say it banally, that there is an inter-com system with the Trinity, too, so that the powers of each belong to all and you cannot cut up the reality of God simply along these modal lines.[114]

In his stress on the fact that "the life of each is a function of all" or that "the powers of each belong to all" Sittler follows both Gregory of Nyssa, who in *Concerning We Should Not Think of Saying That There Are Not Three Gods* argues that there is one energy or activity involving all three persons of the God-head, and also Augustine, who in book 15 of *On the Trinity* presents the triad *memoria, intelligentia,* and *voluntas* as a help in understanding the Trinity while also insisting that these features are interchangeable in God and so cannot be confined to a single member of the Trinity.

With his emphasis on divine unity, however, Sittler leaves himself open to the charge of modalism. While rightly emphasizing the single action of God in all three persons-- thus disavowing the view of the Trinity that exclusively identifies love with the first person, grace with the second person, and communion with the third person--Sittler fails to specify clearly what distinguishes the persons of the Trinity from each other. As he says in the quote above, "there is a legitimacy to dividing things up that way," i.e., dividing the Trinity up in terms of love, grace, and communion, but Sittler never addresses *exactly why* that is a legitimate way to speak of the Trinity. Sittler refers to the "all-engendering Father," the "absolutely obedient Son," and the "illuminating and empowering Spirit," apparently implying that there are certain differences between the divine persons, but he does not explicate the basis for this claim. In what respects, if any, are the persons of the Trinity different?

114Sittler, "Speeches," 42.

In short, Sittler emphasizes the unity and oneness of God, affirming a form of trinitarian *perichoresis* or mutual indwelling. But his emphasis on oneness tends to imperil his ability to affirm any significant divine threeness, thereby leading to the impression that he espouses a form of modalistic monarachianism. The problem with this is not simply that Sittler's view of the Trinity is "heterodox"; the problem is that Sittler explicitly wishes "to honor the richness and operational adequacy of the traditional confessions of the trinity" and affirm "the interior relations of Father, Son, and Spirit in a manner that preserves faith's intentions."[115] Insofar as his Trinity leans too far in the direction of divine oneness without also adequately affirming divine threeness, contrary to his own design Sittler risks losing touch with "the traditional confessions" and "faith's intentions." More attention must be given to the distinctive persons within the community of love that is God if Sittler is to make good on his intention to honor the orthodox confessions of the trinity.

Sittler is, nevertheless, correct in his assesment of the importance--indeed necessity--of the doctrine of the Trinity. Sittler argues that the doctrine of the Trinity is necessary for at least three reasons: 1) to express adequately the scope of grace; 2) to develop coherently a cosmic christology; and 3) to ground sufficiently an ecological theology. For example, with respect to the first claim, given the scope of grace evident in scripture, Sittler is justified in arguing that "nothing short of the dogma of the Holy Trinity was adequate to set it forth."[116] Since Christ is seen as the manifestation of grace and incarnation of God, a strict monotheism was unable to do justice to the New Testament witness to God as creator, redeemer, and sanctifier. Some reformulation of theology was necessary. As Sittler argues: "The doctrine of the Trinity arose precisely because of the magnitude of the Christian community's claim about Christ. The community knew that if God is subtracted from Jesus the remainder is not Jesus."[117]

---

[115]Sittler, "The Presence and Acts," 91.
[116]Sittler, *Essays*, 48.
[117]Sittler, "Scope," 331.

The Cosmic Christ

With regard to christology, Sittler is honest enough to acknowledge the genuine plurality in the New Testament and thus recognize the always alluring temptation toward "dogmatic arrangement." He admits that there is no single or simple way of speaking of God in Christ. Yet he also rightly insists that there is "a christological momentum" or "directionality" toward a cosmic christology. Hence it is "legitimate to see a growing magnitude in the christological utterances of the New Testament"--"an ever-widening orbit of christological meaning, scope, and force."[118] In short, there is, says Sittler, a "rhetoric of cosmic extension." As indicated in chapter three, this conclusion is shared by a number of biblical scholars. Despite the diversity of images of the person of Christ and views of the work of Christ in the New Testament, there are good grounds for asserting a cosmic christology.

In seeking to develop a christology adequate to this "rhetoric of cosmic extension" as well as intelligible in the twentieth century, Sittler articulates his "cosmic christology" or "christology for nature." Moira Creede's fine analysis of Sittler's christology is helpful at this point. Employing Rahner's distinction between "metaphysical" and "saving-history" types of christologies, Creede describes the former as *Logos* christology and the latter as Lord christology.[119] The *Logos* tradition, with its emphasis on the pre-existent Word, is a christology from above, while the Lord tradition, with its emphasis on the earthly Jesus, is a christology from below. *Logos* christology is primarily ontological in character while Lord christology is primarily functional in character. *Logos* christology stresses the antecedent glory of Christ while Lord christology stresses the subsequent glory of Christ. And *Logos* christology concentrates on the person of Christ and creation in Christ, while Lord christology concentrates on the work of Christ and redemption.

---

[118]Sittler, *Essays*, 11.
[119]Creede, "Logos and Lord," 238ff.

According to Creede, Sittler articulates "a *Logos*-Lord christology."[120] In other words, Sittler combines elements from these two different christological traditions. That in itself is not unique since the above ideal types are in various ways combined by many theologians. But Sittler joins these traditions in ways especially helpful for an ecological theology. First, Sittler "inverts the traditional emphasis given to person and work in *Logos* christology and maintains that we should see *Logos* christology as primarily an assertion of the cosmic significance of the *work* of Christ."[121] *Logos* christology is "a doctrine of the person of Christ which was given in answer to the problem of interpreting the work of Christ to the Greek world."[122] So Sittler takes a typical feature of Lord christology and makes it central to *Logos* christology.

Second, Sittler "expands the scope of redemption to include the whole creation, emphasizing always the cosmic dimensions of Christ's lordship."[123] If redemption is cosmic in scope, then there is "a universality [to Christ] which brings this viewpoint [Lord christology] very close to *Logos* christology."[124] In other words, Sittler incorporates a typical characteristic of *Logos* christology into Lord christology. Creede concludes that "so closely, then, do the functional and ontological christologies come to one another that they seem interpenetrating rather than parallel."[125] In sum, Sittler brings together important aspects of each type so as to fuse the two into a single perspective.

Creede's analysis is both accurate and perceptive. It, furthermore, illuminates a number of problems in Sittler's attempt to fashion a cosmic christology. As mentioned previously, Sittler does not merely distinguish between functional and essential christology, he argues for the former over the latter. Indeed, Sittler strenuously argues that a christology of function is superior to an essential or ontic christology. For example, Sittler claims:

---

[120]Ibid., 241ff.
[121]Ibid., 241.
[122]Ibid.
[123]Ibid., 242.
[124]Ibid.
[125]Ibid.

Classical terms were expressive of bodies; ours must be expressive of functions. Nicaea operated with the discourse of *statics;* contemporary discourse is permeated through and through with a world view which is dynamic. For us, *persons* are not bodies, but units of force and will; all things are not bodies, but aims, means, creations of these units. The classical relationship between bodies was positional; our understanding of relationship is functional. Christology is therefore called upon to transpose an entire theological vocabulary to conform with a thoroughly functionalized understanding.[126]

Sittler also argues that since "the Nicene Christology...is radically reductive of the amplitude and variety of the biblical witness to God's relation of himself to the world in the person and work of Christ," to undertake "a fresh explication of Christology in terms of functions is appropriate to biblical terms of discourse and congruent with what for better or worse we now are."[127] In addition, Sittler contends "that modern biblical and historical understanding joins [sic] to supply us with a way of thinking which at once preserves the religious intention of Nicea and avoids it categories."[128] Indeed, Sittler claims that "if we move toward a christology of function, we still celebrate the doctrine of the Holy Trinity legitimately but we avoid the question of hypostatic union, of essence, which is not necessary for biblical theology."[129] In sum, Sittler argues that a functional christology is more congruent with modern categories of experience, does greater justice to the witness of the Bible, can be articulated in a way that remains faithful to the creeds and hence the tradition, and avoids certain vexing theological problems.

There are, however, as intimated above, a number of problems with Sittler's strong emphasis on a functional christology. First, if the coherence of Sittler's *Logos*-Lord christology depends upon the interpenetration of functional and essential christologies, as Creede maintains, and if Sittler eschews essential christology as fiercely as he does, then it is altogether unclear how his christology can hang together. In other words, if

---

[126]Sittler, "Christology of Function," 122-123.
[127]Ibid., 123.
[128]Ibid.
[129]Sittler, "Speeches," 23.

Sittler repudiates an inextricable feature of one of the two perspectives that comprise his *Logos*-Lord christology, then his creative synthesis is at best unstable and at worst incoherent.

Furthermore, Sittler's emphasis on functional christology can be construed in at least two ways. On the one hand, Sittler seems to suggest that a functional christology is an alternative to *any* ontological or more speculative theological reflection. A properly and modestly biblical christology of function, Sittler argues, can avoid the unnecessary questions of hypostatic union and divine essence. However, such a claim is highly dubious. As John Courtney Murray persuasively argues, in the early church "it was inevitable that the new question [of ontology and divine essence] should have been asked."[130] Sticking to the mostly functional categories of the Bible was impossible. With respect to the Nicence problem of God Murray states: "The answer is given, as it had to be given, not in the empirical categories of experience, the relational category of presence, or, even, the dynamic categories of power and function, but in the ontological category of substance, which is a category of being."[131] In times ancient or modern philosophical questions about divine being are inevitable. The appropriate stance is not to imagine that one can avoid such questions, but rather to reflect on which categories best address these important questions.

On the other hand, at other times Sittler seems to suggest that a functional christology is an alternative not to any and all philosophically oriented christologies, but to the *particular* christology of Nicea and Chalcedon. That is, a functional christology is seen as an alternative to a christology which employs the categories of being and essence. A proper christology, argues Sittler, must employ an alternative set of metaphysical categories, namely, the categories of process, change, becoming, action--in short, categories of doing rather than being. However, this claim, too, is questionable since Sittler seems to assume, with both his reflections on God and on Christ, that doing can somehow be separated from being. But is it valid to assert that "God is what

---

[130]John Courtney Murray, *The Problem of God* (New Haven: Yale, 1964), 41.
[131]Ibid., 45.

God does" without also asserting that God's activity is dependent upon God's being?[132] Can God be exhaustively described merely in terms of divine action? Is Christ who he is *only* because of what he does? Here too Sittler's christology is inadequate.

Sittler gives a number of arguments in support of a cosmic christology. What could be called his "embeddedness argument" begins with anthropological and ontological premises. Sittler first claims that "I am what I am not only as one with, among, and in self-forming transactions with men; I am who and what I am in relation to the web, structure, process and placenta of nature."[133] Sittler then concludes: "If the self is to be redeemed by Christ, *and if that self is unspecifiable* apart from its embeddedness in the world as nature, then 'the whole creation' of the Book of Genesis and of Romans 8 is seen as the logically necessary scope of christological speech."[134] Similar to Allan Galloway, Sittler argues that a cosmic christology can be avoided only if the human is viewed as somehow separate from nature. But since the human cannot be detached from nature, redemption must be cosmic in scope.

Sittler's conclusion that redemption is cosmic is as important for an ecological theology as it is true; however, Sittler's argument is invalid in its present form. More specifically, a crucial additional premise is missing, namely, the assertion that the human person is unitary in some strong sense. In other words, given that the human is redeemed, and given that the human is embedded in nature, it does not follow that redemption is cosmic unless it is also given that the human which is the object of redemption is not a dualistic being, since a dualistic human could be seen as embedded in nature and yet detached from nature as well. Redemption could thus affect only the one part and not the other and would not then be cosmic.

Another argument for cosmic christology given by Sittler stems from his claim that "if the God of our faith is not God of all, he is not God at all."[135] That is, if God is not seen as "the Lord of nature as well as the Redeemer of sinful people in history," then

---

[132]Sittler, *Gravity and Grace*, 83.
[133]Sittler, "Scope," 333.
[134]Ibid.
[135]Sittler, "Speeches," 36.

God is not big enough to really be God.[136] According to Sittler, God is "the God of everything" or God "is not God at all."[137] All creation must come within the purview of God's control and care if God is truly the God of the Christian faith.

This "all-or-nothing argument" has a deceptive simplicity that is attractive. But it defines a cosmic christology into existence rather than actually arguing for it. In sum, the argument claims: 1) if God exists, then God is the Lord of everything, including the natural world; 2) God exists; 3) therefore, God is the Lord of the natural world. The problem is that the first premise begs the question as to whether and how God is Lord of everything and thus how redemption is cosmic. Again, while the conclusion may be true, the argument is not valid and thus not sound.

Sittler is on surer footing when he argues that creation is sacramental. Similar to his arguments with respect to other themes--e.g., the immanence of God in creation, the intrinsically graced character of creation, creation as a theatre of grace--Sittler affirms that the Incarnation also implies that creation is a sign of divine presence. Since the earth is the place where God's glory became flesh, the ineffable meets us through the effable and material. The presence of God is known in and through the material world. Hence creation is not unimportant or expendable but the very means by which humans know God. Thus as Sittler states, his theology is "a theology of the incarnation applied to nature" rather than a theology "derived from nature." It is a theology of and for "nature" and not a natural theology.

Given the crisis of presence that Sittler astutely perceives, this focus on divine presence--especially in the life, death, and resurrection of Jesus--is particularly important. That is to say, a sacramental theology which emphasizes the incarnation is especially appropriate and timely given the felt absence of God in the lives of many people. Furthermore, given the "cruciform character of human existence," a theology which emphasizes presence takes on added significance. Sittler is absolutely right when he claims that "unless the God before whom we sit, and at

---

[136]Ibid.
[137]Ibid.

whom we gaze, and about whom we think--unless that God has the tormented shape of our human existence, he isn't God enough."[138] Because life itself is cruciform, God's action must also be cruciform. As Peter Bakken says, for Sittler "the cosmic Christ must also be the crucified Christ."[139] In other words, the *Logos* must also be the Lord. The cosmic Christ must also be the crucified God. Sittler correctly realizes that these christological images must be combined if justice is to be done to the core of the Christian gospel and the ache of human hearts. As Sittler explicitly affirms when with characteristic elegance he captures the core of the Christian faith:

> At the heart of the Christian message is the affirmation that God himself enters our dying--that God, the Creator of all things, the life of all life, has himself undergone that which is most common to us humans. The one of whom the church says, "In him is the fullness of God," not only died; he died a crucified convict. The Christian faith says that nothing in human experience is outside the experience of God.[140]

Conclusion

As indicated in this chapter, there are both strengths and weaknesses in Sittler's theology. As clearly evidenced by this investigation of anthropology, ontology, and theology, Sittler has much to teach those who wish to develop a Christian ecological theology--about both which paths to pursue and which to avoid. Additonal attention is given in chapter eight to these concerns.

Despite the various problems with and limitations of his theology, however, one cannot deny that Sittler was both prophet and sage on the issue of ecology and theology. He was a prophet for telling forth, as a lonely voice in the wilderness, both the grace and the judgment of a God who creates and redeems *all* that has being. And he was a sage for perceiving and creatively articulating an inclusive vision of mountains and marmots, lakes and loons,

---

138Sittler, *Gravity and Grace*, 34.

139Bakken, "The Ecology of Grace," 406.

140Sittler, *Grace Notes*, 119. See Bakken, "The Ecology of Grace," 404ff for a nice explication of this theme.

humans black, white, red, and brown as lying within the scope of God's embrace. As Peter Bakken asserts, Sittler was "a pioneer in bringing environmental concerns into Christian theology."[141] Indeed, Sittler's greatest contribution to Christian theology is his passionate and eloquent call for a "cosmic christology" in the service of a "christology for nature."

---

[141]Bakken, "The Ecology of Grace," 45.

CHAPTER 7

THE CHALLENGE OF MOLTMANN'S PANENTHEISM: A CRITICAL APPRAISAL

Eschatology is nothing other than faith in the Creator with its eyes turned toward the future.[1]

Jürgen Moltmann

The analysis and evaluation in this chapter, as in the previous two chapters, is divided into three sections: anthropology, ontology, and theology. We first investigate Moltmann's views regarding humankind, then analyze his understanding of creation, and finally examine how Moltmann construes the being and character of God. The intention here is to identify the main claims and central arguments of Moltmann's thought with respect to a Christian ecological theology and to critically evaluate these claims and arguments.

As in chapters five and six, here too evaluation is interspersed with analysis. Where warranted critical questions are raised which point out both the strengths and the weaknesses in Moltmann's theology. While Moltmann makes important contributions toward developing a Christian ecological theology, especially with regard to pneumatology, this analysis and critique also show that there are some significant ambiguities and unresolved tensions in his constructive theological proposals. In short, just as much was learned by examining the theologies of Ruether and Sittler, so also by carefully attending to Moltmann's thought there is much to learn about developing a Christian ecological theology.

---

[1]Moltmann, *God in Creation*, 93.

Anthropology

Body and Soul

As with the previous thinkers the issue of the composition of the human serves as an illuminating point of entry into Moltmann's anthropology. Moltmann firmly rejects traditional dualistic views which posit that the human is composed of body and soul. According to Moltmann, in "dichotomic or trichotomic conceptions, the soul has always already been abstracted from the body or the body has been split off from the soul" and thus "in these patterns we can no longer perceive the total human person."[2] Since "humanity constitutes a unity of body, soul and spirit," typical body/soul dualisms fail to capture adequately the unity of the human person and the wholeness of human existence.[3]

In contrast to dualistic anthropologies which "spiritualize the human subject" and "instrumentalize the human body," Moltmann maintains that "we shall deliberately choose an alternative approach" to the dominant trend of Western anthropology--a trend which "shows a tendency to make the soul paramount over the body."[4] We must begin, states Moltmann, with "the biblical anthropologies of the Old and New Testaments."[5] He claims that "the fundamental anthropological differentiation between soul and body is foreign to the Old Testament tradition" since "soul and body are not analyzed as a person's component parts;" rather, in the Old Testament a person does not have a soul but *is* a soul and a person thinks with the body as well as the mind.[6] We must acknowledge that in a biblical anthropology

> soul and body, the core of the inner life (*Innenzentriering*), and the outward mental horizon (*Aussenhorizont*) are seen as existing in reciprocal relation and mutual interpenetration (*in wechsel-seitigem Zusammenhang und gegenseitiger Durchdringung*). Here

---

[2]Ibid., 244.
[3]Moltmann, *Humanity in God*, 118. See also, Moltmann, *The Way of Jesus Christ*, 265ff.
[4]Moltmann, *God in Creation*, 244-245, 247.
[5]Ibid., 256.
[6]Ibid., 256.

a reduction of the 'human act of living' to thinking and willing, and its localization in the soul or brain, are unknown. There is no 'primacy of soul.' An inner hierarchy, according to which the soul is to be thought of a 'higher' and the body as 'lower', the soul as dominating and the body as subservient, is alien to this way of thinking.[7]

Hence Moltmann argues that "the detachment, degradation and deanimation of the body," found for example in Plato, "means that the notion of 'the immortality of the soul' can hardly be reconciled with the biblical belief in creation."[8] If we take this biblical belief seriously, Moltmann concludes, we must speak of "the animation of the body (*die Beseelung des Leibes*)" and of "the animated body (*der beseelte Leib*)."[9]

One of the reasons such a more unified and less dualistic view of the human person is important, Moltmann argues, has to do with the interconnections between how we view ourselves and how we view the world around us. Moltmann asserts that "the alienation of the human being from his bodily existence must be viewed as the inner aspect of the external ecological crisis of modern industrial society."[10] That is to say, insofar as we see ourselves as "subjects merely of cognition and will" whose bodies are "to be objectified and subdued," to that degree we also will perceive the natural world as something to be controlled and mastered.[11] Therefore Moltmann concludes:

If human society is to find a home in the natural environment, the human soul must correspondingly find a home in the bodily existence of the human person. Unless a person's own physical nature is liberated from its subjugation by the subject, nature in the environmental sense (*Natur in der Umwelt*) will not be liberated from the estrangement brought about by the subjection and exploitation imposed on it. And the reverse is equally true.[12]

---

[7]Ibid., 257.

[8]Ibid., 250.

[9]Ibid., 47, 255. These German expressions are both translated, somewhat misleadingly, "soul and body."

[10]Ibid., 48.

[11]Ibid.

[12]Ibid., 49.

In other words, a necessary condition for the construal of the natural world as a home rather than a frontier to be plundered and pillaged is the liberation of the body, and conversely. Only if we move beyond a dualistic anthropology which devalues corporeality will we both attain greater individual health and achieve any semblance of harmony with our non-human neighbors. We must be at home in our bodies, or more accurately*as* bodies, if we are to experience creation as our home.

Moltmann's attempt to move beyond the influential and largely destructive dualistic anthropologies that we have inherited and continue to perpetuate in the West is much-needed and commendable. Also both necessary and commendable is his retrieval of a more holistic biblical anthropology as one means to criticize the dominant Western tradition. As indicated in previous chapters, there is much scholarly support for Moltmann's contentions about the more integral anthropology found in the Bible, especially in the Old Testament. A functional anthropology in which various anthropological terms refer to the *whole* human person from different perspectives is one alternative approach.[13]

Furthermore, Moltmann perceptively recognizes the deep interconnections between our alienation from our bodies and our alienation from the earth. As long as the implicit if not explicit paradigm is the master-slave relation--whether with regard to aspects of the individual person or with respect to the relation between humans and non-humans--we will most likely continue to abuse both our bodies and the natural world. Moltmann is certainly right in affirming that a view of the body as home is something like a necessary condition for the construal of the world as home.

There are, however, a number of problems with Moltmann's arguments and thus it is unclear whether his own proposal of a more unitary anthropology actually achieves what he intends. For example, while he accepts the claim that "differentiation between soul and body is foreign to the Old Testament tradition"--that a person *is* a body rather than has a body and *is* a soul rather than has a soul--Moltmann nevertheless employs such an

---

[13]See, e.g., G. C. Berkouwer, *Man: The Image of God*, chap. 6 for one such attempt.

"anthropological differentiation."[14] Indeed his whole discussion of "the perichoretic pattern of body and soul" assumes such a distinction. For Moltmann body and soul refer to "inward structures (*Innenstrukturen*)" capable of influencing and informing each other: the body is unconscious, involuntary, and outward, while the soul is conscious, voluntary, and inward.[15] The body is "the periphery" while the soul is "the centre."[16] Moltmann's main concern here is *not* actually to reconceive the categories of body and soul in a manner akin to the Old Testament anthropology he mentions; it is, rather, to reconceive the *relationship between* body and soul in a way that does justice to their "mutual need and mutual interpenetration."[17] It is unclear, however, precisely how this reconception fits with Moltmann's affirmation of a more wholistic, biblically informed anthropology and constitutes an advance over many of the views he criticizes.

In other words, for Moltmann the terms body and soul are not ways of referring to the *whole* human person, as suggested by his comments regarding the Old Testament, but refer to differentiable structures *within* the human person. Hence when he speaks of "the unity of body, soul, and spirit," it is because he is attempting to bring together different components that are in some sense *dis*unified. But this assumption of lack of unity belies his intention to develop a more integral perspective. If Moltmann's claim is that unity itself is constituted by differentiation, then it must be shown more clearly how this claim is coherent with his claims about the anthropological perspective of the Bible. In short, Moltmann's attempt to articulate a more unitary anthropology is hamstrung by his ambiguity about the categories of body and soul. And given that he links the alienation of body and earth, it is unclear whether his "alternative approach" can in fact provide the necessary perspective from which to envision the earth as home.

A key concept in Moltmann's more unified anthropology is the category of spirit (*Geist*). Spirit refers to "the forms of organization and communication of all open systems of matter and

---

[14]Moltmann, *God in Creation*, 259; cf. 260.
[15]Ibid., 259-264.
[16]Ibid., 259.
[17]Ibid., 258.

life."[18] On any level of existence--from matter to humanity to the entire galaxy--there are two fundamental "organizational principles" named by the term spirit, viz., "self-assertion and integration" and "self-preservation and self-transcendence."[19] Spirit is, in short, that which unifies and maintains all beings.

With respect to humans Moltmann claims that it follows from the above definition of spirit that "the human being's consciousness is reflective spirit--a becoming aware (*ein Bewusstwerden*) of the organization of his body and his soul, and an awareness, too, of the vitally necessary forms of communication of the human organism in society and nature."[20] Human embodiment is "embodiment that is pervaded, quickened and formed by the creative Spirit" and thus "the human being is a *spirit-body*."[21] So also "the human being's soul--his feelings, ideas, intentions, and so forth--is a soul that is pervaded, quickened and formed by the creative Spirit" and hence "the human being is *spirit-soul*."[22] In short, Moltmann asserts that the human person is a "*spirit-Gestalt*" in which "body and soul have become united" by the creative Spirit who is "at the same time the cosmic Spirit."[23]

Thus Moltmann argues that "spirit is the quintessence (*Inbegriff*) of the human being's self-organisation and his self-transcendence, his inner and his outward symbioses."[24] We must speak of "a unity of body and soul *in* the spirit" since the "human being's spirit is not identical with the conscious subjectivity of his reason or will" but rather "comprehends the whole unified structure of his body and his soul."[25] The human spirit, insists Moltmann, "does not mean some higher spiritual principle, or some mystical summit of the soul;" rather it refers to "the centre of the whole personal, bodily and spiritual being--the psychosomatic

---

[18]Ibid., 263. See also p. 17 where he states that spirit refers to "the forms of organization and modes of communication in open systems."

[19]Ibid., 17.

[20]Ibid., 263.

[21]Ibid.

[22]Ibid.

[23]Ibid.

[24]Ibid., 18.

[25]Ibid.

totality of the person."[26] The spirit is not a part or an aspect of human functioning but the central unifying principle of organization of the whole.

Moltmann's attempt here to move beyond typical dualisms toward a more unified anthropology is a helpful step in the right direction. As he suggests, the Bible supports his affirmation that the category of spirit does not refer to "some higher spiritual principle" or "mystical summit of the soul." In scripture spirit refers not to "a supersensual divine principle inherent in man," but rather to the *whole* human person "in his natural existence, approached from within," especially as empowered or directed.[27] In short, Moltmann is on solid biblical ground in asserting that spirit refers to the center or totality of the person.

It still unclear, however, whether this move actually gives Moltmann the unified anthropology he desires. With his use of the category of spirit Moltmann has certainly brought body and soul closer together--they are "united"--but they still seem to be in an important sense differentiated parts of the human person. In other words, while spirit enfuses both body and soul, body and soul do not enfuse each other, and thus Moltmann has not precluded the possibility, as he believes he has, of an anthropology which devalues the body. And insofar as Moltmann is right about the interconnections between the alienation and subjugation of body and earth, his anthropology fails to provide a secure basis for construing both our bodies and the earth as home.

Human Uniqueness

Additional insight into Moltmann's anthropology can be gained by exploring how he differentiates humans from non-humans. In order to conceive properly that which distinguishes humans from other creatures, Moltmann begins by affirming the importance and goodness of the body. Despite the above-mentioned unclarity about the precise nature of and relationship

---

[26]Ibid., 101. See also p. 259 where Moltmann asserts that the place of the Spirit "is the whole human organism."

[27]See, e.g., Ridderbos, *Paul*, 120-121; and Wolff, *Anthropology of the Old Testament*, chap. 4.

between body and soul, he insists that whether with respect to creation, reconciliation, or redemption, the Bible affirms that "embodiment is the end of all of God's works."[28] Indeed, he argues that "the special thing about Christian eschatology is its surmounting of the enmity between soul and body, spirit and matter, and its full affirmation of the body and the matter of which earthly things are composed."[29] Moltmann thus not only perceptively links views of the body and views of the earth, but he also rightly emphasizes the centrality and importance of the Christian affirmation of embodiment. In the Christian view of the world, matter matters.

In his affirmation of embodiment Moltmann claims that "it is inconceivable that the alienation of nature brought about by human beings can ever be overcome without the naturalization of the human being himself."[30] A necessary condition for the amelioration of the ecological crisis is that "men and women should find a new understanding of themselves, and a new interpretation of their world in the framework of nature."[31] We must, says Moltmann, replace "the modern metaphysics of subjectivity," which has objectified the natural world and sanctioned its domination, with "a relational metaphysics (*eine Metaphysik der Relativität*) based on the mutual relativity of human beings in the world."[32] In other words, however else we conceive the human being, we must view the human as "nothing other than one of nature's products" in relationship to other creatures.[33] Given what we know of the evolution of creation, we must envision human beings "as belonging within the all-embracing coherences (*Zusammenhängen*) of God's history within the world."[34] Humans are, in short, embedded within the natural world.

Furthermore, this "fellowship (*Gemeinschaft*) of human beings with creation" implies, Moltmann asserts, that the human

---

[28]Moltmann, *God in Creation*, 245.
[29]Moltmann, *The Way of Jesus Christ*, 259.
[30]Moltmann, *God in Creation*, 49.
[31]Ibid., 50.
[32]Ibid.
[33]Ibid.
[34]Ibid., 189.

creature is *imago mundi*.[35] Humans are, as the Genesis 2 creation narrative affirms, not only earth-creatures--*adam* formed from *'adamah*; they are distinctive creatures in the history of the world. Because humans are the highest of evolution's products, humans are the image of the world--"a microcosm in which all previous creatures are to be found again" and "a being that can only exist in community with all other created beings and which can only understand itself in that community."[36] Hence as the embodiment of all other creatures, the human being represents the world. As Moltmann asserts:

> As microcosm the human being represents the macrocosm. As 'image of the world' he stands before God as the representative (*stellvertretend*) of all other creatures. He lives, speaks and acts on their behalf. Understood as *imago mundi*, human beings are priestly creations and eucharistic beings. They intercede before God for the community of creation (*Sie treten vor Gott fur die Schöpfungsgemeinschaft ein*).[37]

Thus because of the very embeddedness of the human being in the world and its place in the history of creation, the human is in an important sense unique vis-a-vis other creatures.

Moltmann is certainly correct to point out the need for some sort of "naturalization of the human being." In the context of the overweening anthropocentrism of the past two centuries, we do need some sort of relational metaphysics which acknowledges that humans are creatures of the earth. Moltmann's contention that humans are *imago mundi* is a creative and helpful way to emphasize the basic continuity of the human creature with other creatures. While humans may be more than bodies, they nonetheless are bodies.

There is, however, a great danger that such a program of "naturalization of the human being" will engage in "nothing buttery" or anthropological reductionism, especially given the modern faith in natural science and its sometimes pretentious claims that humans are, for example, *nothing but* bodies--$19.43

---

[35]Ibid., 186.
[36]Ibid.; cf. 190.
[37]Ibid., 190.

worth of carbon, oxygen, and nitrogen. Moltmann himself appears to engage in such a reductionism when, despite his claims that humans are in various ways more than merely matter, he states that humans are "nothing other than one of nature's products." If this is so, then it is unclear how Moltmann can coherently argue, for example, that the divine Spirit is at work in individual humans, human groups, and humanity in general. In short, while Moltmann's insistence on viewing humans as essentially a part of the natural world is an important factor to consider in developing a Christian ecological theology, there is a danger that humans will be viewed solely or merely in such terms.

In addition to pointing to the role of the human as *imago mundi*, Moltmann argues that there are three other features which distinguish humans from other creatures. First, "the human being is distinguished from the earth by the divine charge 'to subdue that earth'," though Moltmann quickly adds that this charge "means nothing but the injunction to eat vegetable food."[38] This command, in other words, does not as is often thought license the domination of the earth. Of all the creatures, only humans, Moltmann affirms, are given this charge. Second, the human being "is distinguished from the animals because he is supposed to give them their names."[39] Again Moltmann is quick to add that while this act of naming is an obvious act of rule, it is does not necessarily involve enmity between humans and animals. That is, this part of the narrative implies no permission to exploit non-human creatures. And third, with reference to Gen. 2:18 Moltmann posits that "unlike animals, the human being is a social being who is dependent on the help of others."[40] The fact that humanity is essentially *co*-humanity distinguishes humans from other creatures.

Understanding these distinguishing characteristics--both those due to what humans have in common with other creatures and those which are uniquely human--is an important ingredient in properly understanding that humans are made in the image of God. States Moltmann:

---

[38]Ibid., 188.
[39]Ibid.
[40]Ibid.

It is only when we become aware of the things which human beings have in common with other creatures, and the things that differentiate them, that we can understand what the human being's designation to be the image of God really means (Gen. 1:26). This designation certainly sets him apart from the rest of creation. Not even the angels are said to be in the image of God. But the designation is not identical with the natural differences between human beings and animals, and is in no way intended to interpret these differences.[41]

The *imago Dei* resides in the fact that "human beings are God's proxy in his creation, and represent him."[42] Humans represent God's glory and will and "intercede for God before the community of creation" and as such are "God's representatives on earth."[43]

Thus Moltmann concludes that humans are the priests of creation. Properly understood, humans "stand before God on behalf of creation, and before creation on behalf of God."[44] While "all God's creatures are fundamentally eucharistic beings," the human being "is able--and designated--to express the praise of all created things before God" and so "acts as a representative for the whole creation."[45] So also, the human being is God's "counterpart" in creation, called to cultivate and protect the garden that is the earth.[46] In sum, humans have a double-role: they are "at once *imago mundi* and *imago Dei*."[47]

Moltmann's thesis regarding the content of the *imago Dei* is supported by many biblical scholars.[48] Rather than identifying the *imago* with some property, e.g., reason, language, moral agency, Moltmann maintains that the *imago Dei* refers to a task or function, namely, representing God as God's vicegerent. Besides

---

[41]Ibid.

[42]Ibid., 190.

[43]Ibid. Also, Moltmann stresses repeatedly that the *whole* human person images God; see, e.g., pp. 219-221, 225, 227, 240.

[44]Ibid.; cf. 228.

[45]Ibid., 71.

[46]Ibid., 188, 30.

[47]Ibid., 190.

[48]See, e.g., Wolff, *Anthropology of the Old Testament*, 160-161; Westermann, *Creation*, 58-59; Gerhard VonRad, *Genesis*, rev. ed. (Philadelphia: Westminster, 1972), 57-58.

being more faithful to the biblical text, this interpretation has the advantage of allowing Moltmann to emphasize the priestly character of humanity not only with respect to the continuity of humans with creation, but also with regard to the fact that humans are a divine counterpart in creation. In other words, if God is most essentially a God of unfathomable love, especially as manifest in the suffering servant Jesus, and if we are to represent *this* God in our dealings with other creatures, then any form of human domination or exploitation of the natural world is strictly forbidden. Like the Orthodox theologian Paulos Gregorios-- himself influenced by Gregory of Nyssa in this regard--Moltmann emphasizes the role of humanity as a priest, mediating between God and creation, and in so doing provides a strong basis for judging human misuse of creation illicit.[49] Moltmann's contention that humans have a double-role as both *imago mundi* and *imago Dei* thus is a potent resource for a Christian ecological theology.

If humans have this priestly role, then Moltmann further concludes that "in a Christian doctrine of creation human beings must neither disappear into the community of creation, nor must they be detached from that community."[50] Neither a one-with- nature-primitivism which completely subsumes humanity into creation, nor a brave-new-world-technocism which lifts humanity completely out of creation is adequate. We must rather, says Moltmann, acknowledge both that "as the image of God, the human being has his special position in creation" and also that "he stands together with all other earthly and heavenly beings in the same hymn of praise of God's glory."[51] In other words, only a position which affirms *both* the commonality *and* the distinctiveness--the continuity and uniqueness--of humanity vis-a- vis the rest of creation is acceptable. However the specific details of such an anthropology are worked out, Moltmann offers both sage

---

[49]Paulos Gregorios, *The Human Presence* (Geneva: World Council of Churches, 1978), 64; cf. 8. Moltmann refers to the resources of the Orthodox tradition when on p. 71 of *God in Creation* he affirms that the monastic traditions of the Orthodox church, along with the Hasidic traditions of Judaism, "must be rediscovered." It is precisely the concepts of humanity as priest and creation as eucharistic that Moltmann has in mind here.

[50]Moltmann, *God in Creation*, 190.

[51]Ibid., 31.

counsel and a stiff challenge for constructing a biblically and ecologically informed theology.

Moltmann persuasively argues that only a theocentric perspective meets this challenge. Neither a cosmocentric nor an anthropocentric viewpoint is adequate since the former fails to preserve human uniqueness while the latter fails to preserve the continuity that humans have with all creation. In contrast, the "theocentric biblical world picture (Weltbild) gives the human being, with his special position in the cosmos, the chance to understand himself as a member of the community of creation (Schöpfungsgemeinschaft)."[52] In contrast to both cosmocentrism and anthropocentrism, a theocentric worldview affirms that while "the human being is certainly the living thing with the highest development known to us," nonetheless the crown of creation is not humanity but the sabbath.[53] That is to say, that for which humans are created is the feast of creation in which God is praised. As Moltmann insists:

> The enduring meaning of human existence lies in its participation (Teilnahme) in this joyful paean of God's creation. This song of praise was sung before the appearance of human beings, is sung outside the sphere of human beings, and will be sung even after human beings have--perhaps--disappeared from this planet. To put it without the images of biblical language: the human being is not the meaning and purpose of the world. . . Theologically speaking, the meaning and purpose of human beings is to be found in God himself, like the meaning and purpose of all things.[54]

Moltmann is, in my view, profoundly correct in his insistence that we must "overcome the old anthropocentric world picture by a new theocentric interpretation of the world of nature and human beings."[55]

---

[52]Ibid. The term Schöpfungsgemeinschaft is one of Moltmann's favorite expressions; see also, e.g., 38, 69ff, 101, 186-187.

[53]Ibid., 197. See chapter 11 for an extensive presentation on the sabbath of creation.

[54]Ibid.

[55]Ibid. On p. 139 Moltmann similarly contends that anthropocentrism must be "replaced by a new cosmological theocentrism" in which "the creatures of the natural world are not there for the sake of human beings" but "human beings are there for the sake of the glory of God, which

Moltmann is not alone in this belief. Paul Santmire, for example, shares Moltmann's basic position when he argues that both cosmocentrism with its "ethic of adoration" and anthropocentrism with its "ethic of exploitation" are problematic perspectives.[56] Neither a view in which the nonhuman is exalted over the human nor a view in which humanity is exalted over other creatures is adequate since both assume a strong dualism between "nature" and "history"--inevitably placing one in a hierarchical relation over the other and thereby undercutting any integral position. In contrast, Santmire argues for a theocentric perspective in which both nonhuman and human creatures stand as siblings before God. This approach, Santmire maintains, warrants "an ethic of responsibility" in which humans are called to the three-fold role of overlord, caretaker, and wondering onlooker.[57] In affirming a theocentric perspective, each in their own distintive way, both Moltmann and Santmire are pointing to a more promising approach to a Christian ecological theology.

Ontology

Like Ruether and Sittler, Moltmann makes numerous assumptions with respect to ontology. Indeed, of the three thinkers here examined Moltmann has the most explicit and developed ontology. Given the close connection between ontological and theological questions, an analysis and evaluation of Moltmann's ontology will allow us to understand his theology more deeply.

The Coherence of Creation

Like many today Moltmann acknowledges and emphasizes the coherence of reality. The world is one unitary organic whole. For example, Moltmann claims that "the perception of the divine

---

the whole community of creation extols." See also, Moltmann, *The Way of Jesus Christ*, 195, 276.

[56]See, e.g., Santmire, *Brother Earth*, chaps. 1-2.

[57]Ibid., chap. 9. There are obvious similarities here with the work of James Gustafson; see, e.g., Gustafson, *Ethics from a Theocentric Perspective*, vol. 1.

Spirit in all things gives rise to a new view of the world: the mechanistic and atomistic picture of the world is replaced by a view of the world in terms of organism and energy."[58] The world is not a place of essentially unrelated and independent parts, but a place characterized by unity and interdependence and "the community of all creatures with one another and God."[59] Modern science, Moltmann asserts, gives us a similar view of the earth. With reference to the Gaia hypothesis Moltmann claims that "the earth is like one living organism, an open system which breaths in energy and regulates itself."[60] Humans are therefore "dependent on the functioning of the comprehensive organism earth."[61]

With his use of the metaphor of organism, Moltmann implies, among other things, that the world is an integral and interdependent whole. As stated in the previous chapters, this way of picturing the world represents a considerable advance over other more common ways of envisioning the world, e.g., as a machine, since it does more justice not only to modern science but also to the Christian scriptures. It is, for example, more in harmony with both the deliverences of the science of ecology and the vision of Psalm 104. The view of the world as coherent and unitary has, moreover, the signal advantage of providing a much more adequate basis for a sound ecological ethic.[62]

This emphasis on the coherence and unity of creation requires Moltmann to repudiate the typical dualism between nature and history and thus re-envision the relationship on a different and more adequate basis. As he states: "Ever since the beginning of the experiment we know as modern times, history (*Geschichte*) and nature (*Natur*) have continually been defined over against one another."[63] They have, for example, often been viewed in terms of the master-slave relation. Moltmann rightly argues that "human history runs its course within the great, comprehensive ecosystem

---

[58]Moltmann, *Creating a Just Future*, 57.
[59]Ibid.
[60]Ibid., 79.
[61]Ibid., 80. Moltmann refers to the earth as an organism three more times on this same page.
[62]See, e.g., Merchant, *The Death of Nature*, 293ff.
[63]Moltmann, *God in Creation*, 137; cf. 31, 38.

'earth'" and hence "history" and "nature" are inextricably linked.[64] Since human history must be seen within the larger history of the earth, we must "integrate that concept [history] into the wider concept of nature."[65]

Moltmann is equally forceful about the inadequacies of the typical categories of history and nature with respect to christology. "A post-modern christology," asserts Moltmann, "places human history ecologically in the framework of nature" and "integrates human history in the natural conditions in which it is embedded."[66] Indeed, he declares that "the growing ecological awareness about the nature of the earth on which human history is played out is going to supercede the paradigm 'history'."[67] Therefore Moltmann argues:

> History and nature must not be defined over against one another. They must be seen in the light of one another, in their reciprocal dependence (*in ihrer wechselseitigen Angeweisenheit aufeinander*), just as mind and body cannot be defined over against one another in an individual life, but must be seen as going hand in hand, if the person is not to be destroyed. And just as the human being's mind or spirit is embedded in his bodily nature and is wholly dependent on it, human history is wholly embedded in the natural conditions which provide its framework, and is dependent on these. It is not human history that is all-comprehensive. The ecological conditions of the nature of the earth are much more so...Theology must go deeper than this [the paradigm of history], and look beyond the world of history to the ecological conditions of history in nature.[68]

However, as with his attempt to rethink anthropology, Moltmann's attempt to reconceive the categories of nature and history reveals a number of ambiguities and tensions. For while he speaks of integrating the concept of history into the concept of nature because nature and history are "inextricably linked," Moltmann's main intention seems to be *not* a basic redefinition of the terms but a reconception of their inter-relationship. As with his views on body, soul, and spirit--where his basic concern is with

---

[64]Ibid., 138.

[65]Ibid., 125.

[66]Moltmann, *The Way of Jesus Christ*, xvi.

[67]Ibid., 215.

[68]Ibid., 246-247; cf. 270-272, 283.

conceiving their relationship in a more mutual and non-
hierarchical way--with respect to nature and history Moltmann is
most concerned with not defining them "over against one another."
Thus it is unclear, despite his contentions to the contrary, whether
he actually intends to rethink the very relata of the relationship
itself. For example, he often uses the terms in traditional ways that
suggest precisely the kind of dualism which he wishes to move
beyond.[69] In short, while Moltmann wishes to supercede the
traditional paradigm of history, it is not clear that he goes as
"deep" as he thinks he does or as deep as he must.

Despite these problems, Moltmann's emphasis on the
coherent unity of creation, especially in light of his theocentrism,
leads him to affirm that "nature" must be viewed as creation. To
put the challenge succinctly: "The sciences have shown us how to
understand creation as nature. Now theology must show how
nature is to be understood as God's creation."[70] Moltmann lists
four necessary aspects to this understanding of the natural world
as God's creation: creation is contingent; humans and non-humans
are one community of creation; creation includes heaven as well as
earth; and creation is fallen. Given the overwhelming temptation
at least since the Enlightenment to view creation as autonomous--
for example, either as mere material "nature" or as quasi-divine
"Nature"--Moltmann's insistence that the natural world be
understood as creation is a necessary and important corrective.

However, there are a number of serious problems with
Moltmann's affirmations regarding the terms nature and creation.
In Moltmann's view "nature means the reality of that world which
is no longer God's good creation and is not yet God's kingdom."[71]
Nature is "the term and concept which sums up the experience of
creation in its present condition. The 'time of nature' is a kind of
winter of creation. Nature is frozen, petrified creation. It is God's
creation, alienated from the source of its life."[72] In other words,

---

[69]See, e.g., Moltmann, *God in Creation*, 63, 137-138, and Moltmann,
The Way of Jesus Christ, 245, 306-307.

[70]Moltmann, *God in Creation*, 38.

[71]Ibid., 59; cf. 53, 70.

[72]Moltmann, *The Way of Jesus Christ*, 253.

nature is creation under "the conditions of sin and corruption."[73] By contrast, creation is the "manifestation of the hidden subject nature in a reconciled, redeemed and hence newly created cosmos."[74] That is, "the coming of Christ in glory is accompanied by a transformation of the whole of nature into its eternal discernible identity as God's creation."[75] And so Moltmann asserts that

> today the essential point is to understand this knowable, controllable and usable nature *as God's creation* and to learn to respect it as such. The limited sphere of reality which we call 'nature' must be lifted into the totality of being (*muss in die Gesamtheit des Seienden aufgehoben werden*) which is termed 'God's creation.'[76]

Moltmann thus argues that "it is not possible for a biblically determined Christian theology to see the present condition of the world as pure divine 'creation'" and view creation as good.[77] To construe the world as nature, in Moltmann's view, means "discerning 'nature' as the enslaved creation that hopes for liberty."[78] Using traditional categories, Moltmann views creation itself as 'fallen' in some sense--enslaved and longing for freedom. Creation is faulted, alienated, enslaved.

Moltmann is following the mainstream of the Christian tradition in his affirmation that creation is in some sense faulted. All is not right with the world. It is enslaved and alienated and "under the conditions of sin and corruption." However, Moltmann's understanding of this affirmation raises a number of important questions. For example, why employ the categories nature and creation in such a way that the former is *by definition* sinful while the latter is *by definition* redeemed? Why not speak of fallen creation and redeemed nature, as well as redeemed creation and fallen nature (redundant expressions for Moltmann), thereby allowing the distinction between creation and nature to be used for

---

[73]Moltmann, *God in Creation*, 59.
[74]Moltmann, *The Way of Jesus Christ*, 280.
[75]Ibid; cf. Moltmann, *Creating a Just Future*, 60.
[76]Moltmann, *God in Creation*, 21; cf. 32.
[77]Ibid., 39.
[78]Ibid. See also, Jürgen Moltmann, *The Crucified God*, 24, 39, 101, 335.

other purposes than to distinguish between that which is faulted and that which is not? Furthermore, what exactly is meant in the assertion that "nature must be lifted into the totality of being which is termed God's creation"? In what precise sense is the term *aufheben* used here? For example, does it mean the "transformation of the whole of nature" or does it mean a "newly created cosmos"?[79] In other words, is there a basic continuity or discontinuity between this present fallen world and the future redeemed world?

Additional insight regarding these questions is gained in understanding how Moltmann more exactly describes the fallenness of creation. According to him, the precise nature of this fallenness or enslavement is found in the fact that "nature" is transient and subject to death.

> Nature has fallen victim to transience (*Vergänglichkeit*) and death. It has not fallen through its own sin, like human beings. To talk about 'a fallen nature' is therefore highly dubious. And yet a sadness lies over nature which is the expression of its tragic fate and its messianic yearning. It is enslaved and wishes to be free, for it is transitory (*vergänglich*) and wishes for 'an abiding habitation.'[80]

Citing Romans 8:19-21, a favorite text in this regard, Moltmann contends that "enslavement through the bondage of transience (*Vergänglichkeit*) and a yearning openness for the future of the kingdom of God's glory, determine the present condition of the world;" indeed, with reference to this text in Romans he speaks of "the curse of transience (*der Fluch der Vergänglichkeit*)."[81] Creation must be redeemed "from the fetters of the transience of the times (*aus den Fesseln der Vergänglichkeit der Zeiten*)."[82] Thus, for Moltmann, mortality does not properly belong to creaturely finitude--for either human or non-human creatures--but is something to which creation has somehow fallen victim. While the

---

[79]Moltmann, *The Way of Jesus Christ*, 280.

[80]Moltmann, *God in Creation*, 68.

[81]Ibid., 68, 189. See also p. 60 where Moltmann states that "all earthly things and all living things can be discerned in their forfeiture to transience and in their hope for liberation to eternity."

[82]Moltmann, *The Way of Jesus Christ*, 304; cf. 258.

origin of death is unclear, Moltmann posits that "the death of all the living can neither be called 'the consequence of sin,' nor can it be termed 'natural.' It is a destiny (*Schicksal*) to which everything living is subjected, and which hence spurs us on to yearn for cosmic deliverance."[83] In sum, creation has inexplicably yet tragically become enslaved to transience and death and therefore yearns to be free--to participate in an abiding form of existence. The world is fated to evanescent temporal existence, and yet longs for some kind of perpetual existence.

Moltmann's claims here, however, raise a number of significant problems. First of all, if creation as we now know it is "under the conditions of sin and corruption," and if these enslaving conditions are defined in terms of transience and death, then it follows that salvation must be either some form of atemporal existence, e.g., eternality, or some form of perpetual temporal existence, e.g. everlastingness. In other words, if the faultedness of creation is its temporary or momentary or non-abiding character, then the only salvific response to such a fault is some sort of eternal or everlasting mode of being. If Moltmann intends the former, then it is quite unclear how such an appeal to atemporality can easily fit with his own emphasis on temporal categories in theology, especially with respect to God. That is, if salvation lies in a form of eternal or timeless existence--since creation is under the "bondage" and "curse" of transience, then how can that concept of salvation be internally consistent with an eschatological perspective, especially one which speaks of the "history of God"?

Moltmann must, therefore, mean that salvation involves some form of everlasting existence in time. It is, however, unclear whether Moltmann affirms this option. For example, he argues that in the eschatological "kingdom of glory" creation will be "eternal (*ewig*)."[84] "Temporality," claims Moltmann, "is the nature of this aeon, not the coming one" and so we must speak of "relative eternity or aeonic time" in attempting to describe the age to come.[85] But Moltmann also affirms that "in the kingdom of glory there will

[83]Ibid., 169-170.
[84]Moltmann, *God in Creation*, 184.
[85]Moltmann, *The Way of Jesus Christ*, 158.

be time and history, future and possibility;" these, however, will obtain "to an unimpeded degree and in a way that is no longer ambivalent."[86] Hence he claims that "instead of timeless eternity (*zeitloser Ewigkeit*) it would be better to talk about 'eternal time' (*ewiger Zeit*)" and "the 'eternal history' (*ewigen Geschichte*) of God, human beings and nature" since in the future of creation there will be "change without transience (*Veranderung ohne Vergehen*), time without the past (*Zeit ohne Vergangenheit*), and life without death."[87] There are a number of pressing questions that are prompted by these claims. For example, what does relative eternity or eternal time or eternal history mean? Does it make sense to speak of time without the past or change without transience? The main point here, though, is that Moltmann's claims are if not incoherent at least in need of much greater clarity.

In any case, according to Moltmann what creation must be saved from is not disobedience and its effects or the powers of evil, but transience and death. That existents come into being, exist, and cease to be is the evil to be overcome. As he asks in response to the views of Augustine: "What meaning can the creation of transience have? If death is already the destiny (*das Schicksal*) of creation itself, not only the destiny of sin, then created existence is not anything we can possibly affirm."[88] In other words, it is impossible to affirm creation if it is essentially transient and if death is a necessary feature of creaturely existence. But this is an eminently debatable claim, occasioning a number of questions. For example, why does it follow that created existence cannot be affirmed if death, e.g., biological death, is a natural feature of creation? Indeed, how is it possible to have life unless some things die-- unless, for example, plants die, decompose, and provide nourishment for other forms of life? Is it possible to have a world like ours without there being non-abiding or short-lived creatures? Is it correct to insist that death *per se*--the death of micro-organisms and stalks of wheat and seventeen-year cicadas--is

---

[86]Moltmann, *God in Creation*, 213.
[87]Ibid.
[88]Ibid., 117.

what constitutes the faultedness of creation? As Wesley Granberg-Michaelson affirms:

> If death within creation--meaning the death of biological organisms--is not the result of human sin, it must have been present from the beginning of creation. Biological death, then, is part of the *goodness* of creation. The cosmos, the world, and all within it, pronounced "good" or "right" even before the advent of humanity, was created by God in include biological death. An ecological understanding of creation lends insight into what at first seems outlandish--God's creation of death. Every living organism, we discover, is given life because of death. It survives because some other part of creation has relinquished its life. The trout lives because the stone fly dies. The osprey lives because the trout dies. You and I live because countless plants and animals die....
> So at every level--from within the cellular life of organisms, to relationships between organisms, to the overall life of ecosystems--life is made possible by death. We can say that this is part of the Creator's intention.[89]

In short, Moltmann's conclusion that creation cannot be affirmed if it is transient and subject to death does not necessarily follow.

The above analysis points to what is one of the most fundamental problems with Moltmann's views on creation, namely, the conflation of creation and fall and consequent *inability* ultimately to affirm creation. In other words, for Moltmann creation is *necessarily* faulted since sin as death and transience is ontologically *constitutive* of creation itself. As a result, Moltmann is unable, despite his best intentions, to affirm creation. If creation is essentially faulted, then only some new creation can provide an adequate solution to the reality of sin; but to posit the necessity of a new creation is precisely to undercut the goodness and acceptability of this creation. In addition to being self-stultifying, this position contravenes a central tenet in the Christian tradition. Brian Walsh puts this point well when he states that rather than viewing sin "as an alien intruder into God's good creation," with Moltmann "sin is seen as ontologically constitutive of transitorily 'burdened'

---

[89]Granberg-Michaelson, *A Worldly Spirituality*, 198-199.

creatureliness."[90] But such a view flies in the face of the standard Christian understanding of sin. As Langdon Gilkey insists:

> Because sin is an estrangement of our essential structure, an alienation from our nature, a misuse of freedom in which freedom itself is bound, it is not possible to describe it in ontological terms-- for ontology knows only structure and not its misuse. Among the most important things a Christian interpretation says of history is that that which is fated or evil in experience, while an undoubted part of the concrete actuality of history, is not the result of its ontological and so its "necessitating" structure. Rather, this strange, "fallen" aspect of concreteness is the creation of sin, of a warped human freedom, and not of God, of time, of the structure of our finitude or of nexorable natural or social forces.[91]

Despite contentions to the contrary, in Moltmann's view we do *not* live in a fundamentally good though alienated creation; rather, creation itself is *by nature* warped and burdened by the transience of matter. Thus the "sadness" which lies over the natural world is not a result of the alienation of a good creation, but a consequence of there being any creation at all. The "tragedy in creation" does not refer to what the Christian tradition typically affirms by "the fall"--that evil is an alien intruder into and a perversion of an essentially good creation.[92] The tragedy of creation for Moltmann is that the creation of this world necessarily entails the creation of a faulted world--a world subject to transience and death. In Moltmann's view of creation there is a kind of metaphysically necessary fault.

The validity of this analysis is supported by Moltmann's repeated references to and readings of Romans 8:19ff.[93] Moltmann interprets the groaning of creation in this text to be due to "enslavement to the bondage of transience." Creation yearns to be

---

[90]Brian Walsh, "The Theology of Hope and the Doctrine of Creation: An Appraisal of Jürgen Moltmann," *The Evangelical Quarterly* 59 (January 1987): 62-63.

[91]Gilkey, *Reaping the Whirlwind*, 256-257.

[92]Moltmann, *The Way of Jesus Christ*, 170. See, e.g., Langdon Gilkey, *Maker of Heaven and Earth* (Garden City: Doubleday, 1959), chap. 7 for a lucid account of the traditional Christian view of creation and fall.

[93]See, e.g., Moltmann, *The Future of Creation*, 12, 129; and Moltmann, *God in Creation*, 39, 60, 67-68.

free from the "forfeiture to transience." The text, however, does not attribute the groaning of creation to any such inherent imperfection of creation; rather it finds the reason for the groaning of creation in human sin. As Walsh rightly affirms:

> Romans 8:19ff portrays the groaning of creation in terms of Adam's sin, not the inherent structure of creatureliness....Romans 8 does not present a creation which is constitutively fallen but one that has been 'subjected to futility, not of its own will but by the will of him who subjected it in hope.' And the 'bondage to decay' surely does not refer to the ontological structure of a temporal and transient creatureliness, but is a metaphor for the break in the harmony of creation occasioned, according to Genesis 3, by human sin.[94]

Creation is cursed not because it is transient, but, as Genesis 3:17 suggests, because of human sin.

The Mutability of Creation

In addition to his emphasis on the unity and coherence of creation, Moltmann places great stress on the dynamic and developmental character of creation. For example, as indicated in chapter four, Moltmann claims that *creatio originalis* implies *creatio mutabilis*--a creation "open for history" and "aligned in the direction of the future." To use one of his own favorite expressions, creation is "an open system"--a non-deterministic communicative system in which real change occurs as future states are actualized over time. And so creation is dynamic and in process. Creation is, as Moltmann affirms, a *fieri*, not a *factum*.

---

[94]Walsh, "Theology of Hope and the Doctrine of Creation," 64. Given this misreading of Romans 8:19ff, it is not surprising that, as Walsh perceptively observes, "one finds few references to creation praising God, its Creator in Moltmann's writings." Therefore Walsh rhetorically asks: "Could it not be that Moltmann's doctrine of creation does not emphasize the element of creational praise and thanksgiving because he has ontologically structuralized the directional question of sin, and has thereby fused creation into the fall?" In other words, Walsh is suggesting that the reason Moltmann rarely refers to creation's praise of God--praise found, e.g., in Psalms 19, 65, 93, 98, 104, and 148, among other places--is because he views creation as essentially faulted or imperfect.

Moltmann affirms that creation is not only dynamic but developmental, i.e., changing in a particular direction. For example, with his concept of *creatio continua* as *creatio anticipativa* he emphasizes the developmental nature of the world. As outlined previously, continuous creation, for Moltmann, means not only continuous divine preservation and sustenence but also the initiation of the consummation of creation. God innovates as well as preserves, and so creation evolves. Creation is, in keeping with Moltmann's orientation, eschatological.

Given this eschatological understanding of creation, Moltmann describes "God's activity in history" as consisting "essentially in opening up systems which are closed in on themselves."[95] Indeed, the full flourishing of creation is the complete openness of all things, since the new creation is characterized by "the openness *par excellence* of all life systems."[96] According to Moltmann, we must envision the "kingdom of glory, which completes the process of creation through the indwelling of God,...as the openness of all finite life systems for the fullness of life."[97] Hence he concludes: "We can, therefore, call salvation in history the divine opening of 'closed systems.' The closed or isolated person is freed for liberty and for his own future."[98] So also the closed non-human system finds salvation through being opened up and freed for its own future.

As is obvious, this understanding of salvation implies that sin is essentially the state of being closed off or closed down or isolated. As Moltmann maintains:

> Having called creation in the beginning a system open for time and potentiality, we can understand sin and slavery as the self-closing of open systems against their own time and their own potentialities. If a person closes himself against his potentialites, then he is fixing himself on his present reality and trying to uphold what is present, and to maintain the present against possible changes.[99]

---

[95]Moltmann, *God in Creation*, 211. On p. 212 Moltmann speaks of "the opening up in time of closed systems."

[96]Ibid., 213.

[97]Ibid., 214.

[98]Moltmann, *The Future of Creation*, 122. For other references to sin as isolation, see Moltmann, *The Way of Jesus Christ*, 254, 283.

[99]Moltmann, *The Future of Creation*, 122.

Sin is the human form of fallenness in which one fixes on the present in order to preclude any possible future change. However creation, too, can be characterized in this way. In presenting an analogy between human and non-human creatures, Moltmann identifies being closed-in and isolated as the essence of creational faultedness, and further posits that these qualities are manifest in the transience of the world.

> Because in human beings faith brings liberation from the closed-in isolation (*Abgeschlossenheit*) which is sin, in nature too the isolation (*Abgeschlossenheit*) of the life systems can be seen as their 'bondage' to transience (*Knechtschaft unter der Vergänglichkeit*), and 'openness' is recognizably their living character."[100]

Using metaphors from the seasons, Moltmann describes nature or fallen creation as "frozen and petrified" and the time of nature as "a kind of winter of creation."[101] By contrast, "the divine energy" which we call the Holy Spirit--"the Spirit of the new creation of nature"--brings "all living creatures into the springtime of eternal life."[102] Like a dormant plant or hibernating animal, nature is closed down and fixed in a state of relative immutability.

Moltmann's eschatological perspective, with its insistence on the open-ended and historical character of creation, contains important insights. The mechanistic cosmology of previous centuries has been found wanting and appropriately been replaced by more dynamic ontological models which emphasize contingency and novelty. The unhistorical outlook of the past which viewed reality primarily in terms of static order or structure has rightly been superceded by perspectives which more adequately acknowledge historicity and change. With his stress on indeterminateness and temporality--on the future possibilites and

---

100Moltmann, *God in Creation*, 69. In a similar vein, on p. 209 of *The Trinity and the Kingdom* Moltmann claims that divine providence "means that God keeps the world's true future open for it through the gift of time, which works against all the world's tendencies to close in on itself, to shut itself off."

101Moltmann, *The Way of Jesus Christ*, 253.

102Ibid., 253-254.

the processive nature of being--Moltmann captures both of these features of the world.

There are, however, numerous problems with Moltmann's eschatological orientation. For example, in defining sin as closedness and salvation as openness Moltmann baptizes change in itself as a necessary good. Fixation on the present is necessarily bad, while change *per se* is necessarily good. But is it the case that "trying to uphold what is present" is necessarily evil, while being "open for time and potentiality" is necessarily good? Gilkey offers a trenchant critique of such a perspective:

> It is important to note...that sin is *not* merely undue attachment to the past and the closing off of an open future. Sin arises as well in the way we deal with an open future, in the warping use we make of even the most novel possibilities introduced into history. For it is precisely the "openness" of a future that is menace as well as possibility; that very openness thus breeds our deepest anxieties as well as our expectation of new possibilities, and leads both revolutionary and conservative forces to become infected by self-concern and the securing and defence of their worlds. It is the openness, the contingency, the risk and the demand, of the future that tempts us to sin as well as beckons us to new creative possibilities.[103]

Moltmann assumes that change, any change, will necessarily secure salvation, and so further assumes that the future is necessarily salvific. But, like his mentor Reinhold Niebuhr, Gilkey reminds us that the future is ambiguous. The openness of the future means the possibility for sin as well as redemption. As Walsh rightly insists: "Openness to the future *per se* is no guarantee of redemption beause it is precisely this openness which affords us with the freedom which has the potential to sin."[104]

William French astutely identifies this same problem. Moltmann's stress on the "openness of nature," says French, "is reductionistic in that it suggests both an unwarranted moral affirmation of transformation and change and a moral denigration for the preservation of order and stable structure."[105] As French

---

[103]Gilkey, *Reaping the Whirlwind*, 258.
[104]Walsh, "Theology of Hope and the Doctrine of Creation," 63.
[105]French, "Returning to Creation," 84.

quite naturally asks: "Before we dash to transform, I would like to know specifically what we are transforming, why, and to what end....We may 'transform' the Amazon jungle into teak furniture, but is this theologically, ethically, or ecologically a good transformation or bad?"[106] Moltmann's discussion of the openness of creation suffers because normative categories are absent, or more accurately, because Moltmann assumes that process, change, and the future itself are necessarily normative. Thus while he speaks against the exploitation of creation--employing certain moral norms like peace, justice, symbiosis[107]--it is difficult to see how these norms have a legitimate basis in his theology.

There are further problems with Moltmann's theology, especially with his concept of *creatio nova*. As indicated in chapter four, *creatio nova* signifies "the consummated new creation of all things." It is quite unclear, however, what the *novum* here precisely means. Is what exact sense is the new creation new? On the one hand Moltmann suggests that there is significant *continuity* between old and new creation since the new creation is a *renewal* or transformation of the old. For example, he claims that "the glorification of God at the End-time in the Spirit and through the Spirit is to be understood as a world-embracing and world-renewing event."[108] In the eschaton the world will be transformed into the home of God. The coming kingdom of God, posits Moltmann, "will renew heaven and earth."[109] Therefore we must conclude: "Faith in God the Creator cannot be reconciled with the apocalyptic expectation of a total *annihilatio mundi*. What accords with this faith is the expectation and active anticipation of the *transformatio mundi*."[110] Thus the person who believes in God the

---

[106]Ibid.

[107]See, e.g., Moltmann, *The Future of Creation*, 128-130; *God in Creation*, 23ff; *Creating a Just Future*, 14, 40.

[108]Moltmann, *The Future of Creation*, 94.

[109]Moltmann, *God in Creation*, 55.

[110]Ibid., 93. See also *The Way of Jesus Christ*, 258 where Moltmann states that with the transformation of "vulnerable human nature" into "eternally living, immortal human nature" the "non-human nature of the earth is transformed as well."

creator is a person of hope--a hope which "commits him to faithfulness to the earth (*verpflichet ihn auf die Treue zur Erde*)."[111] Moltmann continues this emphasis on continuity with respect to christology. For example, he affirms that the process of resurrection begun in Christ "indicates that the hope of resurrection is not related to a different life" but rather that "it is this mortal life which is going to be different."[112] Properly conceived, the hope of resurrection "is directed, not towards a different world but towards the redemption of this one."[113] Thus Moltmann insists that the future general resurrection of the dead is "a *transition* (*Übergang*), not a total breach and a new beginning" and so is best spoken of as a "transformation (*Verwandlung*)" and "transfiguration (*Verklärung*)" rather than "a breaking off and a new beginning."[114] As Moltmann acknowledges in his interpretation of 1 Corinthians 15:

> The eschatological new creation of this creation must surely presuppose *this whole* creation. For something new will not *take the place* of the old; it is *this same 'old' itself* which is going to be created anew (*Es tritt a nicht am Ende etwas Neues an die Stelle des Alten, sondern dieses Alte wird neugeschaffen*).[115]

In sum, Moltmann takes the *novum* in the new creation to be the *renewal* of this present world.

However, Moltmann also clearly asserts that the *novum* of the new creation is something *absolutely* new and that consequently there is a basic *dis*continuity between old and new creation. For example, Moltmann claims that with the resurrection of Jesus "everything is changed" and so we must speak of the new creation as a creation "*ex nihilo*."[116] The resurrection of Christ implies "an *annihilatio* such as descends on all being in the end of all things;" it is "a *nova creatio per annihilationem nihili*."[117]

111Moltmann, *God in Creation*, 93.
112Moltmann, *The Way of Jesus Christ*, 242.
113Ibid.
114Ibid., 249-250.
115Ibid., 262.
116Moltmann, *The Future of Creation*, 161-163.
117Ibid., 163.

Therefore Moltmann concludes: "The new creation does not emerge out of the restoration of the old creation; it follows from creation's end. Out of 'the negation of the negative' a being arises that has overcome the conflict between being and non-being and hence is absolutely new."[118] The *novum* of the new creation is fundamentally new.

Lest these remarks be viewed as aberrations, in his more recent work Moltmann makes similar claims. For example, in speaking of the *theologia gloriae* of the new creation he refers to "the radical new creation of the created being (*die gründliche Neuschöpfung des Geschöpfes*)."[119] The new creation is significantly different than the old creation. In fact, using artistic metaphors, Moltmann contends that since God does not yet dwell in creation, the world is "a sketch or design for the kingdom of God."[120] In yet other terms, creation is a parable of the coming glory since, Moltmann rhetorically asks, "does not everything passing remain merely a parable of what is immortal?"[121] Indeed, the new creation represents "a qualitatively new, redeeming future (*einer qualitativ neuen, erlösenden Zukunft*)."[122] In the new creation, according to Moltmann, the old creation will be "caught up and absorbed in its fulfillment (*wird aufgehoben*);" when the kingdom is fully consummated, creation will be "discarded (*abgetan*)."[123] In short, the *novum* of the new creation does not represent the renewal but rather the annihilation or abolition of creation. And so Moltmann contradicts his claim that the new creation is in basic continuity with the old creation.

Brian Walsh also puts his finger on this problem in Moltmann's theology when he asks: "Is the 'new' which eschatological language anticipates a totally new of the future or a realization of the possibilities of the past and present? Moltmann's answer has not been clear."[124] Walsh points to the tension in

---

[118]Ibid., 164.
[119]Moltmann, *God in Creation*, 59.
[120]Ibid., 62.
[121]Ibid.
[122]Ibid.
[123]Ibid., 63. See also pp. 133-134 where Moltmann's distinction between *futurum* and *adventus* reflects this same emphasis on discontinuity.
[124]Walsh, "Theology of Hope and the Doctrine of Creation," 56.

Moltmann's claims that the new creation both preserves and destroys creation: "If the new is totally new and even a *novum ex nihilo* or a *creatio nova*, then how can it take up and preserve the old within itself?"[125] In other words, to bring up a question posed earlier, what exactly does Moltmann mean by *aufheben*?

James Carpenter identifies this problem as well. He argues that Moltmann's views present "a real difficulty" because "creation in the beginning and in the present is devalued" given Moltmann's overwhelming emphasis on the future.[126] As Carpenter rightly insists:

> That God's openness in the world becomes manifest in Christ is basic to the church's faith, but that openness should not be considered as openness solely toward the future; it should be seen as the disclosure of what in some basic sense has ever been so, even if considered more fully so after Christ's advent in history.[127]

Furthermore, to insist as Moltmann does that with Christ creation is absolutely new is "to take him [Christ] out of the context of life" and "to divorce him from prior history."[128] This move, argues Carpenter, "is theologically dubious, if not inadmissible" because it is "Docetic in fundamental tendency and implication."[129] If Christ's death and resurrection are "the absolutely new," then they are "too new to be appropriated in experience and made the basis for hope, at least for those to whom its Docetic and Gnostic tendencies are unacceptable."[130] Moltmann's theology undercuts the Christian hope of redemption and bodily resurrection.

As suggested previously, Moltmann is driven to this problem because of his conflation of creation and fall. If creation is essentially faulted, then only a radically new creation can provide an adequate solution to such faultedness. So despite his intention to affirm the goodness of creation and his assertions that the new creation is a transformation or renewal of creation, Moltmann is

---

[125]Ibid., 57.
[126]Carpenter, *Nature and Grace*, 87.
[127]Ibid., 88.
[128]Ibid., 92.
[129]Ibid.
[130]Ibid.

unable consistently to speak of "faithfulness to the earth." As Walsh
accurately concludes, Moltmann "does not sufficiently account for
the fall."[131] If, on the other hand, creation is viewed as essentially
good, then "while the *novum* of the new creation will be
undoubtedly surprising, it will be qualitatively different from a
creatio ex nihilo or a *creatio nova* because it will not itself be
either *ex nihilo* or totally *nova*."[132] If, in other words, sin is viewed
as an alienation of a good (though undeveloped) creation, then the
new creation can justifiably be seen as the renewal and
transformation rather than abolition of this world.

Theology

As in the previous chapters, in this final section two central
theological issues are jointly considered, namely, the attributes and
action of God. And as before, discussion about the being and action
of God involves some treatment of the relationship between God
and creation. More exactly, using traditional categories, questions
about divine transcendence or absoluteness and divine immanence
or relatedness are at the forefront of this inquiry.

As in the sections on Reuther and Sittler, one important
criterion of adequacy here is whether or not *both* transcendence
and immanence are sufficiently addressed. To repeat the
formulation of Bernard McGinn: "Every Christian theology of
creation has to insist not only that God is absolutely different from
creation, but also that he is related to it in an essential way."[133]
Thus both transcendence and immanence are necessary features of
an adequate Christian ecological theology.

The Trinitarian Creator

As indicated in chapter four, Moltmann is clearly aware of
the issue of divine absoluteness and relatedness. Indeed it is
precisely his awareness of the crucial importance of these

131Walsh, "Theology of Hope and the Doctrine of Creation," 67.
132Ibid., 59.
133McGinn, "Do Christian Platonists Really Believe in Creation," 210.

categories that enables him to identify certain defects in traditional theology. For example, Moltmann correctly perceives that there has been in Western Christian thought in the last centuries an over-emphasis on God's absoluteness. Many Christians have been and are *de facto* deists. He is also correct in perceiving the links between this view of God and creation--a view in which creation has been evacuated of divine presence--and the contemporary ecological crisis. A world-view which envisions God bringing creation into being and then going on holiday, leaving the world to its own machine-like devices, implicitly if not explicitly invites human exploitation of creation. Hence Moltmann's insistence that we need "a new kind of thinking about God"--a kind of thinking in which the presence of God in the world is heartily acknowledged--should be heeded.

Given the overemphasis on divine transcendence in the history of Christian thought, with the consequent legitimation of ecological exploitation, Moltmann seeks a way to emphasize divine immanence without necessarily sacrificing transcendence. As mentioned previously, Moltmann argues that the distinction between God and creation "is a truth that must not be surrendered" as we find ways to "perceive and teach God's immanence in the world." The God who is other than the world must be conceived in intimate and integral relation to the world. And so Moltmann speaks of the impossibility of having transcendence without immanence or immanence without transcendence since there is a "dialectical structure of transcendence and immanence." They are "mutually related" in such a way as to be necessary conditions each for the other.

One of Moltmann's most significant contributions lies in this persistent affirmation that Christian theology must take with *equal* seriousness *both* divine transcendence and immanence. As Moltmann reminds us, both deism and pantheism, the views of Newton and Spinoza, are inadequate positions. In keeping with the criterion stated above--articulated by Gilkey, McGinn, Neville, and many others--Moltmann rightly affirms both "the fundamental distinction between creation and Creator" and "the presence of God in the world." And so Moltmann provides a helpful service in his criticism of both those who fail to preserve the proper distinction between God and creation and those who fail to integrally relate God and creation.

One of the reasons why Moltmann strongly resists any view which slights divine transcendence is his belief in divine freedom. Moltmann affirms that the God who creates does so freely. The world "was neither created out of pre-existing matter nor out of the divine Being itself" but rather was "called into existence by the free will of God: *creatio e libertate Dei.*"[134] But by divine freedom Moltmann does not mean "the absolute power of disposal," since such a concept of freedom "is hardly appropriate for the God who is love."[135] In other words, like most theists Moltmann asserts that even God is not free to do absolutely anything. Divine omnipotence is not absolutely unqualified. For example, God "does not have the choice between being love and *not* being love" since God's essential being is love.[136] This absence of choice is not a limitation of divine freedom since, like Augustine, Moltmann affirms that "freedom of choice is by no means freedom's highest stage."[137] Genuine freedom is freedom only for the good. We must "understand true freedom as being the self-communication of the good."[138]

Moltmann thus concludes that "when we say that God created the world 'out of freedom', we must immediately add 'out of love'."[139] For if "God's freedom is not the almighty power for which everything is possible" but rather is love or "the self-communication of the good," then that "God creates the world out of freedom" necessarily entails that God "creates it out of love."[140] Hence *creatio e libertate Dei* implies "*creatio ex amore Dei.*"[141] Put in other terms: "But if God *is* love, then his liberty cannot consist of loving or not loving. On the contrary, his love is his liberty and his liberty is his love. He is not compelled to love by any outward or inward necessity. Love is self-evident for God."[142] Moltmann

---

[134]Moltmann, *God in Creation*, 75.
[135]Moltmann, *The Trinity and the Kingdom*, 54.
[136]Ibid., 54-55.
[137]Ibid., 55.
[138]Ibid.
[139]Moltmann, *God in Creation*, 75.
[140]Ibid., 75-76.
[141]Ibid., 76.
[142]Moltmann, *The Trinity and the Kingdom*, 151.

succinctly captures the kernal of the matter when he insists: "For God it is axiomatic (*selbstverständlich*) to love, for he cannot deny himself. For God it is axiomatic to love freely, for he is God."[143]

The insistence that God is love is perhaps Moltmann's central affirmation with respect to God. For example, in contrast to both the Reformed doctrine of the decrees, with its emphasis on divine will, and the neo-platonic doctrine of emanation, with its emphasis on divine nature, Moltmann argues that "the unity of will and nature in God can be appropriately grasped through the concept of love" since "God loves the world with the very same love which he eternally *is*."[144] Indeed, avers Moltmann, the "supreme New Testament statement" is that "God is love."[145] So in contrast to any view which identifies the divine life with divine creativity, Moltmann asserts that "it is more appropriate if we view the eternal divine life as a life of eternal, infinite love, which in the creative process issues in its overflowing rapture from its trinitarian perfection and completeness."[146] In short, for Moltmann God is "the overflowing love from which everything comes."[147]

Moltmann's assertion of the freedom of God, and so also the contingency of creation, rightly affirms a number of important features of the classical Christian doctrine of creation and concept of God. More exactly, Moltmann affirms the "three main concepts that make up the idea of creation:" that "God alone is the source of all that there is in the created universe;" that creation is "dependent upon God, and yet is real, coherent, and 'good';" and that God acts freely and purposively.[148] Likewise, Moltmann's affirmation of the unfathomable depths of divine love captures a central biblical and Christian attribute of God. As Gilkey states, that God creates "solely because of the divine purpose of love" is "the most fundamental knowledge that Christians have of God and of the

---

[143]Ibid., 107.

[144]Moltmann, *God in Creation*, 85; cf. Moltmann, *The Trinity and the Kingdom*, 57ff.

[145]Moltmann, *God in Creation*, 85.

[146]Ibid., 84. See also, Moltmann, *The Future of Creation*, 86 for this metaphor of God as fountain of "overflowing abundance, of perfection that communicates itself."

[147]Moltmann, *God in Creation*, 15.

[148]Gilkey, *Maker of Heaven and Earth*, 47.

character of his actions."[149] Love, especially suffering love, says Gilkey, is "the deepest clue to divinity."[150]

But Moltmann's views on divine freedom and the contingency of creation exhibit an inner tension. With his principle of the diffusiveness or self-communication of the good Moltmann stands in the Dionysian tradition exemplified, for example, by Bonaventure. One problem with this tradition, however, is that creation is sometimes viewed as necessary rather than contingent. If God is love, and if love is ultimate goodness, and if the nature of ultimate goodness is that it must go out of itself to an other, then there must be some other to God; therefore creation is necessary. Moltmann accepts most of this argument, but rejects the conclusion. He affirms the premises that "for God it is axiomatic to love" and that love as a form of goodness is necessarily diffusive or "overflowing," and thus he accepts the contention that there must be some other for God. But because of both his affirmation of *creatio ex nihilo* and his doctrine of the Trinity Moltmann denies the conclusion that creation is necessary. For Moltmann the necessary other for God is within the being of God. The overflowing love of God expresses itself in a community of love which the triune God is.[151]

Moltmann, however, also maintains that creation is in fact necessary and *not* contingent. For example, while he claims that God communicates his love "not out of compulsion and not out of some arbitrary resolve, but out of the inner pleasure of his eternal love," he also argues that for God not to "call to life his Other, man, as his image" would "contradict the love which God is."[152]

---

[149]Ibid., 73.

[150]Ibid., 214.

[151] On p. 147 of *Our Idea of God* (Downers Grove: Intervarsity Press, 1991), Thomas Morris puts this point especially well: "The eternally existing relations among these members of the divine *Trinity* are thought to encompass precisely the sort of communications of love and sharings of goodness that the legitimate insight behind the principle of diffusiveness requires. So in order for divine goodness to be expressed in an interpersonal way, it was not necessary for God to bring about the existence of a contingent universe containing created persons. It is expressed quite naturally in intra-trinitarian relations."

[152]Moltmann, *The Trinity and the Kingdom*, 58.

Like many influenced by the Dionysian tradition, Moltmann contends that God's love is imperfect unless it "leads God out of himself."[153] Approvingly quoting Isaak Dorner, Moltmann posits that love "does not yet find the real place of its activity in God himself, but only where there is purely free, primal giving, only where there is pure neediness in the receiver."[154] Love, even the divine love within the Trinity itself, is incomplete. So Moltmann concludes: "God 'needs' the world and man. If God is love, then he neither will nor can be without the one who is his beloved." Intra-trinitarian love is insufficient. God cannot exist without creation. Creation is necessary in order to complete divine love.

This claim, however, contradicts Moltmann's claims about the contingency of creation and the freedom of God. Furthermore, as Morris perceptively observes, the belief that an internal or intra-trinitarian expression of divine love is insufficient to satisfy the requirements of diffusiveness and that some external manifestation of divine love is necessary--this belief demands assent to something more than the principle of diffusiveness. Some sort of "principle of plenitude" is required, i.e., some belief that perfect love necessarily expresses itself in *as many ways* as possible. But, as Morris shows, there are a number of problems with this principle, e.g., it entails too much and is too indeterminate, and so "there is no compelling reason to follow those who believe that God must have created some contingent universe or other."[155]

This inner tension is also evident in Moltmann's espousal of panentheism. While Moltmann intends with his form of panentheism to articulate a more satisfactory way to preserve divine transcendence while emphasizing divine immanence, it is not clear that he is successful. For example, Moltmann argues on the one hand that the intra-trinitarian *perichoresis* is an "archetype" for the understanding the relationship between God and creation. As indicated in chapter four, the relationship between

---

[153]Ibid.

[154]Ibid. See also p. 108 where Moltmann says that "the idea of the world is already inherent in the Father's love for the Son" since the love of God must communicate itself to that which is genuinely other than God.

[155]Morris, *Our Idea of God*, 149.

254   The Greening of Theology

God and creation must therefore be characterized in terms of "mutual need and mutual interpenetration"--"the mutuality and the reciprocity of love." It necessarily involves a "reciprocal indwelling." It is a *Gemeinschaftverhältnis* and so a fellowship "without privileges and without subordinances (*ohne Privilegien und ohne Abhängigkeiten*)."[156]

Yet Moltmann asserts that while "the relationship between God and creation has a *reciprocal* character"--such that not only does God put his impress on the world but the "world puts its impress on God too"--nonetheless the world "certainly does not do so in the same way."[157] The world does *not* affect God in the same way that God affects the world. While God is not indifferent to the world, the world still "represents an object (*Gegenstand*), a counterpart (*Gegenüber*)" to God.[158] And so Moltmann rather cryptically declares that while "God and the world are related to one another through the relationship of their mutual indwelling and participation" nevertheless "God's indwelling in the world is divine in kind" while "the world's indwelling in God is worldly in kind."[159] Clearly there is a need here for greater clarity on what precisely the relationship between God and creation is. What does it mean to say, as Moltmann frequently does, that God is *in* the world and the world is *in* God?

There are also problems with Moltmann's use of the concept of *zimzum*. Moltmann employs this concept as a way of more precisely explaining his version of panentheism. The world is "in God" because and only because God has withdrawn himself and provided a space for creation to be. Thus, so he argues, "creation outside of God exists simultaneously *in* God." However, putting aside the fact that this theory of creation suggests a kind of *creatio de Deo* or theogeny which Moltmann disavows,[160] it is unclear whether Moltmann can, despite his intentions, actually affirm creation. If, as Moltmann maintains, the self-limitation of God and

[156]Moltmann, *The Trinity and the Kingdom*, 157.
[157]Ibid., 98-99. On p. 3 Moltmann clearly states: "The relationship between God and man is not a reciprocal relationship between equals."
[158]Ibid., 99.
[159]Moltmann, *God in Creation*, 150.
[160]See, e.g., Moltmann, *God in Creation*, 75.

the creation of a primordial *nihil* is a necessary condition for the world to exist, and if redemption is the refilling of that space, then how can the fundamental distinction between God and creation be preserved in the eschatological redemption of all things? Can creatureliness *per se* be affirmed in Moltmann's doctrine of creation? Walsh puts this point particularly well. Describing Moltmann's view he says:

> Redemption, then is not primarily a restoration of a covenantal relationship broken in history, but a 're-filling' of that space, an overcoming of God's self-limitation by means of an *annihilatio nihili*. But if this *nihil* was for some reason necessary for the *creatio originalis* then how can the God/creation distinction still be maintained when this *nihil* is vanquished and God is all in all? Is the distinction between pantheism and panentheism only semantic?[161]

While Moltmann claims that the eschatological kingdom "does not imply a pantheistic dissolution of creation in God," it is not evident whether his doctrine of creation actually allows him to affirm creation.[162]

Returning to Moltmann's basic claim that God is preeminently love, this necessarily implies, for Moltmann, that God is a suffering God. He contends that the usual assertion of the apathy of God "only really says that God is not subjected to suffering in the same way as transient, created beings," and so "does not exclude the deduction that in another respect God certainly can and does suffer."[163] Thus Moltmann argues that "if God were incapable of suffering in every respect, then he would also be incapable of love;" however, "if he is capable of loving something else, then he lays himself open to the suffering which love for another brings him."[164] In other words, since "love is acceptance of the other without regard to one's own well-being," love necessarily entails the possibility of suffering, and since God is

161Walsh, "Theology of Hope and the Doctrine of Creation," 75.
162Moltmann, *God in Creation*, 89.
163Moltmann, *The Trinity and the Kingdom*, 23.
164Ibid; cf. 32.

love, God is at least capable of suffering.[165] The possibility of suffering is a necessary condition for the ability to love, and since God is love, God must be able to suffer. Thus Moltmann concludes that while "God does not suffer out of deficiency of being, like created beings," God does suffer "from the love which is the superabundance and overflowing of his being."[166] Moltmann's argument here is as elegant as his conclusion is profound.

Given that God is able to suffer, Moltmann further concludes that, in contrast to both atheism and traditional theism, "God and suffering are no longer contradictions; rather "God's being is in suffering and the suffering is in God's being itself, because God is love."[167] In short, God is for Moltmann the crucified God. And as Moltmann eloquently reminds us: "The symbol of the cross in the church points to the God who was crucified not between two candles on an altar, but between two thieves in the place of the skull, where the outcasts belong, outside the city."[168] God the Father himself suffered on the cross of Jesus, and God continues to suffer in the crosses of today--in South Africa, Mexico, Chicago.[169] Therefore, as Moltmann simply puts it, "the history of the world is the history of God's suffering."[170] Or as he affirms, quoting Dietrich Bonhoeffer: "Only the suffering God can help us."[171]

The Spirit in the Trinity

As explicated in chapter four, Moltmann's understanding of the Trinity as communal, social, and family-like implies some concept of person, especially divine person. Moltmann acknowledges this when he affirms that his concept of unitedness

---

[165]Moltmann, *The Crucified God*, 230. On the same page Moltmann says that "the one who is capable of love is also capable of suffering."

[166]Moltmann, *The Trinity and the Kingdom*, 23. See also, Moltmann, *The Future of Creation*, 93.

[167]Moltmann, *The Crucified God*, 227; cf. 214, 253.

[168]Ibid., 40.

[169]Ibid., 192, 200ff.

[170]Moltmann, *The Trinity and the Kingdom*, 4. See also Nicholas Wolterstorff, *Lament for a Son*, 91.

[171]Moltmann, *Experiences of God*, 17. Bonhoeffer's quote is from *Letters and Papers from Prison*, (New York: Macmillan, 1972), 361.

"presupposes the personal self-differentiation of God, and not merely a modal differentiation, for only persons can be at one with one another."[172] Moltmann defines a person as an independent subject or agent. For example, he argues that it is permissible to call the Holy Spirit a "divine person" only if the Spirit is an "independent subject of his own acts (*eines selbständigen Subjektes von Handlungen*)."[173] The Holy Spirit must be understood "not as an energy" but as "a subject"--"as the centre of the act, which is to say as 'person'."[174] Moltmann thus not only helpfully distinguishes between energy and agency, but properly describes persons, including the Holy Spirit, as necessarily characterized by intentions as well as energy. The Spirit is a person.

But a person is not merely an agent, for Moltmann, but an agent intrinsically related to an other. In contrast to the "individualistic reduction" of the concept of person common today, in which the term 'person' means an individual essentially *un*related to any other, Moltmann recaptures a pre-modern understanding of person and persuasively argues that "without the social relation there can be no personality."[175] He insists, for example, that "men and women can only become persons in relation to other men and women."[176] The concepts of person and individual, in other words, must be distinguished since the concept of person, properly understood, is a relational concept, while the concept of individual is not.

It follows that if God is personal, then God is essentially relational. The three persons of the Trinity, claims Moltmann, are not only in some sense distinct from one another, but "are just as much united with one another as in one another, since personal character and social character are only two aspects of the same thing."[177] Because "being a person in this respect means existing-

---

[172]Moltmann, *The Trinity and the Kingdom*, 150.
[173]Ibid., 125.
[174]Ibid., 126; cf. 142-143. On p. 171 Moltmann defines divine persons, following the classic definition given by Boethius, as the "individual, unique, non-interchangable subjects of the one, common divine substance, with consciousness and will."
[175]Ibid., 145.
[176]Ibid., 156.
[177]Ibid., 150.

in-relationship (*In-Beziehungen-Existieren*)," Moltmann argues: "The three divine Persons exist in their particular, unique natures as Father, Son, and Spirit in their relationships to one another, and are determined through these relationships. It is in these relationships that they are persons."[178]

Moltmann claims that "this relational understanding of the person...takes us beyond the 'substance' thinking of Boethius" since it engenders a more felicitous way of speaking about both divine unity and diversity.[179] More exactly, Moltmann argues that "the three divine Persons possess the same individual, indivisible and one divine nature, but they possess it in varying ways."[180] That is, in the Trinity there is only one divine nature, but there are three distinctive and person-constituting relations, viz., *paternitas*, *filatio*, and *spiratio*. One must distinguish, in other words, between two natures: a divine nature which the three persons have in common and a person nature which is unique to each member of the Trinity. As Moltmann states, the members of the Trinity "have the divine nature in common; but their particular individual nature is determined in their relationship to one another."[181] He concludes:

> The constitution of the Persons and their manifestation through their relations are two sides of the same thing. The concept of substance reflects the relations of the Person to the common divine nature. The concept of relation reflects the relationship of the Persons to one another....The trinitarian Persons *subsist* in the common divine nature; they *exist* in their relations to one another.[182]

Moltmann is quite helpful in speaking of divine unity and diversity in these terms since the distinction between kind essence and person essence is a useful one.[183] A kind essence is a cluster of

---

[178]Ibid., 172.
[179]Ibid.
[180]Ibid.
[181]Ibid.
[182]Ibid., 173.
[183]For elaboration of this distinction see, e.g., Thomas Morris, *Our Concept of God*, chap. 9; Edward Wierenga, *The Nature of God: An Inquiry into Divine Attributes* (Ithaca: Cornell, 1989), 11; Ronald Feenstra and Cornelius Plantinga, eds., *Trinity, Incarnation, and Atonement:*

properties individually necessary and jointly sufficient for membership in a natural kind, e.g., humanness, tree-ness, divinity. An individual *exemplifies* a kind essence. In contrast, an individual essence is a cluster of properties essential for an individual to be the particular entity that it is, e.g., Jürgen Moltmann, that birch tree, the Holy Spirit. An individual *is* an individual essence. Thus, as Moltmann says, each of the three persons of the Trinity possesses a divine nature or essence and each person also possesses a unique individual, or more properly, personal nature or essence constituted by the inter-relationships within the Trinity. In this way justice can be done to both the unity and plurality of the Trinity and one can speak coherently both of what is distinctive of each person of the Trinity and of what each person has in common.

Moltmann proceeds to argue that "the doctrine of *the Trinity of love* carried on the development of the concept of Person, and took it one step further."[184] He contends that in the theology of Richard of St. Victor, for example, "every divine Person exists in the light of the other and in the other" because of "the love they have for one another."[185] Moltmann further claims that Hegel "picked up this idea and deepened it" since he affirmed that "it is the nature of the person to give himself entirely to a counterpart, and to find himself in the other most of all."[186] The concept of person is thus not only relational, but necessarily implies a relationship of self-giving love. In sum, Moltmann claims:

> The substantial understanding of person (Boethius) and the relational understanding of person (Augustine) was now expanded by the historical understanding of person (Hegel). The Persons do not merely 'exist' in their relations; they realize themselves in one another by virtue of self-surrendering love.[187]

Thus Moltmann insists that the category of change must be added to the categories of person and relation if the life of the Trinity is to

---

Philosophical and Theological Essays (Notre Dame: University of Notre Dame, 1989), 28-29.

[184]Moltmann, *The Trinity and the Kingdom*, 173.
[185]Ibid.
[186]Ibid., 174.
[187]Ibid.

be adequately expressed. We must be able to talk of "the history of God (*die Geschichte Gottes)*" and "God's passion for his Other."[188]

Given this understanding of the Trinity as a community of persons existing in love--of "the love story of the God whose very life is the eternal process of engendering, responding and blissful love"--Moltmann argues that the inner trinitarian life not only "does not correspond to the solitary human subject in his relationship to himself," but that it does not "correspond, either, to a human subject in his claim to lordship over the world."[189] Rather, the perichoretic life of the Trinity "only corresponds to a human fellowship of people without privileges and without subordinances (*eine menschliche Personengemeinschaft ohne Privilegien und ohne Abhängigkeiten).*"[190] Among the persons of the Trinity there are no isolated individuals nor any relations of hierarchy or subordination. And if there is this mutuality and reciprocity within the God-head, and if the relations within the Trinity are a paradigm for human relationships, then the doctrine of the Trinity must "point towards a community of men and women without supremecy and without subjection (*eine menschliche Gemeinschaft ohne Vorherrschaft und Unterwerfung)*" and therefore point beyond "dependency, helplessness, and servitude (*Abhängigkeit, Ohnmacht, und Knechtschaft).*"[191] The social Trinity, Moltmann contends, "replaces the principle of power by the principle of concord and replaces authority and obedience with "dialogue, consensus, and harmony."[192]

Moltmann rightly emphasizes ethical norms like harmony, fellowship, and community and justifiably condemns the oppression and subjugation of humans by other humans, especially when legitimated on putatively Christian grounds. There can be no truck with such religiously sanctioned forms of oppression. However, a number of questions arise with respect to Moltmann's claims here. For example, is all power necessarily evil, or only a misuse of power? Is authority *per se* necessarily pernicious, or only

---

[188]Ibid.
[189]Ibid., 157.
[190]Ibid.
[191]Ibid., 192; cf. 198, 211.
[192]Ibid., 202.

when it is abused? Is obedience in itself necessarily a bad thing, or only obedience in certain forms or to certain causes? God, after all, calls Christians to a life of obedience. Moltmann often seems to assume that power, authority, and obedience *per se* are the problem, rather than their all too common misuse.

Furthermore, as stated previously, it is unclear how exactly the divine perichoresis can and should function as an "archetype" for either God's relationship to creation or relationships among creatures. Does the analogy between the relationships *ad intra* and the relationships *ad extra* imply that it is inappropriate to speak of *any* hierarchy or subordination between God and the world or with respect to different creatures in the world? Given the nature of God, the world, and its various creatures--even on Moltmann's terms--it would seem incredible to affirm, for example, that all relationships between humans and plants should exhibit "reciprocity" and "mutual indwelling." In fact Moltmann himself speaks of certain kinds of priority or subordination relations within as well as outside of the Trinity.[193]

Also, with respect to the relation between God and creation, Moltmann's assertion that the Spirit is the "bridge" between God and the world as a whole--the "immanent transcendence in all things"--is problematic. It is, for example, unclear exactly what Moltmann means with his claim that God "creates out of the powers and energies of his own Spirit." If he means to posit some sort of *creatio de Deo*, then he appears to contradict his own affirmation of *creatio ex nihilo*. If he intends to stand by *creatio ex nihilo*, then he needs to specify further what the "out of" means in his statement that God creates out of the powers of the Spirit. Moltmann is clearly wrestling with important ontological and theological issues. He wants to incorporate the strengths of the emanation tradition, e.g., its insistence on a non-arbitrary divine presence in creation, into a doctrine of creation which preserves divine freedom. But if "creation is a kind of outpouring of the Spirit," it is unclear whether he can achieve his own intentions.

---

[193]See, e.g., Moltmann, *The Trinity and the Kingdom*, 94-95, and *God in Creation*, 188, 203ff.

Despite these problems, with both his social theory of the Trinity and concept of creation in the Spirit Moltmann does a great service in emphasizing the immanence of God in creation. In an age in which the Spirit is often conceived of as some amorphous cosmic energy and creation is usually seen as mere "nature," Moltmann reaffirms a classic and much-needed view of the Holy Spirit. As Calvin rightly affirms, "it is the Spirit who, everywhere diffused, sustains all things, causes them to grow, and quickens them in heaven and in earth."[194] And so Moltmann's central claim that "creation in the Spirit is the theological concept which corresponds best to the ecological doctrine of creation which we looking for and need today" has considerable appeal.[195] Insofar as the ecological crisis stems from a view of creation as evacuated of divine presence, a theological perspective like Moltmann's which affirms the sustaining presence of God the Spirit in all things and envisions creation as the home and dwelling of God has much to offer. If, as the epigraph at the beginning of chapter four puts it, "the whole creation is a fabric woven and shot through by the efficacies of the Spirit," then we have good reason to see the world "charged with the grandeur of God."[196]

Conclusion

As indicated in this chapter, there are both assets and liabilities in Moltmann's theology. As clearly revealed by this inquiry into his anthropology, ontology, and theology, Moltmann's theological reflections are highly instructive--concerning both fruitful possibilities and likely problems--for those desiring to articulate a Christian ecological theology. Greater attention is given in the last chapter to these strengths and weaknesses.

The criticisms leveled against Moltmann's thought in this chapter, however, should not detract from or in any way diminish his creative, thought-provoking, and in many ways pioneering systematic work. While there may be problems with his theology,

---

[194]Calvin, *Institutes of the Christian Religion*, 1.13.14.
[195]See ch. 4, footnote 146.
[196]From "God's Grandeur," by Gerard Manley Hopkins.

his is one of those relatively rare theological perspectives which--
because of its subtlety and thoroughness as well as its openness and
irenic spirit--encourages, indeed forces, critical engagement with
one's own assumptions and arguments. In so doing, his theology
also opens up the possibilities for dialogue. As A. J. Conyers notes,
Moltmann "more than any other theologian that comes to mind
draws dialogue partners as a magnet draws iron filings," and so
"his insights have penetrated so many and such varied circles of
current thought."[197] His considerable constructive contributions
aside, that his theology serves as an opportunity for critical self-
clarification and fosters greater dialogue is itself no meager
accomplishment.

---

[197]Conyers, *God, Hope, and History*, xi.

CHAPTER 8

TOWARD A CHRISTIAN ECOLOGICAL THEOLOGY

Any error about creation also leads to an error about God.[1]

Thomas Aquinas

I confess, of course, that it can be said reverently, provided that it proceeds from a reverent mind, that nature is God; but because it is a harsh and improper saying, since nature is rather the order prescribed by God, it is harmful in such weighty matters, in which special devotion is due, to involve God confusedly in the inferior course of his works.[2]

John Calvin

Who, finally is my *neighbor*, the companion whom I have been commanded to love as myself?... He is the near one and the far one, the one removed from me by distances in time and space...the unborn generations who will bear the consequences of our failures, future persons for whom we are administering the entrusted wealth of nature and other greater common gifts. He is man and he is angel and he is animal and he is inorganic being, all that participates in being.[3]

H. Richard Niebuhr

The task in this last chapter is to gather together in a coherent and clear way the most important insights of the previous chapters in order to provide the basis for a more adequate Christian ecological theology. This task involves critically comparing the views of Ruether, Sittler, and Moltmann and ferreting out the relative strengths and weaknesses of each perspective. To facilitate this endeavor I present these conclusions as a series of propositions or theses.

---

[1]Thomas Aquinas, *Summa Contra Gentiles*, II.3.
[2]John Calvin, *Institutes of the Christian Religion*, I.5.5.
[3]H. Richard Niebuhr, *The Purpose of the Church and Its Ministry* (New York: Harper and Row, 1956), 38.

In addition, this chapter is a continued defense of the overall thesis of this project, namely, that the fundamental concepts of human, world, and God must be reconceived in certain ways. This chapter is, then, an attempt to argue for certain necessary changes in anthropology, ontology, and theology. More exactly, a Christian ecological theology will be adequate to both its own tradition and the current ecological crisis only if it moves beyond the dualism of nature and history, accounts adequately for the responsiveness of creation, and takes seriously the doctrine of the trinity.

Anthropology: Beyond the Dualism of Nature and History

The first proposition is that an adequate Christian ecological theology must develop and persuasively articulate an integral anthropology. This claim is supported by all three of the thinkers examined in this project. For example, Ruether, Sittler, and Moltmann all repudiate the typical dualism of body and soul and seek to construct a more holistic view of the human person. Ruether rejects dualism because it legitimates both the subjugation of women and the exploitation of the earth. Sittler disavows dualism because it is contrary to both the witness of the Bible and the conclusions of modern science. And Moltmann repudiates dualism, in addition to the above reasons, because seeing the world as home will occur only if we are at home in our bodies. In their rejections of typical anthropological dualisms, all three thinkers rightly emphasize the interconnections between how we see ourselves and how we see the world of which we are a part.

Ruether is especially helpful in this regard for she presents a persuasive argument that links the dualism of body and soul with the domination of both women and earth. Ruether argues that if the soul or spirit is viewed as not merely different than but of higher value than the body, and if the body represents matter, then that which is identifed with the body--the earth, women--will be devalued and dominated. It is no coincidence that we speak of the "rape" of both women and the earth. The fear of the body and the fear of finitude and the attempt to control and conquer the body, matter, and the natural world must somehow be overcome. Hence, as Ruether claims, a more ecologically adequate theology is possible only if bodiliness is affirmed, and bodiliness can be affirmed only if a more unitary view of the human person is adopted. Hilde Hein represents this typically feminist perspective when she argues that the dichotomy of spirit and matter, or soul and body, must be rejected if philosophy is to be liberated and spirituality properly conceived.[4] In short, these thinkers provide backing for the affirmation that a Christian ecological theology must incorporate a more holistic anthropology--one which does not sanction the domination of women or the earth.

Ruether, Sittler, and Moltmann also all illustrate various problems with the attempt to formulate a more satisfactory anthropology. For example, Ruether wishes to affirm a more holistic anthropology, but her own proposal lacks the sufficient development and precision to function usefully as an alternative paradigm. Admittedly Ruether's major contribution does not lie in systematic articulation; but if an ecological theology is to take seriously her perceptive analyses and conclusions, then greater attention must be given to the development of a more sophisticated philosophical and theological anthropology that specifies in some detail just what a more integral or holistic view of the human person looks like.[5]

Similarly, Sittler is instructive not only because he points to the biblical testimony regarding anthropological holism and the embeddedness of humanity in the bio-physical world, but also because the weaknesses in some of his arguments highlight the need for better arguments. Merely asserting that humans are embedded in the natural order is insufficient to warrant the claim that humans are unitary. It must be acknowledged that Sittler's signal contribution is the presentation not of rigorous arguments

---

[4]Hilde Hein, "Liberating Philosophy: An End to the Dichotomy of Spirit and Matter," in *Beyond Domination*, 125-128.

[5]For one attempt at specifying such a model, see Arnold DeGraaff, "Towards a New Anthropological Model," in *Hearing and Doing*, eds. John Kray and Anthony Tol (Toronto: Wedge, 1979), 97-118. For two other very helpful works, see John Cooper, *Body, Soul, and Life Everlasting;*, especially chap. 10, and also C. Stephen Evans *Preserving the Person* (Grand Rapids: Baker, 1977), chap. 11.

but of an eloquent vision of creation graced by God; however, an ecological theology must give adequate attention to more precise argumentation as well as to the larger vision.

So also, Moltmann is instructive because of both the liabilities and the assets of his view. For example, like Sittler Moltmann retrieves the more holistic categories from the Bible in his attempt to fashion a theological anthropology. And his emphasis on humans as the priests of creation is a helpful way of speaking of the human responsibility to represent God in creation. However, the unresolved ambiguities in Moltmann's theological anthropology regarding the categories of body, soul, and spirit lead to the conclusion that greater attention must be given to this crucial issue of definition. In sum, a Christian ecological theology must seek greater precision, clarity, and sophistication in constructing an integral anthropology.

Second, an adequate Christian ecological theology must acknowledge the link between ecological degradation and social injustice, and correlatively, ecological wholeness and social justice. With this claim all three thinkers concur. As Ruether persuasively argues, for example, the renewal of the earth and the emancipation of women are interdependent. We must think in terms of the concept of ecojustice if we are to address adequately either the concerns of the environmental movement or the goals of the various movements for human liberation. Sittler too recognizes the interconnections between the domination of non-humans and humans. As he succinctly states: "All abuse is a distortion of right use, for persons as for all things."[6] The degradation of forests and lakes is of a piece with the exploitation of women and the poor. And Moltmann, likewise, throughout his writings points to the need for an expansive ethical orientation which includes justice for both non-humans and humans. For example, he argues that "we shall not be able to achieve social justice without justice for the natural environment, and we shall not be able to achieve justice for

---

[6]Sittler, *Essays*, 133.

nature without social justice."[7] The concept of ecojustice is a necessary feature of any fully adequate ecological theology. With their insistence on viewing ecological wholeness and social justice as integrally related, these theologians join a growing chorus of thinkers who affirm the necessity of some such concept as ecojustice within Christian theology and ethics. For example, Ian Barbour maintains: "Poverty and pollution are linked as products of our economic institutions. Exploitation of man and of nature are two sides of the same coin; they reflect a common set of cultural values and a common set of social structures."[8] Norman Faramelli argues that "economic or distributive justice must become an active component in all ecology debates."[9] Peri Rasolondraibe reiterates such a judgment when he claims that "any environmental activism which does not address such [social] injustice...is indeed naive."[10] William Gibson affirms conversely that "there cannot possibly be any serious commitment to economic justice that is not inclusive of ecological responsibility."[11] James VanHoeven argues that traditional theologies of creation must be rethought in such a way that they affirm that "ecological threats and injustice are inseparable."[12] Or as David Tracy and Nicholas Lash simply state: "The struggle for justice must also include the struggle for ecology."[13] Charles Birch puts this point perhaps as clearly as possible: "It is a cock-eyed view that regards ecological liberation as a distraction from the task of liberation of the poor. One cannot

---

[7]Moltmann, *The Future of Creation*, 130. See also, Moltmann, *The Crucified God*, 332, 336; *The Experiment Hope* (Philadelphia: Fortress, 1975), 176; *The Church in the Power of the Spirit* (New York: Harper and Row, 1977), 174; *On Human Dignity* (Philadelphia: Fortress, 1984), 28; *God in Creation*, 24, 320; and *The Way of Jesus Christ*, 212, 255.

[8]Barbour, *Western Man and Environmental Ethics*, 4. See also Norman Gottwald, "The Biblical Mandate for Eco-Justice Action," in *For Creation's Sake*, 32-44.

[9]Barbour, *Western Man and Environmental Ethics*, 188.

[10]Peri Rasolondraibe, "Environmental Concern and Economic Justice," *Word and World* 11 (Spring, 1991): 150.

[11]William Gibson, "Eco-Justice: New Perspective for a Time of Turning," in *For Creation's Sake: Preaching, Ecology, and Justice*, ed. Dieter Hessel (Philadelphia: The Geneva Press, 1985), 25.

[12]VanHoeven, "Renewing God's Creation," 141.

[13]Tracy and Lash, *Cosmology and Theology*, 90.

be done without the other. It is time to recognize that the liberation movement is finally one movement."[14] In short, any adequate Christian ecological theology must also be a liberation theology.

Third, an adequate Christian ecological theology must resist the individualism of modernity and, in contrast, creatively present a vision and corresponding set of practices which emphasize the multifaceted relational character of human existence in the world. Ruether, Sittler, and Moltmann all reach this conclusion and provide impressive support for this politically unpopular claim. Ruether's communitarian perspective, for example, calls into question many of the assumptions of the modern vision of the good social order while also attempting to incorporate typical liberal ideals like equality and liberty into an alternative vision which emphasizes community and mutuality. She mentions many concrete, practical steps that enhance community--between humans and the earth as well as among people. This resistence, it should be emphasized, must include *practices* which initiate people into earth-friendly ways of living or the acids of individualism will continue to eat away at well-intentioned efforts to establish and maintain community.

Mention of practices or habitual patterns of behavior leads directly to an important though largely unexplored topic, namely, ecological virtues. If certain practices are to be established, then habitual dispositions to act must be shaped in and with and for the Christian community. James Nash offers one of the few discussions of this issue and presents nine traits of character or virtues which merit inclusion in a Christian ecological theology and ethic. They are: sustainability, adaptability, relationality, frugality, equity, solidarity, biodiversity, sufficiency, and humility.[15] Each of these deserves more than a mere mention, but the point here is simply that with this claim concerning individualism and community, as with all of the other propositions in this chapter, the actions which flow from the theology necessarily imply an ethic--an ethic characterized by certain virtues.

---

[14]Charles Birch, "Creation, Technology, and Human Survival," *Ecumenical Review* 28 (1976): 76.

[15]Nash, *Loving Nature*, 63-67.

With his intrinsically relational concept of person, Sittler too reminds us that humans are constituted not only by their relationships with other people but also by their relationships with the non-human world. As he repeatedly says, "the world of nature is...also a self-constituting datum" of human identity and existence.[16] And Moltmann also emphasizes the inextricably communal character of human being and action when he argues that as *imago mundi* the human is "a being that can only exist in community with all other created beings and which can only understand itself in that community."[17] In sum, these thinkers all agree that any adequate ecological theology must transcend individualistic views of creaturely flourishing with a perspective which gives much greater attention to the relational nature of both human and non-human existence.

Fourth and finally with respect to anthropology, an adequate Christian ecological theology must move beyond the typical dualism between nature and history. Ruether, Sittler, and Moltmann all strenuously insist that this is one of the central requirements of any adequate Christian ecological theology. Ruether gives five cogent arguments for why this dualism must be rejected: 1) this dualism is false because the natural world is historical in its own right; 2) this dualism is false because the natural world is indelibly affected by human agency and thus a part of human history; 3) this dualism is false because, as corporeal, humans are embedded in the natural order; 4) this dualism has led to disastrous consequences since it has sanctioned various forms of exploitation; 5) this dualism conflicts with the biblical emphasis on a single all-embracing covenant. For these reasons, Ruether justifiably insists that these two categories must be reconceived.

Sittler, likewise, employs some of the same arguments to back the claim that these categories must be rethought. We must, says Sittler, speak of "the world-as-nature" and "the world-as-history" rather than of nature and history. He observes that Christians especially have been tempted by this dualism since "Christianity

---

[16]Sittler, "The Presence and Acts," 131.
[17]Moltmann, *God in Creation*, 186.

proudly presents itself as a historical religion."[18] The assumption in this view is that history is defined as and limited to *human* history and thereby set over against nature. Consequently redemption and grace extend only as far as history, i.e., humanity. As Sittler rightly notes, this assumption is "a fundamental misunderstanding."[19] History must be redefined as inclusive of all being and nature must be reconceived as inclusive of human being. These revisions are fully compatible with the claim that Christianity is a historical religion. Indeed they more accurately capture the comprehensive biblical vision of the redemption of bodies, of grace for a groaning creation, and of shalom for all of God's creatures.

Support for this claim is found in Moltmann's theology also, for he vigorously repudiates the typical view in which nature and history are defined over against each other. For many of the same reasons given by Ruether and Sittler--e.g., because creation is coherent, because human history is part of the overarching history of creation, because humans are embodied creatures--Moltmann concludes that the traditional modern paradigm must be replaced by a view in which human history is integrated into "the wider concept of nature."[20] A post-modern ecological theology must move beyond the dualism of nature and history.

A large number of other thinkers also argue that a necessary condition for any adequate Christian theology is the rejection of this dualism and the attempt to articulate a different view of the relationship between what typically is referred to with the terms history and nature. For example, Sallie McFague proposes as one of her four criteria for a "theology of nature pertinent to the closing years of the twentieth century" that "it needs to see human life as profoundly interrelated with all other forms of life, refusing the traditional absolute separation of human beings from other creatures."[21] Likewise one of the conclusions William French

---

[18]Sittler, "Ecological Commitment," 176.

[19]Ibid.

[20]Moltmann, *God in Creation*, 125.

[21]Sallie McFague, "Imaging a Theology of Nature: The World as God's Body," in *Liberating Life: Contemporary Approaches to Ecological Theology*, eds. Charles Birch, William Eakin, and Jay McDaniel (Maryknoll: Orbis, 1990), 203.

reaches is that "the conceptual reification of the polarization of history and nature no longer makes sense."[22] Any adequate ecological theology must reject these categories as typically defined. Ian Barbour concurs when he asserts that "the Christian tradition has too often set man apart from nature."[23] In contrast we must affirm the unity of the human and nonhuman worlds, while nevertheless recognizing the distinctive features of humankind. As Barbour maintains: "These distinctive features of human existence can be acknowledged without denying man's fundamental unity with nature."[24] As David Tracy and Nicholas Lash succinctly state: "History cannot be understood without nature" and thus "contemporary Christian theology needs to recover a theology of nature--even to develop an adequate theology of history."[25]

While the call to abandon the dualism of nature and history is abundantly clear, the specific contours of an acceptable alternative paradigm are as yet unclear, as evident by the various problems with the constructive proposals offered by Ruether, Sittler, and Moltmann. For example, with her emphasis on the continuity between humans and non-humans Ruether fails to specify precisely the distinction between human action and the events of the natural world. What are the *differentiae* that distinguish humans from other creatures? What are the properties, functions, features that all and only humans have that allow us, while acknowledging the similarities between human and non-human creatures, nonetheless to do justice to the undeniable differences?

So too with Sittler there is much clarity regarding what he rejects and why, but there is precious little with respect to what he proposes as an alternative perspective. His suggestion that the earth might better be envisioned as sibling--sister or brother--is helpful as far as it goes, but in the end it does not go very far. Such

---

[22]French, "Christianity and the Domination of Nature," 563.
[23]Barbour, "Attitudes Toward Nature and Technology," 152.
[24]Ibid., 155.
[25]Tracy and Lash, *Cosmology and Theology*, 87, 89. On the opening page of *On Nature* (Notre Dame: University of Notre Dame, 1984), editor Leroy Rouner states that the interest in integrating the categories of nature and history is "the dominant theme" in the volume.

a revisioning of our non-human neighbors is an important dimension of a constructive alternative to the unhelpful dualism of nature and history, but much more work in philosophical and theological anthropology and in ontology is necessary. The same basic conclusion obtains for Moltmann: while it is clear what he wishes to reject, it is less clear what he offers as a alternative and whether his alternative, insofar as it is clear, is persuasive. For example, how *exactly* are we to integrate the concept of history into the "wider concept of nature"? What *precisely* does it mean to posit that history and nature must be seen in their "reciprocal dependence"? And does Moltmann actually redefine the terms nature and history or does he merely reconceive the relationship between them but in such a way that they continue to present the same intractable problems?

In sum, these three thinkers point out many of the inadequacies with regard to theological anthropology. In so doing, they provide grounds for one of the basic claims of this endeavor, namely, that the fundamental concept of the human must be reconceived. In addition, with their creative (even if in some respects inadequate) constructive proposals, they offer some specific ways in which this category can and should be revised if theology is to be adequate to the tasks and the challenges at hand.

Ontology:
The Responsiveness of Creation

One of the reasons for some of the problems outlined above, e.g., the ambiguity concerning the relationship between nature and history, is that the *concept* of nature itself is ambiguous. The ambiguity to which I refer here is *not* that there are different *views* of nature (which there are), but that the idea itself is capable of being understood in more than one way. For example, in his famous study *The Idea of Nature* R. G. Collingwood traces three different views of nature in the history of Western culture: nature as organism, as machine, and as evolving process.[26] But Collingwood himself often confuses two particular concepts of nature. Most often nature means the *totality* of reality; it is defined, as he himself says, in terms of cosmology. However, nature also means the non-human *part* of reality. And these are only two of several concepts of nature often not distinguished from one another. As indicated with respect to Ruether, Sittler, and Moltmann--who exhibit this problem in varying degrees--the failure to distinguish properly between different concepts of nature lies at the heart of a number of other issues.

Others have observed this same problem. Claude Stewart, for example, explicitly focuses on this question about the nature of "nature" and identifies at least three main usages of the term. According to Stewart nature can mean: 1) "that which stands over against 'culture' or human artifice"; 2) "the totality of structures, processes, and powers that constitute the universe," not including God; and 3) the totality of reality including God.[27] Stewart concludes that because of this ambiguity surrounding the concept of nature there is "considerable confusion concerning precisely what the theologian of nature is about."[28] Declares Stewart:

> None of the theologians of nature taken for our examination and few, if any, other significant contributors to the literature falling under the rubric of the theology of nature engage in a sustained critical treatment of the concept of nature....We conclude, therefore, that one of the immediate duties of the theologian of nature is to engage in a critical examination of the concept of nature.[29]

Paulos Gregorios echoes Stewart when he states that "it is the very concept of nature itself that is problematic."[30] He identifies five different concepts of nature: 1) that which happens without human intervention, e.g., the laws of nature; 2) the non-human part of creation, e.g., birds, plants, air; 3) that which is beyond the

---

[26]R. G. Collingwood, *The Idea of Nature* (Oxford: Oxford University, 1960). Carolyn Merchant's fine study *The Death of Nature* is also very helpful in this regard.

[27]Stewart, *Nature in Grace*, 239; cf. 155.

[28]Ibid., 237.

[29]Ibid., 238.

[30]Gregorios, *The Human Presence*, 17.

realm of human agency, e.g., nature as opposed to history or
culture; 4) that which is within the range of ordinary human power,
e.g., nature as opposed to supernature or grace; and 5) the given
structure or constitution of a person or thing, e.g., human nature,
feline nature, the nature of zinc.[31] Gregorios further argues that
only the last concept is found in the Bible and that the most common
concepts--nature as the whole of creation and nature as the non-
human aspects of creation--are "a Hellenic legacy in western
Christian thought" which assume "the absence of the notion of God
who created and sustained the cosmos."[32] In other words, the most
common concepts of nature entail certain metaphysical
assumptions which should not go unchallenged by Christians.

Gordon Kaufman also notes that there are different concepts
of nature--three basic concepts in his view. Nature can refer to 1)
"the essential qualities or properties" of a particular existent or
that which constitutes a person or thing; 2) "the totality of powers
and processes that make up the universe;" and 3) "that which exists
independently of all human artifice."[33] Kaufman observes that the
ambiguity of the concept arises from the complexity of that which
we try to designate with the term since

> in a very real sense man is a natural being, is a part of nature and
> sustained by it...and yet man is able to distance himself from nature
> sufficiently to conceive it as something over against him which he
> perceives and on which he can work, which he transforms through
> his activity into the "artificial" or "unnatural" reality which we call
> "culture."[34]

Kaufman, like Gregorios, further argues that the concept of nature
has an "implicit metaphysic"--naturalism or the view that the
universe is without purpose, value, and meaning--which implies
that for Christian theologians "the concept will have to be
subjected to careful scrutiny and used only with the greatest care"

---

[31]Ibid., 18.
[32]Ibid., 21, 23. See also Paulos Gregorios, "New Testament Foundations for Understanding the Creation," in *Tending the Garden*, 85-87.
[33]Gordon Kaufman, "A Problem for Theology: The Concept of
Nature," *Harvard Theological Review* 65 (1972): 339-341.
[34]Ibid., 343.

since "the metaphysical tendencies implicit in it are not obviously congruent with those of Christian faith."[35]

At least two important conclusions can be drawn from this discussion. First, an adequate Christian ecological theology must give greater attention to clarifying the concept of nature itself. Some typology, like those mentioned above, is required in order to bring greater clarity to the discussion. This implies, as stated previously, that more work must be done specifying in precisely what ways humans are similar to and different from other creatures. Using Kaufman's language, we must specify more exactly in what ways the human is "a part of nature" and in what ways the human is "able to distance himself from nature." My own suggestion here, following Gregorios, is that the term "nature" refer to the essence of an individual existent and that the adjective "natural" refer to nonhuman creatures. So one could speak of the nature of a marmot or a mountain or a meadow--all of which are features of the natural world. My argument for adopting such terminology follows, but whatever the specific proposal it is clear that this conceptual confusion must end. Greater clarity on the very concept of nature itself is badly needed.

The second conclusion drawn from the above discussion is that an adequate Christian ecological theology must challenge the metaphysical assumptions implicit in certain concepts of nature. As both Kaufman and Gregorios suggest, the term nature and the various concepts associated with it are laden with metaphysical assumptions, some of which conflict with basic beliefs of the Christian faith. For example, the notion that the cosmos exists without God or that while God exists the universe is nevertheless meaningless or autonomous or purposeless--all these conflict with central Christian beliefs about God and creation. I have, for example, in this work generally avoided the term "nature" since it can all too easily connote not the resplendent creation of the God of grace and love, but a godless self-regulating machine. I have eschewed the expression "theologian of nature" for the same reason. Language is important and terms or concepts which run counter to Christian faith must be revised or rejected.

---

[35]Ibid., 347-348.

Of the three thinkers dealt with here, Sittler offers the most vigorous support for this claim. As he insists, insofar as the concept of nature implies something autonomous and separate from God, it should be rejected in favor of the concept of creation, since the concept of creation "contains and requires a God-postulation."[36] Like Sittler, Robert Quam argues that whether one uses the term "nature" or "creation" is *not* just a "manner of speaking" since these terms "suggest differing assumptions about both environment and humans" and "significantly different" assumptions about God.[37] So also Loren Wilkinson argues that neither "natural resources" nor "the environment" nor "nature" are biblically adequate expressions for what more properly goes by the name creation.[38]"Nature" must be construed as *creation* in any adequate Christian theology. Hence the concept of nature must not only be clarified, but clarified in certain ways, viz., in harmony with basic Christian beliefs.

The above remarks lead to a third conclusion, namely, that an adequate Christian ecological theology must be theocentric. Sittler and Moltmann, and to some degree Ruether, concur on the truth and importance of this claim. Only such a perspective, for example, can avoid both the assumption that the world is autonomous and the assumption that the world is divine and thus preclude both a naturalism which divests creation of its grace-full character and a romanticism which re-enchants creation with some sort of quasi-divine status. As Sittler reminds us: "The world is not God, but it is God's."[39] Only such a theocentrism--in which God is affirmed as the source of being and existence, of ultimate meaning and value-- is able both to preserve human uniqueness and affirm the interdependence of creation and thereby avoid both an anthropocentrism that fails to acknowledge the commonality of humans with other creatures and a cosmocentrism that refuses to admit human distinctiveness. In the words of Moltmann: "The *theocentric* biblical world picture gives the human, with his special position in the cosmos, the chance to understand himself as a

---

[36]Sittler, *Essays*, 99.
[37]Quam, "Creation or Nature?," 131-132.
[38]Wilkinson, *Earthkeeping in the Nineties*, 347-350.
[39]Sittler, "Ecological Commitment," 178.

member of the community of creation."[40] Only a theocentric perspective not only informs us of our true identity as children of the Redeemer who is also our Creator but also reveals the identity of our non-humans neighbors as creatures of the same God. As Sittler states, echoing Augustine and Calvin: "Knowing *who* we are is a reality that depends finally on *whose* we are."[41] We are God's and the creatures of the earth are our sisters and brothers.

In addition to Sittler and Moltmann many others support this claim about the superiority of a theocentric perspective. For example, Paul Santmire asserts that neither cosmocentrism with its "ethic of adoration" nor anthropocentrism with its "ethic of exploitation" is adequate since both tacitly assume a dualism between nature and history, differing only in which has priority.[42] Wes Granberg-Michaelson insists that "creation has value because of its relationship to God, rather than its utility for humanity" since the world "was created by God, is constantly sustained by God, and gives glory to God."[43] Hence Granberg-Michaelson concludes: "A theocentric, rather than an anthropocentric, view lies at the heart of an environmental ethic built on this [biblical] foundation."[44] And Richard Young, as the subtitle of his book indicates, cogently argues that a theocentric perspective offers the best approach to solving today's ecological problems.[45]

A fourth conclusion that emerges from this inquiry is that an adequate Christian ecological theology must conceive of creation as coherent and interdependent. Ruether, Sittler, and Moltmann all stress, appealing to both science and scripture, that creation is a unified whole of interdependent parts. And in his survey and

---

[40]Moltmann, *God in Creation*, 31.

[41]Sittler, *Grace Notes*, 113.

[42]Santmire, *Brother Earth*, chaps. 1-2; see also Santmire, "The Future of the Cosmos and the Renewal of the Church's Life with Nature," in *Cosmos as Creation*, 270.

[43]Wesley Granberg-Michaelson, "Renewing the Whole Creation," *Sojourners* (February-March 1990): 12; see also "At the Dawn of a New Creation," *Sojourners* (November 1981); and "Earthkeeping: A Theology for Global Sanctification," *Sojourners* (October 1982).

[44]Granberg-Michaelson, "Renewing the Whole Creation," 12.

[45]Richard Young, *Healing the Earth: A Theocentric Perspective on Environmental Problems and Their Solutions* (Nashville: Broadman and Holman, 1994).

analysis Stewart also concludes that the most adequate theologies "emphasize the organic interdependence of all things."[46] Barbour draws attention to this fact as well when he argues that in addition to being based in scripture an adequate ecological theology must be informed by modern science. And one of the conclusions of modern science, he states, is that "nature is an interacting community" and "an integrated ecosystem."[47] We must, in short, speak of "the interdependence of living things" and "man's unity with nature."[48]

More easily intellectually assented to than experientially grasped, these claims that creation hangs together and displays intricate and complex patterns of mutual dependence are crucial ingredients in any adequate ecological theology. Moreover, widespread acknowledgment that this is how the world works is doubtless a necessary condition for genuine or lasting progress in ameliorating contemporary ecological degradation. We are all in this together--one community of creation. Whether in the textual witness of the Psalms or in the topographical witness of the landscape, we must grasp these central truths.

A fifth conclusion to emerge from this investigation is that an adequate Christian ecological theology must conceive of creation in terms of dynamic temporal process. All of the thinkers examined in this project emphasize this feature of created reality, as do both Stewart and Barbour, among others. For example, Stewart finds that, in addition to emphasizing the interdependence of creation, the most adequate theologies "replace the traditional static understanding of 'nature'...with a view of nature as complexifying temporal process."[49] So also, Barbour maintains that "nature as dynamic process" is one of the significant concepts from science that must be incorporated into a ecological theology.[50] As Moltmann succinctly puts it: creation is *fieri*, not *factum*. It is not only coherent and interdependent but dynamic and developing.

As the many questions in the previous three chapters attest, however, there is much more work to be done in clarifying these

[46]Stewart, *Nature in Grace*, 240.
[47]Barbour, *Earth Might Be Fair*, 7.
[48]Ibid.
[49]Stewart, *Nature in Grace*, 239.
[50]Barbour, *Earth Might Be Fair*, 7.

concepts. For example, with respect to Ruether's insistence that because of the interdependent nature of creation hierarchy *per se* must be discarded, Richard Mouw argues that while many types of hierarchy should be summarily rejected, e.g., patriarchy, certain forms of hierarchy are necessary ingredients in any adequate Christian theology. For example, he insists that "the Creator-creature distinction is basic to biblical religion" and thus that "God is in a very crucial sense infinitely 'higher' than we are."[51] Mouw perceptively observes that "an affirmation of one very important form of hierarchy is implied by the insistence on the part of many feminist theologians that an emphasis on divine *transcendence* must be maintained."[52] Or with regard to Moltmann's concept of eschatology--with its emphasis on the openness of nature and the dynamic character of creation--William French asserts that Moltmann "overemphasizes the 'openness' of nature, its open history, its evolution, its 'subjectivity'" and hence "fails to do justice to the relative 'closedness' of the ecosystem, to its fragile balance and stable structures that sharply limit the range of adaptability of the biosphere."[53] In sum, the claims that creation is coherent, interdependent, dynamic, and developmental themselves require further development.

All of the above contentions may perhaps best be summarized by the claim that an adequate Christian ecological theology must take more seriously the responsiveness of creation. That is to say, the common view of the natural world as essentially autonomous and unresponsive--as "nature"--must be replaced by a perspective in which the natural world is seen as grace-full and response-able. All creation is a place of grace. And all creatures respond to the call of God to be and become, each in their own creature-specific way. If these claims were taken more seriously, the concept of nature could be clarified in some important ways, the natural world would necessarily be construed as the creation of a God of goodness and grace, and thus a form of theocentrism would be maintained, and

[51]Richard Mouw, *The God Who Commands: A Study in Divine Command Ethics* (Notre Dame: University of Notre Dame, 1990), 163.
[52]Ibid., 162.
[53]French, "Returning to Creation," 83.

the coherence and dependence as well as the dynamic and developmental nature of creation could better be highlighted.

Of the authors here studied Sittler especially supports this claim that creation is intrinsically grace--that creation is not a stage for grace but itself a form and a result of grace. Sittler, furthermore, with his image of non-human creatures as siblings and companions gives prominence to a kind of response-ability appropriate to non-human creatures. For example, he contends:

> Man is not alone in this world, not even when his aloneness is unalleviated by the companionship of the fellowman. The creation is a community of abounding life--from the invisible microbes to the highly visible elephants, the vastness of the mountains, the sweep of the seas, the expanse of land. These companions of our creaturehood are not only *there*; they are there as things without which I cannot be at all! They surround, support, nourish, delight, allure, challenge, and talk back to us.[54]

Sittler does not specify the precise sense in which non-human creatures "talk back," but he intends that this rather "unscientific" claim be taken quite seriously. As mentioned already, Paul Santmire argues that because of "a certain *mysterious activity*" of non-human creatures we must introduce a third type of basic relationship in addition to the I-Thou and I-It relations identified by Buber, namely, the I-Ens relation. Like Sittler and Santmire, Walsh, Karsh, and Ansell also insist that Christian theology must give more attention to the responsiveness of all creatures and of creation as a whole to God's multifaceted call to be and become.[55] If we are to acknowledge a way of relating to our non-human neighbors that is not captured by traditional concepts and thus be enabled to speak more fully of the responsiveness of creation, then some new language is required.

Others who attest to the responsiveness of creation could be cited, e.g., John Muir, Aldo Leopold, Barbara McClintock, but the

---

[54]Sittler, "Evangelism and the Care of the Earth," 102.

[55]For example, on p. 16 of "Trees, Forestry, and the Responsiveness of Creation," Walsh, Karsh, and Ansell conclude that trees are "responsive agents."

basic point is perhaps clearest in the Bible itself. For example, the Psalmist exultantly sings:

> Let the heavens be glad, and let the earth rejoice;
> Let the sea roar, and all that fills it;
> let the field exult, and everything in it.
> Then shall all the trees of the forest sing for joy
> before the LORD; for he is coming,
> for he is coming to judge the earth.
> He will judge the world with righteousness,
> and the peoples with his truth.
>
> Psalm 96:11-13

Or as the prophet joyously and hopefully exclaims in describing his vision of restoration and abundant life:

> For you shall go out in joy, and be led back in peace;
> the mountains and the hills before you
> shall burst into song,
> and all the trees of the field
> shall clap their hands.
> Instead of the thorn shall come up the cypress;
> instead of the brier shall come up the myrtle;
> and it shall be to the LORD a memorial,
> for an everlasting sign that shall not be cut off.
>
> Isaiah 55: 12-13

Should these texts be "demythologized" as usual and read as merely poetic hyperbole and personification? Or do such typically modern readings represent a debilitating form of "cultural autism"? In other words, do such readings blind us to the biblical testimony of the covenant solidarity of all creatures? Do they make us deaf to the actual experiences of creaturely response-ability and kinship?[56] These are not trivial or hypothetical or irrelevant questions. A Christian ecological theology must wrestle with these and other such questions of ontology. In sum, these reflections provide warrant for one of the basic claims of this endeavor, namely, that the way we think about the world must be reexamined.

---

[56]Ibid., 13.

Theology:
The Social Trinity

As mentioned previously one of the central issues with respect to theology proper is how best to conceive of the relations of God to the world and the world to God. As Robert Neville states, this question is a "central issue" in theology and philosophy, usually presented in terms of "the speculative problem of the transcendence and presence (or immanence) of God."[57] God is, the Christian tradition insists, both qualitatively different than and essentially related to creation.

Langdon Gilkey nicely summarizes a number of the important issues at stake in this discussion. While the Christian doctrine of creation emphasizes both "the ontological transcendence of God and the goodness or value of creation," says Gilkey, these affirmations "were qualified by their apparent opposites--the divine immanence in the world and the ambiguity of creation."[58] Thus, Gilkey argues:

> The *immanence* of God in creation follows as a polar concept to the divine transcendence, as the symbol of providence is entailed in that of creation. God is both transcendent to creation and therefore absolute, and at the same time immanent and participating in or relative to creation.[59]

---

[57]Neville, *God the Creator*, 1-2.

[58]Gilkey, "Creation, Being, and Non-Being," in *God and Creation*, 228

[59]Ibid., 229. Gilkey contends (pp. 230-231) that this claim has a number of important implications for the "interrelations between God, the human, and nature." For example, he argues that in such a view of God and creation "nature and humankind are implicitly and deeply related to one another; both have value as God's creation; both reflect the divine life, order, and 'glory'--if not the divine image--and both participate in the divine purpose of redemption and reunion." The fact that these affirmations have "remained at best implicit, at worst forgotten and overlooked" because of the emphasis on human history in no way abrogates their truth or importance. This fact, rather, raises the central question of "how can we reevaluate radically the status, role, and value of nature, which we have overlooked, and yet preserve the affirmation of history and of the human-- on which most of our culture's real values rest?"

The Christian doctrine of creation rejects both a monism, which views the plurality other than God as a part of God or as unreal, and a dualism, which views God as merely one finite factor among others. As Gilkey observes:

> Theologians of creation have all teetered on a thin line between monism and dualism, each leaning towards one or the other of these poles. Some have emphasized more the *presence* of God in creation and so the continuing and pervasive dependence of finitude on God (and tended) towards monism (Augustine, Luther, Scheiermacher, Tillich). Others have emphasized the *distinction* between the transcendent God and creation and thus tended towards dualism (Thomas, Calvin, Barth). All alike, however, have in the end illustrated the dialectical, paradoxical notion implicit in creation: the world is totally and essentially dependent on God (*non ex materia*), and yet the world is not identical with God (*non de Deo*). Correspondingly, God transcends the world as distinct from it, and yet God is immanent within the world as the source of its being, as the principle of its life and order, and as the ground of its hope for fulfillment.[60]

In other words, to state the first proposition concerning theology, an adequate Christian ecological theology must reject both ontological monism and ontological dualism while yet affirming both divine immanence and divine transcendence--the presence of God in creation and also the basic ontological distinction between God and creation.

Ruether, Sittler, and Moltmann all support this claim. That is, they all attempt to articulate a view of God which rejects both monism and dualism and affirms both divine transcendence and immanence. And in so doing they try to reconceive God in such a way as to move beyond the eclipse of creation and validate the natural world. Ruether, for example, with her concept of God as Primal Matrix affirms the need to preserve divine transcendence while attempting to recapture the presence of God in, with, and

---

[60]Ibid. In a very helpful article on the doctrine of creation *ex nihilo*, David Kelsey concurs with Gilkey on these matters and further argues that the affirmation of these beliefs regarding God and creation necessarily implies certain attitudes toward God, e.g., reverence, gratitude, and certain dispositions toward creation, e.g., respect, care; see Kelsey, "The Doctrine of Creation from Nothing," in *Evolution and Creation*, ed. Ernan McMullin (Notre Dame: University of Notre Dame, 1985), 179-180.

under creation. With his stress on divine grace and nature as grace, Sittler, too, affirms God's immanence in and with creation while also insisting on the fundamental distinction between God and creation. And Moltmann affirms divine transcendence even though his emphasis on the nature and function of the Holy Spirit is, among other things, designed to reconceive God as profoundly present in creation. A Christian ecological theology must strive to preserve both divine transcendence and immanence, absoluteness and relatedness, as it seeks to explain the mystery of the relationship between God and the world.

There are, however, numerous problems with these attempts to walk, as Gilkey puts it, the "thin line between monism and dualism." Given that these three thinkers all emphasize divine immanence, the problems not surprisingly stem from a failure to maintain a sufficiently strong distinction between God and creation. In other words, one or more of McGinn's "four D's"-- dependence, distinction, decision, and duration--is sacrificed in the attempt to reconceive the relation between God and creation in a way which does more justice to divine presence in creation. For example, Ruether calls into question the basic distinction between God and creation with her version of panentheism. At times she seems to fuse God with creation in such a way that immanence engulfs transcendence and God and creation become virtually indistinguishable. Moltmann, similarly, with his explicit embrace of a form of panentheism seems, despite claims to the contrary, to deny both the absolute distinction between God and creation and the free decision by God to create the world.

This tendency to fudge on the God-creation distinction in the otherwise admirable effort to stress divine relatedness to creation leads to a second proposition, namely, that an adequate Christian ecological theology must not just emphasize both divine transcendence and immanence (as asserted above), but must affirm that God's relatedness actually *depends* upon God's otherness. In other words, divine transcendence and immanence are not, as is often assumed, contradictory or incompatible, as if one entails the contrary of the other. Rather, as Loren Wilkinson suggests, "God is lovingly involved with creation *because* God is other than his creation."[61] That is, it is impossible for God to be intimate with creation unless God is transcendent to creation since the kind of loving intimacy predicated of the biblical God is possible only of an agent who is not identical or coextensive with the other. In short, divine immanence is contingent upon divine transcendence.

The central question here concerns which model of or analogy for the God-world relationship is best able to express God's intimate relatedness to the world and yet also maintain a strong distinction between God and creation. Both Claude Stewart and Ian Barbour provide helpful typologies of common models of the God-creation relation. Stewart lists five basic types: 1) the deistic model in which God is likened to an inventor and the world is analogous to a machine; 2) the dialogic model in which the relationship between God and the world is viewed as a relationship between two persons; 3) the monarchical model in which God is akin to a king and the world is his subject; 4) the processive-organic model in which God is to the world as an individual is to a community; and 5) the agential model in which the God-world relation is analogous to the relationship between an agent and the agent's actions.[62] Stewart not only identifies but critiques these different models, exhibiting their respective strengths and weaknesses. He further argues that a synthesis of the monarchical, processive-organic, and agential models is the most satisfactory position, though in his view "the agential model performs more of the functions requisite to an adequate theology of nature, with fewer of the liabilities, than any of the other models of the God-world relationship" and thus "the most promising path-- the best way forward--lies in the development of a theology of nature rooted in the agential model."[63]

Barbour also furnishes a useful typology of models. His list consists of eight types arranged in three groups.[64] In the group he calls "classical theism" there is: 1) the classical or monarchical model in which the relationship between God and creation is like that between a ruler and his kingdom; 2) the deist model in which

---

[61]Wilkinson, *Earthkeeping in the Nineties*, 278.
[62]Stewart, *Nature in Grace*, chap. 6.
[63]Ibid., 280-281.
[64]Barbour, *Religion in an Age of Science*, chap. 9.

God is like a clockmaker and the world is like a clock; and 3) neo-
Thomist model which posits that God is to the world as a worker is
to a tool. Barbour makes various criticisms of these three types--
that they cannot adequately explain human freedom, that they are
patriarchical, that they are too static and do not take evolution
seriously enough--and thus considers a set of alternative models: 4)
the kenotic model in which God is like a parent and the world is like
a child; 5) the existentialist model in which God is to the world as a
person is to an object; 6) the linguistic model which envisions God
as an agent and the world as an action; and 7) the embodiment
model in which the world is construed as the body of God. Barbour
also offers various criticisms, pointing to both the assets and
liabilities of each type. In the end Barbour presents an eighth
model--that of process theism--in which God is analogous to the
leader of a community, which is the world. Barbour concludes that
"the process model thus seems to have fewer weaknesses than the
other models considered here."[65]

While Stewart and Barbour advocate the agential and
process models, respectively, the embodiment model also finds
many supportive voices. For example, Sallie McFague argues that
viewing the world as God's body more adequately captures the
immanence of God vis-a-vis creation without necessarily reducing
God to the world.[66] Grace Jantzen contends that construing the
world as the body of God provides a better understanding of
typical divine attributes like omnipotence and omnipresence and

---

[65]Ibid., 270. Barbour's process orientation is also evident in the classic
work *Issues in Science and Religion* (New York: Harper and Row, 1966),
439ff. There are many others who propose the process model as the best
model. Perhaps the best known theologian is John Cobb; see, e.g., with
respect especially to ecological concerns, *Is It Too Late?: A Theology of
Ecology* (Beverly Hills: Bruce, 1972); and *Process Theology as Political
Theology* (Philadelphia: Westminster, 1982).

[66]McFague, *Models of God*, 69ff. McFague actually combines the
embodiment model with the agential model. For example, on pp. 72-73 she
argues that in such a "panentheistic" model, i.e., the embodiment model,
"God remains as the agent, the self, whose intentions are expressed in the
universe," and on pp. 78ff she insists that we must speak of God in agential
terms as, e.g., mother, lover, and friend. Indeed the entire second half of the
book elaborates on these agential models of God as mother, lover, and
friend.

also is "able to provide a better account not only of immanence but even of transcendence than we could do on the model of cosmic dualism."[67] And Jay McDaniel asserts that while "there can and should be a variety of images, some traditional and some not" to describe the relationship between God and the world, viewing God as "the heart of the universe" and creatures as "the body of this heart" is a model which has much to commend.[68]

This is not the place to engage in an extensive discussion of this important and complex issue. However, it seems to me that Stewart's claim that the agential model is the most promising is on the mark. For example, compared to the process and embodiment models, the agential model better preserves important claims about divine freedom and grace (and the rest of McGinn's "four D's") and is thus most in harmony with scripture and tradition. The agential model also seems best able to redeem the claim that divine immanence is contingent upon divine transcendence. That is, by speaking of God as an agent who intends and brings to completion certain actions, this model shows promise not only in linking divine relatedness and otherness, but in showing how the former is dependent upon the latter.

One perceptive and well-argued attempt to develop this model in some detail and defend it against various objections is that of Thomas Tracy. In essence Tracy argues that "conceiving of God as the perfection of agency opens up a path between process theology and classical theism, and nicely balances some of their contrasting strengths and weaknesses."[69] In contrast to those who advocate the embodiment model, Tracy defends a view of God as an *un*embodied agent. His attempt to forge a mediating alternative which combines the best of both classical theism and process theology is quite suggestive and merits much greater attention than it has heretofore received. Regardless of which specific model is employed, however, an adequate Christian ecological theology

---

[67]Grace Jantzen, *God's World, God's Body* (Philadelphia: Westminster, 1984), 101-102.

[68]Jay McDaniel, *Of God and Pelicans: A Theology of Reverence for Life* (Louisville: Westminster/John Knox, 1989), 48.

[69]Thomas Tracy, *God, Action, and Embodiment* (Grand Rapids: Eerdmans, 1984), 148.

must give serious attention to this issue of models for the God-world relation and, in particular, to the topic of divine agency.[70] More precisely, to reiterate the second conclusion of this section, an adequate Christian ecological theology must affirm that divine immanence depends on divine transcendence.

The third claim advanced here is that an adequate Christian ecological theology must re-envision God as mother as well as father. To attend to models of the relationship between God and creation is implicitly if not explicitly to attend to models of God. And for much too long the predominant if not exclusive model of God has imaged God as male. God is (perhaps) like a mother, the argument goes, but God *is* a father.[71] The witness of both scripture and tradition, however, suggests otherwise.The three thinkers examined in this endeavor all bear eloquent witness to the claim that God must be imaged in more gender inclusive ways. Indeed, one of the central desiderata of Ruether, and one of her most important contributions to Christian theology, is the affirmation that God must be conceived of as mother as well as father. As Ruether argues, so long as the image of father connotes such "masculine" traits like distance and independence, then viewing God exclusively in terms of father, or other male images like king, will emphasize God's transcendence and otherness rather than God's immanence and relatedness, thereby evacuating the world of divine presence and concern and so legitimating the exploitation of the earth. On the other hand, a more inclusive view that employs female images for God would better emphasize the presence of God in and love of God for creation and thus foster an attitude of

---

[70]While some impressive and insightful work has already been accomplished, much remains to be done, especially with respect to the concerns specific to an ecological theology. Examples of recent important works concerned with divine agency are: William Alston, *Divine Nature and Human Language: Essays in Philosophical Theology* (Ithaca: Cornell, 1989); Brian Hebblethwaite and Edward Henderson, eds., *Divine Action: Studies Inspired by the Philosophical Theology of Austin Farrer* (Edinburgh: T and T Clark, 1990); Thomas Morris, ed., *Divine and Human Action: Essays in the Metaphysics of Theism* (Ithaca: Cornell, 1988); Kathryn Tanner, *God and Creation in Christian Theology: Tyranny or Empowerment?* (Oxford: Basil Blackwell, 1988); and Tracy, *God, Action, and Embodiment.*

[71]For example Donald Bloesch, *Is the Bible Sexist?* (Westchester, IL: Crossway, 1982).

respect and care for the earth. In short, the exclusive reliance upon patriarchal images of God must give way to a more inclusive view of the first person of the Trinity which embraces images of God as caregiver and nurturer.

Moltmann seconds Ruether's insistence that we must speak of God as mother as well as father. For example, he argues that in the trinitarian understanding of God we must speak of God the father as "a motherly Father" since "a father who both *begets* and *gives birth* to his son is no mere male father."[72] Moreover, God should be understood not only "as the motherly Father of the only Son he has brought forth" but "at the same time as the fatherly Mother of his only begotten Son."[73] In other words, according to Moltmann the doctrine of the Trinity itself "makes a first approach towards overcoming sexist language in the concept of God."[74] And while the image of mother is, perhaps, one of the most important female images for God, it is certainly not the only one. The Bible is full of many rich non-sexist images that express the care and concern of God.[75]

The fourth proposition is that an adequate Christian ecological theology must include a christology as expansive in scope as the cosmos itself. This is one of Sittler's major contributions--the articulation of a view of the person and work of Christ which includes the entire symphony of creation. In contrast to traditional christology which typically limits its scope to (human) history, both scripture and science, says Sittler, conspire to force an expansion of the typical christological categories in the direction of a "christology for nature." As Sittler clearly insists in a summary of his famous New Delhi address: "Only a Christology capable of administering the cosmic scope of biblical and catholic Christ-

---

[72]Jürgen Moltmann, "The Motherly Father: Is Trinitarian Patripassianism Replacing Theological Patriarchicalism?" in *God As Father?*, 53.

[73]Moltmann, *The Trinity and the Kingdom*, 164.

[74]Ibid., 165.

[75]See, e.g., Virginia Ramey Mollenkott, *The Divine Feminine: The Biblical Imagery of God as Female* (New York: Crossroad, 1987), and Leonard Swidler, *Biblical Affirmations of Women* (Philadelphia: Westminster, 1979).

testimony would be adequate to the question about Christ and his meaning as it is necessarily put by men of modernity."[76]

Moltmann endorses Sittler's move to a cosmic christology. Indeed, in a chapter entitled "The Cosmic Christ" Moltmann argues that "concern about the things of Christ therefore requires us to go beyond the christology developed in modern times, which was a christology in the framework of history, and compels us to develop a *christology of nature.*"[77] We need, he states, to "enquire again into the wisdom of ancient cosmic christology."[78] After a discussion of Sittler's contribution Moltmann concludes: "Christology can only arrive at its completion at all in a cosmic christology. All other christologies fall short."[79] Thus Sittler and Moltmann, among others, point to another important desideratum for an ecological theology. In short, a view of the second person of the Trinity which focuses exclusively on humanity must be replaced by a christology that is cosmic in scope and includes within its purview not merely human history but the entire natural world.

This insistence that the scope of christology must be expanded leads to a fifth claim, namely, that an adequate Christian ecological theology must affirm that the Christian God is a suffering God. Sittler and Moltmann, of the three theologians examined here, emphasize and provide support for this claim. As Sittler declares, because of the "cruciform character of human existence" life must be addressed "if it is to be savingly struck, in an action which itself is cruciform."[80] It is in the "ineffable, inexplicable, almost unimaginable suffering" of Jesus that we fellow sufferers discover "the heart of the Christian message," namely, that "God himself enters our dying--that God, the Creator of all things, the life of life, has himself undergone that which is most common to us humans."[81] "The Christian faith," affirms Sittler, "says that nothing in human experience is outside the experience of God." And so Sittler's

---

[76]Sittler, *Essays*, 8.

[77]Moltmann, *The Way of Jesus Christ*, 274; see also, Moltmann, *God in Creation*, 94-95, 170-171.

[78]Moltmann, *The Way of Jesus Christ*, 274.

[79]Ibid., 278; cf. 194, 255-256, and especially 286ff.

[80]Sittler, "The Cruciform Character of Human Existence," 20.

[81]Sittler, "Speeches," 28, and *Grace Notes*, 119.

cosmic Christ is a crucified God. The Maker of the universe is a suffering servant. The cross is the central symbol of Christian faith, concludes Sittler, "because the whacks of life take that shape." And so "unless you have a crucified God, you don't have a big enough God."[82] Only a suffering God can help.

Moltmann is one of the most well-known thinkers who contend that God is a suffering God. He argues that the fact that God is love necessarily implies that God is not an apathetic but a suffering God. The possibility of suffering is a necessary condition for the ability to love. Moltmann further argues that God's suffering does not, like our suffering, originate from some deficiency or lack of perfection; rather God's pathos and thus passibility stem from "the superabundance and overflowing of his being."[83] God's suffering is evidence of the unbounded and irrepressible care exhibited by the community of love God is. Thus "God and suffering are no longer contradictions;" rather, claims Moltmann, "God's being is in suffering."[84] God's suffering is a kind of divine perfection--a perfection of love.

Sittler and Moltmann are by no means alone in their repudiation of divine apathy and advocacy of divine passibility and hence in their support of the claim that God suffers. In a fascinating historical study Joseph Hallman shows that there is a significant tradition within Christianity that diverges from the mainstream belief in divine impassibility. From Clement of Alexandria and Origen to Tertullian and Lanctantius, from Athanasius and Gregory of Nyssa to Hilary of Potiers and Augustine, Hallman shows how belief that God changes--more specifically that God suffers--has been affirmed.[85] For example, Hallman refers to a part of Origen's homily on Ezekiel 6:6 where Origen states:

> The Redeemer descended to earth out of sympathy for the human race. He took our sufferings upon Himself before He endured the cross--indeed before He even deigned to take our flesh upon Himself: if He he had not felt these sufferings He would not have

---

82Sittler, *Grace Notes*, 118-119.
83Moltmann, *The Trinity and the Kingdom*, 23.
84Moltmann, *The Crucified God*, 227.
85Joseph Hallman, *The Descent of God: Divine Suffering in History and Theology* (Minneapolis: Augsburg/Fortress, 1991).

come to partake of our human life. What was this passion which He suffered for us beforehand? It was the passion of love. But the Father himself, the God of the universe, who is full of longsuffering and plenteous in mercy and sympathy, does He not also suffer in a certain way? Or know you not that He, when he concerns Himself with human things, knows human suffering?[86]

So Sittler and Moltmann are simply joining their voices to the (too often unheard) voices of the communion of saints.

Paul Fiddes also argues that an adequate concept of God must include the attribute of divine suffering. Fiddes lists four main reasons for rejecting impassibility and accepting passibility: 1) suffering compassion is a necessary implication of love; 2) the cross of Jesus is of central significance to the character of God; 3) the problem of human suffering demands divine identification with suffering; and 4) the interdependence of reality requires a suffering God.[87] Fiddes, furthermore, argues that this view of God as passible is fully consonant with most of the traditional beliefs about God in the Christian tradition, e.g., belief in the transcendence of God, the aseity of God, creation *ex nihilo*.[88] With the help of Moltmann in particular Fiddes develops a trinitarian theology which satisfies the demand "for a suffering which penetrates to the inner being of a God who still remains transcendent."[89]

---

[86]Quoted from Moltmann, *The Future of Creation*, 69; also in Hallman, *The Descent of God*, 40.

[87]Paul Fiddes, *The Creative Suffering of God* (Oxford: Clarendon, 1988), chap. 2. In chapter one Fiddes identifies "four major contributions" to the issue of divine passibility in the contemporary debate: 1) *Kreuzestheologie*, e.g., Moltmann; 2) process theology, e.g., Cobb; 3) the "death of God" theology; and 4) classical theism. While finding theology from the cross and process theology to be mutually corrective and the most promising possibilities, Fiddes nonetheless declares on p. 15 that "a theology of a suffering God needs to weave all four of these strands into a pattern, or to use another image, it must stand where four ways cross."

[88]Ibid., 110.

[89]Ibid., 135. In his careful study of divine impassibility, *Divine Impassibility: An Essay in Philosophical Theology* (Cambridge: Cambridge University, 1986), Richard Creel distinguishes between four aspects of impassibility--nature, will, knowledge, and feeling--and concludes that God is passible, but only with respect to knowledge. Creel's arguments against divine impassibility of feeling are not as sound as his arguments for divine impassibility of nature and will; however, regardless of whether one agrees

In sum, an adequate Christian ecological theology must include a cosmic christology, but a cosmic christology must also be a *theologia crucis*. And as indicated above, this claim itself entails a reconception of divine perfection. Divine perfection need not necessarily mean absolute changelessness or invulnerability or imperviousness to suffering. Rather, as Langdon Gilkey states, "this whole identification of perfection with security and invulnerability was rejected" in light of the cross of Christ and so perfection "took on an entirely new meaning."[90] "The message of the cross," according to Gilkey, "was that the perfection of God in history, and the perfect obedience of man to God, are revealed by just that suffering love, even in the face of death."[91] Expressing the heart of the matter clearly and succinctly, as usual, Gilkey says:

> To the amazement of all, the disciples and enemies of Christ alike, the divine power reveals itself in precisely that which is most vulnerable and powerless: self-giving love. Truly here was one of the most radical transformations of values in all historical experience: not the avoidance of suffering, but its willing acceptance in love, became the deepest clue to divinity.[92]

The sixth proposition with respect to theology proper is that an adequate Christian ecological theology must give greater attention to the Holy Spirit. While reconceiving God as mother as well as father and viewing the person and work of Christ in cosmic terms are necessary, they are not sufficient. Also required is an overcoming of the eclipse of the Spirit evident in much of modern

---

with him in every respect Creel is most instructive in his basic contention that in any discussion of divine impassibility or passibility the distinct meanings of the terms must first be clarified.

[90]Gilkey, *Maker of Heaven and Earth*, 214.

[91]Ibid.

[92]Ibid. See also, "Creation, Being, and Non-Being," 233, where Gilkey states that it is no surprise that most theologians in this century have questioned the priority of the definition of God as Absolute Being and have, rather, "empathized with Moltmann's effort to understand the divine nature also in terms of the divine suffering present in and revealed through the crucifixion."

For an eloquent, profound, and poignant expression of the truth that suffering love is the deepest clue to divinity, see Nicholas Wolterstorff, *Lament for a Son* (Grand Rapids: Eerdmans, 1987).

theology. Moltmann in particular is of great assistance on the topic of pneumatology. With his emphasis on creation in the Spirit, creation as the home of the Spirit, the cosmic presence of the Spirit, the Spirit as bridge and bond, Moltmann points to the central theological importance of the reality and role of the Holy Spirit. An ecological theology will be deficient if it fails to affirm and articulate the being and action of the Spirit. Moltmann is right to claim that, properly conceived, a pneumatological doctrine of creation is an ecological doctrine of creation.

Moltmann's insistence on the importance of the Spirit is reiterated by many others. Wesley Granberg-Michaelson, for example, argues that "a fresh understanding of the Holy Spirit is central to the church's faith and witness on behalf of renewing the whole creation."[93] Paul Fries maintains that only a "consistently trinitarian perspective" which affirms that "the Holy Spirit is the integrity of creation" will be able to break the bonds of the conceptual dualisms that chain our thinking.[94] And James VanHoeven claims that "a Spirit-recast theology of creation opens possibilities for 'untraditional thinking' about nature," e.g., viewing the natural world as more than simply "the stage for the divine-human drama."[95] In short, the typical view of the Holy Spirit as unimportant must be replaced by a vigorous acknowledgement that the Spirit is the authentic and pervasive presence of God in creation.

In summary with regard to these last four conclusions, Ruether's claim that God is like a mother as well as like a father, Matrix as well as Creator; and Sittler's claim that Christ is cosmic, Lord of nature as well as history, agent of creation as well as redemption; and Moltmann's claim that the Holy Spirit permeates creation--in, with, and under all being: these three claims are necessary if not sufficient conditions for an adequate Christian ecological theology.

A seventh conclusion, implied by the claims summarized above, is that the doctrine of the Trinity must play a pivotal role in

---

[93]Granberg-Michaelson, "Renewing the Whole Creation," 13.

[94]Fries, "Explorations in the Spirit and Creation," 12.

[95]VanHoeven, "Renewing God's Creation," 148. See also George Hendry, *Theology of Nature* (Philadelphia: Westminster, 1980), chaps 7, 9.

any adequate Christian ecological theology. In other words, if those claims are indeed necessary for the development of an adequate ecological theology, then a doctrine of the Trinity is entailed. Various other arguments can be given to back this contention. Sittler argues, for example, that only a doctrine of the Trinity is able to express adequately the scope of grace. That is, if creation and not just human history is the place of grace, then a three-personed God is required to understand the expansiveness of grace as the energy of God's love. Sittler also contends that only with a doctrine of the Trinity can one develop coherently a cosmic christology. No pale monotheism can do justice to the claims that God was in Christ reconciling the entire cosmos back to himself or that God tented among us full of grace and truth. Without the doctrine of the Trinity an ecological theology is doomed to failure.

Moltmann, too, vigorously argues that any non-trinitarian perspective is seriously deficient. Indeed, this claim is the burden of his *The Trinity and the Kingdom* . Only a fully trinitarian concept of God is consonant with the revelation of God as not only Creator but incarnate Son and indwelling Spirit. A Christian theology is authentically Christian only if God is viewed in terms of Father, Son, and Spirit. Or as Paul Fiddes simply puts it, in working out a theology in which God is both passible and transcendent, "I have found the concept of God as Trinity indispensable."[96] Langdon Gilkey once again captures the essence of the matter:

> Nevertheless its [the Trinity's] permanent theological importance is that it represents an intellectual formulation of the very heart of the Church's faith, and that the Christian confidence in victory over the power of evil is based on the Church's certainty of its truth....The basic religious affirmation of the doctrine of the Trinity is that the love of Christ and the grace of the Holy Spirit manifest and represent the love and grace of the power of all being and of all existence. Now if this conjunction of the power of all being with the love of Christ is not made, the Christian Gospel--and one could say all hope in life itself--falls apart.[97]

---

[96]Fiddes, *The Creative Suffering of God*, 110; see also p. 131 where he argues that a Trinitarian theology is "more successful" than process theology in accomplishing this task of "preserving both the transcendence of God and a suffering which inhabits every corner of his Being."

[97]Gilkey, *Maker of Heaven and Earth*, 211.

Christian hope depends upon the trinitarian conviction that the unexpected grace which catches us and lovingly holds us above the abyss is the very power which fuels the universe. Moltmann's claim, however, is not just that the doctrine of the Trinity is essential, but that a *particular* doctrine of the Trinity is indispensable, namely, a *social* theory of the Trinity. Only a "social doctrine of the Trinity" adequately expresses "the history of the Trinity's relations of fellowship" within the Godhead itself, with humans, and with all creation.[98] Moltmann's claim is, in my judgement, persuasive and leads to the eighth and last proposition: an adequate Christian ecological theology must adopt a social trinitarian model. Not just an affirmation of the Trinity, but a view of the Trinity as a perichoretic community of love is the most promising path to take in forging an ecological theology.

This assertion of the necessity of a social theory of the Trinity must be viewed in the context of the various kinds of models of the Trinity in the Christian tradition. There are three main types: *nonpersonal* or natural models, *intra-personal* or psychological models, and *inter-personal* or social models. The first type may be found, for example, in Justin Martyr's claim that the Son is to the Father as a kindled fire is to the fire which is its source. Athenagoras, Tertullian, and Origen all argue that the relation between Son and Father is analogous to that of sunlight and sun. And both Gregory of Nanzianus and the Pseudo-Dionysius find the trinitarian relations exemplified in the mingling of three lights or three suns. Dionysius of Alexandria, in contrast, states that the relationships of plant to root and stream to fountain best describe the relationship of Son to Father. Light is obviously a common analogy from the natural world used to describe the inner-trinitarian relations.

The most common intra-personal models, as the name implies, have to do with some analogy between parts or aspects of the human person. For example, Athenagoras, Tertullian, Origen, and Hippolytus all employ an analogy between word and speaker, or mind and thinker, or will and actor to refer to the relationship

---

[98]Moltmann, *The Trinity and the Kingdom*, 19.

between the Son and the Father. Victorinus describes the three trinitarian *personae* in terms of *esse, vivere,* and *intelligere*. In his *De trinitate* Augustine, as is well-known, speaks of the first, second, and third persons of the Trinity with two sets of terms: *mens, notitia,* and *amor,* and *memoria, intelligentia,* and *voluntas*. This way of referring to the Trinity influenced Thomas Aquinas to speak of the Trinity as akin to being, intellect, and will or love.

The inter-personal or social type, in contrast to the types above, employ analogies of human relationships to articulate the inner-trinitarian reality. The most common metaphor is found is the New Testament, especially in the gospel of John, namely, that of son and father. Origen also images the relation between second and first persons of the Trinity in terms of the relation between child and parent, while the Pseudo-Dionysius uses the relationship between a student and Christian teacher. Perhaps the most pervasive expression of this type is the view that the Trinity is analogous to love between people. Richard of St. Victor, Alexander of Hales, Bonaventure, and Karl Barth are just a few of the theologians who describe the Trinity as a three-way relation of love between persons.[99]

It is this inter-personal or social model that I refer to in my eighth and final proposition. Moltmann is most helpful here. For Moltmann, God is best seen as analogous to a family. God is constituted by three persons or intrinsically related agents with a common divine essence or nature. While possessing a common divine-nature, each person has a distinctive person-nature determined by the unique relations with the other persons. God is, therefore, essentially relational.[100] These perichoretic relations are,

---

[99]For a relatively brief yet accurate survey of most of these views of the Trinity, see Christopher Kaiser, *The Doctrine of God* (Westchester: Crossway, 1982). For a much more extensive treatment see Edmund Fortman, *The Triune God: A Historical Study of the Doctrine of the Trinity* (Philadelphia: Westminster, 1972). For helpful analyses of past and present thinkers on this issue see *One God in Trinity*, eds. Peter Toon and James Spiceland (Westchester: Cornerstone, 1980), and Ted Peters, *God as Trinity* (Louisville: Westminster/John Knox, 1993). .

[100]A number of thinkers argue that this feature of God's being implies that God can be *essentially* relational *without* being *necessarily* related to *creatures*. That is, God's being can be constituted by relations

furthermore, characterized by mutuality, reciprocity, and fellowship. In sum, God is a community of love. To capture the reality of God we must speak, affirms Moltmann, of "the love story of the God whose very life is the eternal process of engendering, responding and blissful love."[101]

David Brown also presents a social theory of the Trinity and cogently defends it against various criticisms. Brown argues that a proper concept of person--one, for example, that distinguishes between individuality and individualism--renders a social theory of the Trinity coherent and can successfully escape the charge of tritheism.[102] Cornelius Plantinga likewise articulates "a strong or social theory of the Trinity" and ably defends it against "the usual objection that theories of this kind are tritheistic."[103] He persuasively argues that a social theory may be coherently stated and adequately defended if the proper definitions are adhered to and if assumptions about divine simplicity are reformulated.

The significance of a social theory of the Trinity for a Christian ecological theology, as explained in chapter four, lies in the fact that such a view of God helps ground a theology of relationship and an ethic of care. As Moltmann insists, if within God "there is no one-sided relationship of superiority and subordination, command and obedience, master and servant" but there exists rather "the mutuality and the reciprocity of love" and

---

(within the Trinity) and God can still create *ex nihilo*. For example, Thomas Tracy states that "one may be convinced, following Whitehead, that internal relation to other subjects is a necessary condition for being a subject at all;" but "we should note the possibility of granting that relatedness is an essential structure of God's life and yet arguing that God's life is complete apart from his relation to his creatures, since the relatedness that is an essential property of God might not be his relatedness to creatures." See Tracy, *God, Action, and Embodiment*, 178. Thomas Morris makes the same argument on pp. 177-179 of *Our Idea of God*, as does Paul Fiddes in his own way on p. 143 of *The Creative Suffering of God*. This is, in my view, a strong argument which rebuts the contention that God is internally relational only if somehow internally related to the world.

[101]Moltmann, *The Trinity and the Kingdom*, 157.

[102]See, e.g., Brown, "Trinitarian Personhood and Individuality," in *Trinity, Incarnation, and Atonement*; and also David Brown, *The Divine Trinity* (London: Duckworth, 1985).

[103]Plantinga, "Social Trinity and Tritheism," in *Trinity, Incarnation, and Atonement*, 22.

thus if all God's relations cannot but be characterized by a "perichoretic relationship of fellowship," then the relation between God and creation must also be understood in terms of such relations of fellowship.[104] In other words, if the very being of God is constituted by relationships and if these relationships necessarily involve mutuality and fellowship, then the relationship of God with creation must also be of the same nature. And if the God-creation relation is of such a character, then given the admonition that faithful discipleship requires Christians to be God-like, the only adequate Christian ecological ethic is an ethic of respect and care.[105] Those like Moltmann who insist on the need not just for the doctrine of the Trinity but for a fully social theory of the Trinity provide yet another important desideratum for a Christian ecological theology.

Conclusion

There is, of course, much more that could and should be said on each of the three topics explored in this chapter. As Henry James reportedly said: an author does not finish a book, he merely gives up and stops writing. So it is with this endeavor. It is time to give up and stop writing. From what has been said, however, a number of things are clear. First, the three thinkers examined here have much to contribute to the development of a Christian ecological theology. Rosemary Radford Ruether, Joseph Sittler, and Jürgen Moltmann each in their own way provide valuable and greatly-needed resources for disciplined reflection in light of the Christian faith on the pressing social and ecological issues we face today. It is also clear that there are problems with their theologies, and that more work is required to construct a perspective which is faithful to both Christian scripture and tradition, informed by the insights of contemporary science, and understandable and compelling to both Christians and non-Christians alike.

104Moltmann, *God in Creation*, 16-17, 258.

105For a very stimulating and helpful presentation of an ethic of care, see Max Oelschlaeger, *Caring for Creation: An Ecumenical Approach to the Environmental Crisis* (New Haven: Yale, 1994).

In addition, the conclusions of this chapter, and of this project as a whole, are a reminder of a famous line from Joseph Wood Krutch's 1954 essay entitled "Conservation is Not Enough." One of the main spokespersons for Aldo Leopold's "land ethic," Krutch states that in the contemporary world "the thing which is missing is love, some feeling for, as well as some understanding of, the inclusive community of rocks and soils, plants and animals, of which we are a part."[106] Like Sittler, Krutch laments the absence of a beholding, of a "feeling for" things natural. And also like Sittler Krutch insightfully concludes that such wonder and care requires greater first-hand acquaintance with that community of creation we so often blithely call "nature." Until we discover or recapture a "feeling for" our non-human neighbors--a love based on genuine understanding--we will continue to rape, pillage, and plunder the earth. Gerard Manley Hopkins' poem "God's Grandeur" is an eloquent expression of a love for things natural rooted in an understanding of the natural world as the creation of a loving God.

> The world is charged with the grandeur of God.
> It will flame out, like shining from shook foil;
> It gathers to a greatness, like the ooze of oil
> Crushed. Why do men then now not reck his rod?
> Generations have trod, have trod, have trod;
> And all is seared with trade; bleared, smeared with toil;
> And wears man's smudge and shares man's smell: the soil
> Is bare now, nor can foot feel, being shod.
>
> And for all this, nature is never spent;
> There lives the dearest freshness deep down things;
> And though the last lights off the black West went
> Oh, morning, at the brown brink eastward, springs--
> Because the Holy Ghost over the bent
> World broods with warm breast and with ah! bright wings.

Finally, all three of the theologians here investigated concur that the church has too long been on the sidelines with respect to ecological issues. In contrast, given both the crisis of our age and the demands of biblical faith, Christians must enthusiastically and vigorously act in ways consonant with a Christian ecological

---

[106]Joseph Wood Krutch, quoted in Nash, *The Rights of Nature*, 75.

theology--the kind of theology indicated in these pages. As Sittler reminds all Christians:

> If *in piety* the church says, "The earth is the Lord's and the fulness thereof" (Ps. 24:1), and *in fact* is no different in thought and action from the general community, who will be drawn by her word and worship to "come and see" that her work or salvation has any meaning? Witness in saying is irony and bitterness if there be no witness in doing.[107]

And lest we be overwhelmed by the enormity of the task, the (paraphrased) words of Edmund Burke stand as a fitting challenge: No one made a greater mistake than he who did nothing because he could do only a little.

---

[107]Sittler, "Evangelism and the Care of the Earth," 104.

SELECT BIBLIOGRAPHY

Adams, Carol, ed. *Ecofeminism and the Sacred.* New York: Continuum, 1993.

Alpers, Kenneth. "Starting Points for an Ecological Theology: A Bibliographical Survey." *Dialog* 9 (Summer 1970): 226-235.

Alston, William. *Divine Nature and Human Language: Essays in Philosophical Theology.* Ithaca: Cornell University Press, 1989.

Andersen, Svend, and Peacocke, Arthur, eds. *Evolution and Creation.* Aarhus: Aarhus University Press, 1987.

Anderson, Bernhard. *Creation in the Old Testament.* Philadelphia: Fortress, 1984.

_____. *Creation versus Chaos.* Philadelphia: Fortress, 1987.

Arts, Herwig. *Moltmann et Tillich: les fondements de l'esperance chretienne.* Gembloux: Duculot, 1973.

Attfield, Robin. *The Ethics of Environmental Concern,* second edition. Athens, GA: University of Georgia Press, 1991.

_____. "Western Traditions and Environmental Ethics." In *Environmental Philosophy: A Collection of Readings,* pp. 201-230. Edited by Robert Elliot and Arran Gare. University Park: Penn State University Press, 1983.

Austin, Richard. *Baptized into Wilderness: A Christian Perspective on John Muir.* Atlanta: John Knox, 1987.

_____. *Beauty of the Lord: Awakening the Senses.* Atlanta: John Knox, 1988.

_____. *Hope for the Land: Nature in the Bible.* Atlanta: John Knox, 1988.

Bakken, Peter. "The Ecology of Grace: Ultimacy and Environmental Ethics in Aldo Leopold and Joseph Sittler." Ph.D. dissertation, University of Chicago, 1991.

Barbour, Ian. "Attitudes Toward Nature and Technology." In *Earth Might Be Fair: Reflections on Ethics, Religion, and Ecology*, pp. 146-168. Edited by Ian Barbour. Englewood Cliffs: Prentice Hall, 1972.

_____. *Issues in Science and Religion*. New York: Harper and Row, 1966.

_____. *Religion in an Age of Science*. San Francisco: Harper and Row, 1990.

_____. *Technology, Environment, and Human Values*. New York: Praeger, 1980.

_____, ed. *Western Man and Environmental Ethics: Attitudes Toward Nature and Technology*. Reading, MA: Addison-Wesley, 1973.

Barnette, Henlee. *The Church and the Ecological Crisis*. Grand Rapids: Eerdmans, 1972.

Barth, Karl. *Church Dogmatics*. Edinburgh: T. and T. Clark, 1975.

Basinger, David. *Divine Power in Process Theism: A Philosophical Critique*. Albany: State University of New York Press, 1988.

Bauckham, Richard. *Moltmann: Messianic Theology in the Making*. Hants: Marshall Morgan and Scott, 1987.

_____. *Word Biblical Commentary 50: Jude and 2 Peter*. Waco: Word, 1983.

Bavinck, Herman. "Common Grace." Translated with an introduction by Raymond Van Leeuwen. *Calvin Theological Journal* 24 (April 1989): 35-65.

_____. *Philosophy of Revelation*. Grand Rapids: Baker, 1979.

Beaty, Michael, ed. *Christian Theism and the Problems of Philosophy*. Notre Dame: University of Notre Dame, 1990.

Becker, Ernest. *The Denial of Death*. New York: Macmillan, 1973.

_____. *Escape From Evil*. New York: Macmillan, 1975.

Bellah, Robert, et al. *Habits of the Heart: Individualism and Commitment in American Life*. New York: Harper and Row, 1985.

Berkhof, Hendrikus. *The Doctrine of the Holy Spirit*. Grand Rapids: Eerdmans, 1962.

_____. "God in Nature and History." In *God, History, and Historians: Modern Christian Views of History*, pp. 291-328. Edited by C. T. McIntire. New York: Oxford University Press, 1977.

Berkouwer, G. C. *General Revelation*. Grand Rapids: Eerdmans, 1955.

_____. *Man: The Image of God*. Grand Rapids: Eerdmans, 1962.

Berry, Thomas. *The Dream of the Earth*. San Francisco: Sierra Club, 1988.

Berry, Wendell. "A Secular Pilgrimage." In *Western Man and Environmental Ethics*, pp. 132-155. Edited by Ian Barbour. Reading, MA: Addison-Wesley, 1973.

_____. *The Unsettling of America: Culture and Agriculture*. San Francisco: Sierra Club, 1977.

Binns, Emily. *The World as Creation: Creation in Christ in an Evolutionary World View*. Wilmington: Michael Glazier, 1990.

Birch, Charles. "Creation, Technology, and Human Survival: Called to Replenish the Earth." *Ecumenical Review* 28 (1976): 66-79.

Birch, Charles, Eakin, William, McDaniel, Jay, eds. *Liberating Life: Contemporary Approaches to Ecological Theology*. New York: Orbis, 1990.

Bloesch, Donald. *Is the Bible Sexist?* Westchester, IL: Crossway, 1982.

Boff, Leonardo. *Trinity and Society*. Maryknoll: Orbis, 1988.

Bonifazi, Conrad. *A Theology of Things: A Study of Man in his Physical Environment*. Philadelphia: Lippincott, 1967.

Bonhoeffer, Dietrich. *Letters and Papers From Prison*, enlarged edition. New York: Macmillan, 1972.

Bowman, Douglas. *Beyond the Modern Mind: The Spiritual and Ethical Challenge of the Environmental Crisis*. New York: Pilgrim, 1990.

Bratton, Susan Power. *Christianity, Wilderness, and Wildlife: The Original Desert Solitaire*. Scranton: University of Scranton Press, 1993.

Brauer, Jerald. "In Appreciation of Joseph Sittler." *The Journal of Religion* 54 (April 1974): 97-101.

Bring, Ragnar. "The Gospel of the New Creation." *Dialog* 3 (Autumn 1964): 274-282.

Brown, David. *The Divine Trinity*. London: Duckworth, 1985.

_____. "Trinitarian Personhood and Individuality." In *Trinity, Incarnation, and Atonement*, pp. 48-78. Edited by Ronald Feenstra and Cornelis Plantinga. Notre Dame: University of Notre Dame Press, 1989.

Brueggemann, Walter. *Genesis*. Atlanta: John Knox, 1982.

_____. *The Land*. Philadelphia: Fortress, 1977.

Bruner. Frederick Dale. *A Theology of the Holy Spirit: The Pentecostal Experience and the New Testament Witness*. Grand Rapids: Eerdmans, 1970.

Burnham, Frederic, McCoy, Charles, and Meeks, M. Douglas, eds. *Love: The Foundation of Hope: The Theology of Jürgen Moltmann and Elisabeth Moltmann-Wendel*. San Francisco: Harper and Row, 1988.

Burrell, David. "Creation or Emmanation: Two Paradigms of Reason." In *God and Creation: An Ecumenical Symposium*, pp. 27-37. Edited by David Burrell and Bernard McGinn. Notre Dame: University of Notre Dame Press, 1990.

Burrell, David, and McGinn, Bernard, eds. *God and Creation: An Ecumenical Symposium*. Notre Dame: University of Notre Dame, 1990.

Burtness, James. "All the Fullness." *Dialog* 3 (Autumn 1964): 257-263.

Callicott, J. Baird. *In Defense of the Land Ethic: Essays in Environmental Philosophy*. Albany: State University of New York Press, 1989.

_____. "Traditional American Indian and Traditional Western European Attitudes Towards Nature: An Overview." In *Environmental Philosophy: A Collection of Readings*, pp. 231-259. Edited by Robert Elliot and Arran Gare. University Park: Penn State University Press, 1983.

Calvin, John. *Institutes of the Christian Religion*. Translated by Ford Lewis Battles and edited by John McNeill. Philadelphia: Westminster, 1960.

Capps, Walter. *Time Invades the Cathedral: Tensions in the School of Hope*. Philadelphia: Fortress, 1972.

Carmody, John. *Ecology and Religion: Toward a New Christian Theology of Nature*. New York: Paulist, 1983.

Carpenter, James. *Nature and Grace: Toward an Integral Perspective*. New York: Crosroad, 1988.

Carr, Anne. *Transforming Grace: Christian Tradition and Women's Experience*. San Francisco: Harper and Row, 1988.

Chodorow, Nancy, "Family Structure and Feminine Personality." In *Women, Culture, and Society*, pp. 43-66. Edited by Michelle Zimbalist Rosaldo and Louise Lamphere. Stanford: Stanford University Press, 1974.

Chopp, Rebecca. *The Praxis of Suffering: An Interpretation of Liberation and Political Theologies*. Maryknoll: Orbis, 1986.

Cobb, John, Jr. *Is It Too Late?: A Theology of Ecology*. Beverly Hills: Bruce, 1972.

_____. *Process Theology as Political Theology*. Philadelphia: Westminster, 1982.

Cohen, Jeremy. *"Be Fertile and Increase, Fill the Earth and Master It": The Ancient and Medieval Career of a Biblical Text*. Ithaca: Cornell University Press, 1989.

_____. "The Bible, Man, and Nature in the History of Western Thought: A Call for Reassessment." *The Journal of Religion* 65 (April 1985): 155-172.

Collingwood, R. G. *The Idea of Nature*. London: Oxford University Press, 1945.

Compton, John. "Science and God's Action in Nature." In *Earth Might Be Fair*, pp. 33-47. Edited by Ian Barbour. Englewood Cliffs: Prentice Hall, 1972.

Conyers, A. J. *God, Hope and History: Jürgen Moltmann and the Christian Concept of History*. Macon: Mercer, 1988.

Cooper, John. *Body, Soul, and Life Everlasting: Biblical Anthropology and the Monism-Dualism Debate*. Grand Rapids: Eerdmans, 1989.

Creede, Moira. "Logos and Lord: A Study of the Cosmic Christology of Joseph Sittler." Ph.D. dissertation, Louvain, 1977.

Creel, Richard. *Divine Impassibility: An Essay in Philosophical Theology.* Cambridge: Cambridge University Press, 1986.

Cromie, Thetis. "Feminism and the Grace-Full Thought of Joseph Sittler." *The Christian Century* (April 9, 1980): 406-408.

Daly, Lois. "God, Creation, and Nature." Ph.D. dissertation, University of Chicago, 1984.

DeGraaff, Arnold. "Towards a New Anthropological Model." In *Hearing and Doing,* pp. 97-118. Edited by John Kray and Anthony Tol. Toronto: Wedge, 1979.

Derr, Thomas. *Ecology and Human Liberation: A Theological Critique of the Use and Abuse of Our Birthright.* Geneva: World Council of Churches, 1973.

DesJardins, Joseph. *Environmental Ethics: An Introduction to Environmental Philosophy.* Belmont, CA: Wadsworth, 1993.

Deuser, Hermann, Martin, Gerhard, Stock, Konrad, and Welker, Michael, eds. *Gottes Zukunft-- Zukunft der Welt: Festschrift fuer Jürgen Moltmann zum 60 Geburtstag.* Muenchen: Chr. Kaiser Verlag, 1986.

Devall, Bill, and Sessions, George. *Deep Ecology: Living As If Nature Mattered.* Salt Lake City: Gibbs M. Smith, 1985.

DeWitt, Calvin. "Assaulting the Gallery of God: Human Degradation of Creation." *Sojourners* (February-March 1990): 19-21.

_____. "The Church's Role in Environmental Action." *Word and World* 11 (Spring 1991): 180-185.

_____, ed. *The Environment and the Christian: What Can We Learn from the New Testament?* Grand Rapids: Baker, 1991.

Diemer, Johann. *Nature and Miracle.* Toronto: Wedge, 1977.

Dinnerstein, Dorothy. *The Mermaid and the Minotaur: Sexual Arrangments and Human Malaise.* New York: Harper and Row, 1976.

Ditmanson, Harold. "The Call for a Theology of Creation." *Dialog* 3 (Autumn 1964): 264-273.

Dubos, René. "Franciscan Conservation versus Benedictine Stewardship." In *Ecology and Religion in History,* pp.114-136. Edited by David and Eileen Spring. New York: Harper and Row, 1974.

Duchrow, Ulrich, and Liedke, Gerhard. *Shalom: Biblical Perspectives on Creation, Justice, and Peace.* Geneva: World Council of Churches, 1987.

Dunn, James D. G. *Jesus and the Spirit.* Philadelphia: Westminster, 1975.

Dyrness, William. "Stewardship of the Earth in the Old Testament." In *Tending the Garden: Essays on the Gospel and the Earth,* pp. 50-65. Edited by Wesley Granberg-Michaelson. Grand Rapids: Eerdmans, 1987.

Elder, Frederick. *Crisis in Eden: A Religious Study of Man and Environment.* Nashville: Abingdon, 1970.

Elliot, Robert, and Gare, Arran, eds. *Environmental Philosophy: A Collection of Readings.* University Park: Penn State University Press, 1983.

Elsdon, Ron. *Bent World: A Christian Response to the Environmental Crisis.* Downer's Grove: Intervarsity, 1981.

Engel, David. "Elements in a Theology of Environment." *Zygon* 5 (September 1970): 216-227.

Evans, C. Stephen. *Preserving the Person: A Look at the Human Sciences.* Grand Rapids: Baker, 1977.

Faricy, Robert. *Wind and Sea Obey Him: Approaches to a Theology of Nature.* London: SCM, 1982.

Feenstra, Ronald, and Plantinga, Cornelius, eds. *Trinity, Incarnation, and Atonement: Philosophical and Theological Essays.* Notre Dame: University of Notre Dame Press, 1989.

Feuerbach, Ludwig. *The Essence of Christianity.* New York: Harper and Row, 1957.

Fiddes, Paul. *The Creative Suffering of God.* Oxford: Clarendon, 1988.

Fiorenza, Elizabeth Schussler. *In Memory of Her: A Feminist Theological Reconstruction of Christian Origins.* New York: Crossroad, 1983.

Fortman, Edmund. *The Triune God: A Historical Study of the Doctrine of the Trinity.* Philadelphia: Westminster, 1972.

Foster, Michael. "The Christian Doctrine of Creation and the Rise of Modern Science." In *Creation: The Impact of An Idea*, pp. 29-53. Edited by Daniel O'Connor and Francis Oakley. New York: Scribners, 1969.

Fox, Matthew. *The Coming of the Cosmic Christ*. San Francisco: Harper and Row, 1988.

_____. *Original Blessing: A Primer in Creation Spirituality*. Santa Fe: Bear and Co., 1983.

Frankena, William. "Ethics and the Environment." In *Ethics and Problems of the 21st Century*, pp. 3-19. Edited by Kenneth Goodpaster and Kenneth Sayre. Notre Dame: University of Notre Dame Press, 1979.

French, William. "Christianity and the Domination of Nature." Ph.D. dissertation, University of Chicago, 1985.

_____. "Returning to Creation: Moltmann's Eschatology Naturalized." Review of Jürgen Moltmann's *God in Creation*. *The Journal of Religion* 68 (January 1988): 78-86.

_____. "Subject-centered and Creation-centered Paradigms in Recent Catholic Thought." *The Journal of Religion* 70 (January 1990): 48-72.

Fries, Paul. "Explorations in the Spirit and Creation." *Perspectives/Reformed Journal* 6 (January 1991): 10-13.

Galloway, Allan. *The Cosmic Christ*. New York: Harper and Brothers, 1951.

George, K. M. "Toward a Eucharistic Ecology." *Reformed Journal* 40 (April 1990): 17-22.

Gibbs, John. "Pauline Cosmic Christology and Ecological Crisis." *Journal of Biblical Literature* 90 (December 1971): 466-479.

Gibson, William. "Eco-Justice: Burning Word." *Foundations* 20 (October-December 1977): 318-327.

_____. "Eco-Justice: New Perspective for a Time of Turning." In *For Creation's Sake: Preaching, Ecology, and Justice*, pp. 15-31. Edited by Dieter Hessel. Philadelphia: Geneva, 1985.

Gilkey, Langdon. "Creation, Being, and Nonbeing." In *God and Creation: An Ecumenical Symposium*, pp. 226-245. Edited by David Burrell and Bernard McGinn. Notre Dame: University of Notre Dame Press, 1990.

_____. "God." In *Christian Theology: An Introduction to its Traditions and Tasks*, revised ed, pp. 88-113. Edited by Peter Hodgson and Robert King. Philadelphia: Fortress, 1985.

_____. *Maker of Heaven and Earth*. Garden City: Doubleday, 1959.

_____. *Message and Existence: An Introduction to Christian Theology*. New York: Seabury, 1981.

_____. *Naming the Whirlwind: The Renewal of God-Language*. Indianapolis: Bobbs-Merrill, 1969.

_____. *Reaping the Whirlwind: A Christian Interpretation of History*. New York: Seabury, 1976.

Glacken, Clarence. *Traces on the Rhodian Shore: Nature and Culture in Western Thought from Ancient Times to the End of the Eighteenth Century*. Berkeley: University of California Press, 1967.

Goodpaster, Kenneth, and Sayre, Kenneth, eds. *Ethics and Problems of the 21st Century*. Notre Dame: University of Notre Dame, 1979.

Gosling, David. "Towards a Credible Ecumenical Theology of Nature." *Ecumenical Review* 38 (July 1986): 322-331.

Gottwald, Norman. "The Biblical Mandate for Eco-Justice Action." In *For Creation's Sake: Preaching, Ecology, and Justice*, pp. 32-44. Edited by Dieter Hessel. Philadelphia: Geneva, 1985.

Goudzwaard, Bob. *Capitalism and Progress: A Diagnosis of Western Society*. Grand Rapids: Eerdmans, 1979.

Gould, Carol, ed. *Beyond Domination: New Perspectives on Women and Philosophy*. Totowa, NJ: Rowman and Allanheld, 1983.

Granberg-Michaelson, Wesley. "At the Dawn of the New Creation." *Sojourners* (November 1981): 12-16.

_____. "Called to be Caretakers." *The Church Herald* (November 19, 1982): 8-10.

_____. "Earthkeeping: A Theology for Global Sanctification." *Sojourners* (October 1982): 20-24.

_____. *Ecology and Life: Accepting Our Environmental Responsibility*. Waco: Word, 1988.

314   The Greening of Theology

_____. "Renewing the Whole Creation." *Sojourners* (February-March 1990): 10-14.

_____, ed. *Tending the Garden: Essays on the Gospel and the Earth.* Grand Rapids: Eerdmans, 1987.

_____. *A Worldly Spirituality: The Call to Redeem Life on Earth.* San Francisco: Harper and Row, 1984.

Gray, Elizabeth Dodson. "A Critique of Dominion Theology." In *For Creation's Sake*, pp. 71-83. Edited by Dieter Hessel. Philadelphia: Geneva, 1985.

_____. *Green Paradise Lost: Re-Mything Genesis.* Wellesley: Roundtable, 1981.

Green, Michael. *I Believe in the Holy Spirit.* Grand Rapids: Eerdmans, 1975.

Gregorios, Paulos. *The Human Presence: An Orthodox View of Nature.* Geneva: World Council of Churches, 1978.

_____. "New Testament Foundations for Understanding Creation." In *Tending the Garden: Essays on the Gospel and the Earth*, pp. 83-92. Edited by Wesley Granberg-Michaelson. Grand Rapids: Eerdmans, 1987.

Gunton, Colin. *Christ and Creation.* Grand Rapids: Eerdmans, 1992.

Gustafson, James. *Ethics From a Theocentric Perspective: Theology and Ethics.* Chicago: University of Chicago Press,1981.

_____. "Interdependence, Finitude, and Sin: Reflections on Scarcity." *The Journal of Religion* 57 (April 1977): 156-168.

_____. *A Sense of the Divine: The Natural Environment from a Theocentric Perspective.* Cleveland: Pilgrim Press, 1994.

Gutierrez, Gustavo. *A Theology of Liberation*, second edition. Maryknoll: Orbis, 1988.

_____. *We Drink From Our Own Wells.* Maryknoll: Orbis, 1984.

Hall, Douglas. *Imaging God: Dominion as Stewardship.* Grand Rapids: Eerdmans, 1986.

_____. *The Steward: A Biblical Symbol Come of Age.* Grand Rapids: Eerdmans, 1990.

Hallman, Joseph. *The Descent of God: Divine Suffering in History and Theology.* Minneapolis: Augsburg/Fortress, 1991.

Harding, Sandra. "Is Gender a Variable in Conceptions of Rationality?: A Survey of Issues." In *Beyond Domination: New Perspectives on Women and Philosophy,* pp. 43-63. Edited by Carol Gould. Totowa, NJ: Rowman and Allanheld, 1983.

_____. *The Science Question in Feminism.* Ithaca: Cornell University Press, 1986.

Hargrove, Eugene. *Foundations of Environmental Ethics.* Englewood Cliffs: Prentice Hall, 1989.

_____, ed. *Religion and Environmental Crisis.* Athens, GA: University of Georgia Press, 1986.

Harrisville, Roy. "The New Testament Witness to the Cosmic Christ." In *The Gospel and Human Destiny,* pp. 39-63. Edited by Vilmos Vajta. Minneapolis: Augsburg, 1971.

Hart, John. *The Spirit of the Earth: A Theology of the Land.* New York: Paulist, 1985.

Hayes, Zachery. *What Are They Saying About Creation?.* New York: Paulist, 1980.

Headington, Charles. "Americans in the Wilderness: A Study of Their Encounters With Otherness from the Initial Contact Through Henry David Thoreau." Ph.D. dissertation, University of Chicago, 1985.

Hebblethwaite, Brian, and Henderson, Edward, eds. *Divine Action: Studies Inspired by the Philosophical Theology of Austin Farrar.* Edinburgh: T. and T. Clark, 1990.

Hefner, Philip. "Can a Theology of Nature be Coherent with Scientific Cosmology?" In *Evolution and Creation,* pp.141-151. Edited by Svend Andersen and Arthur Peacocke. Aarhus: University of Aarhus Press, 1987.

_____. "The Politics and the Ontology of Nature and Grace." *The Journal of Religion* 54 (April 1974): 138-153.

_____, ed. *The Scope of Grace: Essays on Nature and Grace in Honor of Joseph Sittler.* Philadelphia: Fortress, 1964.

Hein, Hilde. "Liberating Philosophy: An End to the Dichotomy of Spirit and Matter." In *Beyond Domination: New Perspectives on Women and Philosophy*, pp. 123-141. Edited by Carol Gould. Totowa, NJ: Rowman and Allenheld, 1983.

Hendry, George. *Theology of Nature*. Philadelphia: Westminster, 1980.

Hepp, Valentine. *Calvinism and the Philosophy of Nature*. Grand Rapids: Eerdmans, 1930.

Hessel, Dieter, ed. *For Creation's Sake: Preaching, Ecology, and Justice*. Philadelphia: Geneva, 1985.

Hinsdale, Mary Ann. "Ecology, Feminism, amd Theology." *Word and World* 11 (Spring 1991): 156-164.

Hodgson, Peter, and King, Robert, eds. *Christian Theology: An Introduction to its Traditions and Tasks*, second edition. Philadelphia: Fortress, 1985.

Holmes, Arthur. *Contours of a World View*. Grand Rapids: Eerdmans, 1983.

Houston, James. *I Believe in the Creator*. Grand Rapids: Eerdmans, 1980.

Jaggar, Alison. "Human Biology in Feminist Theory: Sexual Equality Reconsidered." In *Beyond Domination: New Perspectives on Women and Philosophy*, pp. 21-41. Edited by Carol Gould. Totowa, NJ: Rowman and Allanheld, 1983.

James, William. *The Varieties of Religious Experience*. New York: The New American Library, 1958.

Jantzen, Grace. *God's World, God's Body*. Philadelphia: Westminster, 1984.

Jegen, Mary Evelyn. "An Encounter with God." *Sojourners* (February-March 1990): 15-17.

Jegen, Mary Evelyn, and Manno, Bruno, eds. *The Earth Is the Lord's: Essays On Stewardship*. New York: Paulist, 1978.

Johnson, Edward. "Treating the Dirt: Environmental Ethics and Moral Theory." In *Earthbound: New Introductory Essays in Environmental Ethics*, pp. 336-365. Edited by Tom Regan. New York: Random House, 1984.

Joranson, Philip, and Butigan, Ken, eds. *Cry of the Environment: Rebuilding the Christian Creation Tradition*. Santa Fe: Bear and Co., 1984.

Kaiser, Christopher. *Creation and the History of Science*. Grand Rapids: Eerdmans, 1991.

_____. *The Doctrine of God*. Westchester: Crossway, 1982.

Kaufman, Gordan. *God the Problem*. Cambridge: Harvard University Press, 1972.

_____. "A Problem for Theology: The Concept of Nature." *Harvard Theological Review* 65 (1972): 337-366.

Keller, Evelyn Fox. *Reflections on Gender and Science*. New Haven: Yale University Press, 1985.

Kelsey, David. "The Doctrine of Creation From Nothing." In *Evolution and Creation*, pp. 176-196. Edited by Ernan McMullin. Notre Dame: University of Notre Dame Press, 1985.

Kohak, Erazim. *The Embers and the Stars: A Philosophical Inquiry into the Moral Sense of Nature*. Chicago: University of Chicago Press, 1984.

Kray, John, and Tol, Anthony, eds. *Hearing and Doing: Philosophical Essays Dedicated to H. Evan Runner*. Toronto: Wedge, 1979.

Kuyper, Abraham. *The Work of the Holy Spirit*. Grand Rapids: Eerdmans, 1979.

Lane, Beldon. *Landscapes of the Sacred: Geography and Narrative in American Spirituality*. New York: Paulist, 1988.

Lee, Charles. "Evidence of Environmental Racism." *Sojourners* (February-March 1990): 21-25.

Leopold, Aldo. *A Sand County Almanac*. New York: Ballantine, 1970.

Limberg, James. "The Responsibility of Royalty: Genesis 11 and the Care of the Earth." *Word and World* 11 (Spring 1991): 124-130.

Limouris, Gennadios, ed. *Justice, Peace, and the Integrity of Creation: Insights from Orthodoxy*. Geneva: WCC, 1990.

Linzey, Andrew. *Christianity and the Rights of Animals*. New York: Crossroad, 1987.

Lønning, Per. *Creation--An Ecumenical Challenge?: Reflections Issuing from a Study by the Institute for Ecumenical Research Strasbourg, France*. Macon: Mercer, 1989.

Lutz, Paul, and Santmire, H. Paul. *Ecological Renewal*. Philadelphia: Fortress, 1972.

Malchow, Bruce. "Contrasting Views of Nature in the Hebrew Bible." *Dialog* 26 (Winter 1987): 40-43.

McCoy, Marjorie Casebier. "Feminist Consciousness in Creation: 'Tell Them the World Was Made for Women Too.'" In *Cry of the Environment*, pp. 132-147. Edited by Philip Joranson and Ken Butigan. Santa Fe: Bear and Co., 1984.

McDaniel, Jay. *Of God and Pelicans: A Theology of Reverence for Life*. Louisville: Westminster/John Knox, 1989.

McFague, Sallie. *The Body of God: An Ecological Theology*. Minneapolis: Augsburg/Fortress, 1993.

_____. "Imaging a Theology of Nature: The World as God's Body." In *Liberating Life: Contemporary Approaches to Ecological Theology*, pp. 201-227. Edited by Charles Birch, William Eakin, and Jay McDaniel. Maryknoll: Orbis, 1990.

_____. *Models of God: Theology for an Ecological, Nuclear Age*. Philadelphia: Fortress, 1987.

McGinn, Bernard. "Do Christian Platonists Really Believe in Creation?" In *God and Creation: An Ecumenical Symposium*, pp. 197-225. Edited by David Burrell and Bernard McGinn. Notre Dame: University of Notre Dame Press, 1990.

McHarg, Ian. "The Place of Nature in the City of Man." In *Western Man and Environmental Ethics*, pp. 171-186. Edited by Ian Barbour. Reading, MA: Addison-Wesley, 1973.

McKibben, Bill. *The Comforting Whirlwind: God, Job, and the Scale of Creation*. Grand Rapids: Eerdmans, 1994.

_____. *The End of Nature*. New York: Doubleday, 1989.

McMullin, Ernan, ed. *Evolution and Creation*. Notre Dame: University of Notre Dame Press, 1985.

Meeks, M. Douglas. *The Origins of the Theology of Hope*. Philadelphia: Fortress, 1974.

Meland, Bernard. "Grace: A Dimension Within Nature?" *The Journal of Religion* 54 (April 1974): 128-137.

_____. "New Perspectives on Nature and Grace." In *The Scope of Grace: Essays on Nature and Grace in Honor of Joseph Sittler*, pp. 141-161. Edited by Philip Hefner. Philadelphia: Fortress, 1964.

Merchant, Carolyn. *The Death of Nature: Women, Ecology, and the Scientific Revolution*. San Francisco: Harper and Row, 1980.

Metz, Johannes-Baptist, and Schillebeeckx, Edward, eds. *God As Father?* New York: Seabury, 1981.

Meyendorff, John. *Byzantine Theology: Historical Trends and Doctrinal Themes*. New York: Fordham University Press, 1979.

Mitcham, Carl, and Grote, Jim. *Theology and Technology: Essays in Christian Analysis and Exegesis*. Lanham: University Press of America, 1984.

Mollenkott, Virginia Ramey. *The Divine Feminine: The Biblical Imagery of God as Female*. New York: Crossroad, 1987.

Moltmann, Jürgen. "The Alienation and Liberation of Nature." In *On Nature*, pp. 133-144. Edited by Leroy Rouner. Notre Dame: University of Notre Dame Press, 1984.

_____. *The Church in the Power of the Spirit: A Contribution to Messianic Ecclesiology*. Translated by Margaret Kohl. New York: Harper and Row, 1977.

_____. *Creating a Just Future: The Politics of Peace and the Ethics of Creation in a Threatened World*. Translated by John Bowden. Philadelphia: Trinity, 1989.

_____. "Creation and Redemption." In *Creation, Christ, and Culture*, pp. 119-134. Edited by Richard McKinney. Edinburgh: T. and T. Clark, 1976.

_____. *The Crucified God: The Cross of Christ as the Foundation and Criticism of Christian Theology*. Translated by R. A. Wilson and John Bowden. New York: Harper and Row, 1974.

_____. *Experiences of God*. Translated by Margaret Kohl. Philadelphia: Fortress, 1980.

_____. *The Experiment Hope*. Translated by M. Douglas Meeks. Philadelphia: Fortress, 1975.

_____. *The Future of Creation*. Translated by Margaret Kohl. Philadelphia: Fortress, 1979.

_____. *God in Creation: A New Theology of Creation and the Spirit of God*. Translated by Margaret Kohl. San Francisco: Harper and Row, 1985. Translation of *Gott in der Schöpfung: Okologische Schöpfungslehre*. München: Chr. Kaiser Verlag, 1985.

_____. "God Means Freedom." In *God and Human Freedom: A Festschrift in Honor of Howard Thurman*, pp. 10-22. Edited by Henry James Young. Richmond, IN: Friends United, 1983.

_____. *Mensch: Christliche Anthropologie in den Konflikten der Gegenwart*. Guetersloh: Guetersloher Verlagshaus Mohn, 1983.

_____. "The Motherly Father: Is Trinitarian Patripassianism Replacing Theological Patriarchalism?" In God As Father?, pp. 51-56. Edited by Johannes-Baptist Metz and Edward Schillebeeckx. New York: Seabury, 1981.

_____. *On Human Dignity*. Translated by M. Douglas Meeks. Philadelphia: Fortress, 1984.

_____. *The Power of the Powerless*. Translated by Margaret Kohl. San Francisco: Harper and Row, 1983.]

_____. "Reconciliation with Nature." *Word and World* 11 (Spring 1991): 117-123.

_____. "The Scope of Renewal in the Spirit." *Perspectives* (January 1991): 14-17.

_____. *Theology of Hope: On the Ground and the Implications of a Christian Eschatology*. Translated by James Leitch. New York: Harper and Row, 1967.

_____. *Theology Today: Two Contributions Toward Making Theology Present*. Translated by John Bowden. London: SCM, 1988.

_____. *The Trinity and the Kingdom*. Translated by Margaret Kohl. New York: Harper and Row, 1981. Translation of *Trinität und Reich Gottes: Zur Gotteslehre*. München: Chr. Kaiser, 1980.

_____. *The Way of Jesus Christ: Christology in Messianic Dimensions*. Translated by Margaret Kohl. San Francisco: HarperCollins, 1990. Translation of *Der Weg Jesu Christi: Christologie in messianischen Dimensionen*. München: Chr. Kaiser, 1989.

Moltmann, Jürgen, and Moltmann-Wendel, Elisabeth. *Humanity in God.* London: SCM, 1983.

Moncrief, Louis. "The Cultural Basis of Our Environmental Crisis." In *Western Man and Environmental Ethics,* pp. 31-42. Edited by Ian Barbour. Reading, MA: Addison-Wesley, 1973.

Monsema, Stephen, ed. *Responsible Technology.* Grand Rapids: Eerdmans, 1986.

Montague, George. *The Holy Spirit: Growth of a Biblical Tradition.* New York: Paulist, 1976.

Morris, Thomas, ed. *Divine and Human Action: Essays in the Metaphysics of Theism.* Ithaca: Cornell University Press, 1988.

_____. *Our Idea of God: An Introduction to Philosophical Theology.* Downers Grove: Intervarsity Press, 1991.

Morse, Christopher. *The Logic of Promise in Moltmann's Theology.* Philadelphia: Fortress, 1979.

Moule, C. F. D. *Man and Nature in the New Testament.* Philadelphia: Fortress, 1967.

Mouw, Richard. *The God Who Commands: A Study in Divine Command Ethics.* Notre Dame: University of Notre Dame Press, 1990.

Muir, John. *My First Summer in the Sierra.* San Francisco: Sierra Club, 1988.

Murphy, Charles. *At Home On Earth: Foundations for a Catholic Ethic of the Environment.* New York: Crossroad, 1989.

Murray, John Courtney. *The Problem of God.* New Haven: Yale University Press, 1964.

Nash, James. *Loving Nature: Ecological Integrity and Christian Responsibility.* Nashville: Abingdon, 1991.

Nash, Roderick. *The Rights of Nature: A History of Environmental Ethics.* Madison: University of Wisconsin Press, 1989.

_____. *Wilderness and the American Mind.* New Haven: Yale University Press, 1973.

Nash, Ronald, ed. *Process Theology.* Grand Rapids: Baker, 1987.

Neville, Robert. *Creativity and God: A Challenge to Process Theology.* New York: Seabury, 1980.

_____. *God the Creator: On the Transcendence and Presence of God.* Chicago: University of Chicago Pres, 1968.

Niebuhr, H. Richard. *The Purpose of the Church and Its Ministry.* In collaboration with Danial Day Williams and James Gustafson. New York: Harper and Row, 1956.

O'Conner, Daniel, and Oakley, Francis, eds. *Creation: The Impact of an Idea.* New York: Scribners, 1969.

O'Donnell, John. *The Mystery of the Triune God.* London: Sheed and Ward, 1988.

_____. *Trinity and Temporality: The Christian Doctrine of God in the Light of Process Theology and the Theology of Hope.* Oxford: Oxford University Press, 1983.

Oelschlaeger, Max. *Caring for Creation: An Ecumenical Approach to the Environmental Crisis.* New Haven: Yale University Press, 1994.

Ortner, Sherry. "Is Female to Male as Nature Is to Culture?" In *Women, Culture, and Society,* pp. 68-87. Edited by Michelle Rosaldo and Louise Lamphere. Stanford: Stanford University Press, 1974.

Pannenberg, Wolfhart. "The Doctrine of the Spirit and the Task of a Theology of Nature." *Theology* 75 (January 1972): 8-21.

Passmore, John. *Man's Responsibility for Nature: Ecological Problems and Western Traditions.* New York: Scribners, 1974.

Peacocke, Arthur. *Creation and the World of Science.* Oxford: Clarendon, 1979.

Pepper, Stephen. *World Hypotheses.* Berkeley: University of California Press, 1942.

Peters, Ted, ed. *Cosmos as Creation: Theology and Science in Consonance.* Nashville: Abingdon, 1989.

_____. "Creation, Consummation, and the Ethical Imagination." In *Cry of the Environment,* pp. 401-429. Edited by Philip Joranson and Ken Butigan. Santa Fe: Bear and Co., 1984.

_____. *God As Trinity: Relationality and Temporality in Divine Life.* Louisville: Westminster/John Knox, 1993.

Plantinga, Alvin. "Advice to Christian Philosophers." In *Christian Theism and the Problems of Philosophy*, pp. 14-37. Edited by Michael Beaty. Notre Dame: University of Notre Dame, 1990.

Plantinga, Cornelius. "Social Trinity and Tritheism." In *Trinity, Incarnation, and Atonement*, pp. 21-47. Edited by Ronald Feenstra and Cornelius Plantinga. Notre Dame: University of Notre Dame, 1989.

Polkinghorne, John. *Science and Creation: The Search for Understanding.* Boston: Shambhala, 1988.

_____. *Science and Providence: God's Interaction with the World.* Boston: Shambhala, 1989.

Premasagar, P. V. "Jesus: Cosmic Christ or a Man of History?" *Indian Journal of Theology* 24 (July-December 1975): 104-107.

Quam, Robert. "Creation or Nature?: A Manner of Speaking." *Word and World* 11 (Spring 1991): 131-136.

Rabuzzi, Kathyrn Allen. "The Socialist Feminist Vision of Rosemary Radford Ruether: A Challenge to Liberal Feminism." *Religious Studies Review* 15 (January 1989): 4-8.

Rae, Eleanor, and Marie-Daly, Bernice. *Created In Her Image: Models of the Feminine Divine.* New York: Crossroad, 1990.

Rahner, Karl. *Foundations of Christian Faith: An Introduction to the Idea of Christianity.* New York: Crossroad, 1987.

Ramsey, William. *Four Modern Prophets.* Atlanta: John Knox, 1986.

Rasmussen, Larry. "Creation, Church, and Christian Responsibility." In *Tending the Garden: Essays on the Gospel and the Earth*, pp. 114-131. Edited by Wesley Granberg-Michaelson. Grand Rapids: Eerdmans, 1987.

Rasolondraibe, Peri. "Environmental Concern and Economic Justice." *Word and World* 11 (Spring 1991): 147-155.

Regan, Tom, ed. *Earthbound: New Introductory Essays in Environmental Ethics.* New York: Randon House, 1984.

Regan, Tom, and Singer, Peter, eds. *Animal Rights and Human Obligations*, 2nd ed. Englewood Cliffs: Prentice-Hall, 1989.

Reumann, John. *Creation and New Creation: The Past, Present, and Future of God's Creative Activity*. Minneapolis: Augsburg, 1973.

Ridderbos, Herman. *Paul: An Outline of His Theology*. Grand Rapids: Eerdmans, 1975.

Rolston, Holmes, III. *Environmental Ethics: Duties to and Values in the Natural World*. Philadelphia: Temple University Press, 1988.

_____. *Science and Religion: A Critical Survey*. New York: Random House, 1987.

Rosaldo, Michelle Zimbalist, and Lamphere, Louise, eds. *Women, Culture, and Society*. Stanford: Stanford University Press, 1974.

Rouner, Leroy, ed. *On Nature*. Notre Dame: University of Notre Dame Press, 1984.

Ruether, Rosemary Radford. "The Biblical Vision of the Ecological Crisis." *The Christian Century* (November 22, 1978): 1129-1132.

_____. *Disputed Questions: On Being a Christian*. Maryknoll: Orbis, 1989.

_____. "The Female Nature of God: A Problem in Contemporary Religious Life." In *God As Father?*, pp. 61-66. Edited by Johannes-Baptist Metz and Edward Schillebeeckx. New York: Seabury, 1981.

_____. "Feminist Interpretation: A Method of Correlation." In *Feminist Interpretation of the Bible*, pp. 111-124. Edited by Letty Russell. Philadelphia: Westminster, 1985.

_____. "A Feminist Perspective." In *Doing Theology in a Divided World*, pp. 65-71. Edited by Virginia Fabella and Sergio Torres. New York: Orbis, 1985.

_____. *Gaia and God: An Ecofeminist Theology of Earth Healing*. San Francisco: HarperCollins, 1992.

_____. "In What Sense Can We Say That Jesus Was the Christ?" *The Ecumenist* 10 (January-February 1972): 17-24.

_____. *Liberation Theology: Human Hope Confronts Christian History and American Power*. New York: Paulist, 1972.

_____. "Mother Earth and the Megamachine." *Christianity and Crisis* (December 13, 1971): 267-272.

_____. *New Women/New Earth: Sexist Ideologies and Human Liberation*. New York: Seabury, 1975.

_____. "Paradoxes of Human Hope: The Messianic Horizon of Church and Society." *Theological Studies* 33 (June 1972): 235-252.

_____. "Rich Nations/Poor Nations and the Exploitation of the Earth." *Dialog* 13 (Summer 1974): 201-207.

_____. *Sexism and God-Talk: Toward a Feminist Theology*. Boston: Beacon, 1983.

_____. "Sexism, Religion, and the Social and Spiritual Liberation of Women Today." In *Beyond Domination: New Perspectives on Women and Philosophy*, pp. 107-122. Edited by Carol Gould. Totowa, NJ: Rowman and Allanheld, 1983.

_____. "Sexism and the Theology of Liberation." *The Christian Century* (December 12, 1973): 1224-1229.

_____. *To Change the World: Christology and Cultural Criticism*. New York: Crossroad, 1981.

_____. "Triple Oppression: Sex, Class, Race." In *God and Human Freedom: A Festschrift in Honor of Howard Thurman*, pp. 32-43. Edited by Henry James Young. Richmond, IN: Friends United, 1983.

_____. "Women, Ecology, and the Domination of Nature." *The Ecumenist* 14 (November-December 1975): 1-5.

_____. *Women-Church: Theology and Practice of Feminist Liturgical Communities*. San Francisco: Harper and Row, 1985.

_____. *Womanguides: Readings Toward a Feminist Theology*. Boston: Beacon, 1985.

Ruether, Rosemary Radford, Rabuzzi, Kathryn Allen, and Chopp, Rebecca. "Rosemary Radford Ruether: Retrospective." *Religious Studies Review* 15 (January 1989): 1-11.

Russell, Letty, ed. *Feminist Interpretation of the Bible*. Philadelphia: Westminster, 1985.

_____. *Human Liberation in a Feminist Perspective: A Theology*. Philadelphia: Westminster, 1974.

Russell, Robert. "Cosmology, Creation, and Contingency." In *Cosmos As Creation*, pp. 177-209. Edited by Ted Peters. Nashville: Abingdon, 1989.

Russell, Robert, Stoger, William, Coyne, George, eds. *Physics, Philosophy, and Theology: A Common Quest for Understanding*. Vatican City State: Vatican Observatory, 1988.

Rust, Eric. *Nature and Man in Biblical Thought*. London: Lutterworth, 1953.

_____. *Nature--Garden or Desert? An Essay in Environmental Theology*. Waco: Word, 1971.

_____. *Science and Faith: Towards a Theological Understanding of Nature*. New York: Oxford University Press, 1967.

Santmire, H. Paul. *Brother Earth: Nature, God, and Ecology in Time of Crisis*. New York: Thomas Nelson, 1970.

_____. "Ecology and Ethical Ecumenics." *Anglican Theological Review* 59 (January 1977): 98-101.

_____. "Ecology, Justice, and Theology: Beyond the Preliminary Skirmishes." *The Christian Century* (May 12, 1976): 460-463.

_____. "The Future of the Cosmos and the Renewal of the Church's Life with Nature." In *Cosmos as Creation: Theology and Science in Consonance*, pp. 265-282. Edited by Ted Peters. Nashville: Abingdon, 1989.

_____. "Healing the Protestant Mind: Beyond the Theology of Human Domination." unpublished manuscript prepared for the "Theology and Ethics Symposium: New Perspectives on Ecojustice." Chicago, 1990.

_____. "Historical Dimensions of the American Crisis." In *Western Man and Environmental Ethics*, pp. 66-92. Edited by Ian Barbour. Reading, MA: Addison-Wesley, 1973.

_____. "I-Thou, I-It, and I-Ens." *The Journal of Religion* 48 (July 1968): 260=273.

_____. "Reflections on the Alleged Ecological Bankruptcy of Western Theology." In *Ethics for Environment: Three Religious Staregies*, pp. 23-45. Edited by Dave Steffenson, Walter Herrscher, and Robert Cook. Green Bay: University of Wisconsin at Green Bay Press, 1973.

_____. "Studying the Doctrine of Creation." *Dialog* 21 (Summer 1982): 195-200.

_____. "Toward a New Theology of Nature." *Dialog* 25 (Winter 1986): 43-50.

_____. *The Travail of Nature: The Ambiguous Ecological Promise of Christian Theology*. Philadelphia: Fortress, 1985.

Santmire, H. Paul, and Lutz, Paul. *Ecological Renewal*. Philadelphia: Fortress, 1972.

Scheffczyk, Leo. *Creation and Providence*. Translated by Richard Strachan. New York: Herder and Herder, 1970.

Schmemann, Alexander. *For the Life of the World*. New York: National Student Christian Federation, 1963.

Schreiner, Susan. *The Theatre of His Glory: Nature and Natural Order in the Thought of John Calvin*. Grand Rapids: Baker, 1991.

Schuurman, Egbert. *Technology and the Future: A Philosophical Challenge*. Toronto: Wedge, 1980.

Scott, Nathan. "The Poetry and Theology of Earth: Reflections on the Testimony of Joseph Sittler and Gerard Manley Hopkins." *The Journal of Religion* 54 (April 1974): 102-118.

Simonson, Conrad. *The Christology of the Faith and Order Movement*. Leiden: Brill, 1972.

Sittler, Joseph. *The Anguish of Preaching*. Philadelphia: Fortress, 1966.

_____. "An Aspect of American Religious Experience." *Proceedings of the Twenty-Sixth Annual Convention of the Catholic Theological Society*. Bronx: Catholic Theological Society of America, 1972.

_____. "Called to Unity." *Southeast Asia Journal of Theology* 3 (April 1962): 6-15.

_____. *The Care of the Earth and Other University Sermons*. Philadelphia: Fortress, 1964.

_____. "Christian Higher Education as Liberation." *Brethern Life and Thought* 8 (Autumn 1963): 4-8.

_____. "A Christology of Function." *Lutheran Quarterly* 6 (May 1954): 122-131.

_____. "Commencement Address." *The Chicago Lutheran Seminary Record* 64 (November 1959): 34-37.

_____. "The Cruciform Character of Human Existence." *The Chicago Lutheran Seminary Record* 54 (October 1949): 18-21.

_____. "Depersonalization." In *The Layman and the Church*, pp. 161-169. Edited by Andrew Buehner. St. Louis: Lutheran Academy for Scholarship, 1967.

_____. *The Doctrine of the Word in the Structure of Lutheran Theology.* Philadelphia: The Board of Publication of the United Lutheran Church in America, 1948.

_____. "Ecological Commitment as Theological Responsibilty." *Zygon* 5 (June 1970): 172-181.

_____. *The Ecology of Faith.* Philadelphia: Muhlenberg Press, 1961.

_____. "Eschatology and the American Mind." *Charisteria Iohanni Kopp Octogenario Oblata* (November 9, 1954): 137-147.

_____. *Essays on Nature and Grace.* Philadelphia: Fortress, 1972.

_____. "Ethics and the New Testament Style." *Union Seminary Quarterly Review* 13 (May 1958): 29-36.

_____. "Evangelism and the Care of the Earth." In *Preaching in the Witnessing Community*, pp.100-104. Edited by Herman Stuempfle. Philadelphia: Fortress, 1973.

_____. "God, Man, Nature." *The Pulpit* 24 (August 1953): 16-17.

_____. *Grace Notes and Other Fragments.* Selected and edited by Robert Herhold and Linda Marie Delloff. Philadelphia: Fortress, 1981.

_____. *Gravity and Grace: Reflections and Provocations.* Edited by Linda Marie Delloff. Minneapolis: Augsburg, 1986.

_____. "In the Light of Our Biblical Tradition." In *What is the Nature of Man?: Images of Man in Our American Culture*, pp. 185-194. no editor. Philadelphia: The Christian Education Press, 1959.

_____. "Intercommunion and the Cultural Reality." In *The Future of Empirical Theology*, pp. 307-320. Edited by Bernard Meland. Chicago: University of Chicago Press, 1969.

_____. "Joseph Sittler." *Criterion* (Winter 1967): 20-23.

_____. "Nature and Grace: Reflections on an Old Rubric." *Dialog* 3 (Autumn 1964): 252-256.

_____. "The Necessity of Faith." *The Christian Scholar* 38 (September 1955): 198-205.

_____. "The Perils of Futurist Thinking." In *Shaping the Future*, pp. 66-82. Edited by John Roslansky. Amsterdam: North Holland, 1972.

_____. "The Presence and Acts of the Triune God in Creation and History." In *The Gospel and Human Destiny*, pp. 90-135. Edited by Vilmos Vajta. Minneapolis: Augsburg, 1971.

_____. "The Scope of Christological Reflection." *Interpretation* 26 (July 1972): 328-337.

_____. "The Shape of the Kerygma." *The Chicago Lutheran Seminary Record* 56 (Juy 1951): 31-36.

_____. "The Sittler Speeches." In *Center for the Study of Campus Ministry Yearbook 1977-78*, pp. 8-61. Edited by Phil Schroeder. Valparaiso: Valparaiso University, 1978.

_____. *The Structure of Christian Ethics*. Baton Rouge: Louisiana State University Press, 1958.

_____. "Theological Developments of the Lutheran-Catholic Dialogue." *Chicago Studies* 11 (Spring 1972): 45-58.

_____. "A Theology for Earth." *The Christian Scholar* 37 (September 1954): 367-374.

Snyder, Mary Hembrow. *The Christology of Rosemary Radford Ruether: A Critical Introduction*. Mystic, CT: Twenty-Third, 1988.

Soelle, Dorothy with Shirley Cloyes. *To Work and To Love: A Theology of Creation*. Philadelphia: Fortress, 1984.

Sokolowski, Robert. "Creation and Christian Understanding." In *God and Creation: An Ecumenical Symposium*, pp. 179-196. Edited by David Burrell and Bernard McGinn. Notre Dame: University of Notre Dame Press, 1990.

Spring, David and Eileen, eds. *Ecology and Religion in History*. New York: Harper and Row, 1974.

Steck, Odil. *World and Environment*. Nashville: Abingdon, 1978.

Steffenson, Dave, Herscher, Walter, and Cook, Robert, eds. *Ethics for Environment: Three Religious Strategies*. Green Bay: University of Wisconsin at Green Bay Press, 1973.

Stevenson, Leslie. *Seven Theories of Human Nature*. New York: Oxford University Press, 1974.

Stewart, Claude, Jr. "Factors Conditioning Christian Creation Consciousness." In *Cry of the Environment*, pp. 107-131. Edited by Philip Joranson and Ken Butigan. Santa Fe: Bear and Co., 1984.

_____. *Nature in Grace: A Study in the Theology of Nature*. Macon: Mercer University Press, 1983.

Stone, Christopher. *Earth and Other Ethics: The Case for Moral Pluralism*. New York: Harper and Row, 1987.

_____. *Should Trees Have Standing?: Toward Legal Rights for Natural Objects*. Los Altos: William Kaufman, 1974.

Sturm, Douglas. "The Prism of Justice: E Pluribus Unum?" *The Annual of the Society of Christian Ethics 1981*.

Suh, Chul Won. *The Creation-Mediatorship of Jesus Christ: A Study in the Relationship Between the Incarnation and the Creation*. Amsterdam: Rodopi, 1982.

Swidler, Leonard. *Biblical Affirmations of Women*. Philadelphia: Westminster, 1979.

Tanner, Kathryn. *God and Creation in Christian Theology: Tyranny or Empowerment?* Oxford: Basil Blackwell, 1988.

Teilhard de Chardin, Pierre. *The Phenomenon of Man*. Translated by Bernard Wall. New York: Harper and Row, 1961.

Thunberg, Lars. "The Cosmological and Anthropological Significance of Christ's Redeeming Work." In *The Gospel and Human Destiny*, pp. 64-89. Edited by Vilmos Vajta. Minneapolis: Augsburg, 1971.

Tillich, Paul. *Systematic Theology*. 3 vols. Chicago: University of Chicago Press, 1951-1963.

Toon, Peter, and Spiceland, James, eds. *One God in Trinity*. Westchester: Cornerstone, 1980.

Toulmin, Stephen. *The Return to Cosmology: Postmodern Science and the Theology of Nature.* Berkeley: University of California Press, 1982.

Toynbee, Arnold. "The Religious Background of the Present Environmental Crisis." In *Ecology and Religion in History*, pp. 137-149. Edited by David and Eileen Spring. New York: Harper and Row, 1974.

Tracy, David. *The Analogical Imagination: Christian Theology and the Culture of Pluralism.* New York: Crossroad, 1981.

_____. *Blessed Rage for Order: The New Pluralism in Theology.* New York: Seabury, 1975.

_____. *Dialogue With the Other: The Inter-Religious Dialogue.* Grand Rapids: Eerdmans, 1990.

_____. *Plurality and Ambiguity: Hermeneutics, Religion, Hope.* San Francisco: Harper and Row, 1987.

Tracy, David, and Lash, Nicholas, eds. *Cosmology and Theology.* New York: Seabury, 1983.

Tracy, Thomas. "Enacting History: Ogden and Kaufman on God's Mighty Acts." *The Journal of Religion* 64 (January 1984): 20-36.

_____. *God, Action, and Embodiment.* Grand Rapids: Eerdmans, 1984.

Trible, Phyllis. *God and the Rhetoric of Sexuality.* Philadelphia: Fortress, 1978.

Vajta, Vilmos, ed. *The Gospel and Human Destiny.* Minneapolis: Augsburg, 1971.

Van Bavel, T. J. "Kosmische Christologie of Theologie van de Natuur?" *Tijdschrift Voor Theologie* 20 (1980): 280-303.

VanderGoot, Henry, ed. *Creation and Method: Critical Essays on Christocentric Theology.* Washington, DC: University Press of America, 1981.

_____. "Introduction." In Gustaf Wingren, *Creation and Gospel*, pp. xi-li. New York: Edwin Mellon, 1979.

VanderVelde, George, ed. *The Holy Spirit: Renewing and Empowering Presence.* Winfield, BC: Institute for Christian Studies, 1989.

Van Hoeven, James. "Renewing God's Creation: An Ecumenical Challenge." *Reformed Review* 44 (Winter 1990): 137-149.

Van Leeuwen, Mary Stewart. *Gender and Grace: Love, Work, and Parenting in a Changing World.* Downers Grove: Intervarsity, 1990.

Van Melsen, Andrew. *The Philosophy of Nature*, 3rd. ed. Pittsburgh: Duquesne University Press, 1961.

Van Till, Howard. *The Fourth Day: What the Bible and the Heavens Are Telling Us About the Creation.* Grand Rapids: Eerdmans, 1986.

Van Till, Howard, Snow, Robert, Stek, John, and Young, Davis. *Portraits of Creation: Biblical and Scientific Perpsectives on the World's Formation.* Grand Rapids: Eerdmans, 1990.

Vaughan, Judith. *Sociality, Ethics, and Social Change: A Critical Appraisal of Reinhold Niebuhr's Ethics in the Light of Rosemary Radford Ruether's Works.* Lanham: University Press of America, 1983.

Von Rad, Gerhard. *Genesis.* Philadelphia: Westminster, 1961.

Wall, James, ed. *Theologians in Transition.* New York: Crossroad, 1981.

Walsh, Brian. "Theology of Hope and the Doctrine of Creation: An Appraisal of Jürgen Moltmann." *The Evangelical Quarterly* 59 (January 1987): 53-76.

Walsh, Brian, and Middleton, Richard. *The Transforming Vision: Shaping A Christian World View.* Downers Grove: Intervarsity, 1984.

Walsh, Brian, Karsh, Marianne, and Ansell, Nik. "Trees, Forestry, and the Responsiveness of Creation." Unpublished paper.

Weir, Mary Kathryn Williams. "The Concept of Freedom in the Work of Rosemary Radford Ruether." Ph.D. dissertation, University of St. Andrews, 1982.

Westermann, Claus. *Creation.* Translated by John Scullion. Philadelphia: Fortress, 1974.

_____. "Creation and History in the Old Testament." In *The Gospel and Human Destiny*, pp. 11-38. Edited by Vilmos Vajta. Minneapolis: Augsburg, 1971.

Westphal. Merold. *God, Guilt, and Death: An Existential Phenomenology of Religion.* Bloomington: Indiana University Press, 1984.

White, Lynn, Jr. "The Historical Roots of Our Ecologic Crisis." *Science* 155 (1967): 1203-1207.

Wierenga, Edward. *The Nature of God: An Inquiry into Divine Attributes.* Ithaca: Cornell University Press, 1989.

Wildiers, N. Max. *The Theologian and His Universe: Theology and Cosmology from the Middle Ages to the Present.* New York: Seabury, 1982.

Wilkinson, Loren. "Cosmic Christology and the Christian's Role in Creation." *Christian Scholar's Review* 11 (September 1981): 18-40.

_____, ed. *Earthkeeping in the Nineties: Stewardship of Creation.* Grand Rapids: Eerdmans, 1991.

Williams, George. "Christian Attitudes Toward Nature." *Christian Scholar's Review* 2 (Fall 1971 and Winter 1972): 3-35, 112-126.

_____. *Wilderness and Paradise in Christian Thought: The Biblical Experience of the Desert in the History of Christianity and the Paradise Theme in the Theological Idea of the University.* New York: Harper and Row, 1962.

Willis, W. Waite, Jr. *Theism, Atheism, and the Doctrine of the Trinity: The Trinitarian Theologies of Karl Barth and Jürgen Moltmann in Response to Protest Atheism.* Atlanta: Scholars Press, 1987.

Wilson, Garth. "The Doctrine of the Holy Spirit in the Reformed Tradition: A Critical Overview." In *The Holy Spirit*, pp. 57-72. Edited by George VanderVelde. Winfield, BC: Institute for Christiain Studies, 1989.

Wingren, Gustaf. *Creation and Gospel: The New Situation in European Theology.* New York: Edwin Mellen, 1979.

_____. "The Doctrine of Creation: Not an Appendix but the First Article." *Word and World* 4 (Fall 1984): 353-371.

_____. *The Flight From Creation.* Minneapolis: Augsburg, 1971.

Wolff, Hans Walter. *Anthropology of the Old Testament.* Philadelphia: Fortress, 1974.

Wolters, Albert. "Editorial: Worldview and Textual Criticism." *Anakainosis* 2 (June 1980): 1-2.

Wolterstorff, Nicholas. *Lament for a Son.* Grand Rapids: Eerdmans, 1987.

————. *Until Justice and Peace Embrace.* Grand Rapids: Eerdmans, 1983.

Young, Norman. *Creator, Creation, and Faith.* Philadelphia: Westminster, 1976.

Young, Richard. *Healing the Earth: A Theocentric Perspective on Environmental Problems and Their Solutions.* Nashville: Broadman and Holman, 1994.

INDEX